914·2

1001
DAYS
OUT

1001
DAYS
OUT

YOUR COMPREHENSIVE
GUIDE TO THE BEST
ATTRACTIONS IN THE UK

Bath • New York • Singapore • Hong Kong • Cologne • Delhi
Melbourne • Amsterdam • Johannesburg • Auckland • Shenzhen

First published by Parragon in 2010

Parragon
Queen Street House
4 Queen Street
Bath BA1 1HE, UK

ISBN: 978-1-4454-1625-0

Printed in China

All the information given in this book has come directly from
the attractions included and was correct at the time of going to
press. The Publishers will be grateful for any information that
will assist in keeping future editions up to date. While every
care has been taken in the preparation of this book, neither the
Compilers nor the Publishers can accept any liability for any
consequences arising from the use thereof, or the information
contained herein. The price guide, best times to go and the
facilities given should be used as a guide only.

Compiled and Written by Julian Flanders
Designed by Craig Stevens, Carole Melbourne and Nick Heal

Frontispiece:
The cliffs at Land's End

This page:
View of the Three Graces from Liverpool Docks

Important Note for the Reader
We have made every effort to ensure the information in this
guide is accurate and up to date. But things can change very
quickly. Prices and details of opening and closing are
sometimes altered at short notice, and sadly some venues
close unexpectedly. We would therefore urge readers to
check on an attraction's website, the address of which is
included in almost every case, before setting out on a visit.
This will ensure you are aware of any changes in prices or
whether the attraction is open or not, and will avoid
unexpected disappointment or other problems.

Contents

Introduction

Britain is one of the most popular holiday destinations in the world, and it's easy to see why.

Major cities like London, Glasgow and York with their world-famous museums, palaces and stately architecture attract visitors all the year round. There are also Areas of Outstanding Natural Beauty like the Lake District and the Peak District, the Brecon Beacons, the Gower Peninsula in Wales and the Highlands in Scotland – all with their own natural history and wildlife. There are mountains and moors, industrial landscapes, castles, gardens ... and all surrounded by over 3,000 miles of coastline.

But with so many places to choose from, it's hard to know where to begin. *1001 Days Out* will help you do just that. The book is packed with ideas to form the basis of days out in Britain where you can discover the natural beauty, rich heritage and cultural attractions that England, Scotland and Wales have to offer. This practical guide offers a broad selection of attractions ranging from world-famous castles, stately homes and gardens to carefully restored windmills, ancient ruins and rediscovered gardens. But also included are many small and more unusual places to visit. With 1001 entries, all tastes are catered for.

Of course, at any one time, some attractions may be closed for renovation or refurbishment. For this reason a few of the famous and popular attractions you may be expecting to see may not in fact have been included in this edition.

About this guide

This guide covers England, Scotland (including the Northern and Western Islands) and Wales and is arranged in regions, shown on the national map on page viii. The counties within each region, the towns within each county and the attractions within each town are all, where possible, arranged alphabetically. Each attraction also has a reference number so that you can easily find it on the regional map at the beginning of each section.

Understanding the entries

In this fully revised and updated edition we have simplified the information included to make it even easier to use. Coloured boxes and text at the top of each page indicate regions; the numbers in the top corners next to the regional name refer to the numbered attractions on that page. The nearest major town or village is indicated below the name of the attraction. Green bars alongside pictures indicate which attraction is shown. A solid green line indicates the end of one county and the beginning of the next.

Description

Each entry has a description of the attraction that gives a flavour of what visitors may expect to find when they get there. Brief but to the point, this information includes the highlights of what each attraction has to offer. This is generally written with families in mind, but includes information of use to everyone.

Where is it?

These are simple directions, usually for motorists and often simply a road number or an indication of where you are likely to find signs to follow to your intended destination. For attractions in London we have given the name of the nearest Underground station. This information has normally been provided by the attraction itself.

Best time to go

This information is given in the form of seasonal icons:

Spring   Summer   Autumn   Winter

Again, these are intended as a guide only. If a winter icon is not included, it does not necessarily mean that the attraction is closed in the winter months. We have included extra information where possible, particularly if, for example, an attraction is only open two days a week. But we strongly recommend that you check with the relevant website to make sure the attraction you are visiting is open before you travel.

⏱ How long it'll take you

This information is very useful when planning your trip. It is an indication of how long it'll take you to get the best out of your visit.

⭐ Don't miss

All attractions have a core, a unique selling point around which they are based. It is particularly useful for anyone short of time, for example, families with small children who may have to leave at short notice and don't want to miss out on anything. In those cases, we recommend you see this feature first and then take in any others at your leisure.

Price guide

We have included four price categories: free, low, medium and high. These are intended as a guide only. Free attractions do not charge for entry, but there may be car park charges (we have indicated these wherever possible), and some attractions may charge extra for certain things. Otherwise the categories are as follows:

💷 Up to £9.99 per person   💷💷 £10–£19.99   💷💷💷 £20 and up

Prices are correct at time of going to press, but please note that they are subject to change. Some places that do not charge admission may ask for a voluntary donation (we have given this information wherever possible). In some instances discounts may be available to families, groups, local residents or members of certain organisations such as English Heritage and The National Trust. Other attractions, particularly theme parks, offer discounts for advanced bookings on-line, so please check the website when planning your trip.

Website address

The attraction's official website address is given wherever possible. However, if there is no such address, we have given an appropriate website address that should provide any additional information the visitor will need.

Star and feature attractions

We have selected ten five-star attractions that we feel are unmissable. But ten attractions do not do justice to the incredible range of activities available in Britain and so we have also chosen a whole series of other star attractions too, just to help you make your choice.

Have a good day out!

Ⓐ Colour indicating region
Ⓑ Nearest town
Ⓒ Description
Ⓓ Reference number on regional map
Ⓔ Information: location, best time to go, how long it'll take you, don't miss, price guide, website
Ⓕ Five-star attraction
Ⓖ Star attraction

South East

South West

Eastern

East Midlands

West Midlands

Wales

Yorkshire

North West

North East

Scotland

South East

Berkshire
Buckinghamshire
East Sussex
Hampshire and Isle of Wight
Kent
London
Oxfordshire
Surrey
West Sussex

Ightam Mote, Kent

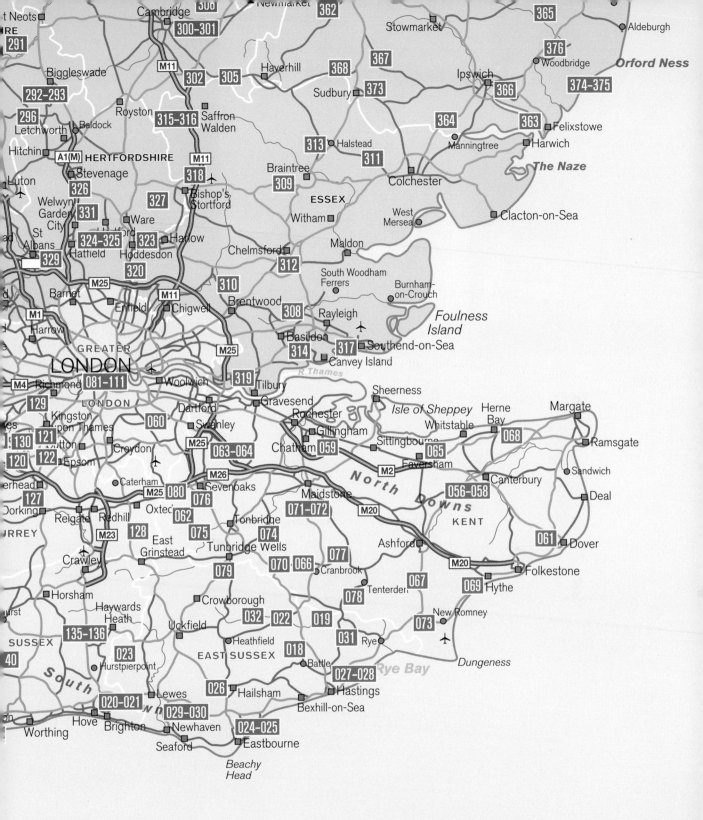

Guide to the **South East**

Go Ape!   001
Bracknell

Go Ape! is a network of rope bridges, trapezes, tunnels and zip wires that stretches for roughly a mile through the tree canopy. You will be trained in the use of harnesses, pulleys, carabiners and safety techniques by qualified instructors before setting out to swing through the treetops on a real, adrenalin-pumping, high-wire forest adventure. This is a unique experience that consists of a giant obstacle course made up of an extensive cat's cradle of ropes, netting, walkways and platforms, set high above the ground in Swinley Forest.

🔍 Just south of Bracknell (shares a car park with the Look Out Discovery Centre)

⚙ ☉ ❧

⏳ 2 hours

⭐ Zip wire thrills

£ £ £

www.goape.co.uk

The Look Out Discovery Centre   002
Bracknell

A hands-on, interactive science and nature exhibition with over 70 fun-filled exhibits for the entire family. The exhibits are themed in the following zones: Sound and Communication, Light and Colour, Forces and Movement, Body and Perception and Woodland and Water Zone. There are a variety of shows throughout the year, based on science topics. They are presented in an exciting and fun way and include shows like Bugs and Beasties and the Big Dinosaur Show. The centre is set in 1,000 hectares of woodland with nature walks, cycle trails and an adventure play area.

🔍 Just south of Bracknell (shares a car park with Go Ape!)

⚙ ☉ ❧ ❄

⏳ 1½ hours

⭐ Interactive science fun

£ £

www.bracknell-forest.gov.uk/leisure

Cliveden   003
Maidenhead

This spectacular house overlooking the Thames was once the glittering hub of society as the home of Waldorf and Nancy Astor. It was later infamously associated with the Profumo Affair. Part of the house is now open to visitors. The estate consists of a series of magnificent formal gardens, which include topiary, and a marvellous collection of sculptures and statues. You can also take in the magnificent views from the estate's celebrated parterre. The estate also features waymarked woodland and riverside walks. There are also new picnic and play areas.

🔍 2 miles north of Taplow

⚙ ☉ ❧ House open Thursdays and Sundays

⏳ 2 hours

⭐ Thameside views

£ £

www.nationaltrust.org.uk

The Living Rainforest   004
Newbury

You can explore a real rainforest without leaving the UK in this incredible tropical glasshouse. Home to over 700 exotic species of plants, animals and birds, this unique conservation project is a charitable organisation run by the Trust for Sustainable Living. As you walk along the tropical trails you will see lizards, monkeys, snakes, crocodiles and butterflies as well as amazing plants like giant lily pads, bananas, vanilla pods, ginger and coffee. This is your chance to get up close and personal with an ecosystem whose very existence is under threat.

🔍 Just off the M4 at junction 13
☀ ◯ ♣ ❄
⏳ 1½ hours
⭐ A real rainforest in the south-east of England
£ £
www.livingrainforest.org

Legoland Windsor   006
Windsor

This well-known attraction continues to be popular. It's well laid out and organised into rides for different age-groups. For the bravest, rides like the Jungle Coaster and the Dragon will blow you away. Tots go mad for Duplo Land and Miniland – the largest Lego brick construction ever made. With educational activities, shows, food and drink counters, Legoland offers a whole day's play for all ages. Continuously updating and developing the park, new additions include Pirates Landing and a Clutch Powers 4D movie adventure.

🔍 2 miles from Windsor with easy access from both the M3 and M4
☀ ◯ ♣
⏳ All day if you wish
⭐ Miniland
£ £ £
www.legoland.co.uk

Bucklebury Farm Park   005
Reading

Over 70 acres of parkland in which to see deer in their natural habitat, take the free tractor and trailer ride to see them at close quarters. There are ponies, donkeys, pigs, wild boar and lots of other animals to feed and a pat-a-pet area with rabbits and guinea pigs. In addition an indoor play area with slides, an outdoor adventure playground, den building, nature trail, woodland walk, pedal go-kart track and large picnic area all combine to make this park one of Berkshire's best kept secrets.

🔍 Off the M4 between Reading and Newbury
☀ ◯ ♣
⏳ 1-2 hours
⭐ Pat-a-pet area
£ £
www.buckleburyfarmpark.co.uk

Windsor Castle   007
Windsor

Rebuilt in 1350, Windsor is the oldest and largest occupied castle in the world. Most of the Kings and Queens of England have had a direct influence on the construction and evolution of the castle, which has been their garrison fortress, home, official palace and sometimes their prison. The magnificent State Apartments are furnished with paintings by Rubens, Rembrandt, Gainsborough and Canaletto. Other highlights include the Semi-State rooms, St George's Chapel, which is home to ten royal tombs (including those of Henry VIII and Charles I), and Queen Mary's doll's house.

🔍 In Windsor town centre
☀ ◯ ♣ ❄
⏳ 2-3 hours
⭐ State Apartments
£ £ £
www.royalcollection.org.uk

California Country Park
008
Wokingham

This park, set within 100 acres of ancient bogland and lowland heath, offers a wealth of walking and wildlife-watching opportunities for visitors. The site was used in the 19th century for brickmaking and in the early 1950s was developed into one of the first holiday camps in England. There are two main walks: the short Longmoor Lake Walk and the longer Woodland Walk, which takes in the 8,000-year-old Longmoor Bog on a specially constructed boardwalk (now a Site of Special Scientific Interest). Other facilities are available in the summer (see website for details).

🔍 Off Nine Mile Ride near Finchampstead
✻ ◉ ❀ ❄
⌛ 2-3 hours
⭐ Tranquil walks
♿
www.wokingham.gov.uk

Buckinghamshire County Museum and Roald Dahl Gallery
009
Aylesbury

Housed in beautifully restored 15th-century buildings, this award-winning museum covers local archaeology, social history, natural history, geology, art works and photographs. You can also visit the Roald Dahl Gallery, which uses the celebrated author's characters to stimulate children's interests in science, history and literature. The kids can boggle their eyes, baffle their brains and let their imaginations run wild with Willie Wonka's inventions, minibeasts inside the Giant Peach, Mr Fox's tunnel, the Twits' upside-down room and the BFG.

🔍 Aylesbury town centre
✻ ◉ ❀ ❄ See website for details
⌛ 2 hours
⭐ Aylesbury's annual Roald Dahl Festival at the end of June/start of July
♿
www.buckscc.gov.uk/museum

Buckinghamshire Railway Centre
010
Aylesbury

This is a working steam museum where you can step back in time as you view the giants of the steam age displayed on the spacious 25-acre site. Exhibits range from express passenger locomotives to the humble shunting engine. Carriages include a dining car from the Royal train of 1901 as well as another reputedly used by General Eisenhower and Winston Churchill among others for wartime planning meetings. On special days you can book in advance for the opportunity to learn how to drive a real steam engine.

🔍 Off the A41 Aylesbury–Bicester Road
✻ ◉ ❀ ❄ See website for details
⌛ 3-4 hours
⭐ Days out with Thomas the Tank Engine
♿
www.bucksrailcentre.org

Tiggywinkles, The Wildlife Hospital Trust
011
Aylesbury

Every year over 5 million wild animals and birds are injured as a direct result of their encounters with human beings. Come to the visitor centre to find out why and learn about the hundreds of sick animals the busiest wildlife hospital in the world cares for. Visit the gardens and wild areas to see some of the other disabled residents who cannot be returned to their original habitats (including hedgehogs, badgers, wild birds, foxes, reptiles and amphibians). The hospital relies on donations to survive.

🔍 At Haddenham, off the A418 from Aylesbury
❄ ⚙ ♣ ❄
⏳ 1–2 hours
⭐ Hands-on training courses for 16–18-year-olds
£
www.sttiggywinkles.org.uk

Waddesdon Manor
012
Aylesbury

This stunning Renaissance-style château was built in 1874 for Baron Ferdinand de Rothschild to display his magnificent collection of art treasures. The 45 rooms are filled with the finest French furniture – including Marie Antoinette's desk – Sèvres porcelain and paintings by English and Dutch Old Masters. There is an additional gallery of contemporary art in the Coach House. The house is set in a beautiful Victorian garden with fountains, statuary and seasonal flower displays. For younger visitors there is a wildlife trail and a woodland playground.

🔍 On A41, 6 miles north-west of Aylesbury
❄ ⚙ ♣ ❄ Admission to house by timed ticket only
⏳ 2–3 hours
⭐ The aviary, stocked with exotic species from Baron Ferdinand's collection
£ £
www.waddesdon.org.uk

Bekonscot Model Village and Railway
013
Beaconsfield

Opened in 1929 Bekonscot is the oldest model village in the world. It's made up of six model towns that combine to create a miniature wonderland depicting rural England in the 1930s set in 1.5 acres of garden. A gauge-1 model railway winds its way through the mini-landscape among castles, thatched cottages and a cricket match on the green. Visitors can stride up and down the high streets and look inside the incredibly detailed models.
The ride-on Bekonscot Light Railway provides an excellent vantage point from which to explore the site.

🔍 In the centre of Beaconsfield
⚙
⏳ 2 hours
⭐ Reputed to be the inspiration for Noddy's Toytown
£
www.bekonscot.co.uk

Wycombe Museum   014

High Wycombe

Set in an 18th-century house, this is a modern museum with a relaxed atmosphere surrounded by beautiful landscaped gardens. Visitors can discover the social history of the Wycombe district through lively, interactive displays. Exhibits mainly cover the area's famous furniture industry, in particular chair making. There is also an area showing the various types of tools and machinery that have been used in the industry over the years. Upstairs there is an interactive section with a diary of annual events aimed at children, and also a small art gallery.

In the centre of Wycombe

1 hour

Marvellous collection of Windsor chairs

www.wycombe.gov.uk/museum

Bletchley Park, National Codes Centre   015

Milton Keynes

Home of Station X and the site of code-breaking activities that had such an effect on the successful outcome of the Second World War. Check out the tales of spies and strategic deception. You may even be the one to discover the whereabouts of genius mathematician Alan Turing's silver, supposedly buried in or near Bletchley Park. There are also exhibitions of wartime toys and working computers, a vintage mini cinema and an outstanding Churchill collection. A programme of lively, exciting events are held on special days throughout the year.

Signposted from Bletchley station, a few miles south of Milton Keynes

See website for details

3-4 hours

Reconstruction of the Bombe Enigma code-breaking machine

www.bletchleypark.org.uk

Xscape – Milton Keynes   016

Milton Keynes

Xscape is a unique family day out. Try indoor skydiving in the incredible Airkix, or hit the Snozone and learn to ski, snowboard or even go tobogganing on the UK's longest real-snow slope or test your nerve on Vertical Chill's 13-metre climbing walls. There is also a state-of-the-art fitness centre. Alternatively, relax at the ten-pin bowling alley, one of the 16 cinema screens or browsing at a range of lifestyle and fashion shopping outlets. When you've done all that you can relax at a number of good quality, high street cafes and restaurants.

Signposted from junction 14 of the M1

Pre-booking essential for the Snozone and Airkix

7-8 hours

'Ski in a Day' programme

www.xscape.co.uk

Emberton Country Park   017
Olney

Emberton Park has turned into a relaxing country tourist attraction. There are 200 acres of beautiful parkland, bordered by the Great Ouse River and including five lakes, in which visitors can camp, go cycling, play in various play areas, study in the conservation area, sail on Heron Lake, enjoy the sun, have a picnic, stroll through the beautiful designated walks before ending up in the local tea rooms. The park also offers day and night fishing and a static caravan park for those who can't bear to leave.

🔍 Near junction 14 of the M1, a mile south of Olney
⚙️
⏳ 3-4 hours
⭐ The fabulous 22-mile circular walk
♿

www.mkweb.co.uk/embertonpark

Bodiam Castle   019
Bodiam

Now a beautiful and tranquil place, Bodiam Castle (built in 1385) was once a formidable defensive barrier. The walls are virtually intact, with ramparts that rise up from the still waters of the moat. Much of the interior is in ruins but you can still see enough to imagine life inside the castle. There are staircases, dungeons and battlements to explore and a marvellous view of the Rother Valley to be seen from the tops of the towers. Enter the castle under its original wooden portcullis – one of the rarest examples of its kind.

🔍 Off A21 near Hurst Green
⚙️
⏳ 1-2 hours
⭐ Picnic with the castle walls reflected in the waters of the moat
♿

www.nationaltrust.org.uk

Battle Abbey and Battlefield   018
Battle

On 14 October 1066, the invading Normans defeated the Anglo-Saxons at the Battle of Hastings – one of the most famous battles in English history. The two armies did not actually fight at Hastings, but north of the town simply named Battle. This is now the site of a popular 100-acre family attraction where you can see a short film that explains what happened, then visit the battlefield and the ruins of the abbey that William the Conqueror built to celebrate his victory. There's also a discovery centre and an activity-based exhibition.

🔍 South end of Battle High Street
⚙️ ✚
⏳ 2 hours
⭐ Stand on the spot where King Harold fell
♿

www.english-heritage.org.uk

Brighton Sea Life Centre 020
Brighton

The world's oldest operating aquarium was first opened in 1872 and today retains much of its original Victorian splendour. The main attraction is an underwater tunnel that takes you deep down beside a tropical reef complete with sharks, sea turtles, a bewildering array of brightly coloured fish, a shipwreck and some breathtaking coral. Other attractions include a rainforest, serpents of the sea, kingdom of the seahorse, piranhas, crabs, rock pools and rays that you can pet. A part of the Sea Life Centre chain, this is regarded as one of the best.

By the pier on Brighton sea front
1–2 hours
The giant sea turtles
www.sealifeeurope.com

The Royal Pavilion 021
Brighton

Built for George, Prince Regent, at the turn of the 19th century, the Royal Pavilion is remarkable for its exotic oriental appearance both inside and out. This magnificent royal pleasure palace was revered by fashionable Regency society and is still a distinctive landmark for Brighton and Hove today. The Pavilion houses furniture and works of art including original pieces lent by HM The Queen and a magnificent display of Regency silver-gilt. The tearoom, with its fabulous balcony, overlooks the Pavilion gardens, which have also been returned to their original Regency splendour.

Brighton town centre
1–2 hours
The incredible Banqueting Room
www.royalpavilion.org.uk

Bateman's 022
Burwash

Home of the famous English writer and poet Rudyard Kipling, author of *The Jungle Book*, the *Just So Stories* and the poem *If* among other classic works, Bateman's provides a fascinating insight into an England that is long gone. The house is preserved exactly as it was when he died in 1936. The 17th-century house is rather austere with its mullioned windows and oak beams, oriental rugs and other artefacts that reflect his association with the East. The house is set in formal gardens with a river flowing through the meadow at the bottom.

Half a mile south of Burwash
1–2 hours
His book-lined study
www.nationaltrust.org.uk

Stoneywish Nature Reserve 023
Ditchling

Within sight of the South Downs, the 50 acres of Stoneywish offer a magical retreat from the rush of modern living. Here you will find a corner of Sussex countryside as it used to be, meadows, wetlands and woodland full of native flowers and a wealth of wildlife, and some tame farm animals. There are gardens and exhibitions for the older visitor to explore, gentle walks for every age and ability and plenty of room for children in the play area. Take a picnic and make it a whole day out.

Just east of Ditchling, off A23
2–3 hours
Shaker-style herb and vegetable garden
www.stoneywish.com

Drusillas Park   024
Eastbourne

Recently rated as the UK's No. 1 attraction by *The Times*, Drusillas Park – normally described as a small zoo – has more than 100 animal species in naturalistic environments including meerkats, otters, monkeys, penguins (see below), bats and lemurs. But 'animal magic' is not all that's on offer at this unique site. There's a free train ride around the park from where you can see all the added attractions in the big adventure playground including the Animal Olympics, Panning for Gold, the Dino Dig, crazy golf and a whole range of play areas.

🔍 Off the A27 between Eastbourne and Lewes
☼ ☉ ♣ ✻
⧖ 4-5 hours
★ Penguin enclosure, which allows you to see them swimming
£ £

www.drusillas.co.uk

Treasure Island   025
Eastbourne

A pirate-themed adventure park that provides swashbuckling fun for all the family in company with a host of characters. The main feature is Long John Silver's shipwreck, which comes complete with walkways, slides and bridges. There is also a large paddling pool, named the 'Splash Lagoon', adventure golf for dads, play areas and sandpits, an indoor soft play area for tots called 'Little Buccaneers', outdoor fun and games for everyone and an indoor state-of-the-art amusement and games arcade for when the weather isn't so clever.

🔍 East end of Eastbourne seafront
☼ ☉ ♣ ✻
⧖ 2-3 hours
★ Long John Silver's shipwreck
£

www.treasure-island.info

Herstmonceux Castle 026
Hailsham

A magnificent moated castle, Herstmonceux is set in beautiful parkland and superb Elizabethan gardens. Built originally as a country home in the mid-15th century, Herstmonceux embodies the history of Medieval England and the romance of Renaissance Europe. However, it was almost demolished during the 18th century as the bricks were used to remodel the nearby Herstmonceux Place. However, the original castle was rebuilt using local craftsmen during the first half of the 20th century. Today it is an international study centre, but the castle and gardens are also open to the public.

🔍 On A22 near Hailsham

☀ ⚙ 🍁

⏳ 2 hours

⭐ Guided tours of the castle

♿

www.herstmonceux-castle.com

Hastings Castle and the 1066 Story 027
Hastings

Strategically sited on a promontory above the town are the ruins of the castle, one of the first built by William of Normandy in 1067 after the Battle of Hastings. Today's visitors can learn about the history of the castle and then explore the fascinating ruins for themselves and enjoy panoramic views over the English Channel. Walk around the ruins of the cloistered chapel, the East Gate and Chapter House. Explore the dungeons carved out of the rock beneath the North Gate, or just relax on the lawns of the Ladies Parlour.

🔍 Overlooks Hastings on east side of town

☀ ⚙ 🍁

⏳ 2 hours

⭐ The 'whispering' dungeons

♿

www.discoverhastings.co.uk

Smugglers Adventure 028
Hastings

Underneath Hastings' West Hill is a network of caves – discovered by accident in the 1780s – that reveal the fascinating story of smugglers on this part of the English coast. This is a spooky experience, best for 8-year-olds and upwards. You walk through a 44-metre tunnel once used by smugglers to store goods such as alcohol, tobacco, paper, silk, sugar and spices. You can also visit the eerie, underground St Clements Chapel, which is believed to be haunted. The caves also served as air-raid shelters during the Second World War.

🔍 Up West Hill (best to take the West Hill Lift as there is no car parking or wheelchair access)

☀ ⚙ 🍁

⏳ 1 hour

⭐ The 'ghost story' wall

♿

www.discoverhastings.co.uk

Newhaven Fort 029
Newhaven

This fine Victorian fortress, built in to the side of chalk cliffs, has been turned into an award-winning attraction that has something for all members of the family. The largest work of defence ever constructed in Sussex, there are tunnels to explore, fine panoramic views from the ramparts and cliff-top gun emplacements to fire the imagination. Visit the on-site military museum and learn about the fort's role in two world wars, then sit inside a street shelter and experience what it was like to be caught in a real air raid.

🔍 Signposted from Newhaven town centre
☀ ⚙ ❁
⏳ 2-3 hours
⭐ Blitz bomb shelter simulation
£
www.newhavenfort.org.uk

Paradise Park 030
Newhaven

The Heritage Trail and gardens make for a great family visit. The Museum of Life is one of the finest exhibitions of its type in the country with life-size moving dinosaurs and a spectacular collection of fossils, minerals and crystals. The new 'Planet Water' zone includes some amazing, rare sea creatures. The delightful gardens are one of Newhaven's hidden secrets with several small lakes, waterfalls and fountains. The Sussex Heritage Trail meanders through the gardens. There's also a miniature railway, play areas, crazy golf and other amusements.

🔍 Take A26 from Newhaven
⚙
⏳ 1-2 hours
⭐ The Dinosaur Safari
£
www.paradisepark.co.uk

Great Dixter 031
Northiam

Without doubt one of the most beautiful places in East Sussex, Great Dixter is actually a Tudor manor house with a 16th-century house (of similar style) moved from Kent and attached by architect Edwin Lutyens in 1912. The gardens, also designed by Lutyens, were taken over in 1954 by the celebrated gardener Christopher Lloyd who was born in the house in 1921 when it was owned by his father. It became his obsession until he died in 2006. The house is fascinating and the gardens gorgeous, particularly in the spring and autumn.

🔍 Off the A28 at Northiam
☀ ⚙ ❁
⏳ 2-3 hours
⭐ Guided tour of the house
£
www.greatdixter.co.uk

STAR ATTRACTION

Bluebell Railway   032

Sheffield Park

The Bluebell Railway, made famous by its appearance in the film *The Railway Children*, operates standard-gauge steam trains through nine miles of scenic Sussex countryside between Sheffield Park, Horsted Keynes and Kingscote. You can visit the engine shed, ride the trains – taking tea or dinner if you choose – visit the stations, see the locomotives and beautifully preserved historic carriages close-up and round off the day with a visit to the Bluebell Railway museum. Pre-booking is advised for all visits and reservations can be made through the website.

🔍 At Sheffield Park just off the A275
☀ ⚙ 🍁
⏳ 1–2 hours
★ 1913 Observation Car
💷 💷

www.bluebell-railway.co.uk

Jane Austen's House Museum   033

Alton

The novelist Jane Austen is known worldwide for her popular novels describing the society of pre-industrial England. She spent the last eight years of her life (1809–1817) at this 17th-century house in Chawton not far from her birthplace in Steventon. She wrote some of her best work at the small round table in the parlour including *Mansfield Park*, *Emma* and *Persuasion*. The museum includes a number of rooms used by Jane, her mother and her sister and holds an extensive collection of family mementoes and documentary material, including manuscripts and copies of letters written by the author.

🔍 Chawton, 2 miles from Alton
☀ ⚙ 🍁 ❄ See website for winter opening hours
⏳ 1 hour
★ Jane Austen's kitchen, only opened to the public in 2009
💷

www.jane-austens-house-museum.org.uk

The Hawk Conservancy Trust   034

Andover

This charity works in the fields of conservation, education, rehabilitation and research into birds of prey. The visitor centre is set in 22 acres of woodland, where there are over 150 birds of prey. There are daily flying demonstrations by hawks, owls and eagles. Special events include Owls by Moonlight, adult and junior experience days and photographic days, which enable the participants to get closer to the birds in a more intimate setting. Extra activities during school holidays and weekends include tractor rides, duck racing, ferret racing, raptor trail and adventure playground.

🔍 Off A303, 4 miles west of Andover
☀
⏳ 3–4 hours
★ The bald eagles in flight
💷 💷

www.hawk-conservancy.org

Beaulieu Abbey and National Motor Museum

035

Brockenhurst

There are three attractions in one at Beaulieu – Palace House, gatehouse for the abbey, set in glorious grounds overlooking the Beaulieu river and home to Lord Montagu; the abbey itself, which was founded in 1204 and though now in ruins still remains an impressive place; and the National Motor Museum, which houses over 250 vehicles that represent every era of motoring. Exhibits include a James Bond experience, a custom car display and a reconstructed 1930's garage. Visitors can also take a monorail ride through the grounds.

🔍 Follow signs from junction 2 of the M27

☼ ☉ 🍁 ❄

⏳ 3-4 hours

⭐ Bluebird, Duncan Campbell's record-breaking jet car

💷 💷

www.beaulieu.co.uk

Osborne House

036

East Cowes

Osborne House, on the Isle of Wight, became Queen Victoria and Prince Albert's country getaway in the mid-1800s. They rebuilt the house to create a family palace of extreme opulence. As you wander around you get a real glimpse into what royal family life was like 200 years ago. Attractions for children include the Swiss Cottage, which is full of child-size furniture. They can also have fun in the play area or enjoy a horse and carriage ride. The house is set in exquisite gardens with majestic views of the Solent.

🔍 1 mile from East Cowes on the Isle of Wight

☼ ☉ 🍁 ❄

⏳ 2-3 hours

⭐ The extravagant Durbar Room

💷 💷

www.english-heritage.org.uk

Exbury Gardens　　037

Exbury

Part of the Rothschild estate, Exbury is a 200-acre informal woodland garden with a large collection of rhododendrons, azaleas, camellias, rare trees and shrubs. The gardens have been planted to reflect the changing moods of the seasons: early spring sees the magnolias and azaleas at their peak. The full bloom of the Exotic and Herbaceous Gardens announce the arrival of summer while autumn brings spectacular displays of colour. If you get tired of walking you can take the 20-minute steam train journey or ride a chauffeur driven buggy to tour the gardens.

🔍 Follow signs from junction 2 of the M27

⚙ ⚙ 🍁

⌛ 2–3 hours

⭐ Autumn display of Japanese maples, deciduous azaleas and dogwoods

💷

www.exbury.co.uk

The Royal Armouries – Fort Nelson　　038

Fareham

Fort Nelson is home to the Royal Armouries' collection of arms and armour, which includes 350 historic big guns. The fort was built in the 1860s as part of a chain of fortifications protecting Portsmouth harbour from a feared French invasion. Covering nearly 19 acres and now fully restored, it sits majestically on top of Portsdown Hill with amazing views of the Solent. You can explore secret underground tunnels or take a tour with an expert guide. There are daily gun salutes; drama and costumed actors bring to life exciting characters from British history.

🔍 Follow signs from junction 11 of the M27

⚙ ⚙ 🍁 ❄

⌛ 2–3 hours

⭐ Free family days out – see website for details

💷

www.armouries.org.uk

The Needles Park   039
Freshwater

The park features a breathtaking chairlift ride to view the Isle of Wight's famous Needles rocks and lighthouse. It also offers a range of other facilities including a sand shop, where visitors can make their own unique souvenir, a traditional carousel and a nine-hole adventure golf with some 3 and 4 par holes. Visitors are also able to watch regular glassblowing demonstrations in Alum Bay Glass and witness the creation of a wide variety of sweets in the island's only sweet factory, whilst enjoying a talk about the process of traditional sweet making.

🔍 Signposted from all main roads on the island
⚙
⏳ 2–3 hours
⭐ The breathtaking chairlift ride
💷
www.theneedles.co.uk

Explosion! The Museum of Naval Firepower   040
Gosport

This museum is set in 18th-century buildings at the Royal Navy's former armaments depot of Priddy's Hard in Gosport. Explosion! traces the development of naval armaments from gunpowder to the Exocet missile. Displays also explore the origins of Priddy's Hard, bringing alive the site's rich history, including the story of how 2,500 women worked on the site during its peak in the Second World War. It describes the role that Priddy's Hard played in naval operations for over 200 years, as well as its importance to the local community.

🔍 Follow signs from junction 11 of the M27
⚙ ⚙ ♣ ❄
⏳ 2–3 hours
⭐ Stunning multimedia film show set in the original gunpowder vault
💷 💷
www.explosion.org.uk

Hurst Castle   041
Lymington

Hurst Castle is situated at the seaward end of a shingle spit, not far from the Isle of Wight, the perfect location to defend the western approach to the Solent. The castle was built by Henry VIII as one of a chain of coastal fortresses. Charles I was imprisoned here in 1648 before being taken to London for trial. The castle was modernised during the Napoleonic wars and again in the 1870s. During the Second World War, Hurst was manned with coastal gun batteries and searchlights. The castle now features exhibitions that tell its story.

🔍 By ferry from Keyhaven or on foot from Milford-on-Sea
⚙ ⚙ ♣ ❄ Check website for winter opening
⏳ 1–2 hours
⭐ Two huge 38-ton cannons
💷
www.hurstcastle.co.uk

Classic Boat Museum   042
Newport

This charitable trust Museum exhibits historic small craft together with topical displays of maritime history as well as marine craft tools. The collection now includes a number of island lifeboats, some classic powerboats and personal craft of Uffa Fox.
The restoration project presently on view, with work in progress, is a launch owned by Mr Frank Beken. A unique feature is that all craft are fully restored and used on the water for rallies. Research work may be undertaken using the computerised archives and the help of friendly volunteers.

🔍 On the quay at Newport harbour
⚙ ⚙ ♣
⏳ 1 hour
⭐ *Gipsy Moth IV* Connection
💷
www.classicboatmuseum.org

Portsmouth Historic Dockyard   043
Portsmouth

There are nine attractions in all at the home of the Royal Navy, including Nelson's flagship HMS *Victory*, the *Mary Rose* museum (the actual ship is not on show until 2012 while a new museum is built around it) and the ironclad HMS *Warrior*. Other attractions are the Royal Naval Museum, Action Stations, Trafalgar Sail and the Dockyard Apprentice, which explains that this place was the world's greatest industrial complex during the 18th and 19th centuries while Britain 'ruled the waves'. There are also harbour tours, which offer informative commentary and fabulous views.

Portsmouth harbour, signposted from junction 12 of the M27

4-5 hours

HMS *Victory*

£ £ £

www.historicdockyard.co.uk

Spinnaker Tower   044
Portsmouth

A contemporary icon on the South coast, this 170-metre tower provides a unique 'window on the sea', offering visitors spectacular views of Portsmouth harbour from a great height. The tower also offers a guarantee that if the three Solent forts are not visible on the day of your visit, then you can claim a ticket for a return visit within three months. The tower can also be hired for special events.

On Portsmouth Historic Seafront

1 hour

Breathtaking views

£

www.spinnakertower.co.uk

Paultons Park 045
Romsey

This is a family theme park situated in the village of Ower, near Romsey. The name derives from the former Paultons Estate, on which the park is situated. The last few years have seen the park transformed from a small local park to a major attraction aimed at family audiences. Now it has over 50 family rides and attractions, including three roller coasters and two water rides, as well as a number of animals, including meerkats, penguins, South African crowned cranes, touracos and over 80 different species of exotic birds.

🔍 Signposted from junction 2 of the M27
✿ ◉ ♣
⌛ 4–5 hours
★ The Cobra roller coaster
£ £
www.paultonspark.co.uk

Isle of Wight Steam Railway 046
Ryde

Take a 5-mile ride behind one of the vintage steam locomotives for a special journey back in time. Breathe in the evocative smells of a real steam railway, while your eyes and ears thrill to the puffing and hissing of the steam engine. Settle back in beautifully restored Victorian and Edwardian carriages and enjoy a unique view of some of the Isle of Wight's unspoilt countryside. The site also has a wagon works to restore carriages and engines and a museum that tells the story of the Island's railway history.

🔍 3 miles from Ryde or Newport
◉ ♣ Check website for other times
⌛ 2–3 hours
★ A first-class Victorian railway journey
£ £
www.iwsteamrailway.co.uk

Isle of Wight Zoo 047
Sandown

The Isle of Wight Zoo is home to one of Britain's largest collection of tigers, many of whom are rescue animals, but also specialises in an expanding population of lemurs. With a number of superb new enclosures modelled on natural habitats, the zoo is a fantastic place to see these wonderful animals relaxing. A number of other animals also live there, including jaguars, monkeys and lions. It's a small zoo but run by knowledgeable keepers for whom education is an important part of their days' work.

🔍 Sandown seafront
✿ ◉ ♣
⌛ 2–3 hours
★ Zena, a rare white Indian tigress
£
www.isleofwightzoo.com

Shanklin Chine   048
Shanklin

A natural, scenic gorge that drops over a 100 feet to the beach has been formed over the last 10,000 years. The gorge has two entrances, one at the top that starts with views of a 45-foot waterfall, and the other that leads from the beach. In between is a place of natural beauty and tranquillity, a haven of rare plants, woodland and wildlife. Shanklin Chine was once a site for shipwrecks and smuggling and was also used for training Commandos during the Second World War.

🔍 Far end of the esplanade or Old Shanklin village
✿ ⚙ 🍁
⏳ 1 hour
★ The majestic waterfall at the top
£
www.shanklinchine.co.uk

Longdown Activity Farm   049
Southampton

A family-run farm that organises a schedule of seasonally based activities every day including bottle-feeding kid goats and calves, feeding the ducks and baby animal encounter where you can cuddle the baby rabbits, guinea pigs, chicks or maybe even a piglet. There are gorgeous kune kune pigs and playful pygmy goats. There are plenty more friendly farm animals to meet including Billy the Shire horse. Lots of fantastic farmyard buildings to explore and loads of indoor and outdoor play areas for the children to run off all their energy.

🔍 Just of A35 between Southampton and Lyndhurst
⚙
⏳ 3 hours
★ Hands-on encounters with furry friends
£
www.longdownfarm.co.uk

Royal Victoria Country Park   050
Southampton

Overlooking Southampton Water, this popular park provides ideal facilities for children to play in a safe environment and peace of mind for their parents. There are nearly 200 acres of parkland, woodland and foreshore to be explored and which are home to a wide variety of wildlife and some spectacular trees and shrubs. The relaxing and happy atmosphere is complemented by a calendar of events, exhibitions, barbecue sites and walks. Set in the grounds of an old military hospital, the newly refurbished chapel hosts an exhibition of its history.

🔍 Follow signs from junction 8 of the M27
⚙
⏳ 3-4 hours
★ See website for a varied calendar of events
£
www.hants.gov.uk/rvcp

Royal Marines Museum   051
Southsea

Housed in what was once Eastney Barracks, the museum celebrates the history of the Royal Marines. Learn about the Marines' globetrotting exploits, and see the difference they have made all round the world – from Trafalgar in 1805, D-Day in 1944, the Falkland Islands in 1982 and Helmand Province in 2010. Find out what it takes to earn a world famous Green Beret and life in the Royal Navy today. Visit the refurbished Medal Room, in which you can review the museum's collection of 8,000 medals including all 10 Victoria Crosses awarded to the Commandos.

🔍 Southsea seafront
✿ ⚙ 🍁 ❄
⏳ 2-3 hours
★ Victoria Cross collection
£
www.royalmarinesmuseum.co.uk

The D-Day Museum and Overlord Embroidery

Southsea

052

The museum tells the story of Operation Overlord from the dark days of 1940 to victory in Normandy in 1944. Its centrepiece is the Overlord Embroidery, a moving tribute to the sacrifices required to defeat Nazi Germany. Visitors can also see a dawn to dusk reconstruction of the Allied landings on D-Day itself. The final image in the exhibition – a photograph of the rows of gravestones in the war cemetery at Ranville in Normandy – is a reminder of the price of victory, which must never be forgotten.

🔍 Clarence Esplanade in the centre of Southsea

❁ ⚙ ♣ ❄

⏳ 1–2 hours

★ Overlord Embroidery

£

www.ddaymuseum.co.uk

INTECH Science Centre and Planetarium

Winchester

053

Intech's aim is to advance the education, knowledge and understanding of the public in basic technological and scientific principles and processes. The stimulating, fun exhibition consists of 100 hands-on interactive exhibits, such as how to bend light and creating your own tornado, which communicate the fundamental principles of science and technology and their applications in industry and the home. In 2008, a state-of-the-art digital planetarium with room for 176 people was added and now presents a range of spectacular shows.

🔍 Off the A31 near Winchester

❁ ⚙ ♣ ❄

⏳ 2–3 hours

★ The digital Planetarium

£

www.intech-uk.com

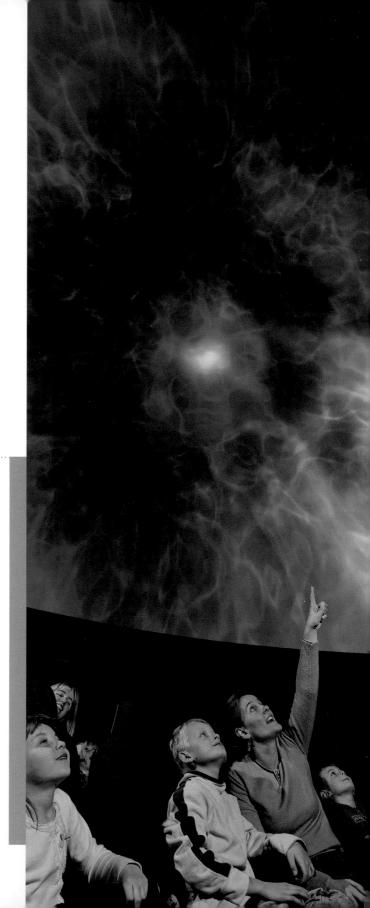

Marwell Wildlife
Winchester

A visit to Marwell Wildlife is a chance to get close to the wonders of the natural world – and play a big part in helping to save them. The 140-acre park is home to over 250 exotic and endangered species, in beautiful, landscaped surroundings. See giraffe, zebra, waterbuck and ostrich roaming wild in the African Valley. Discover the secrets of the rainforest in Tropical World. Marvel at wallabies and kookaburra on the Australian Bush Walk. Dive beneath the surface with the underwater views in Penguin World. There's also a free road train to help you get around.

Follow signs from M3 and M37 near Winchester

3-4 hours

The new Siamang gibbons

www.marwell.org.uk

Fort Victoria Country Park
Yarmouth

Built on the north shore of the Isle of Wight to guard the Solent the remains of Fort Victoria now house a fascinating marine aquarium, an underwater archaeology centre that concentrates on ships claimed by the Island's treacherous waters, a multimedia astrodome planetarium and exhibition area and one of the largest and most advanced model railways in the country. The surrounding Country Park offers seashore and woodland walks and the site is one of the best vantage points for watching the Solent's boats and shipping.

Off the A3054 west of Yarmouth

4-5 hours

Guided woodland and seashore walks

If you do everything

www.fortvictoria.co.uk

Canterbury Tales
Canterbury

This fascinating audio-visual experience, sited in the centre of Canterbury, is one of this historic city's most popular visitor attractions. Step back in time to experience the sights, sounds and smells of the Middle Ages in this stunning reconstruction of 14th-century England. Inside the historic building of St Margaret's Church you can travel back over 500 years to join Geoffrey Chaucer (England's finest poet) and his colourful characters as they tell each other tales on their pilgrimage from London to the shrine of St Thomas Becket in Canterbury Cathedral.

In the city centre, just off the High Street

1 hour

The Miller's Tale

www.canterburytales.org.uk

Howletts, The Aspinall Wild Animal Park `057`
Canterbury

Attractive, well-laid out and full of happy animals in spacious enclosures Howletts is a top quality zoo. From glass-fronted tiger enclosures offering a close encounter with the biggest of cats to gorillas, clouded leopards, monkeys and hundreds of rare and endangered species from around the world. It is also home to the UK's largest herd of African elephants and the black rhino breeding sanctuary. For a close encounter like no other, you can walk alongside, and below, a free roaming family of amazingly agile and lively lemurs.

🔍 On the A2, 3 miles south of Canterbury
⚙
⏳ 2–3 hours
⭐ Big and small cats and gorillas
💷 💷
www.aspinallfoundation.org/howletts

Roman Museum `058`
Canterbury

The museum is underground at the level of the Roman town. It's an exciting mix of excavated real objects, authentic reconstructions and the preserved remains of a Roman town house. A skilful computer program brings together pictures of the excavations on the site, and from the archaeologists' detail it generates images of what the great house found here was like in Roman times. Reconstructions include a Roman market place, with a shoemaker, fabric seller and fruit and vegetable stall. At the end of the museum is the acclaimed 'touch the past' area where visitors can handle real Roman artefacts.

🔍 In Butchery Lane, close to the cathedral
⚙ ⚙ ✿ ❄
⏳ 1 hour
⭐ Town house mosaic
💷
www.canterbury.gov.uk

The Historic Dockyard, Chatham `059`
Chatham

A unique maritime heritage destination brought to life by costumed guides. The Victorian Ropery Tour; Three Historic Warships, Wooden Walls of England, the Royal Dockyard Museum, 3 Slip – The BIG Store and the RNLI Historic Lifeboat Collection are just some of the exciting galleries and attractions to suit all ages. Visit the beautiful Commissioner's garden for a little peace and quiet and allow the children to let off steam in the indoor soft play and outdoor adventure play areas. All tickets are valid for 12 months.

🔍 Follow signs from junction 1 of A2/M2
⚙ ⚙ ✿ ❄
⏳ 2–3 hours
⭐ 3 Slip – The BIG Store: a massive museum for massive things found around the Dockyard
💷 💷
www.chdt.org.uk

Dover Castle `061`
Dover

Commanding the shortest Channel sea crossing, this site has been the UK's most important defence against invasion since the Iron Age. The castle was built by Henry II in the 12th century and reinforced by Henry VIII in the 1530s but has acted as the 'key to England' in many conflicts since then. Today, visitors can experience the majesty of medieval court life within the Great Tower and re-live the turbulent war years in the secret wartime tunnels set deep within the famous White Cliffs. You can also walk round the extensive battlements, the medieval tunnels and Roman lighthouse.

🔍 On the white cliffs just east of the city
✿ ☼ ♣ ❄
⏳ 3–4 hours
⭐ The Great Tower
£ £
www.english-heritage.org.uk/dovercastle

Chislehurst Caves `060`
Chislehurst

Grab a lantern and get ready for an amazing adventure! In these hand-carved caves, dug over 8,000 years in search of lime, chalk and flint, your whole family can travel back in time as you explore the maze of passageways deep in the ground beneath Chislehurst. During a 45-minute guided tour, visit the Caves Church, Druid Altar and Haunted Pool, find out more about the mining, how the caves were used in the war and find out about the scenes filmed there for *Dr Who* and BBC TV's recent *Merlin* series.

🔍 Off the A222, near Chislehurst railway station
✿ ☼ ♣ ❄ School holidays (check website for other opening times)
⏳ 1 hour
⭐ Guided tours
£
www.chislehurstcaves.co.uk

Hever Castle and Gardens `062`
Edenbridge

The oldest part of the castle dates to 1270. In the early 1500s it became the childhood home of Anne Boleyn. From 1557 onwards the castle was owned by a number of families, until in 1903 William Waldorf Astor invested time, money and imagination in restoring the castle and creating the gardens and lake. The castle houses historic Tudor portraits, furniture and tapestries. The magnificent gardens have superb floral displays and a number of water features. Other areas that you can stroll through include the Tudor Garden, Rhododendron Walk and along Anne Boleyn's Walk.

🔍 3 miles south east of Edenbridge, off the B2026
✿
⏳ 3–4 hours
⭐ A stroll through the magnificent gardens to the lake
£ £
www.hevercastle.co.uk

Eagle Heights Wildlife Park `063`
Eynsford

Eagle Heights is one of the UK's largest bird of prey centres, with a current collection of approximately 150 raptors. This includes over 50 species, many of which are now breeding at the centre or can be seen flying in daily demonstrations. The park is also expanding and now includes a number of different species of animals including a new reptile house, cheetahs, meerkats, otters and lizards. The park also runs educational courses, operates as a sanctuary and runs a bird hospital and a breeding programme.

Follow signs from junction 3 of the M25 and the A20

2-3 hours

Zina, the new cheetah cub

www.eagleheights.co.uk

Lullingstone Roman Villa `064`
Eynsford

Lullingstone is one of Britain's most exciting archaeological finds. The villa was built c. AD 75, and extended several times during 300 years of Roman occupation: it includes a room decorated with Christian symbols, among the earliest evidence for Christianity in Britain. Much is still visible today from specially built galleries, including mosaic-tiled floors, wall paintings, and the extensive 4th-century bath complex, built when the villa was at its most prosperous. There is also a display of the skeletal remains found on site.

Follow signs from junction 3 of the M25

Check website for winter opening hours

1-2 hours

Mosaic-tiled floors

www.englishheritage.org.uk

Farming World `065`
Faversham

Farming World is home to hundreds of different animals including beautiful rare-breed pigs, cows, goats, sheep, llamas, alpacas and some really beautiful heavy horses. The farm's ongoing programme of breeding means that there are often piglets, lambs and baby rabbits to be seen in Kid's Corner. You can also see poultry and geese and a number of different species renowned for their ornamental qualities, including pheasants and peafowl. There is also a programme of spectacular flying displays put on by a variety of impressive birds of prey.

On A299 from junction 7 of the M2

2-3 hours

Hawklands flying display

www.farming-world.com

South of England Rare Breeds Centre `067`
Hamstreet

Pigs have pride of place at this friendly and popular attraction in the heart of the garden of England. But there are rare breeds of all kinds here including Bagot goats, brought to Britain by the Crusaders, and Lincoln Longwool sheep that date back to Roman times. These are the ancient breeds from farming's past, with a vital role in farming's future. There are special pens where children can play with piglets and other small animals. Pigs, sheep, goats, cattle, horses, chickens and ducks are here – and others that may surprise you.

Off M20 at junction 10, follow signs to Hamstreet

2–3 hours

Pig racing, see website for details

www.rarebreeds.org.uk

Bedgebury National Pinetum `066`
Goudhurst

Originally a woodland valley walk, the last few years have seen the Pinetum transformed to one of the Kentish Weald's finest visitor attractions. There are new walks, bike trails, an adventure hike and two fantastic play areas for children as well as a top-quality Go Ape! facility. The Pinetum itself is a forest made up of over 10,000 conifers. A walk through the valley provides a haven of beauty and tranquillity throughout the year. For those in search of more energetic pursuits there are walks, cycle tracks, archery, guided tours, mushroom hunts, hidden rope swings and climbing frames.

Follow signs from A21 near Flimwell

2–3 hours

Pinetum valley walk

www.bedgeburypinetum.org.uk

Wildwood `068`
Herne Bay

Wildwood's extensive collection of animals includes badgers, foxes, otters, pine marten and red squirrels that have inhabited Britain for the last 10,000 years as well as animals that have been hunted to extinction in the UK, such as wolves, lynx and beaver. The facility is also involved in conservation work that is helping to restore natural habitats and support endangered native species. There is also an adventure playground and a Wild Fort, and visitors get the chance to meet friendly creatures in the Animal Encounters enclosure.

Off A291 near Herne Bay

2 hours

Wolves and lynxes

www.wildwoodtrust.org

Port Lympne Wild Animal Park | 069
Hythe

One of the best zoos in Southern England, Port Lympne's extensive and beautiful grounds are home to an incredible collection of the world's most exciting animals. Set in 600 acres, the zoo includes Siberian and Indian tigers, Barbary lions, small cats, monkeys and many other rare and endangered species. The park is also home to the largest breeding herd of black rhinos outside of Africa and the largest gorillarium in the world. The African Experience takes visitors across open plains with giraffe, black rhino, wildebeest, zebra, ostrich, antelope and other wildlife roaming free.

🔍 Follow signs from junction 11 of the M20

⚙️

⏳ 3-4 hours

⭐ The Siberian and Indian tigers

💷 💷 (the African Experience is extra)

www.aspinallfoundation.org/portlympne

Bewl Water | 070
Lamberhurst

Originally a reservoir created in the 1970s, Bewl Water has now become a leading visitor facility in the heart of the Weald of Kent. You can bring your own bikes to cycle the 13 miles around the reservoir or hire them on-site. Of course, you can take shorter walks and stop at any number of viewing points along the way. There are also boat rides, sailing, fishing, zip wiring, hydro balling and a tremendous children's play area with a magnificent slide. The reservoir also runs a regular programme of events.

🔍 Off A21 near Lamberhurst

⚙️

⏳ 3-4 hours

⭐ Strolling past the most picturesque stretch of inland water in the south-east

💷

www.bewl.co.uk

Kent Life | 071
Maidstone

A unique open-air living museum that celebrates 150 years of rural Kentish life. Traditional crafts are demonstrated on a 28-acre, working farm created in a series of traditional buildings, including cottages, oast houses and barns that have been rescued and re-erected. There are also animals, birds, a nature trail, boat trips, tractor rides, stilt walking and an exciting children's adventure play area. This is also one of the few places in England where hops are grown, harvested, dried and packed using time-honoured techniques.

🔍 Follow signs from junction 6 of the M20

⚙️ ⚙️ ✤

⏳ 2 hours

⭐ The Victorian farmhouse

💷

www.museum-kentlife.co.uk

29

Leeds Castle   072
Maidstone

Set on two islands in a lake, Leeds is a magnificent castle with significant royal connections. Originally a Norman stronghold, Leeds has since been a residence for six of England's medieval queens, a palace for Henry VIII and a retreat for the rich and powerful. Fully restored by an American heiress in the 1930s, the castle now looks just as a 12th-century fortress should. A tour of the castle is essential to get a real feel of this special place, but the grounds are also very impressive.

🔍 Follow signs from junction 8 of the M20

✳ ◎ ♣ ❄

⏳ 2-3 hours

★ Summer concerts and hot air balloon festival

£ £

www.leeds-castle.com

Romney, Hythe and Dymchurch Railway   073
New Romney

This was the world's smallest public railway when it opened in July 1927. Requisitioned by the War Department in 1940, the railway was gradually reopened when Laurel and Hardy cut the ribbon for the Dungeness section in 1947. It now runs regular passenger services covering a distance of 13½ miles from the picturesque Cinque Port of Hythe to the fishermen's cottages and lighthouses at Dungeness. The railway also runs a full programme of events including 'Drive a Locomotive' days and 1940s weekends and dance nights.

🔍 Stations at New Romney, Dungeness and Hythe all on or near the A259

✳ ◎ ♣ ❄   Check website for timetable

⏳ 2 hours

★ A steam driver experience day

£ £

www.rhdr.org.uk

The Hop Farm Family Park   074
Paddock Wood

Over the last few years the Hop Farm has grown and developed into one of Kent's premier visitor attractions. It hosts a bewildering number of events all year round. At its heart is the World of Activities, which includes over 30 rides and other attractions such as the Leap of Faith, the Magic Factory, Giant Jumping Pillows, a driving school, Shire horse rides and the like. In the centre is a huge outdoor adventure play area with bridges, slides and tunnels. It's well worth booking online for good discounts.

🔍 Follow signs from junction 4 of the M20 and junction 5 of the M25

✳ ◎ ♣ ❄

⏳ 3-4 hours

★ The newly opened Enchanted Kingdom

£ £

www.thehopfarm.co.uk

Ightham Mote 076
Sevenoaks

Dating from 1320, Ightham Mote is a rare example of a medieval moated manor house and is exquisitely beautiful. The inner courtyard, which houses a Grade I listed dog kennel, is reached via a bridge and castellated gatehouse. The exterior of the house, the ancestral home of the Sidney family since 1552, is half-timbered while the interior is unspoiled and includes a fine Great Hall, old chapel, crypt and a Tudor chapel with a hand painted ceiling. The gardens are lovely and include water features, a lakeside and several woodland walks.

🔍 Follow signs from the A25 at Borough Green
✿ ◉ ✚ Weekends only
⌛ 2-3 hours
⭐ The views from the top of the tower
£
www.nationaltrust.org.uk

Penshurst Place and Gardens 075
Penshurst

This medieval manor house was built in 1341. The Baron's Hall, with its 60-foot high, chestnut-beamed roof and trestle tables, is regarded as one of the world's grandest rooms. Other staterooms boast a remarkable collection of tapestries, paintings, furniture, porcelain and armour. Much of the house and gardens remain unchanged since the days when Elizabeth I visited the property. The ten acres of garden retain the original terraces and walls of the 16th century. Designed to be a garden for all seasons, visitors can enjoy a feast of colour and beauty from spring through to autumn.

🔍 Follow signs from Hildenborough on the A21
✿ ◉ ✚
⌛ 2 hours
⭐ The toy museum
£
www.penshurstplace.com

Sissinghurst Castle and Gardens 077
Sissinghurst

Hardly a castle, but it is home to one of the world's most celebrated gardens, created by Vita Sackville-West and her husband, Sir Harold Nicholson in the ruins of a large Elizabethan house. The library and the tower, which are open to the public, include Vita's writing room. The gardens are astonishing, providing colour and fragrance throughout the year. As many people will have seen from the BBC TV series, the new vegetable garden is now in production, supplying fresh produce to the licensed restaurant.

🔍 1 mile east of Sissinghurst on the A262
✿ ◉ ✚ Afternoons are best
⌛ 2-3 hours
⭐ Views of the Weald from the top of the tower
£ £
www.nationaltrust.org.uk

Kent and East Sussex Railway 078

Tenterden

Take a nostalgic trip behind a full-size steam engine on Britain's first light railway. Journey through 10½ miles of unspoilt countryside in the Rother Valley between Tenterden and the Sussex village of Bodiam, via Rolvenden, Wittersham Road and Northiam. You will be thrilled by the sights and sounds of steam engines. As well as the regular services, the railway has a full programme of events including Pullman dining, gala weekends with visiting engines, 1940s weekends and Days Out with Thomas.

🔍 Off Tenterden High Street on A28
⚙ ◎ ♣ Check website for timetable before travelling
⏳ 2 hours
⭐ Travelling in style through the Garden of England
£ £
www.kesr.org.uk

Groombridge Place Gardens and Enchanted Forest 079

Tunbridge Wells

In addition to strolling through the gardens of 17th-century Groombridge Place – the setting for the Sherlock Holmes mystery *The Valley of Fear* – you can also visit a rustic theme park on a hill overlooking the house. This is the Enchanted Forest where you can enjoy exciting playgrounds, huge swings, strange plants, giant rabbits and shy deer. Don't miss the raised wooden adventure boardwalk, the Dinosaur and Dragon Valley, the Serpent's Lair and a canal cruise. There are also flying displays by birds of prey at the Raptor Centre.

🔍 Groombridge is 4 miles west of Tunbridge Wells on B2110
⚙
⏳ 2-3 hours
⭐ Giant rabbits in the Grooms' Village
£ £
www.groombridgeplace.co.uk

Chartwell 080

Westerham

The home of Winston Churchill, Britain's wartime Prime Minister, for over 40 years, Chartwell remains pretty much as it was in his day. With many of his personal possessions and reminders of the man voted greatest Briton of all time, the house enables visitors to capture the mood of some of the key moments in British history. The lakes, populated with his favourite black swans, and the hillside gardens reflect the great statesman's love of the Wealden landscape and nature. Many of his paintings are on show in the studio.

🔍 2 miles south of Westerham. Follow signs from junctions 5 or 6 of the M25
⚙ ◎ ♣
⏳ 2 hours
⭐ The interior of Churchill's stunning home
£ £
www.nationaltrust.org.uk

British Museum
Bloomsbury

The British Museum, founded in 1753 from the collection of Sir Hans Sloane, is home to an unrivalled collection of art and antiquities from ancient and living cultures. Housed in one of Britain's architectural landmarks, the collection – which numbers some 7 million objects – is one of the finest in existence, spanning two million years of human history. Famous objects include the Rosetta Stone, sculptures from the Parthenon, the Elgin Marbles, Leonardo da Vinci's notebook, the Sutton Hoo and Mildenhall treasures and the Portland Vase.

Near Holborn tube station

3-4 hours

The mummies of Ancient Egypt

FREE

www.britishmuseum.org

STAR ATTRACTION

Camden Market
Camden Town

At the cutting edge of street fashion since the 1970s, no trip to London is complete without a visit to Camden Market. In fact there are a number of markets here but it all began in Camden Lock in 1975. Between them, the five markets now draw more than 150,000 people a week with many stalls and shops open every day. You can buy just about anything here – designer and second-hand clothes, home furnishing, unique fabrics and furniture, paintings, prints, handcrafted traditional and contemporary jewellery. Alternatively, you can just stand and stare at the wonderful sights.

Between Camden Town and Chalk Farm tube stations

2-3 hours

The sights and sounds of contemporary London

FREE (unless you buy something)

www.camdenlock.net

Museum of London
City

The Museum of London presents a quarter of a million years of social history in the city. The museum comprises a series of chronological galleries such as the prehistoric city, Medieval London and the Great Fire. A new development sees the opening of four new galleries in 2010, which tell the story of the city from 1666 to the present day. Star exhibits include a reconstruction of the Victorian Vauxhall Pleasure Gardens, the foreboding wooden interior of the Wellclose debtors' prison, and fashions from the 1950s right up to a pashmina from Alexander McQueen's 2008 collection.

Close to Barbican, St Paul's and Moorgate tube stations

2-3 hours

The Lord Mayor's State Coach

FREE

www.museumoflondon.org.uk

St Paul's Cathedral

City

The grave of the architect Sir Christopher Wren is in the south-east corner of the crypt of this, his greatest work. The inscription on it, written by his eldest son, reads, 'Reader, if you seek his memorial – look around you.' If you do so, you will not be disappointed. The distinctive dome on this magnificent cathedral is the most prominent landmark on London's skyline. Its monumental interior, sacred tombs and atmospheric crypt ensure that it remains one of London's major tourist attractions.

Near St Paul's tube station

Monday to Saturday

1 hour

The Whispering Gallery

FREE Guided tours

www.stpauls.co.uk

Buckingham Palace

Green Park

This is the official residence of Her Majesty The Queen. The 19 State Rooms are used extensively to entertain guests on official occasions but are open to the public during August and September. These rooms form the heart of the working palace and are lavishly furnished with some of the greatest treasures from the Royal Collection – paintings by Rembrandt, Rubens and Canaletto; sculpture by Canova; exquisite examples of Sèvres porcelain and some of the finest English and French furniture. Visits end with a walk along the south side of the palace's extensive garden.

Near Victoria, Green Park and Hyde Park Corner tube stations

See website for booking details

1–2 hours

Special exhibition entitled 'The Queen's Year'

www.royal.gov.uk

National Maritime Museum 086
Greenwich

This World Heritage Site comprises the National Maritime Museum, the Royal Observatory and the Queen's House, which constitute one museum working to illustrate the importance of the sea, ships, time and the stars and their relationship with people. Arranged in a series of themed galleries you can recall the romance of the great ocean liners, delve into the traditions of maritime London and study the controversial history of trade across the Atlantic. The Queen's House holds much of the museum's art and the Royal Observatory has a number of galleries dedicated to astronomy and a state-of-the-art Planetarium.

🔍 Near Greenwich main line or Cutty Sark DLR stations
☀ ⚙ ♣ ❄
⏳ 2–3 hours
⭐ Stand on the line where East meets West
FREE There is a charge for the Planetarium
www.nmm.ac.uk

Royal Botanic Gardens 087
Kew

Located in 300 acres of beautiful landscape Kew Gardens sit beside the river Thames at Kew in south-west London. The gardens are a World Heritage Site with six magnificent glasshouses, and are home to a remarkable collection of plants from all over the world including over 14,000 trees. Kew Gardens is a wonderful day out for all. If you haven't been to Kew before, don't miss the 19th-century Palm House, the tropical atmosphere of the Princess of Wales Conservatory, a walk to the iconic pagoda, and a climb up for a birds-eye view at the new Xstrata Treetop Walkway.

🔍 Kew Gardens underground station
☀ ♣
⏳ 2–3 hours
⭐ The Palm House
💷 💷
www.kew.org

Imperial War Museum 088
Lambeth

The Imperial War Museum in London was created in 1917 to collect and display material relating to the First World War. In 1939 the Museum started adding artefacts from the Second World War and eventually it began its current policy of including memorabilia from all modern British conflicts. Inside you will find military vehicles, weapons, war memorabilia, an extensive library open to the public Monday to Saturday, a photographic archive, and an art collection of 20th century and later conflicts, especially those involving Britain, and the British Empire.

🔍 Lambeth North or Waterloo tube stations
☀ ⚙ ♣ ❄
⏳ 2–3 hours
⭐ The walk through a First World War trench
FREE (exhibitions may charge)
www.iwm.org.uk

London Dungeon 089
London Bridge

The London Dungeon is an interactive attraction that dispenses fear and fun in equal doses. Visitors encounter a number of 'horrible' historic events, such as the Great Plague, Jack the Ripper and the Great Fire of London. In all there are 12 shows and two scary rides. The various stories are told by actors as visitors move from room to room – in the dark. The atmosphere is spooky and it is easy to be disoriented, but the laughter makes it a great experience. Make sure you buy tickets online to get the best prices.

🔍 Near London Bridge tube station
☀ ⚙ ♣ ❄
⏳ 1–2 hours
⭐ The Drop Ride to Hell
💷 💷 💷
www.thedungeons.com

Madame Tussaud's   090
Marylebone

Consistently voted London's number one tourist attraction, but not at all popular with Londoners – decide for yourself by visiting the world's most famous waxworks. If you fancy attending an A-list party, going to a star-studded film premiere, challenging your sporting heroes or taking to the stage with music's megastars, being knighted by the Queen or addressing the world's leaders, you can do all these things as you mingle and interact with the world's most famous figures at Madame Tussaud's.

🔍 Near Baker Street tube station
✿ ◉ ♣ ❀
⧗ 2 hours
★ The Chamber of Horrors
💷 💷 💷
www.madametussauds.com

Sherlock Holmes Museum   091
Marylebone

Sherlock Holmes and Doctor John H. Watson lived at 221b Baker Street between 1881 and 1904, according to the stories written by Sir Arthur Conan Doyle. The house was last used as a lodging house in 1936 and the famous first floor study overlooking Baker Street is still faithfully maintained as it was in Victorian Times. Step back in time, and when you visit London, remember to visit the world's most famous address – 221b Baker Street – the official home of Sherlock Holmes.

🔍 Near Baker Street tube station
✿ ◉ ♣ ❀
⧗ 1 hour
★ Wax figures from the best-known stories
💷
www.sherlock-holmes.co.uk

London Zoo
Regent's Park

092

An institution in London since 1828, the zoo sits in the north-eastern corner of the lovely Regent's Park. It's pretty good for an inner-city zoo, and has an impressive range of animals all kept in suitable enclosures. The zoo is big but well laid out and easy to get around. Highlights include the Reptile House, as featured in Harry Potter, the zebras, the Moonlit World, the penguins, the Komodo dragons and, of course, all the big cats you'd expect. There are also regular shows such as Animals in Action, which are popular with children.

Near Camden Town tube station

3-4 hours

The new Rainforest Life exhibit

www.zsl.org

STAR ATTRACTION

BBC Television Centre Tours
Shepherd's Bush

093

Take an exclusive look into the BBC newsroom, see the famous studios and take part in making your own bit of TV in an interactive studio. You'll see memorabilia from programmes such as *EastEnders* and *Doctor Who*, and venture into the dressing rooms that have hosted so many famous guests over the decades. Well-informed guides will entertain you as you walk in the footsteps of your favourite stars. They will make sure that you see the most interesting areas available on the day of your visit, as well as giving you an insight into how TV really works.

Near White City tube station

See website for details

1-2 hours

You never know who you might bump in to!

www.bbc.co.uk/tours

Shakespeare's Globe
South Bank

094

Based under the Globe, this engaging and informative exhibition explores the life of Shakespeare, the London where he lived, and the theatre for which he wrote. It also has a collection of costumes used during recent productions at the theatre. A fascinating guided tour inside the theatre reveals the story of its reconstruction and gives an exciting insight into the working life of the Globe. Tickets include a 30–40 minute guided tour of the theatre, plus an all-day ticket to an exhibition.

Near Southwark tube station

1-2 hours

Cutting edge theatrical effects

www.shakespeares-globe.org

STAR ATTRACTION

The 135-metre high big wheel provides the most **spectacular views** of one of the biggest cities in the world

London Eye
South Bank

Originally chosen as the best of thousands of ideas as to how best to celebrate the Millennium, and erected in 1999, the London Eye soon became and still remains the most popular tourist attraction in London. The 135-metre high big wheel provides the most spectacular views of one of the biggest cities in the world. On a clear day you can see 25 miles in every direction from one of 32 safe and comfortable capsules. Famous landmarks to be seen include Big Ben, Houses of Parliament, St Paul's Cathedral, Buckingham Palace and Westminster Abbey. You can also book a guide, or take a Champagne or Pimm's flight. It is essential to book in advance for all flights, see website for details, and you will need to arrive at least 30 minutes early.

In response to criticism of long queues, a new 4D pre-flight experience has been added for visitors. You will see the first-ever 3D aerial footage of London, which includes the spectacular New Year's Day fireworks, in a breathtaking journey across the city. Boasting added sensory effects, you will feel like you are really there; with wind in your hair, snow falling at your feet, the floor shaking and even a sense of smell, your new perspective on London will be truly memorable.

Near Waterloo tube station

1 hour

Dusk flight, just as London's lights come up

www.ba-londoneye.com

London Sealife Aquarium
South Bank

096

Part of the attractive South Bank complex, the London Aquarium is an impressive attraction. It includes three floors and 14 different tanks including the upper Atlantic, British harbour, Ray pool, Indian Ocean, mid-Pacific, Atlantic, Pacific, coral reef, invertebrates, tropical freshwater, Thames freshwater streams, mangrove and rainforest. The Pacific and Atlantic zones both contain large tanks with numerous species, such as green sea turtles and sharks. Recent additions included a glass tunnel, Shark Walk and a revamped Pacific Ocean tank. In all the facility is home to around 400 species of fish.

Near Westminster tube station

1 hour

The sharks

www.londonaquarium.co.uk

Tate Modern
South Bank

097

Another must see for all visitors to London, Britain's national museum of modern and contemporary art (post-1900) from around the world is housed in the former Bankside Power Station on the banks of the Thames. The awe-inspiring Turbine Hall runs the length of the entire building inside which you can see a permanent collection of amazing works by artists such as Cézanne, Bonnard, Matisse, Picasso, Rothko, Dalí, Pollock, Warhol and Bourgeois. There is also a programme of temporary exhibitions, although they may carry an entrance fee.

Near Southwark tube station

2-3 hours

Matisse, Dalí, Warhol, Rothko

FREE (exhibitions may charge)

www.tate.org.uk

Science Museum 099
South Kensington

The science museum is huge, covering five floors, so don't expect to see it all in one go. Each floor looks at a different aspect of technology and science using displays and interactive information. The ground floor looks at vehicles and space exploration. The first floor is dedicated to food, gas, structural metals and communications. On the second floor you can learn about nuclear power, printing and computing. The third floor looks at photography and optics with electricity and the top two floors concentrate on the science of medicine.

🔍 Near South Kensington tube station

⚙ ◎ ♣ ❄

⌛ 2-3 hours

★ The Launch Pad

FREE (some exhibits may charge)

www.sciencemuseum.org.uk

Natural History Museum 098
South Kensington

Home to one of the largest natural history collections in the world, the entrance hall to this impressive museum is home to an astounding Diplodocus skeleton. The museum is divided into four zones. The green zone concentrates on facts about environment and evolution. The red zone explores our ever-changing planet. In the blue zone you can marvel at the diversity of life from blue whales to the smallest invertebrates. Finally the orange zone takes you into the Darwin centre and the wildlife garden (open between April and October) where you can explore world-class science in action.

🔍 Near South Kensington underground station

⚙ ◎ ♣ ❄

⌛ 2-3 hours

★ The blue whale

FREE

www.nhm.ac.uk

Victoria and Albert Museum 100
South Kensington

Widely regarded as the world's greatest museum of applied and decorative arts, the V&A is home to an amazing array of artefacts from the world's richest cultures. The museum has been entertaining visitors for over 150 years in its 7 miles of corridors, so it must have something for you. Subjects covered include: architecture, Asia, ceramics, contemporary fashion, jewellery and accessories, furniture, glass, history, periods and styles, Metalwork, photography, prints and books, textiles, theatre and performance. Often overlooked in favour of its illustrious neighbours, this museum is well worth a visit.

🔍 Near South Kensington tube station

⚙ ◎ ♣ ❄

⌛ 3-4 hours

★ The Great Bed of Ware

FREE (some exhibitions may charge)

www.vam.ac.uk

Dennis Severs House   101
Spitalfields

18 Folgate Street appears to be a typical Georgian terraced house, until you step behind the front door and are swiftly transported back to the 18th century. Severs moved into the house in 1979 and decided to recreate the home of a fictitious family of Huguenot silk-weavers. As you enter each room there is a sense that the occupants have just slipped out – a half-eaten meal sits on the table and beds are left unmade. The attention to detail is impressive, with what Severs called his 'still-life drama' blurring the line between history and fantasy, truth and imagination.

🔍 10 minutes walk from Liverpool Street tube station
✹ ✺ ♣ ❄ See website for booking details
⏳ 1 hour
★ Silent Night tours
💷 💷
www.dennissevershouse.co.uk

Lord's Tour and MCC Museum   102
St John's Wood

Lord's is one of the most famous sporting venues in the world. Tours start in the MCC Museum, home of the famous Ashes urn as well as paintings, photographs and artefacts that cover 400 years of cricket history and trace the game's development from a rural pastime to a modern international sport. You then visit the famed Long Room, which is lined with portraits of the game's best-known figures, has panoramic views of the pitch and is where players make their way to and from the hallowed turf. Other highlights include the players' dressing rooms and the famous Lord's honours board.

🔍 Near St John's Wood tube station
✺ See website for opening times
⏳ 1–2 hours
★ The famous Ashes urn
💷 💷
www.lords.org

Ragged School Museum   103
Stepney

Housed in what was once London's biggest Ragged School, this popular, family-friendly museum welcomes people of all ages to taste a slice of Victorian life. Located beside the Regent's Canal the museum offers, through role-play, hands-on exhibits and talks, an authentic and memorable experience of the poor of the East End a century ago. The museum includes a reconstructed Victorian classroom, along with features on housing, education and work in the city's poorest parts from the 1880s to 1900.

🔍 Near Mile End tube station
✹ ✺ ♣ ❄ Wednesdays and Thursdays only
⏳ 1 hour
★ Slate writing boards and dunce hats
FREE
www.raggedschoolmuseum.org.uk

Tower Bridge Exhibition `104`
Tower Bridge

Opened in 1894, Tower Bridge is the most famous bridge in the world. Housed inside the bridge's twin towers the Tower Bridge Exhibition explains how the bridge works and tells the history of its construction through film, photographs, information panels and holograms. Enjoy breathtaking panoramic views through special viewing windows on the high-level walkways that sit 45 metres above the River Thames and then visit the original Victorian Steam engines that raised and lowered the bascules (so-called from the French word for see-saw).

🔍 Near Tower Hill and London Bridge tube stations
☀ ◑ ❀ ❄
⧗ 1 hour
★ Unique views of the city from the top of the bridge
♿
www.towerbridge.org.uk

Winston Churchill's Britain at War Experience `105`
Tower Bridge

The intention of this interesting attraction is to explain as closely as possible what life in London was really like during the Second World War. It recreates the London Blitz in all its fury with special effects highlighting the sights and sounds. Visit the London Underground air raid shelter and see where thousands spent sleepless nights. Keep up to date with wartime news in the underground cinema. Enter the BBC radio studio and tune in to Rome, Washington, London and Berlin for the latest messages from Churchill, Roosevelt, Hitler and Lord Haw Haw.

🔍 Near London Bridge tube station
☀ ◑ ❀ ❄
⧗ 1-2 hours
★ Wartime newsreels
♿ ♿
www.britainatwar.co.uk

Tower of London `106`
Tower Hill

Founded by William the Conqueror and modified by successive sovereigns, the Tower of London (which actually has 11 towers) is one of the world's most famous and spectacular fortresses. Discover its history as a palace, fortress, prison, mint, arsenal, menagerie and jewel house. Far more than just a chance to see the famous Crown Jewels, there are talks, Beefeater tours, holiday events and family tours all included in the basic ticket price. Other highlights include Traitors' Gate, the White Tower and the Scaffold Site where seven of the Tower's most important prisoners were executed.

🔍 Near Tower Hill, Fenchurch Street and London Bridge tube stations
☀ ◑ ❀ ❄
⧗ 3-4 hours
★ The Crown Jewels
♿ ♿
www.hrp.org.uk

London Duck Tours
Waterloo

Fast becoming a new favourite on the tourist trail, a Duck Tour is an absolutely unique way to see London. You are rewarded not only with a live guided road tour of the City of Westminster, passing landmarks such as Trafalgar Square, the Houses of Parliament and Big Ben, but you are also treated to an unforgettable trip on the river, without ever leaving the comfort of your seat. All this on a historic vehicle used for the D-day landings in 1944. Tours run every day but it is essential to book.

Near Waterloo tube station

1 hour

★ The water launch at Vauxhall

£ £ £

www.londonducktours.co.uk

National Gallery   107
Trafalgar Square

The National Gallery was built especially for the purpose of showing a national collection of art and opened in 1838; it now houses one of the greatest collections of European painting in the world. The permanent collection spans the period from 1250 to 1900 and includes paintings by artists such as Leonardo da Vinci, Michelangelo, Rembrandt, Rubens, Monet, J.M.W. Turner, Vincent van Gogh and many others. There are also special exhibitions, lectures, 10-minute talks, video and audio-visual programmes, guided tours and holiday events for children and adults.

Near Leicester Square and Charing Cross tube stations

2–3 hours

★ *Sunflowers* by Vincent van Gogh

FREE (some exhibitions may charge)

www.nationalgallery.org.uk

STAR ATTRACTION

Wembley Stadium Tour   `109`
Wembley

Until your dream comes true, there's only one way to experience what it's like winning at Wembley – take the tour. Go behind the scenes and feel the magic in your own unforgettable 90-minute tour. You can sense the history in the England changing room, feel the tension in the players' tunnel, climb the sacred trophy winners' steps and raise the replica FA Cup. Your privileged access to Wembley's historical treasures includes the 1966 World Cup crossbar and the Jules Rimet Trophy commemorating England's World Cup glory.

🔍 Near Wembley Park tube station
✸ ✸ ✿ ❋
⧖ 1–2 hours
★ A glimpse of the brand-new Wembley
£ £
www.wembleystadium.com

Houses of Parliament   `110`
Westminster

Visitors who tour Parliament will follow the processional route taken by Her Majesty the Queen when she performs the State Opening of Parliament. The tours take in the Lords and Commons Chambers plus other highlights such as Westminster Hall, the Queen's Robing Room, the Royal Gallery, Central Lobby and St Stephens Hall. Tours are available all year round (see website for details). UK residents can tour throughout the year but bookings must be made six months in advance through their local MP.

🔍 Near Westminster tube station
✸ ✸ ✿ ❋ See website for details
⧖ 1–2 hours
★ The throne in the Lords chamber
FREE For UK residents (if booked in advance) £ £ For foreign visitors
www.parliament.uk

Westminster Abbey   `111`
Westminster

Kings, queens, statesmen and soldiers, poets, priests, heroes and villains – the Abbey is a must-see living pageant of British history. Every year Westminster Abbey welcomes over one million visitors who want to explore this wonderful 700-year-old building. It has been the site of 38 coronations, houses 17 monarch's graves – including Elizabeth I, Henry V and James I – and those of over 3,000 others including Chaucer, Sir Isaac Newton, Laurence Olivier and Charles Dickens. Thousands more flock to the Abbey for worship at daily services.

🔍 Near St James's Park and Westminster tube stations
✸ ✸ ✿ ❋ Monday to Saturday
⧖ 1–2 hours
★ Poets' Corner
£ £
www.westminster-abbey.org

STAR ATTRACTION

Broughton Castle 112
Banbury

The original medieval house was built in about 1300 by Sir John de Broughton. It stands on an island surrounded by a moat. Enlarged between 1550 and 1600, it was also embellished with magnificent plaster ceilings, splendid panelling and fine fireplaces. The house was captured after the nearby battle of Edgehill in the Civil War. Arms and armour from the period are displayed in the Great Hall. Visitors may also see the gatehouse, gardens and park together with the nearby 14th-century church of St Mary, in which there are many family tombs, memorials and hatchments.

On the B4035, 2 miles south-west of Banbury

Wednesdays and Sundays only

2–3 hours

Locations used for the film *Shakespeare in Love*

www.broughtoncastle.com

Cotswold Wildlife Park and Gardens 113
Burford

Cotswold Wildlife Park is set in 160 acres of parkland and gardens around a listed Victorian Manor House and has been open to the public since 1970. The park is home to a fascinating and varied collection of mammals, birds, reptiles and invertebrates from all over the world and aspires to show animals to people so that they can come to understand and respect all forms of wildlife; to understand what is special about each species, and how the various species have evolved over very long periods of time, adjusting to survive in a huge variety of habitats.

On the A361, 3 miles south of Burford

3–4 hours

Meerkats and the big cats

www.cotswoldwildlifepark.co.uk

Didcot Railway Centre 114
Didcot

Based at Didcot, halfway between Bristol and London, members of the Great Western Society have created a living museum of the Great Western Railway. It is based around the original engine shed and depot to which have been added a typical branch line with a country station and signalling demonstrations and a recreation of Brunel's original broad gauge trackwork. There is a large collection of GWR steam locomotives, carriages and wagons. On Steamdays the locomotives come to life, and you can ride in the 1930s trains.

Follow signs from junction 13 of the M4

Weekends only – see website for other opening days

2 hours

A ride behind Fire Fly – a replica of one of Brunel's broad gauge locomotives

www.didcotrailwaycentre.org.uk

Ashmolean Museum of Art and Archaeology
Oxford
115

Founded in 1683, the Ashmolean is the most important museum of art and archaeology in Britain. The collections span the civilisations of east and west, charting the aspirations of mankind from the Neolithic era to the present day. An innovative approach to displaying the collections has transformed the visitor's experience. Each object's story is traced as a journey of ideas and influences across time and continents, enabling visitors to discover how civilisations developed as part of an interrelated world culture.

🔍 On Beaumont Street in Oxford city centre
☀ ☁ 🍁 ❄ Closed on Mondays
⏳ 2–3 hours
⭐ A death mask of Oliver Cromwell
FREE
www.ashmolean.org

Blenheim Palace
Woodstock
117

Home to the 11th Duke and Duchess of Marlborough, Blenheim was also the birthplace of Sir Winston Churchill. Set in 2100 acres of beautiful parkland landscaped by 'Capability' Brown, the magnificent palace is surrounded by sweeping lawns, award-winning formal gardens and the great lake. Blenheim Palace is a unique example of English Baroque architecture. Inside, the scale of the palace is beautifully balanced by the intricate detail and delicacy of the carvings, the hand-painted ceilings and the amazing porcelain collections, tapestries and paintings displayed in each room.

🔍 Follow signs from junction 9 of the M20
☀ ☁ 🍁 ❄
⏳ 3–4 hours
⭐ Wonderful furniture and paintings
💷 💷
www.blenheimpalace.com

STAR ATTRACTION

Oxford Ghost Trails
Oxford
116

You are hereby cordially invited to join Bill Spectre on a tour of Oxford's ghosts. Illustrated with props and illusions, your costumed guide will entertain and horrify you while guiding you through the streets of this most historic city. You may regret not bringing a camera. The spirits of Oxford are revealed on Friday and Saturday evenings when those on the trail examine the nightmares that lie beneath the dreaming spires of this most edifying city. Join Bill as he lifts the lid on this seat of learning.

🔍 Broad Street or New Road
☀ ☁ 🍁 ❄ See website for details
⏳ 1–2 hours
⭐ Stories of Old Oxford
💷
www.ghosttrail.org

The Oxfordshire Museum   118
Woodstock

This local museum is a hidden gem and well worth a visit. Based in a 16th-century merchant's house – Fletcher's House – it illustrates a wealth of local history in 11 galleries spread over three floors. The museum features collections of local history, art, archaeology, the landscape and wildlife relating to the county of Oxfordshire, and to the town of Woodstock in particular. The museum also runs a regular programme of other exhibitions and events such as: 'Soldiers of Oxfordshire', 'A History of Human Hair' and a dinosaur's birthday party.

🔍 Park Street in Woodstock town centre
⚙ ⊙ ♣ ❄
⌛ 1-2 hours
⭐ Gallery on Roman Oxfordshire
FREE
www.oxfordshire.gov.uk

Painshill Park   120
Cobham

One of Britain's finest landscape parks, Painshill was created by Charles Hamilton, a son of the Earl of Abercorn, between 1738 and 1773. Although he ran out of money before the end of the project he designed and planted an archetypal 18th-century landscape complete with lake, beautiful views and follies. Visitors can see a working vineyard, a gothic temple, a Chinese bridge and a crystal grotto. Hamilton introduced a number of tree species that had been collected in North America and the fruits of some of the seeds he planted in 1748 can still be seen today.

🔍 Off the A3 and the A245 at Cobham
⚙
⌛ 3-4 hours
⭐ The newly restored hermitage
💷
www.painshill.co.uk

Thorpe Park   119
Chertsey

Thorpe Park is the UK's most thrilling theme park with incredible rides including Tidal Wave, Slammer and Rush. The live action horror maze SAW Alive is new for 2010, which joins SAW – The Ride and the 'unholy trinity' of fantastic roller coasters – the ten-looping Colossus, the heart pounding Nemesis Inferno and Europe's tallest and fastest launched roller coaster, Stealth. It's expensive but buying tickets online makes it a much better deal. If you like thrills, you will love this park.

🔍 Follow signs from junctions 11 or 13 of the M25
⚙ ⊙ ♣ ❄
⌛ 5-6 hours
⭐ SAW – The Ride is the park's best-loved ride
💷 💷 💷
www.thorpepark.com

Hampton Court Palace
East Molesey

`121`

Without doubt one of the most affecting of the royal palaces, Hampton Court is most closely associated with Henry VIII. He developed it in grand style after he acquired it from Cardinal Wolsey in the 1520s. You can explore Henry's magnificent State Apartments, feel the heat of the vast Tudor Kitchens, the eerie chill of the Haunted Gallery and then stroll through the elegant baroque apartments and glorious formal gardens before disappearing into the maze, where whispers of the past will haunt every step to the centre of this topiary puzzle.

🔍 Follow signs from junctions 10 and 12 of the M25

⚙

⌛ 3–4 hours

⭐ Guided tour with a costumed guide

💷 💷

www. hamptoncourtpalace.org.uk

Chessington World of Adventures
Epsom

`122`

The biggest theme park in the south of England began life as a zoo, but became a theme park during the 1980s. Today rides include Dragon's Fury, Vampire and Tomb Blaster, and there are gentler rides for the youngsters. The zoo is home to one of the biggest families of gorillas in Europe and some of the world's rarest large cats. Highlights include the Trail of the Kings and the Sea Life centre, which houses sharks and stingrays. The new Wild Asia features a thrilling ride, a jungle bus tour and a colourful maharaja's market.

🔍 Follow signs from the A3 or junctions 9 and 10 of the M25

⚙ ⚙ 🍁 ❄

⌛ 4–5 hours

⭐ KOBRA, the spinning disc ride

💷 💷 💷

www.chessington.com

Runnymede 123
Egham

These historic 'medes' on the banks of the River Thames are where the Magna Carta was sealed by King John in 1215. This great charter was the first step in the formation of the British constitution. Today the beautiful natural landscape has been used to commemorate this and other great moments in world history through a series of memorials designed by Maufe, Jellicoe and Lutyens. The memorials have created an atmosphere of reflection and you can stroll through the ancient woodlands, along the towpaths and in the meadows and remember.

🔍 Follow signs from junction 13 on the M25
⚙
⏳ 1–2 hours
⭐ Magna Carta memorial
FREE Car parking charge
www.nationaltrust.org.uk

Polesden Lacey 125
Guildford

This impressive Regency house is set in beautiful downland countryside with sweeping views across the Surrey Hills. Remodelled between 1906 and 1909 by the great Edwardian hostess, Mrs Ronald Greville, the house is the perfect example of an early 20th century grand house party. A number of her collections are displayed in the reception rooms and galleries, which have been kept as they were. You can also visit the estate, which include a walled rose garden, extensive grounds, lawns and landscaped walks.

🔍 Off the A246 Guildford to Leatherhead road
⚙ ⚙ ♣
⏳ 2–3 hours
⭐ Walled rose garden
♿ ♿
www.nationaltrust.org.uk

Rural Life Centre 124
Farnham

The Rural Life Centre is a museum of country life. It is set in ten acres of field, woodland and barns, and comprises a large number of implements and devices from over 150 years of farming. Many aspects of village and rural life are displayed in realistic individual settings including: farming through the seasons, local hop growing, tools and crafts allied to country industries and needs and the social history of village life from the 1800s.
Reconstructed buildings include a 1947 prefab, village hall, chapel, cricket pavilion, a small Victorian laundry and a corrugated iron schoolroom.

🔍 Off the A287, 3 miles south of Farnham
⚙ Wednesdays to Sundays
⏳ 2–3 hours
⭐ The wheelwright's shop
♿
www.rural-life.org.uk

River Wey and Godalming Navigations and Dapdune Wharf
Guildford

`126`

The Wey was one of the first British rivers to be made navigable, and opened to barge traffic in 1653, linking Guildford to Weybridge on the Thames, and then to London. The Godalming Navigation, opened in 1764, enabled barges to work a further distance upriver. The award-winning visitor centre at Dapdune Wharf tells the story of the Navigations and the people who lived and worked on them. Visitors can see where the huge Wey barges were built and climb aboard *Reliance*, one of three surviving barges.

🔍 Dapdune Wharf is on Wharf Road, off A322 in Guildford
⚙
⌛ 2–3 hours
★ A boat trip on tranquil waters
£
www.nationaltrust.org.uk

Bocketts Farm Park
Leatherhead

`127`

This is a working family farm set in beautiful downland countryside with many friendly farm animals who enjoy being fed and handled. The farm boasts tractor and pony rides, a 70-foot slide and daily pig races. Other activities include goat milking, gold panning, pony rides and the chance to meet film-stars Meryl and Beryl, two beautiful Jersey cows who have come to live here straight after an exhausting schedule working on the second Nanny Mcphee film. A number of play areas complete a grand day out for everyone.

🔍 Follow signs from junction 9 of the M25
⚙
⌛ 2–3 hours
★ The giant Astroslide
£
www.bockettsfarm.co.uk

British Wildlife Centre
Lingfield

`128`

First opened in 1997, the British Wildlife Centre's aim is conservation through education. The first inhabitants were a number of Jersey dairy cows; it is now home to one of the finest collections of native mammals, reptiles and birds in the country, with more than 40 species inhabiting 30 acres. Animals include owls, snakes, deer, otters and polecats. Many are rare in the wild but at the centre you have the chance to observe them close-up. A new walk-through red squirrel centre is now open.

🔍 Follow the A22 south from junction 6 of the M25
☀ ⚙ 🍁 ❄ Weekends or daily in school holidays
⌛ 2–3 hours
★ Red Squirrel Experience
£
www.britishwildlifecentre.co.uk

Ham House and Garden `129`
Richmond

A 400-year-old treasure trove waiting to be discovered and one of a series of grand houses and palaces alongside the River Thames. Ham House and Garden is an unusually complete survival of the 17th century that impressed in its day and continues to today. Rich in history and atmosphere, Ham is largely the vision of Elizabeth Murray, Countess of Dysart, who was deeply embroiled in the politics of the English Civil War and subsequent restoration of the monarchy. The fine interiors and historic gardens make this an unusual and fascinating place to visit.

Follow signs from the A307 between Richmond and Kingston

1-2 hours

Furniture, textiles and paintings

www.nationaltrust.org.uk

Brooklands Museum `130`
Weybridge

Constructed in 1907, Brooklands was the world's first purpose-built motor racing circuit, and was famous for its high-banked curves. During the next 80 years it became the birthplace of British motorsport and aviation, home of Concorde and the site of many engineering and technological achievements. The museum displays a wide range of Brooklands-related motoring and aviation exhibits, ranging from giant racing cars, motorcycles and bicycles to an unparalleled collection of Hawker and Vickers/ BAC-built aircraft, including the only Concorde with public access in south-east England.

Off the B374, follow signs from junction 10 of the M25

3-4 hours

Section of original steep-banked curve

www.brooklandsmuseum.com

RHS Wisley Garden `131`
Woking

Wisley is Britain's best-loved garden. It features 240 acres of richly planted borders, luscious rose gardens and the exotica. With sights to see including the stunning glasshouse (housing over 5,000 different varieties of tropical plant), Battleston Hill, the Fruit Orchard and dramatic rock garden, Wisley has a lot to offer. The garden aims to develop growing skills in the beginner, amateur and professional gardener, and a wide variety of inspirational events for people of all ages take place throughout the year, including family activities during school holidays.

Follow signs from junction 10 of the M25

3-4 hours

The glasshouse

www.rhs.org.uk

Arundel Castle

132

Arundel

The seat of The Dukes of Norfolk and set in 40 acres of sweeping grounds and gardens, Arundel Castle has been open to visitors seasonally for nearly 200 years. It is one of the great treasure houses of England, each having its own unique place in history and is home to priceless works of art. Come and see paintings by Gainsborough, Reynolds and Van Dyck, furniture, tapestries and stained glass, china and clocks, sculpture and carving, heraldry and armour in stunning room settings.

In Arundel, on the A27

1–2 hours

Mary Queen of Scots' prayer book and rosary beads

www.arundelcastle.org

Fishbourne Roman Palace

133

Chichester

Fishbourne Roman Palace was discovered by accident during the digging of a water main trench in 1960. This story is told in an entertaining audio-visual programme, with the addition of fascinating artefacts from the excavations along with plans, reconstruction drawings and models. In the north wing of the palace visitors can see the largest collection of in-situ mosaics in Britain including the famous 'Cupid on a Dolphin' mosaic. Outside, half of the formal garden has been replanted to its original plan as recovered by excavation. Adjacent to it is a Roman Garden Museum.

Follow signs from the A27 and A259

See website for winter opening

2–3 hours

Mosaics

www.sussexpast.co.uk/fishbourne

Weald and Downland Open Air Museum
Chichester

134

Set in rolling countryside this museum gives visitors a chance to wander through a collection of nearly 50 old country buildings dating from the 13th to the 19th centuries. Together they paint a picture of a way of life that's long gone. The buildings include a timber-framed Kentish farmhouse (see below), a medieval shop, a Tudor farm and a Victorian school. Interiors are furnished to show how they were originally used. The whole thing is brought to life with regular demonstrations of traditional rural trades and crafts.

🔍 On the A268. 7 miles north of Chichester
⚙️
⏳ 3-4 hours
⭐ The 15th-century two-storey farmhouse
💷
www.wealddown.co.uk

Borde Hill Garden
Haywards Heath

135

Set in 200 acres of Grade II listed landscape and woodland Borde Hill has one of the finest collections of rare and exotic plants in the South East. At the heart of the garden, Borde Hill House, a Tudor mansion from 1598, provides a stunning backdrop to the formal 17-acre garden comprising a series of linked 'garden rooms', each boasting its own distinctive character and style. In addition are there are woodland and lakeside walks, picnic areas and a new adventure playground.

🔍 2 miles north of Haywards Heath
✳️ ⚙️ 🍁
⏳ 2-3 hours
⭐ the intimate living 'garden room'
💷
www.bordehill.co.uk

Nymans
Haywards Heath

136

Set in the High Weald with splendid views, the garden is a series of experimental designs with spectacular planting and beauty all year. It is easy to lose yourself in its intimate and surprising corners. The house, transformed into a Gothic mansion in the 1920s, burnt down shortly after, leaving romantic ruins. The remaining rooms are charming, filled with flowers from the garden as Anne Messel, Countess of Rosse, had them. Ancient woods beyond the garden dip into the valley, with walks among avenues, wild flowers, lake and cascades.

🔍 On B2114 at Handcross. just off M23/A23
⚙️
⏳ 2-3 hours
⭐ The intriguing ruins of the house
💷
www.nationaltrust.org.uk

Harbour Park `137`
Littlehampton

Harbour Park is a family amusement park right on the beach. It has a variety of indoor and outdoor rides and attractions, which include an arcade and gaming area, Kingdom of Fun play area and the Interactive Chicken Show, plus perennial favourites like the Water Chute, Waltzer, Dodgems, the Hiccup, Crazy Bikes and Caterpillar Rollercoaster. For younger children, there is an array of rides, such as the Fantasy Ride, Panning for Gold, Adventure Golf and Formula Circuit. With its delightful 'New England' fishing village setting, Harbour Park is becoming quite a popular place.

On the seafront at Littlehampton

3-4 hours

The House of Mystery

www.harbourpark.com

Uppark House and Garden `138`
Petersfield

This gem on the South Downs, rescued after a major fire in 1989, houses an elegant Georgian interior with a famous Grand Tour collection, which includes paintings, furniture and ceramics. An 18th-century doll's house with original contents is one of the highlights. The complete servants' quarters in the basement are shown as they were in Victorian days when H.G. Wells' mother was housekeeper. The beautiful and peaceful garden is now fully restored in the early 19th-century Picturesque style, in a downland and woodland setting.

Off the B1246, 5 miles south-east of Petersfield

Sundays to Thursdays

2-3 hours

The doll's house

www.nationaltrust.org.uk

Petworth House and Park `139`
Petworth

Originally constructed in the 13th century, Petworth House was rebuilt around 1670 and altered again in the Victorian era. This grand house sits in an impressive 700-acre deer park, landscaped by 'Capability' Brown and immortalised in the paintings of J.M.W. Turner who was a frequent visitor here. The house contains the National Trust's finest collection of paintings by artists such as Van Dyck and Reynolds, as well as carvings, and sculptures. The kitchens, which include a set of copper cooking pans and utensils numbering over 1,000 pieces, and the service rooms are also fascinating.

On the A272, 5 miles east of Midhurst

2-3 hours

Paintings and sculpture

www.nationaltrust.org.uk

Pulborough Brooks RSPB `140`
Wakehurst

Set in the heart of beautiful countryside, this reserve is a fantastic day out for everyone. Walks lead through hedge-lined paths to viewing areas. If you're new to birdwatching, introductory walks are held throughout the year. In winter, the meadows teem with ducks, geese and swans. In spring, wading birds, such as lapwings and redshanks, breed amongst the pools and ditches, and nightingales and warblers sing from the hedgerows. With a children's play area attracting tits, finches, woodpeckers and nuthatches, and a comprehensive events programme, you won't go short of something to do.

Off the A283, 2 miles south of Pulborough

3-4 hours

Nightingales and barn owls

www. rspb.org.uk

South West

Bristol
Cornwall
Devon
Dorset
Gloucestershire
Somerset
Wiltshire

Bedruthan Steps, Cornwall

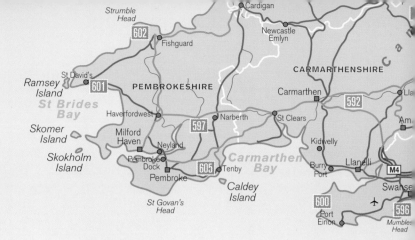
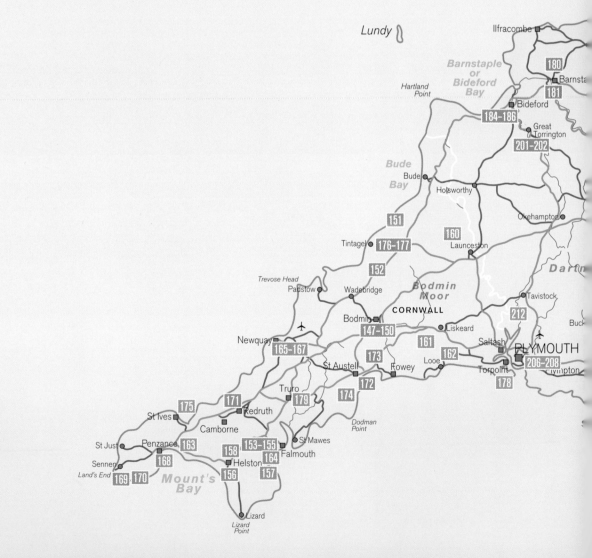

Strumble Head
602
Fishguard
Cardigan
Newcastle Emlyn
CARMARTHENSHIRE
St David's
601
Ramsey Island
St Brides Bay
Haverfordwest
Carmarthen
592
Lla
Skomer Island
597
Narberth
St Clears
Am.
Milford Haven
Neyland
Kidwelly
Skokholm Island
Pembroke Dock
605
Tenby
Carmarthen Bay
Burry Port
Llanelli
M4
Pembroke
Caldey Island
600
Swanse
St Govan's Head
596
Port Einon
Mumbles Head

Lundy
Ilfracombe
Barnstaple or Bideford Bay
180
Barnsta
Hartland Point
181
Bideford
184-186
Great Torrington
201-202
Bude Bay
Bude
Holsworthy
Okehampton
151
160
Darti
Tintagel
176-177
Launceston
152
Tavistock
Trevose Head
Bodmin Moor
Padstow
Wadebridge
212
CORNWALL
Bodmin
147-150
Liskeard
Saltash
PLYMOUTH
Newquay
161
162
206-208
165-167
173
Fowey
Looe
Torpoint
ympton
St Austell
172
178
174
Dodman Point
Truro
179
171
Redruth
175
St Ives
Camborne
St Mawes
St Jus
Penzance
163
153-155
Falmouth
Sennen
168
158
164
Land's End
169 170
Mount's Bay
156
Helston
157
Lizard

159
Isles of Scilly

Lizard
Lizard Point

Guide to the **South West**

At-Bristol

Bristol

At-Bristol is one of the UK's biggest and most exciting interactive science centres. There's lots to do here as exploration and education go hand-in-hand. You can join Morph and friends for a journey through animation past and present and become an animator for the day. Be awed by icy bodies and cosmic rays, get in a spin at the turbulent orb, create your own TV show or cover yourself from head to toe in your own giant bubble. With over 300 hands-on exhibits to explore, live shows and a Planetarium.

Off Anchor road in Bristol city centre

2-3 hours

The Planetarium and the pretend TV studio

www.at-bristol.org.uk

Bristol Ferry Boat Company

Bristol

In business on the water in Bristol for over 30 years, the Bristol Ferry Boat Company runs various ferries, cruises and trips around Bristol's historic harbour and up and down the River Avon. There are a number of private boat trips available, such as booze cruises, commentary tours of the harbour, pirate parties as well as a range of public cruises along the Avon Gorge, to Beeses Tea Gardens and wildlife commentaries around the harbour.

Pick up points are at the official landing stages around the harbour

1-3 hours

Unique views of the city

www.bristolferry.com

Bristol Zoo Gardens

Bristol

Comparatively small in area, Bristol Zoo is rich in animal and plant life with a strong focus on conservation and education. By concentrating on smaller species such as pigmy hippopotamuses and West African dwarf crocodiles this zoo can comfortably accommodate a representative slice of nature. There's an excellent aquarium, reptile house and the Twilight World includes rare mammals such as the aye-aye from Madagascar. The Seal and Penguin Coasts is an exhibit without parallel in the UK, and presents the animals on land and in seawater from above and below the waterline.

Follow signs from junctions 17 or 18 of the M5

2-5 hours

Seal and Penguin Coasts

www.bristolzoo.org.uk

City Museum and Art Gallery `144`
Bristol

Bristol's major museum and art gallery houses an outstanding and diverse range of objects. Visitors can see collections on Ancient Egypt, British birds and mammals, sea dragons, maps of Bristol, incredible fossils and dinosaurs. Other floors have amazing art in stunning galleries where you can see Old Masters; French School painters; a collection of British art; modern art and the Bristol School of Art. Leading off these galleries you can wind your way around the sparkling silver gallery; Chinese glass gallery; Eastern art and ceramics and porcelain.

In Clifton, follow signs from Bristol city centre

2-3 hours

Superb range of temporary exhibitions (see website for details)

FREE

www.bristol-city.gov.uk/museums

The Georgian House `145`
Bristol

The Georgian House is an 18th-century, six-storey townhouse that has been restored and decorated to its original glory. The house was built in 1790 for John Pinney, a wealthy West India slave plantation owner and sugar merchant, it was also where the enslaved African, Pero, lived. It is displayed as it might have looked in the 18th century and provides an insight into life above and below stairs. Imagine the busy kitchen where servants prepared meals, taking a dip in the cold-water plunge pool and relaxing in the elegant upstairs rooms.

Park Street, just up the road from the City Museum and Art Gallery

Saturdays to Wednesdays

1-2 hours

The downstairs kitchen

FREE

www.bristol-city.gov.uk/museums

SS *Great Britain* `146`
Bristol

The world's first great ocean liner is now docked in the original Great Western Dockyard from where she was first launched in 1843. Visitors can experience what life was like on board as the ship sailed between Bristol and New York though she was later pressed into service carrying immigrants from England to Australia.
You can tour the ship, climb the maintop and see the splendour of the first-class cabins as well as the cramped conditions in steerage. You can descend under the glass 'sea' into the dry dock and see state-of-the-art conservation in action.

Bristol Historical Dockyard

2 hours

The glass 'sea'

www.ssgreatbritain.org

STAR ATTRACTION

Bodmin and Wenford Railway   147
Bodmin

This beautiful standard-gauge railway, Cornwall's only full-size railway that still operates on steam, runs a 13-mile round trip from Bodmin General to Bodmin Parkway and back. You'll pass through the beautiful River Fowey valley and stop at Boscarne Junction where you can pick up the historic Camel Trail (see right). It is essential to book your seats and a timetable and full details of fares are available on the website. On Saturdays, trains are normally diesel hauled, however, all trains are in-steam in August.

- On B3268 in Bodmin town
- See website for timetable
- 3-4 hours
- A whole range of special themed days

www.bodminandwenfordrailway.co.uk

Bodmin Jail   148
Bodmin

The original jail was built for King George III in 1779. The jail you see today was built by its prisoners who brought the 20,000 tons of granite from Bodmin's Cuckoo Quarry. During the First World War the jail held state papers and the Doomsday book. You can visit the cold dank cells, look up at the thin light filtering through a small barred window and imagine being sentenced to a spell in such desolation. You can also experience the cold horror of the original hanging pit complete with noose.

- On Berrycoombe Road in Bodmin
- 1-2 hours
- Ghost walks

www.bodminjail.org

Camel Trail   149
Bodmin

The Camel Trail winds through some of Cornwall's most beautiful and little-known countryside. Cornwall County Council converted 11 miles of disused railway beside the River Camel from track bed to trail, linking the towns of Bodmin, Wadebridge and Padstow. An extension follows the river towards Camelford. Visitors can walk, jog or cycle along the trail and enjoy the spectacular scenery of the Camel Valley. The trail is virtually level all the way and vehicles are banned so it is ideal for wheelchair users, pram and buggy pushers and people who have difficulty in walking on uneven surfaces.

- Joining points at Wadebridge, Bodmin or Padstow
- 6-7 hours
- Views of the Camel estuary

FREE

www.thisisnorthcornwall.co.uk/camel_trail.htm

Lanhydrock   150
Bodmin

Lanhydrock is one of the finest houses in Cornwall. Visitors can follow in the footsteps of generations of the Robartes family, walking in the 17th-century Long Gallery among the rare book collection under the remarkable plasterwork ceiling. After a devastating fire in 1881 the house was refurbished in the high-Victorian style, with the latest mod cons. Boasting the best in country-house design and planning, the kitchens, nurseries and servants' quarters offer a thrilling glimpse into life 'below stairs', while the spacious dining room and bedrooms are truly elegant.

- Follow signs from the A30 or A38
- 3-4 hours
- The 900-acre garden

www.nationaltrust.org.uk

Museum of Witchcraft

Boscastle 151

One of the best-known attractions in Cornwall the museum was first opened by Cecil Williamson on the Isle of Man in 1951 and moved to its present location in 1960. Today, the museum houses the world's largest collection of witchcraft related artefacts covering everything from stone circles and sacred sites to ritual magic, charms and spells. Exhibits include 'Images of Witchcraft', 'Devil Worship and Satanism', 'The Hare and Shape Shifting' and the 'Persecution of Witches'. This unique collection is fascinating and well worth a visit.

By the harbour in Boscastle

1 hour

A genuine Bezoar stone, made famous by Harry Potter

www.museumofwitchcraft.com

The Arthurian Centre

Camelford 152

Marked by a stone carrying a Latin inscription which dates back to the 6th century, the Arthurian Centre is located at Slaughterbridge on the site believed to be where Arthur and Mordred fought their last battle which ended the fellowship of the Round Table in AD 537. The centre itself is dedicated to telling the stories of King Arthur and includes fabulous exhibits of photographs, texts, illustrations and paintings. The centre is ten minutes from Tintagel.

Off the A39 at Slaughterbridge

1–2 hours

On-site archaeological dig

www.arthur-online.co.uk

Falmouth Art Gallery

Falmouth 153

Falmouth Art Gallery has one of the leading art collections in Cornwall and features work by Old Masters, major Victorian artists, British Impressionists, leading maritime artists and contemporary painters and printmakers. Artists whose works are on show include Sir Frank Brangwyn, Sir Edward Coley Burne-Jones, Charles Napier Hemy, Dame Laura Knight, Sir Alfred Munnings, William Strang, Henry Scott Tuke, John William Waterhouse RA and George Frederick Watts. The gallery also runs regular free workshops for schools, families and community groups.

The Moor, in Falmouth town centre

1 hour

The print collection

FREE

www.falmouthartgallery.com

Pendennis Castle

155

Falmouth

Pendennis Castle was built by Henry VIII to defend against possible attack by Spain and France. Throughout its 450-year history, Pendennis Castle has faced new enemies, right up to the Second World War. Today, visitors can see a Tudor gun deck in action and experience the sights and sounds of battle in the interactive exhibition at the Royal Artillery Barracks. Explore the cells of the First World War guardhouse, and relive the drama of an enemy attack on the Second World War observation post, and then descend through secret tunnels to the big guns of Half Moon Battery.

🔍 Pendennis Head, 1 mile south-east of Falmouth

⚙️

⏳ 2-3 hours

⭐ Royal Artillery Barracks

♿

www.english-heritage.org.uk

National Maritime Museum Cornwall

154

Falmouth

This museum's mission is to promote an understanding of boats and their place in people's lives. At the heart of its collection are 140 small boats including racing craft, working boats, fishing vessels and record breakers like Ben Ainslie's Laser. There are also galleries devoted to the maritime history of Cornwall. These cover topics such as Cornish fishing, trading, boatbuilding, wrecks and emigration. It also features exhibits on Falmouth's famous packet ships, and local heroes Sir Robin Knox-Johnson and Ellen MacArthur.

🔍 Southern end of the harbourside

⚙️ ⚙️ ♣️ ❄️

⏳ 2-3 hours

⭐ Views over Falmouth harbour

♿

www.nmmc.co.uk

Flambards Experience

156

Helston

A family run theme park, Flambards has been entertaining visitors for 34 seasons. With huge undercover areas in case of bad weather, it has internationally acclaimed, award-winning exhibitions, exciting rides, family shows, live entertainment and glorious gardens. Top of the list come the Victorian Village and Britain in the Blitz. The rides are good too and include the new giant Skyraker 101, the fantastic Extreme Force, the mighty Thunderbolt, and the Hornet rollercoaster amongst others. The key to this park is the variety of things on offer with something for all tastes.

🔍 Follow signs from the A394

⚙️ ⚙️ ♣️

⏳ 4-5 hours

⭐ Mark's Ark animal encounters

♿ ♿

www.flambards.co.uk

National Seal Sanctuary   157
Helston

Located on the beautiful Helford Estuary, the Seal Sanctuary was founded in 1958. It has wonderful facilities including nursery pools, convalescence and resident pools as well as a specially designed hospital. Many seals have been rescued over the years and most are released back into the ocean after being nursed back to health. However, some are never strong enough to return to their natural habitat and therefore make the sanctuary their permanent home. The sanctuary holds a variety of other animals including Californian and Patagonian Sea Lions and even occasionally dolphins and turtles.

Take the A3083 (signposted Lizard) to the B3293 into the village of Gweek

2 hours

New otter facility

www.sealsanctuary.co.uk

Poldark Mine   158
Helston

The site of tin mining from prehistoric times, Poldark boasts one of the Europe's finest underground mine tours. The tour offers a fascinating insight into the life and works of 17th- and 18th-century Cornish tin miners who worked 100 feet underground. Set in the beautiful Wendron Valley, Poldark Mine was originally known as Wheal Roots and changed it's name in recent times to reflect it's connections with the *Poldark* TV drama. There are other things here too including a museum and a wide range of local craft shops.

On B3297, 2 miles from Helston

1-2 hours

One of the most atmospheric mine tours in Europe

www.poldark-mine.co.uk

Isles of Scilly Museum   159
Isles of Scilly

The severe gales of the winter of 1962 yielded up some remarkable Romano-British finds on St Mary's, causing some residents to establish a local museum. Initially the only viable option was a temporary display in the Wesleyan Chapel during the summer months. After much fundraising the present Museum was built. It opened to the public on 15 July 1967. Today's collections are extremely diverse, including material from many wrecks; a wild flower display (during the summer months); Romano-British artefacts; stuffed birds; local art and much more.

St Mary's, 10 minutes walk from Hugh Town harbour

1-2 hours

The Bryher sword and mirror

www.iosmuseum.org

The Tamar Otter and Wildlife Centre

160

Launceston

Situated on the banks of the River Waveney, the centre offers visitors a rare chance to see otters at close quarters along with other wetland wildlife. The informative visitor centre explores the lives and habitats of otters and the conservation issues surrounding them. There are Fallow Deer in a woodland enclosure and you will see Wallabies and Muntjac Deer roaming around the grounds. There are also owl aviaries, peacocks and a variety of waterfowl on the two lakes. There is a woodland walk and a waterfall in the Old Quarry.

On the B3254 at North Petherwin, 5 miles north-west of Launceston

2 hours

Biggy and Smalley – the hand-reared otters

www.tamarotters.co.uk

Porfell Wildlife Park and Sanctuary

161

Liskeard

At Porfell you will meet wallabies, marmosets, snakes, lemurs, meerkats, porcupines and, of course, Bert the capybara as well as all your favourite farmyard animals and pets. Learn about wild exotic animals like the coati. These are just a few of the interesting varieties of exotic, wild and domesticated animals to be seen within the 15 acres of sloping fields bounded by streams and a varied woodland. Experience the pleasure and unique experience of close contact with these animals in this lovely natural environment.

 Take the A387 then the B3359 and follow the signs

2–3 hours

The raccoons and the meerkats

www.porfellanimalland.co.uk

The Monkey Sanctuary Trust

162

Looe

The Monkey Sanctuary is situated in beautiful woodlands overlooking Looe Bay in south-east Cornwall. Visitors can see Amazon woolly monkeys in their own spacious territory at this environmentally aware centre. Talks are given throughout the day about the monkeys and their threatened rainforest habitat. Although the sanctuary focuses on the continued care and management of the woolly monkey colony, it is also involved in the rescue and rehabilitation of ex-pet capuchin, macaque and patas monkeys.

Follow signs from B387, 4 miles from Looe

Mondays to Thursdays

2 hours

Woodland walks

www.monkeysanctuary.org

St Michael's Mount `163`
Marazion

Still home to the St Aubyn family as well as a small community, this iconic rocky island is crowned by a medieval church and castle – with the oldest buildings dating from the 12th century. Immerse yourself in history, wonder at the architecture and discover the legend of Jack the Giant Killer. Look down on the sub-tropical terraced garden and enjoy the breathtaking views of spectacular Mount's Bay. If the weather is favourable, take a short evocative boat trip to the island, or at low tide enjoy the walk across the causeway.

🔍 On A397, off the coast at Marazion

⚙ ⚙ ♣

⌛ 2-3 hours

⭐ Your first sight of the island

£

www.stmichaelsmount.co.uk

Dairyland Farm World `165`
Newquay

Dairyland Farm World is a fabulous all-weather family day out with attractions suitable for all age groups. Its aim has always been to promote a better understanding of farming and country life and there is no better way of doing this than getting visitors to be as hands-on as possible. This is a real working farm and children will love the endless list of attractions on offer – from pony rides to tractor rides, bottle-feeding to milking. With so many animals to choose from, including lambs, pigs, rabbits, chinchillas and chipmunks, youngsters are sure to find one to pet and feed.

🔍 On the A3058, 4 miles from Newquay

⚙

⌛ 2-3 hours

⭐ Daily milking sessions

£

www.dairylandfarmworld.com

Trebah Garden `164`
Mawnan Smith

Trebah is a dramatically beautiful 28-acre sub-tropical garden. The steeply wooded ravine descends to a private, secluded beach on the historic Helford River. A stream cascades over waterfalls, through ponds full of giant Koi carp and exotic water plants, through two acres of blue and white hydrangeas spilling out over the beach. Glades of huge hundred-year-old tree ferns mingle with a forest of rhododendrons, magnolias and camellias under a canopy of ancient oaks and beeches. This is truly a garden for all seasons with colour and scent throughout the year.

🔍 Follow signs from junction of A39 and A394, near Falmouth

⚙

⌛ 2-3 hours

⭐ Dramatic spring or autumn displays

£

www.trebah-garden.co.uk

Newquay Zoo Environmental Park `166`
Newquay

Set in sub-tropical lakeside gardens Newquay Zoo is home to over 130 species of animal such as African lions, penguins, meerkats and red pandas. It also plays a vital role in breeding programmes for endangered animals such as Sulawese crested black macaques and ring-tailed lemurs. Other highlights include feeding time talks and animal encounters where you can meet some of the animals. This award-winning zoo is fun for all age groups with plenty of delights for children including the Tarzan trail, a play area and the dragon maze.

🔍 Follow signs from A3075 in Newquay

⚙ ⚙ ♣ ❄

⌛ 2-3 hours

⭐ African savannah viewing platform

£ £

www.newquayzoo.org.uk

Trerice House

167

Newquay

The most hidden of 'hidden' gems, this is the finest and best-preserved Elizabethan manor house in Britain. Behind the Dutch style gabled facade are ornate fireplaces, elaborate plaster ceilings, and a collection of English oak and walnut furniture of the highest quality, interesting clocks and Stuart portraits. Of particular note is the magnificent Great Chamber. The summer flowering garden is unusual in content and layout and there is an orchard planted with old varieties of fruit. There beautiful borders in front of the house, which feature rare and unusual plants, shrubs and climbers.

🔍 Take A392 and A3058, 3 miles south-east of Newquay

✿ ◎ ♣

⧗ 2 hours

★ Barrel ceiling in the Great Chamber

£

www.nationaltrust.org.uk

Isles of Scilly Travel

168

Penzance

Travel to the Isles of Scilly, either by air on a 20-seat Skybus or on the sea aboard *Scillonian III*, a comfortable 600-capacity passenger ferry with a bar, buffet and comfortable seating. The company offers standard single and return journeys as well as regular day trips to St Mary's, Tresco, Bryher, St Agnes and St Martins. *Scillonian III* sails past Newlyn, Mousehole, the Minack Theatre and Wolf Rock Lighthouse. An informative commentary is broadcast during the start of your trip. Your first glimpse of the islands, as you approach through Crow Sound or around St Mary's, is magical.

🔍 At Penzance Quay, Land's End or Newquay

✿ ◎ ♣ ❄ Not Sundays

⧗ 15 minutes/3 hours

★ Spectacular views of the Cornish countryside

£ £ £

www.islesofscilly-travel.co.uk

Land's End Visitor Centre `169`
Penzance

Land's End is one of Britain's best-loved landmarks, famous for its unique location, natural beauty and stunning scenery. There is plenty to offer those seeking a full day out – explore the cliff top trails, natural splendour, visit the five fantastic value family attractions – including the End-to-End Story, Air Sea Rescue and the new 4D film experience *The Curse of Skull Rock* – and wander around the West Country Shopping Village.

At the end of the A30

2–3 hours

The Land's End signpost

www.landsend-landmark.co.uk

Minack Theatre `170`
Porthcurno

Surely one of the most spectacular theatres in the world – an open-air auditorium carved into the cliffs high above Porthcurno's sandy cove. Founded and largely built by Rowena Cade in the 1930s, its remarkable story is now told in an exhibition in the visitor centre. You can visit the theatre during the day to soak up the atmosphere of this remarkable place and you can buy tickets for evening performances during the summer season of plays, opera and musicals, which runs from May to September.

Off the A30, 3 miles from Land's End

See website for opening times

2 hours

The spectacular panoramas

www.minack.com

Cornish Mines and Engines `171`
Redruth

Learn about the history of Cornwall's industrial heritage at this Cornish Mining World Heritage site. Find out what life was like for the local miners of tin, copper and china clay. See two great beam engines, preserved in their towering engine houses, which are a reminder of Cornwall's days as a world-famous centre of industry, engineering and innovation. There are films, displays, models and knowledgeable guides who can help visitors discover the whole dramatic story of Cornish mining.

On the A3047, 2 miles west of Redruth

Closed Tuesdays and some Saturdays

2–3 hours

Giant engines of a bygone industry

www.nationaltrust.org.uk

Charlestown Shipwreck and Heritage Centre `172`
St Austell

The exhibitions here reflect village life in charming, unspoiled Charlestown, its history, shipwrecks and the once thriving local China Clay industry. The exhibition includes maritime artefacts dating back to 1715 and one of the largest underwater diving equipment collections in the country, including suits used for treasure seeking and naval purposes. Exhibits include local shipwrecks and some of the precious treasures recovered from them, Nelson and HMS *Victory*, the *Titanic* and the Royal Yacht *Britannia*.

Follow signs from the A390 at St Austell

2–3 hours

The collection of recovered artefacts

www.shipwreckcharlestown.com

Eden Project – the **'Eighth Wonder of the World'**

The Eden Project
St Austell

173

Cornwall's best-known tourist attraction is much more than just a big green theme park. Its aim is to ensure that visitors come away with a better understanding of the environment and their interaction with it. Dubbed the 'Eighth Wonder of the World', the Eden Project opened in March 2001, since then it has had more than 8 million visitors.

Sited in a former china clay pit at Bodelva, near St Austell, it consists of three biomes (a biome is a large naturally occurring community of flora and fauna occupying a major habitat). In the Mediterranean Biome you can take a colourful, sensory journey through the Mediterranean-type climates of the world, including South Africa and California. In the Rainforest Biome you can trek through the steamy rainforests of Malaysia and West Africa. The Outdoor Biome consists of over 30 acres of gardens, which are planted to provide glorious seasonal displays.

At the heart of the project is the Core, one of the world's most sustainable buildings, which is used as an education centre. Its design is based on how plants grow and inside it features a whole range of innovative energy and water saving techniques.

🔍 Follow signs from the A390 at St Austell

⚙ ⚙

⏳ 4-5 hours

★ The world's largest greenhouse

💷 💷

www.edenproject.com

Lost Gardens of Heligan
St Austell

174

The award-winning Lost Gardens of Heligan, asleep for more than 70 years, are the scene of the largest garden restoration project in Europe. In 1991, the gardens lay under a blanket of bramble, ivy, rampant laurel and fallen timber. A year later, the gardens were opened to enable the public to share in the excitement of their discovery. There are two and a half miles of footpaths, rockeries, summer houses, a crystal grotto, an Italian garden, a wishing well and a superb collection of walled gardens. Remarkably much of the original plant collection has survived, sometimes to record sizes.

🔍 Follow signs from B3273 near St Austell

⚙ ⚙

⏳ 3-4 hours

★ The Lost Valley and the Jungle

💷 💷

www.heligan.com

Tate St Ives
St Ives

175

Tate St Ives presents 20th-century art in the context of Cornwall. At the heart of the programme of displays and activities is a body of work for which the town of St Ives is internationally known – the modernist art produced by artists associated with the town and its surrounding area from the 1920s onwards. The gallery also presents work by contemporary artists, often responding to the gallery's displays or to the broader Cornish scene. The Barbara Hepworth Museum and Sculpture Garden opened in 1976 is also part of Tate St Ives.

🔍 In St Ives town centre

⚙ ⚙ ♣ ❄

⏳ 2-3 hours

★ Ben Nicholson's paintings

💷

www.tate.org.uk/stives/

Cornish Coastal Path Walk   `176`

Tintagel

This beautiful, exhilarating walk, which explores places involved in the legend of King Arthur, takes in some of the world famous Cornish Coastal Path. Starting at King Arthur's Great Halls, you head straight for Tintagel Island and then head north along the cliffs. You will see Merlin's Cave, Barras Nose, Lye Rock and the Little Sisters. Bear right past Firebeacon Hill and inland to Trevalga village past the manor house. From there you can return to Tintagel inland. On the way walkers are able to take in the spectacular rugged geology and abundant flora.

🔍 Starts at Tintagel, on the B3263

⚙️

⏳ 5–6 hours

⭐ Bring Arthur's legend to life

FREE

www.visitboscastleandtintagel.com

STAR ATTRACTION

Tintagel Castle   `177`

Tintagel

With its spectacular location on Cornwall's dramatic and windswept Atlantic coastline, Tintagel is a place of magic and myth where the legend of King Arthur was born. This historic spot is rich in flora and fauna and provides a breeding ground for sea birds, lizards and butterflies. Tintagel Castle is Cornwall's most iconic site. A stronghold of the Earls of Cornwall, the castle was built in the 13th century. Now in ruins, it still has the power to inspire.

🔍 Tintagel Head, 600 metres from village

☀️ ⚙️ ♿

⏳ 1 hour

⭐ Dramatic coastline views

£

www.english-heritage.org.uk

Mount Edgcumbe House and Park   `178`

Torpoint

Mount Edgcumbe is the Tudor home of the Earls of Mount Edgcumbe. The house is located on a peninsula that extends into the River Tamar and gives fine views over Plymouth Sound. The house is filled with family possessions, including paintings by Sir Joshua Reynolds and William van der Velde, 16th-century tapestries and 18th-century Chinese and Plymouth porcelain. The garden contains ancient and rare trees including a 400-year-old lime and a splendid Lucombe oak.

🔍 Take Torpoint or Cremyll foot ferry from Plymouth

☀️ ⚙️ ♿ Sunday to Thursday

⏳ 2–3 hours

⭐ 800-acre country park in which the house is set

£

www.mountedgcumbe.gov.uk

Royal Cornwall Museum `179`
Truro

This is the oldest museum in Cornwall and the largest centre for the exhibition of Cornish culture. It has a permanent display on the history of Cornwall from the Stone Age to the present day, as well as the natural history of Cornwall, a world famous collection of minerals, a pre-eminent collection of ceramics, and a changing display of fine and decorative art. The museum also has a diverse range of temporary exhibitions, from photographs to textiles, Old Master drawings, contemporary art and natural history.

🔍 In Truro town centre
☼ ⚙ ♣ ❄
⏳ 2-3 hours
⭐ Unwrapped Egyptian mummy
FREE Some exhibitions may charge
www.royalcornwallmuseum.org.uk

Barnstaple Heritage Centre `181`
Barnstaple

Situated in a listed building on Queen Anne's Walk on the historic riverfront, Barnstaple Heritage Centre explores the town's rich and vibrant past. The fixed hands-on exhibition takes visitors through the major periods of a rich history. A combination of touch-screen computers, information panels and atmospheric mock-ups help bring history to life. The exhibition includes medieval and Civil War displays. An audio-visual presentation, computerised heritage trail map and extensive picture database are particular features.

🔍 On the riverfront in Barnstaple town centre
☼ ⚙ ♣ ❄
⏳ 1-2 hours
⭐ The Tarka Gallery
♿
www.devonmuseums.net

Arlington Court `180`
Barnstaple

This charming Regency house contains a variety of treasures collected by the Chichester family including antique furniture, shells and model ships. The 2,700 acre-estate and gardens nestle in the thickly wooded valley of the River Yeo. The gardens are largely informal but include a small Victorian garden with conservatory, basket beds, herbaceous borders and ornamental pond, leading to a partially restored, walled kitchen garden with its greenhouse built to original design. The damp, mild climate provides perfect growing conditions for a wide range of plants including hydrangeas and rhododendrons.

🔍 On the A39, north of Barnstaple
☼ ⚙ ♣
⏳ 3 hours
⭐ The Carriage Museum
♿
www.nationaltrust.org.uk

The Beer Quarry Caves `182`
Beer

Conducted tours by trained guides give visitors an hour-long tour of this vast man-made complex of underground caverns created by centuries of quarrying the famous Beer Stone. The underground quarry, first worked by the Romans, supplied stone for 24 cathedrals including Exeter and St Paul's, parts of Westminster Abbey, the Tower of London, Hampton Court and Windsor Castle. Quarried by hand, the smallest blocks weighing 4 tons, the stone was carted on horse-drawn wagons and barges from Beer beach to its destination, sometimes involving journeys of several hundred miles.

🔍 Follow signs from Beer town centre
☼ ⚙ ♣ ❄
⏳ 1-2 hours
⭐ Beer Quarry bats
♿
www.beerquarrycaves.fsnet.co.uk

Pecorama Pleasure Gardens 183
Beer

Situated high on the hillside above the picturesque fishing village of Beer, Pecorama is home to the famous model railway exhibition and the Beer Heights Light Railway. The exhibition displays wonderful detailed layouts in many different scales, some with push button controls enabling children to operate the trains. The gardens themselves are lovely for strolling around and have a number of play areas, other activities like face painting and there is also an open-air theatre that runs a variety of entertainment during the summer months. You can explore the gardens on the ride-on light railway.

🔍 In Beer town centre

⚙️

⏳ 3-4 hours

⭐ Themed display gardens

💷

www.peco-uk.com

Lundy Island 185
Bideford

Lundy Island lies in the Bristol Channel, about 11 miles off the coast of North Devon. Three miles long and half a mile wide, this granite outcrop rises 400 feet above sea level and is a place of outstanding natural beauty, with tremendous views of England, Wales and the Atlantic. You can take a day trip to this beautiful, peaceful and unspoiled place. Visitors can see three lighthouses (two in use), a castle, church, shop, tavern, working farm, several handsome houses and cottages and a population of about 18.

🔍 Boat trips aboard the MV *Oldenburg* leave from Bideford

⚙️

⏳ 4-5 hours

⭐ Fantastic array of wildlife

💷 💷 💷

www.lundyisland.co.uk

The Big Sheep 184
Bideford

This sheep-based theme park provides a programme of events held throughout the day, which include bottle-feeding lambs and sheep shearing demonstrations. There are lots of opportunities to meet different breeds of sheep and cuddle the lambs at pet's corner. The absolute highlight of the day is the sheep racing. The sheep have little knitted jockeys on their backs, and then they race along a course while you cheer on your favourite. You can even place a bet on your fancied racer. The attraction also includes Ewetopia, an indoor playground for children and adults.

🔍 Off the A39, 2 miles west of Bideford

⚙️

⏳ 2-3 hours

⭐ Sheep milk fudge

💷 💷

www.thebigsheep.co.uk

The Golden Hind 187
Brixham

This full-size replica of Sir Francis Drake's original Tudor galleon offers a unique insight into life on board a 16th-century sailing ship. You can explore the cramped decks and the accommodation below and learn about all aspects of a sailor's life, from his food, health, pay and punishment. In the Education Centre onshore, visitors will gain an understanding and appreciation of Drake's hero status and the skills he showed in his achievement of circumnavigating the world between 1577 and 1580, well before the advent of steam power.

In Brixham harbour

1-2 hours

Details of the treasures brought back by the ship

www.goldenhind.co.uk

The Milky Way Adventure Park 186
Bideford

This is a good family day out at a good price as all rides are inclusive. The park has major rides and a range of different shows including Merlin from *Britain's Got Talent* with death defying escapology. Rides include Devon's biggest roller coaster, Dodgems, Clone Zone and the interactive alien ride. For little ones there's the special Big Apple roller coaster, soft play, ball pools, mini ride on tractors, railway, slides and Time Warp – the biggest adventure play area in Cornwall. Archery, golf, laser shooting and bird of prey displays are also on offer.

Off the A39, 10 minutes drive from Bideford towards Clovelly

3-4 hours

The Cosmic Typhoon rollercoaster

www.themilkyway.co.uk

Buckfast Abbey 188
Buckfastleigh

Buckfast Abbey is a beautiful living Benedictine Monastery. Home to a Roman Catholic community of Benedictine Monks, it is difficult to leave without being touched by the serenity of the place. The first monastery was built here in 1018; however, it was suppressed like so many others by Henry VIII in 1539. Refounded in 1882, the beautiful and architecturally stunning Abbey church was rebuilt by the monks themselves. Buckfast Abbey offers visitors fascinating and insightful presentations and displays about monastic life.

Off the A38, near Buckfastleigh

Check website for opening times

2-3 hours

The marble flooring

FREE

www.buckfast.org.uk

South Devon Railway 189
Buckfastleigh

Steam services run on a former branch line of the Great Western Railway through scenic countryside along the River Dart between Buckfastleigh and Totnes via Staverton. At Buckfastleigh station the goods shed has been converted into a railway museum dedicated to the Great Western and to its builder Isambard Kingdom Brunel. On display are Great Western engines, rolling stock, and other items such as dining car equipment. It is also home to 'Tiny' – the only surviving locomotive from Brunel's original broad gauge rail system.

- Buckfastleigh station on the A38
- Check website for timetables
- 2-3 hours
- A whole range of special events
- £ £

www.southdevonrailway.org

Bicton Park Botanical Gardens 190
Budleigh Salterton

Spanning nearly 300 years of horticultural history, these magnificent gardens are set in East Devon's picturesque Otter Valley, between Exeter and southwest England's Jurassic Coast. The superbly landscaped park combines 18th-century tranquillity with modern amenities to provide all year round enjoyment for gardeners and other leisure lovers, including historic glasshouses, a countryside museum, the Bicton Woodland Railway train ride, nature trail, maze, mini golf, indoor and outdoor children's play complexes and ice-free skating.

- Follow signs from junction 30 of the M5
-
- 3-4 hours
- The historic Palm House
- £

www.bicton gardens.co.uk

Diggerland 191
Cullompton

This small theme park is like a Disneyland full of diggers, dumper trucks and brightly painted machines with scoops, cranes, lifts ... and dirt. There's lots of mud, big tyres, frantic lever twiddling and children screaming with joy. The action spreads across big safe fields, man-made ponds and off-road tracks. For small boys especially, it's a dream-come-true chance to dig a hole in a muddy field with a JCB, take scary rides in a digger's shovel, drive their own dumper truck, ride pedal-powered diggers, and enjoy gentle trips on a 'digger train'.

- On B31281, near Cullompton
- Weekends and school holidays only
- 3-4 hours
- Ride your own JCB
- £ £

www.diggerland.com

Blackpool Sands 192
Dartmouth

Blackpool Sands is an award-winning beach in an unspoiled, sheltered beach among evergreens and pines. Despite its name, it is a shingle beach, privately managed and great for families with turquoise blue sea giving it an almost Mediterranean feel. The beach has superb facilities, sand pits, showers and toilets. It is cleaned regularly and dogs are not allowed. There's a lifeguard patrol and its perfect for swimming in clear waters. There is also a watersports centre where you can hire equipment for kayaking, surfing, snorkelling and other sports.

- On the A379, 3 miles from Dartmouth
-
- 3-4 hours
- Rockpool rambles
- **FREE** (but there are car parking charges)

www.blackpoolsands.co.uk

Dartmouth Castle

193

Dartmouth

Built by 14th-century merchants (led by John Hawley, Mayor of Dartmouth) to protect themselves from invasion, this brilliantly positioned castle juts out into the middle of the narrow entrance of the Dart Estuary. It is said that Hawley was the inspiration for Chaucer's Shipman in *The Canterbury Tales*. Incorporating the fine church of St Petrox, the castle saw action during the Civil War, and continued in service right up until the Second World War. Visitors can inspect the Victorian 'Old Battery' with its remounted heavy guns, guardrooms and there's a maze of passages to explore.

On the B3025, 1 mile south-east of Dartmouth

1–2 hours

Riverboat trip from the town to the castle

www.english-heritage.org.uk

Castle Drogo

194

Drewsteignton

Inside this remarkable granite building, set above the Teign Gorge, is a surprisingly warm and comfortable family home. Commissioned by retail tycoon Julius Drewe, and designed by Sir Edwin Lutyens, the castle harks back to a romantic past, while its brilliant design heralds the modern era. Behind the imposing facade, poignant family keepsakes sit alongside 17th-century tapestries. The dramatic Dartmoor setting can be appreciated from the delightful formal garden and walks into a rhododendron valley. Tours and fun activities are arranged throughout the year.

Off the A382, near Exeter

2–3 hours

Arts and Crafts-inspired gardens

www.nationaltrust.org.uk

Crealy Adventure Theme Park 195
Exeter

This country-based theme park is divided into six realms of 'fun, magic and adventure'. The Adventure Realm includes a number of exciting rides, such as the Tidal Wave log flume and the Maximus rollercoaster. The Adventure Zone has the Meteorite Drop Tower and the two big ball pools. In the Animal Realm visitors can stroke and cuddle friendly animals. The Natural Realm offers glorious countryside in which to stroll. There is also the Action Realm, Magic Realm and Farming Realm.

On the A3052, near Clyst St Mary
Check website for winter opening
3-4 hours
The new Vortex ride

www.crealy.co.uk

STAR ATTRACTION

Exeter Cathedral 196
Exeter

For centuries this medieval cathedral with its two massive towers and its West Front decorated with sculptures has dominated the city. Inside are treasures in abundance: an astronomical clock more than 500 years old, the Great Organ and the Minstrels' Gallery with carvings of angels playing 14th-century instruments. There is a huge window with 19 full-length figures including Sidwel, the local saint. Around the nave are cushions, on the original stone plinths, which depict the history of the cathedral, city and county from Roman times to the present day.

Exeter city centre
1 hour
The spectacular vaulted ceiling

www.exeter-cathedral.org.uk

Killerton 197
Exeter

Killerton is a beautiful agricultural estate covering over 6,000 acres, with walks through park, woodland and Devon countryside. The estate was the ancestral home of the Acland family who acquired Killerton at the time of the Civil War. Later embellishments to the house almost conceal its original central block, which was built in 1778-79. The interior was redesigned in the 1890s and again in 1924 after a fire. Today, the house is furnished as a family home, depicting the way of life in a country house between the First and Second World Wars.

Off the B3181, 6 miles from Exeter
2-3 hours
The superb costume collection

www.nationaltrust.org.uk

Powderham Castle

198

Exeter

Powderham Castle is situated in 600 acres of beautiful parkland beside the Exe estuary. Visit a succession of magnificent halls and staterooms filled with lavish furnishings, tapestries and historic portraits of the Courtenay family, whose home this has been for over 600 years. Guided tours reveal secret doors, stunning castle rooms, amazing architecture and intriguing stories that really bring the history to life. Outside visitors are welcome to explore extensive grounds full of natural rugged beauty and relax in the peaceful surroundings.

🔍 On the A379, 8 miles south of Exeter

⚙ ◎ 🍁

⏳ 2-3 hours

⭐ Newly opened Victorian kitchen

♿

www.powderham.com

Exmouth Model Railway

199

Exmouth

Fourteen years in construction and now 40-years-old, this model railway attracts visitors from all over the world. Visitors can see the British countryside in miniature as 20 trains weave their way through 115 scale miles of varied landscape – the villages, towns, stations, traffic, people and even birds in the trees all authentic to the last meticulous detail. All the locomotives and rolling stock feature British Railways past and present and so children have a chance to see some of the famous trains of the past – as well as the latest diesels.

🔍 On Exmouth seafront

⚙ ◎ 🍁

⏳ 1 hour

⭐ The largest '00' gauge model railway in the world

♿

www.exmouthmodelrailway.co.uk

Stuart Line Cruises and Boat Trips
Exmouth

200

This company runs a wide range of boat trips in Devon from relaxing cruises on the River Exe to exhilarating trips along Jurassic Coast and Day Trips to Torquay, Brixham and Sidmouth. The majority of these trips embark from Exmouth, some depart from other Devon Towns – check the website for details. You could also ride at speed on a fully coded and certified RIB. The boat can hold up to 12 people and reach speeds of 60mph on calm seas. Everyone must wear a self-inflating life jacket and the crew are highly trained for your safety.

🔍 On the seafront at Exmouth marina
⚙ ◎ ♣
⏳ 1–3 hours
⭐ Jurassic Coast Cruise
♿
www.stuartlinecruises.co.uk

Dartington Crystal
Great Torrington

201

Dartington is internationally known for handmade contemporary glassware. At the visitor centre you can learn about 40 years of history through the company timeline, then watch the expert Master Engraving demonstration; even buy that special piece and have it personalised. You might choose to have your hand or foot cast in glass or have a go at glassblowing for yourself. Visitors are then invited to follow the Factory Experience and watch award-winning craftsmen at work, transforming hot molten crystal into elegant shapes, perfecting an art that's 3,000 years old.

🔍 Off the A386, in Great Torrington
⚙ ◎ ♣ ❄ See website for opening times
⏳ 1–2 hours
⭐ The factory tour
FREE With website printout coupon
www.dartington.co.uk

RHS Garden Rosemoor
Great Torrington

202

Set deep in the lovely North Devon countryside, RHS Garden Rosemoor is a 65-acre garden of national importance. You do not have to be a keen gardener to appreciate the beauty and diversity of Rosemoor, which was gifted to the RHS by Lady Ann Berry in 1988. Whatever the season, the garden is a unique and enchanting place that people return to time and again for ideas, inspiration or simply to enjoy a marvellous day out. An exciting and diverse range of events also takes place throughout the year for all the family.

🔍 Follow signs on the A361 from South Molton
⚙ ◎ ♣
⏳ 2–3 hours
⭐ The rose gardens
♿
www.rhs.org.uk

Lynton and Lynmouth Cliff Railway

203

Lynmouth

No family trip to the picturesque towns of Lynton and Lynmouth would be complete without a trip on this world famous, water operated cliff railway – the best, most exciting and most eco-friendly way to travel between these two historic towns. It will be one of the highlights of your day. Enjoy stunning views of the North Devon Coastline as you glide up and down the 862-foot length of track; from Lynmouth nestling at the foot of the cliffs to Lynton perched 500 feet above.

🔍 At the west end of Lynmouth seafront

⚙ ◎ 🍁

⏳ 1 hour

⭐ Stunning view

♿

www.cliffrailwaylynton.co.uk

Tuckers Maltings

204

Newton Abbot

You can take a guided tour of England's only malthouse open to the public and watch Victorian machinery producing malt. Visitors can enjoy guided tours around the malthouse and learn more about the fascinating process of turning barley into malt for brewing. This fascinating tour also gives visitors the opportunity to sample some real ale. There is also a speciality bottled beer shop where visitors can browse over 200 rare bottled beers and even take some home.

🔍 Near the railway station in Newton Abbot

⚙ ◎ 🍁

⏳ 1-2 hours

⭐ Samples of real ale from the nearby Teignworthy Brewery

♿

www.tuckersmaltings.com

Paignton Zoo Environmental Park

205

Paignton

One of Britain's biggest zoos, Paignton is home to some of the planet's rarest and most amazing creatures. Discover all your favourites, like gorillas and orang-utans, elephants and giraffes, lions, tigers and rhinos. And be ready for a few surprises. Don't forget the plants – there are hundreds of rare, special and beautiful specimens around the site. A must-see is Crocodile Swamp. Here, amid the lush tropical foliage and steamy atmosphere, you'll come face-to-face with Cuban, Nile and saltwater crocodiles plus large snakes, turtles and fish.

On the A3022, 1 mile from Paignton town centre

⚙ ⚙ ♣ ❄

⏳ 3–4 hours

★ Crocodile Swamp

💷 💷

www.paigntonzoo.org.uk

National Marine Aquarium

206

Plymouth

The aquarium comprises a total of 50 live exhibits including three massive tanks. Over 4,000 animals from 400 species are displayed in realistic habitats from local shorelines to coral reefs. The aquarium is made up of six main zones: the Shallows, Atlantic Reef, Ocean Drifters, Atlantic Ocean, Weird Creatures and Coral Seas. Each zone is packed full of amazing marine creatures. Visitors will go on a journey from the local shorelines, to the deeper waters off the coast, stop by the Atlantic Ocean and discover the unexplored depths in the wreck.

Follow signs from the A374 in Plymouth

⚙ ⚙ ♣ ❄

⏳ 1–2 hours

★ The Wall of Ocean

💷 💷

www.national-aquarium.co.uk

Plymouth Hoe

207

Plymouth

Plymouth has played a big part in Britain's maritime history. A stroll around the Barbican, the old harbour area, contains some of the city's oldest streets and is home to a number of sights such as the Gin Distillery, the National Maritime Museum and the Mayflower Steps near where the Pilgrims set off on the *Mayflower* for the New World in 1620. A short walk from here is Plymouth Hoe, a large south-facing public space with spectacular views of Plymouth Sound where you can see more historical landmarks as well as a great deal of seagoing activity.

On the seafront

⚙ ⚙ ♣ ❄

⏳ 1–2 hours

★ Smeaton's Tower lighthouse

FREE Car parks charge

www.plymouthbarbican.com

Sound Cruising `208`
Plymouth

Plymouth Sound is one of the most beautiful natural harbours in the world. This established company run regular boat trips from the pontoons near the Mayflower Steps in the Barbican. There are both ferries and cruises, which include a variety of scenic routes such as the dockyard, the warships, the Calstock and Tamar Valley and Morwellham Quay. The highlight is perhaps the harbour cruise, which takes in the beautiful views of Plymouth Sound, passing Smeaton's Tower, Drakes Island and the beautiful Mount Edgcumbe Park in Cornwall.

Madeira Road, Plymouth Barbican

1-3 hours

The harbour cruise

www.soundcruising.com

Seaton Tramway `209`
Seaton

These narrow gauge heritage trams run between Seaton, Colyford and Colyton in East Devon's Axe Valley, travelling alongside the River Axe estuary through two nature reserves and giving an unrivalled view of the abundant wading bird life. The trams are open-topped when the weather is fine but the company also runs elegant, enclosed saloon cars if its cold and rainy. The coastal resort of Seaton is now a gateway town to the Jurassic Coast, while Colyton, with the babbling River Coly flowing through its heart and tiny streets, galleries, shops and pubs, is another must-see for visitors.

Follow signs from the A3052 or A358

See website for timetable and bookings

2 hours

Tour of the Depot complex

www.tram.co.uk

Norman Lockyer Observatory and James Lockyer Planetarium `210`
Sidmouth

Established in 1912, the Norman Lockyer Observatory is a historic working optical observatory and an educational centre for science, especially astronomy, meteorology, amateur radio and sciences of the coast and countryside. Today, it offers visitors the opportunity to observe planets, moon and sunspots through a variety of Victorian telescopes. The Planetarium guarantees a spectacular trip to the North Pole and the Equator at night. There is also a radio room where visitors can talk to people all over the world.

Follow signs from the A3052, 1 mile east of Sidmouth

Check website for details

2-3 hours

Incredible celestial views

www.normanlockyer.org

Quince Honey Farm `211`
South Molton

This marvellous and world-renowned attraction allows access to the hidden lives of the world's latest endangered species. Visitors can stand and watch these wild and wonderful creatures from the distant past. The unique design of the indoor apiary allows close up viewing in complete safety. The glass booths expose the working colonies of honeybees without interfering with their natural lifestyle. Founded in 1949 the farm has grown over the years until today it is the largest honey farm in the country. The large exhibition halls were added in 1980 when the farm moved to its current site.

Just off the A361 in South Molton

2-3 hours

Honey, from the hive to the jar

www.quincehoney.co.uk

Morwellham Quay   `212`
Tavistock

Despite being 23 miles from the sea, Morwellham Quay was the Empire's greatest copper port in the time of Queen Victoria. Today the 1860s are recreated with a Tamar ketch moored at the quay, shops, cottages and costumed staff to act as guides. Visitors can dress up themselves, visit a Victorian school and a farm complete with original farm machinery. The highlight is a train ride along the banks of the River Tamar and then deep underground into a copper mine. Here, in a real abandoned workplace, displays illustrate the harsh working conditions of Victorian copper miners.

🔍 On the A390, 4 miles from Tavistock
✳ ⚙ ❧
⏳ 2-3 hours
⭐ Narrow gauge mine railway
♿
www.morwellham-quay.co.uk

Grand Pier   `213`
Teignmouth

The Grand Pier in Teignmouth was constructed between 1865 and 1867 and sits in the middle of a traditional English seafront. It is easy to while away a few hours on the pier which offers all sorts of traditional seaside amusements, video games, simulators, old-fashioned handle-pull fruit machines, games and gamblers, two lane ten pin bowling and a dance machine. On the Fun Deck there is a children's rollercoaster, pirate ship, mini railway, radio controlled boating pool and formula 1 children's go-karts.

🔍 On Teignmouth seafront
✳ ⚙ ❧
⏳ 1-2 hours
⭐ Traditional English seaside atmosphere
FREE Charges for individual rides
www.whatsonsouthwest.co.uk

Babbacombe Model Village   `214`
Torquay

Take time out from the hustle and bustle of everyday life and feel on top of the world as you see it recreated in miniature. Thousands of miniature buildings, people and vehicles capture the essence of England's past, present and future. It's not just the humour, nor the animation – it has a life of its own. This charming 1:12 scale model is set in award-winning gardens two miles from Torquay harbour. There are also a number of indoor exhibitions including a new illuminated and animated Victorian winter village scene.

🔍 Follow signs from Torquay town centre
✳ ⚙ ❧
⏳ 2 hours
⭐ Summer evening opening
♿
www.babbacombemodelvillage.co.uk

Torquay Museum   `215`
Torquay

Devon's oldest museum, opened in 1845, holds an impressive collection of objects and artefacts relating to natural history, palaeontology, archaeology, social history, ethnography, Torquay pottery and pictorial records and archives relating to the Torbay area. Highlights include Britain's only permanent gallery dedicated to Agatha Christie, the world famous crime writer who was born in Torquay. It features a vast collection of photographs and images. Visitors can see some of her personal effects, from an original manuscript and handwritten notes to some of her clothes and dozens of first editions of her novels.

🔍 Near Torquay harbour
✳ ⚙ ❧ ✳
⏳ 1-2 hours
⭐ The new Explorers gallery
♿
www.torquaymuseum.org

Torre Abbey 216
Torquay

Torre Abbey is the oldest building in Torquay. It has a story spanning 800 years and was once the most important abbey of its kind in England, the brothers who lived here then were known as the White Canons. Following a massive three-year restoration project visitors can now explore the most ancient and hallowed parts of the building where some stunning finds have been unearthed. The abbey is also home to an impressive art collection, which includes a number of important Pre-Raphaelite works by Holman Hunt and Edwin Burne-Jones.

🔍 On the A3022 near Torquay seafront
☼ ⚙ ♣ ❄
⏳ 2–3 hours
★ The Italian Blue Room
♿

www.torre-abbey.org.uk

Berry Pomeroy Castle 217
Totnes

Tucked away in a steep wooded valley, this is the perfect romantic ruin. Within the 15th-century defences of the Pomeroy family castle looms the dramatic ruined shell of its successor, the great Elizabethan mansion of the Seymours. Begun c.1560 and ambitiously enlarged from c.1600, their mansion was intended to become the most spectacular house in Devon, a match for Longleat and Audley End. Never completed, and abandoned by 1700, it became the focus of blood-curdling ghost stories, recounted in the audio tour.

🔍 Off the A385, 2 miles east of Totnes
☼ ⚙ ♣
⏳ 1–2 hours
★ Woodland walks provide fine views of the ruins from below
♿

www.english-heritage.org.uk

Elizabethan House Museum   218
Totnes

Totnes Museum is contained within an authentic Elizabethan merchant's house, built around 1575 for the Kelland family. The three-storey, half-timbered, 13-room house retains many features dating back to the Elizabethan period and has been painstakingly restored. The museum's collections, dating from 5,000 BC, relate to the social, cultural, economic history of Totnes and include a room dedicated to the life and work of Charles Babbage (pioneer of the programmable computer) who, some say, was born in the town. In addition there is a Courtyard and Tudor herb garden to explore.

🔍 On Fore Street in Totnes town centre
✷ ◎ ✦
⏳ 1–2 hours
★ The superb Tudor kitchen
♿
www.devonmuseums.net/totnes

Dorset Belle Cruises   219
Bournemouth

Take a glorious coastal or harbour cruise on a number of routes linking Bournemouth, Swanage and Poole Quay as well as Brownsea Island and the Isle of Wight. There are day and evening trips around the islands, along the Jurassic Coast, past the Isle of Purbeck and Old Harry Rocks, and up the Wareham River. For the more adventurous there's also the ride of a lifetime on *Shockwave* – a twin jet-powered speedboat that hits 40 knots.

🔍 Sailings from Bournemouth Pier, Poole or Swanage
✷ ◎ ✦
⏳ 1–3 hours
★ 135 million-year-old coastline
♿ ♿
www.dorsetbelles.com

Oceanarium, The Bournemouth Aquarium   220
Bournemouth

This aquarium enables visitors to take an underwater adventure around the waters of the world and come face to face with hundreds of awesome creatures. Home to a myriad of species from flamboyant clownfish and tiny terrapins, to stunning sharks and the infamous piranha, which are housed in 10 spectacular recreated environments. This is a fully interactive experience with feeding demos and talks, a walk-through underwater tunnel and exhibits to help you discover more about the fascinating underwater world.

🔍 Follow signs from Bournemouth town centre
✷ ◎ ✦ ✲
⏳ 2–3 hours
★ The Great Barrier Reef exhibit
♿
www.oceanarium.co.uk

Palmers Brewery   221
Bridport

The charming brewery, in the hands of the Palmer family for over a hundred years, runs guided tours that tells the brewery's story – a true English story: of tradition, of community, of commerce and of survival. The tour takes visitors behind the scenes in the historic buildings, to watch every stage of the centuries-old brewing process. The tour ends with a beer tasting (or a soft drink) in the Conference Room, where you will receive an inscribed certificate and commemorative glass tankard. You can book tours in advance on the website.

🔍 On the B3157 West Bay Road, off the A35 at Bridport
✷ ◎ ✦
⏳ 2 hours
★ The impressive Tun Room
♿
www.palmersbrewery.com

Dinosaur Museum   222
Dorchester

The only museum on mainland Britain dedicated to dinosaurs; the award-winning Dinosaur Museum is a treat, especially for children. The museum combines life-sized reconstructions of dinosaurs with fossils and dinosaur skeletons to create an exciting hands-on experience. Multimedia displays tell the story of the giant prehistoric animals and their enthralling world millions of years ago. Visitors can also see and touch life-size reconstructions of a T-Rex, Stegosaurus and Triceratops.

🔍 In Dorchester town centre
✹ ◉ ♣ ❄
⏳ 1–2 hours
★ A real dinosaur skeleton
♿
www.thedinosaurmuseum.com

Thomas Hardy's Cottage   223
Dorchester

Thomas Hardy was born in 1840 in this small cob and thatch cottage, which was built by his great-grandfather and is little altered since the family left. The dwelling is set in a charming cottage garden, which backs on to Egdon Heath. Most of Hardy's writing was done in a small upstairs room with a window seat. The window gave a view over Blackdown. His early novels *Under the Greenwood Tree* and *Far from the Madding Crowd* were written here. Hardy left the cottage in 1860 when he moved to London.

🔍 In Higher Bockhampton, off the A35, 3 miles north east of Dorchester
✹ ◉ ♣
⏳ 1 hour
★ The quiet solitude of Hardy's early life
♿
www.nationaltrust.org.uk

The Tutankhamun Exhibition   224
Dorchester

The exhibition features Tutankhamun's major treasures meticulously recreated, wherever possible, in their original materials. In addition, the ante-chamber and burial chamber of the young pharaoh's tomb have been accurately recreated together with all the tomb furniture and treasures, making it possible for you to experience the wonder of discovery just as Howard Carter did when he discovered it in 1922. Visitors can also see an exact anatomical recreation of Tutankhamun's mummy, which still lies in his tomb and cannot be seen by the public.

🔍 In Dorchester town centre
✹ ◉ ♣ ❄
⏳ 1 hour
★ The golden Death Mask
♿
www.tutankhamun-exhibition.co.uk

Zorbing South UK `225`
Dorchester

Zorbing is the latest adrenaline-surging fix of fun. Ride in a gigantic 3 metre-high PVC ball down a 200-metre run – the longest in the world. Options include tandem and triple-harnessed rides for families who want to tumble head-over-heels together. You could also go for hydro-zorbing when you travel unharnessed in a zorb filled with hot or cold water. It's like a cross between a waterslide and a rollercoaster. Best of all, there's no dizziness. There is an under-6 age restriction and it is essential to book at all times.

Off the A35, 3 miles from Dorchester

1-2 hours

The on-site farmhouse restaurant

www.zorbsouth.co.uk

Jurassic Coast Walk `226`
Lulworth

With stunning views of magnificent cliffs and unspoiled beaches you can take in some of the country's most dramatic scenery along Dorset's Jurassic Coast. Starting at the Lulworth Heritage Centre in Lulworth Cove, walkers make their way around the cove up onto the cliff-top path, heading east. This exhilarating walk will take you through a fossil forest, past Mupe Rocks, Flower's Barrow Iron-Age fort, Wheelbarrow Bay and on into Tyneham Village. You will then have to double back to return to the start.

In Main Road, West Lulworth

4-5 hours

The 135 million-year-old fossil forest

FREE

www.lulworth.com

Lyme Regis Museum   228
Lyme Regis

Built on the site of the home of Lyme's renowned fossilist Mary Anning, the museum is one of the architectural gems of this peaceful town and is packed with fascinating displays. The collections are unusually rich for a small museum though it has a lot of good stories to tell. Lyme's lively local history is well represented by maritime and domestic objects, and illustrated by paintings, prints and photographs. The area is noted for its fossils, displayed in the geological galleries, and the town's literary connections, from Jane Austen to John Fowles, are illustrated in the Writers Gallery.

🔍 In Lyme Regis town centre, next to the Guildhall

⚙ ◎ ♣

⏳ 1-2 hours

★ The Mary Anning collection

💷

www.lymeregismuseum.co.uk

Lulworth Castle and Park   227
Lulworth

Surrounded by beautiful parkland with views of the Jurassic Coast, this 17th-century hunting lodge – built by Thomas Howard, 3rd Lord Bindon in order to entertain hunting parties for the King and Court – has remained in the same family since 1641. Since a devastating fire in 1929, the mock-castle has been restored externally and consolidated inside by English Heritage. The displays, interpretation panels, gallery and unique basement-to-tower interior reveal secrets from the past.

🔍 Off the B3070; 3 miles north-east of Lulworth Cove

⚙ ◎ ♣ ❄

⏳ 2-3 hours

★ Jousting shows in August

💷

www.lulworth.com

Brownsea Island   229
Poole

Just a short boat trip from Poole or Bournemouth, Brownsea Island offers a varied and beautiful landscape for enjoying the wonders of nature; from the patchworks of woodland, heath and grassy fields in the peaceful and secluded interior, to the cliffs and beaches of the coastline, which offer breathtaking views across the harbour to the Purbeck Hills and Studland Bay. Visitors can enjoy fine walks and spectacular views of Poole Harbour. The island is a haven for wildlife including red squirrels, Sika deer and a variety of wading birds.

🔍 By boat from Poole, Bournemouth or Swanage

⚙ ◎ ♣

⏳ 3-4 hours

★ Waymarked trails

💷 💷

www.nationaltrust.org.uk

Chesil Beach
230

Portland

You can't swim here, you can't surf here, but Chesil Beach is one of the most famous beaches in Britain. In fact, this 18-mile long band of shingle is actually a tombolo – a thin strip of shingle joining two bits of land together – in this case Portland and Abbotsbury. For much of its length it is separated from the mainland by an area of saline water called the Fleet Lagoon. Its appeal is its beauty, often at its best when the weather conditions are not, and the huge range of wildlife that make their homes here.

🔍 You can access the beach on foot from Portland

✿ ✿ ✿ ✿

⏳ 2–3 hours

⭐ Exhilarating walks

FREE

www.chesilbeach.org

Sherborne Abbey
231

Sherborne

A trip to the picturesque medieval town of Sherborne would not be complete without a visit to its glorious cathedral. The building was founded in 705. Bishop Alfwold subsequently rebuilt at a later stage, but the period of history most represented in the abbey is from 1475–1504 and was the work of Abbot Ramsam. It was he who created the perpendicular style Norman nave and the fantastic vaulted ceiling. Most of the stained glass is 19th century. In the north and south aisles are several interesting tombs, including that of a 13th-century abbot.

🔍 In Sherborne town centre

✿ ✿ ✿ ✿

⏳ 1–2 hours

⭐ The spectacular fan-vaulted ceiling

FREE Donations encouraged

www.sherborneabbey.com

Studland Beach and Nature Reserve   232
Studland

A glorious slice of natural coastline in Purbeck featuring a four-mile stretch of golden, sandy beach, with gently shelving bathing waters and views of Old Harry Rocks and the Isle of Wight. Ideal for water sports and includes the most popular naturist beach in Britain. The heathland behind the beach is a haven for wildlife and features all six British reptiles. Designated trails through the sand dunes and woodlands, allow for exploration and spotting of animals as well as a wealth of wild flowers. Studland was the inspiration for Toytown in Enid Blyton's *Noddy*.

Access by ferry from Sandbanks or Poole to Shell Bay

3-4 hours
A fabulous walk and a picnic
FREE Car parking charges
www.nationaltrust.org.uk

Durlston Country Park   233
Swanage

Durlston Country Park is a fabulous 280-acre countryside paradise, consisting of sea-cliffs, coastal limestone downland, hay meadows, hedgerows and woodland. With stunning views, walking trails, the historic Great Globe, superb geology and fascinating wildlife and bird life there is always something different to see. The Visitor Centre includes live video of seabirds and dolphin sounds from an underwater hydrophone. There are also daily/monthly displays providing topical information for visitors. There are self-guided trails but see the website for details of guided walks/events programme.

Follow signs from Swanage

3-4 hours
Incredible bird life
FREE Car parking charges
www.durlston.co.uk

The Tolpuddle Martyrs Museum   234
Tolpuddle

This small museum celebrates events in 1834: when six farm workers from the tiny village of Tolpuddle were sentenced to seven years' transportation, a massive protest swept across the country. Thousands of people marched through London and many more organised petitions and protest meetings to demand their freedom. Their 'crime' was to take an oath of solidarity in forming a trade union. The protest campaign proved successful and they returned home in triumph. Their story is now part of the development of a free and democratic society.

Tolpuddle village centre

1-2 hours
The Festival, on the third Sunday in July
FREE
www.tolpuddlemartyrs.org.uk

Corfe Castle   235
Wareham

One of Britain's most majestic ruins and once a controlling gateway through the Purbeck Hills, the castle boasts breathtaking views and several waymarked walks. The demolition of the castle in 1646 by the Parliamentarians marked the end of a rich history as fortress and royal residence. With its fallen walls and secret places, it is a giant playground for children of all ages. The crumbling ruins and subtle invasion by plants and animals, along with its almost ethereal quality as light and weather change, all contribute to the unique atmosphere of the castle.

On the A351, follow signs from Wareham

1-2 hours
Guided tours (see website for details)

www.nationaltrust.org.uk

Monkey World `236`
Wareham

The 65-acre park at Monkey World is a sanctuary for over 230 rescued primates from all over the world. Living in the park is the largest group of chimpanzees outside Africa. Orang-utans, gibbons and other primates inhabit spacious enclosures in a natural setting. As well as completing the world's largest primate rescue operation of 88 capuchin monkeys, it also provides a home for woolly monkeys, lemurs and stump-tailed macaques. Take the woodland walk, drop in on the regular keepers talks or let off steam in the 'Great Ape' play area.

Follow signs from the A352

2 hours

The massive children's play area

www.monkeyworld.org

Abbotsbury Swannery `237`
Weymouth

First established by Benedictine Monks in the 1040s, Abbotsbury Swannery is the only place in the world where visitors are able to walk through the heart of a colony of nesting Mute Swans. You can help hand feed the 600 swans at midday and 4.00 p.m. each day, or get lost in the giant maze (the largest willow maze in Dorset), swing on the swinging nests play area. Located on the dramatic Dorset Coast, this unique natural wildlife habitat is also popular with filmmakers and has been used as a location for *Harry Potter* filming.

On the B3157, between Weymouth and Bridport

1–2 hours

Hatching time (mid-May to end-June)

www.abbotsbury-tourism.co.uk

Brewers Quay `238`
Weymouth

Brewers Quay is a converted Victorian brewery. It is now an indoor shopping complex with speciality shops, heritage and science exhibits. In front of Brewers Quay is Hope Square, with cafes, bars and bistros. Visitors can tour the brewery, visit Weymouth Museum, 'Discovery' – an interactive science centre – and 'Timewalk', a tourist attraction that takes visitors through the history of Weymouth from the Black Death (which was introduced to England by rats on a boat coming into Weymouth harbour) through King George's seaside visits and into more modern times.

Weymouth harbour

2–3 hours

Live music, beer festivals (see website for details)

FREE Attractions will charge

www.brewers-quay.com

Sea Life Park `239`
Weymouth

Weymouth Sea Life Park is unique among this network of attractions in that its numerous marine life exhibitions are housed both indoors and out. Outdoors, visitors will find otter, seal and Humboldt penguin sanctuaries; Adventure Island – with four children's rides and Splash Lagoon, complete with water jets and slide. Indoor exhibits include a Tropical Shark Nursery; the spectacular Turtle Sanctuary with its amazing Ocean Tank; and one of the first National Seahorse breeding and conservation centres.

Follow signs from Weymouth town centre

2–3 hours

The turtles

www.sealife.co.uk

Badbury Rings `240`
Wimborne

The road leading to the Kingston Lacy estate is lined with beech trees (supposedly one for every day of the year, but in fact many more than 365), but dominating the landscape here is the Iron Age hill fort of Bradbury Rings. It dates from around 800 BC and was in use by an ancient Dorset tribe known as the Durotriges until it was attacked and sacked by Roman Legionaries in about 43 AD. The impressive earthworks comprise three ramparts and are over 300 feet high, providing spectacular views from the top.

🔍 Off the B3082, near Wimborne
✿ ◯ ♣ ✻
⏳ 1–2 hours
⭐ Spectacular views
FREE
www.theheritagetrail.co.uk

Kingston Lacy `241`
Wimborne

Home of the Bankes family for more than 300 years, this striking 17th-century house is noted for its lavish interiors. The outstanding art collection includes paintings by Rubens, Van Dyck, Titian and Brueghel, with the largest private collection of Egyptian artefacts in the UK. Outside, stroll across the beautiful lawns towards the restored Japanese tea garden. There are several waymarked walks through the surrounding parkland, with its fine herd of North Devon cattle, and the 8,500 acre estate is dominated by the Iron Age hill fort of Badbury Rings, home to fourteen varieties of orchid.

🔍 On the B3082, near Wimborne
✿ ◯ ♣
⏳ 3 hours
⭐ The outstanding art collection
♿ ♿
www.nationaltrust.org.uk

Berkeley Castle 242
Berkeley

This stunning medieval castle, stately home of the Berkeley family for 900 years is steeped in history. It is where Edward II was murdered, where the Barons of the West gathered before the signing of the Magna Carta and where Queen Elizabeth I hunted and played bowls. It is filled with treasures – paintings by English and Dutch masters, tapestries, furniture of an interesting diversity, silver and porcelain. Particularly interesting is the Norman Keep. The castle is surrounded by sweeping lawns, terraced Elizabethan gardens and Queen Elizabeth I's bowling green.

- Off the A38, west of Dursley
- 2–3 hours
- The cell where Edward II was murdered

www.berkeley-castle.com

Cotswold Motoring Museum and Toy Collection 243
Bourton-on-the-Water

The Cotswold Motoring Museum is a fascinating journey through the 20th century. Though the main focus is on motoring, the museum is full of the everyday paraphernalia that made motoring so popular including picnic sets from the 1920s, alongside caravans, radio sets, gramophones and knitted swimsuits. The museum has an extensive toy collection including teddy bears, aeroplanes and cars, and is also home to *Brum*, the little yellow car from the TV series that was filmed here.

- Bourton town centre
- 1–2 hours
- James Hunt's Formula 1 car

www.cotswold-motor-museum.com

Cheltenham Art Gallery and Museum 244
Cheltenham

A museum filled by generous local residents who have donated their collections over the last hundred years. Exhibits include a world-famous Arts and Crafts Movement collection inspired by William Morris; the story of Edward Wilson, a son of Cheltenham, and his explorations with Scott of the Antarctic; a collection of important Dutch 17th- and 19th-century paintings, rare Oriental porcelain and English ceramics; the social history of Cheltenham, Britain's most complete Regency town, and archaeological treasures of the Cotswolds.

- Cheltenham town centre
- 1–2 hours
- Arts and Crafts collection
- **FREE** Donations appreciated

www.cheltenhammuseum.org.uk

Chedworth Roman Villa 245
Cheltenham

The remains of one of the largest Roman villas in the country provide a fascinating insight into 4th-century Roman Britain. The site was discovered in 1864 on the Earl of Eldon's estate by a local gamekeeper, and subsequently excavated by his estate workers. More than a mile of wall survives, along with beautiful mosaics, two bathhouses, hypocausts, a water shrine and latrine. Visitors to the museum will discover artefacts from the villa, and an audio-visual presentation brings history to life. The ruins nestle in a wooded combe in the heart of the Cotswolds, with beautiful woodland walks.

- On the A429, 3 miles north-west of Fossebridge
- 2–3 hours
- Marvellous mosaics

www.nationaltrust.org.uk

Hidcote Manor Garden 246
Chipping Campden

Hidcote is one of England's great gardens. Designed and created by the horticulturist Major Lawrence Johnston in the Arts and Crafts style, it is made up of exquisite garden rooms, each possessing its own special character. Visitors will discover rare shrubs and trees, outstanding herbaceous borders and unusual plant species. The garden changes in harmony with the seasons, from vibrant spring bulbs to autumn's glorious Red Border. Nestled in the Cotswolds with sweeping views across the Vale of Evesham, Hidcote is appealing all year round.

🔍 Off the B4081, 4 miles north-east of Chipping Campden

✿ ◎ ♣

⏳ 2–3 hours

★ The new Kitchen Garden

£

www.nationaltrust.org.uk

Puzzlewood 248
Coleford

This pre-Roman, open cast iron-ore mine is set in 14 acres of ancient woodland – an area that has remained unaltered since it was transformed into tranquil woodland walks in the 1800s. It has been open to the public for some 50 years. Pathways take you through deep ravines and passageways, over bridges and between moss-covered rocks, forming a very unusual maze. The wood has been used recently for filming for *Dr Who* and *Merlin*. When you've finished walking there's a whole lot of farm animals that you can meet and pet.

🔍 Follow signs from Coleford

✿ ◎ ♣

⏳ 2 hours

★ The indoor wood puzzle

£

www.puzzlewood.net

Dean Heritage Centre 247
Cinderford

The Forest of Dean's local heritage museum comprises five galleries that explore the history of the forest from the Ice Age to the present day. For families there are dressing up clothes, craft activities, and trails around the museum to occupy everyone – not to mention the adventure playground. Visitors can then step outside into the woodlands to experience the lives of charcoal burners, traditional cottage-dwellers, and free miners. Explore a Victorian Foresters' cottage, free mine entrance and charcoal burners camp. A waterwheel and beam engine are also on show.

🔍 On the B4227, near Soudley

✿ ◎ ♣ ❄

⏳ 2 hours

★ A walk in the marvellous woodlands

£

www.deanheritagemuseum.com

Clearwell Caves

249

Coleford

Mining in the Forest of Dean is believed to have started over 7,000 years ago as people migrated back to the area after the last Ice Age. Large-scale, iron-ore mining continued until 1945. Clearwell Caves are now a working mining museum where visitors can see nine impressive caverns with geological and mining displays. Iron ore from the caves has been used over many centuries to make tools, weapons and machinery. These mines are an important part of the Forest of Dean's history and environment.

🔍 Follow signs from Coleford

⚙ 🅿 ♣

⏳ 1–2 hours

⭐ The deep level tour

£

www.clearwellcaves.com

Gloucester's Waterways Walk

250

Gloucester

The River Severn flows right by the city and its famous docks, once bustling with commercial shipping, are now busy with pleasure boats. You can walk from the docks, past Gloucester lock and along the original riverside quay. Cross the river at Westgate Bridge and again at Over Bridge. Head back along the river to Lower Parting, which is a marvellous place from which to view the Severn Bore (see www.severn-bore.co.uk for details of when it's happening). Turn left; staying on Alney Island and you'll arrive at the old Llanthony Lock from where you will be able to see your starting point.

🔍 Follow signs to Historic Docks from the city centre

⚙ 🅿 ♣

⏳ 3 hours

⭐ The old docks

FREE

www.gloucesterdocks.me.uk

Sezincote House and Garden   251

Moreton-in-Marsh

Built in 1810 in a Moghul style of Rajasthan (a mixture of Hindu and Muslim) by Charles Cockerell, who had worked in India, Sezincote House is an extraordinary site nestling in the Cotswold Hills. The house, with a central dome, minarets, peacock-tail windows, jail-work railings and pavilions, is set within a romantic water garden with many rare plants, pools, waterfalls, a grotto and a temple to the Hindu sun god. It is claimed that Sezincote was the inspiration for the Brighton Pavilion.

🔍 On the A44, west of Moreton-in-Marsh
☼ ◎ ✿
⌛ 2 hours
★ Tea and cake is served on guided tours
£

www.sezincote.co.uk

Wellington Aviation Museum   252

Moreton-in-Marsh

This small museum is dedicated to all those who served or who passed through RAF Moreton-in-Marsh, on one of the many training courses for RAF bomber command during the Second World War. The museum holds a huge range of artefacts from the war years. Visitors will see propellers and wheels from the principle aircraft at Moreton-in-Marsh, the Vickers-Armstrong Wellington. There is also a casing for the 4000 lb bombs dropped by the aircraft and a whole tail section of one aircraft, showing the famous Barnes Wallis-designed geodetic structure, which made the aircraft so strong and easy to repair.

🔍 On the A44, north-east of Cheltenham
☼ ◎ ✿
⌛ 1 hour
★ Personal wartime stories
£

www.wellingtonaviation.org

Cherney House Gardens   253

North Cherney

This beautiful 'secret' garden sits high above the Churn Valley in the heart of the Cotswolds. It has many features included a lovely walled garden with lots of old-fashioned roses, a well-labelled herb garden and a kitchen garden. Organic in approach, plants tumble happily over each other and fill the air with perfume. The orchard is rich in fruit. Snowdrops give way to daffodils and carpets of bluebells follow early spring flowers. The summer is a tapestry of shape and colour that changes with the parkland trees to the rich colours of autumn.

🔍 Off the A435, up past North Cherney Church
☼ ◎ See website for details
⌛ 1-2 hours
★ Walks marked in surrounding woodland
£

www.cerneygardens.com

WWT Slimbridge   254

Nympsfield

With an astounding array of wildlife from water voles to waders, hares to dragonflies, Slimbridge is home to the world's largest collection of swans, geese, ducks and flamingos. This beautiful and internationally renowned reserve has something to offer visitors during every season from downy duckling days in spring to breathtaking swan feeds in winter. Visitors can take a canoe trail through the grounds or let the kids splash and stomp in their wellies at Welly Boot Land, an exciting new outdoor play area. See some new resident otters and beavers in Back from The Brink.

🔍 Follow signs from junctions 13 or 14 of the M5
☼ ◎ ✿ ❄
⌛ 3-4 hours
★ Meet the flamingos
£

www.wwt.org.uk/visit-us/slimbridge

Police Bygones Exhibition   255

Tetbury

Housed in Tetbury's original police station, complete with cells and a former magistrate's court, is this interesting exhibition which tells the story of the Gloucestershire Constabulary, first founded in 1839 despite a petition raised by the people of Compton Greenfield against the necessity of forming a police force in Gloucestershire at all. A number of displays of photographs and equipment show the history of policing. In the first floor courtroom there is a complete magistrates court with a display using models and depicting a hearing, as it would have been in the late 1940s or early 1950s.

🔍 Near Tetbury town centre

❀ ❀ ♣ ❄

⏳ 1 hour

★ Exhibition of restraint equipment

FREE Donations appreciated

www.visittetbury.co.uk/police-museum

Westonbirt Arboretum   256

Tetbury

Westonbirt Arboretum is a wonderful world of trees. There are 18,000 of them from all over the world, planted from 1829 to the present day, producing 600 acres of beautifully landscaped Cotswold countryside. Visitors to Westonbirt can wander where they please along 17 miles of paths or simply sit in a leafy glade and admire some of the tallest, oldest and indeed the rarest trees and shrubs of their kind in the world. There is also an extensive array of wild flowers, fungi, birds and animals on display throughout the year.

🔍 On A433, 3 miles south of Tetbury

❀ ❀ ♣ ❄

⏳ 2–3 hours

★ The autumn leaf colour display

♿

www.forestry.gov.uk/westonbirt

Assembly Rooms 258
Bath

The Assembly Rooms were at the heart of fashionable Georgian society, the perfect venue for entertainment. When completed in 1771, they were described as 'the most noble and elegant of any in the kingdom'. The Ball Room, Octagon, Tea Room and Card Room of this magnificent building were used for dancing, music, card playing, tea drinking and conversation. On the lower ground floor visitors can see the Fashion Museum, which includes an internationally renowned collection of fashionable dress and a regular programme of other exhibitions.

In Bath city centre

1-2 hours

The exquisite chandeliers

FREE Fashion Museum

www.nationaltrust.org.uk

Sudeley Castle and Gardens 257
Winchcombe

Sudeley's glorious gardens are among the very best in England, from the centrepiece Queens' Garden, billowing with hundreds of varieties of old fashioned roses, to the Herbal Healing Garden. The castle houses fascinating exhibitions that explore Sudeley's history and the prominent characters that have visited or lived at the castle. Although the castle remains a family home, the 16th-century west wing houses the exhibitions, and visitors can also explore St Mary's Church where Katherine Parr lies buried, the gardens, Pheasantry, medieval ruins and adventure playground.

On the B4362, 8 miles north-east of Cheltenham

2-3 hours

Connoisseur tours (see website for more information)

www.sudeleycastle.co.uk

Bath Balloons 259
Bath

Bath is pretty spectacular from the ground, but little can compare with the city from the air. Taking off from the launch site in Royal Victoria Park, you'll rise alongside Bath's famous Royal Crescent, Bath Abbey and the Roman Baths into the heart of the honey-coloured Georgian skyline, with views in every direction. Every flight is one of discovery – lively, informative and a uniquely individual experience. You won't want it to end, but when it does, you will come gently back down to earth, landing somewhere in the rolling countryside of Somerset, Wiltshire or the Cotswolds.

Near Bath city centre

3-4 hours

The breathtaking view

www.balnet.co.uk

Prior Park Landscape Garden　261
Bath

One of only four Palladian bridges of this design in the world can be crossed at Prior Park, which was created in the 18th century by local entrepreneur Ralph Allen, with advice from 'Capability' Brown and the poet Alexander Pope. The garden is set in a sweeping valley where visitors can enjoy magnificent views of Bath. Restoration of the 'Wilderness' has reinstated the Serpentine Lake, Cascade and Cabinet. Nearby is the Bath Skyline, a six-mile circular route encompassing beautiful woodlands and meadows, an Iron Age hill fort, Roman settlements and 18th-century follies.

🔍 Take a bus from Bath Spa station (the park has no parking)
❀ ❀ ❀
⌛ 1–2 hours
★ Fabulous views of Bath
£
www.nationaltrust.org.uk

Bath Walking Tours　260
Bath

You can take a free walking tour around Bath led by the Mayor's Honorary Guides. Tours leave Abbey Churchyard, outside the Pump Rooms, at 10.30 a.m. every day and at 2.00 p.m. from Sunday to Friday. Additional tours leave at 7.00 p.m. on Tuesdays, Fridays and Saturdays from May to September. You don't need to book but tours are very popular. Among other things, visitors will see the Roman Baths, Medieval Baths, the 16th-century abbey, the site of the coronation of the first King of England, superb 18th-century architecture, the Royal Crescent and the King's Circus.

🔍 Bath city centre
❀ ❀ ❀ ❄
⌛ 2 hours
★ Informative guides
FREE Guides will not accept tips
www.bathguides.org.uk

Thermae Bath Spa　262
Bath

Using the warm, mineral-rich waters, which the Celts and Romans enjoyed over 2,000 years ago, Thermae Bath Spa is Britain's original and only natural thermal Spa. Thermae is a remarkable combination of old and new where historic spa buildings blend with the contemporary design of the New Royal Bath. Choose a 2-hour or 4-hour spa session, which includes full access to the warm waters and flowing curves of the Minerva Bath, a series of aromatic steam rooms and the open-air rooftop pool with spectacular views across the skyline of Bath.

🔍 Follow signs from city centre
❀ ❀ ❀ ❄
⌛ 2–6 hours
★ The Minerva Bath
£ £ £ Booking essential
www.thermaebathspa.com

The Herschel Museum of Astronomy `263`

Bath

The home of a distinguished family of astronomers. It was from here that William Herschel discovered the planet Uranus in 1781. His observations helped double the known size of the solar system. Following a tradition of the great astronomers of the Renaissance he pushed forward the science of building telescopes. His sister Caroline also made a huge contribution to the field of astronomy. Set in a small Georgian house with period interiors and displays of astronomical artefacts.

Bath city centre

1–2 hours

William's famous telescope

www.bath-preservation-trust.org.uk

Brean Leisure Park `264`

Brean Sands

Fun City at Brean Leisure Park on Brean Sands is the biggest theme park in the south-west. There are over 30 rides and attractions, including roundabouts, waltzers, dodgems and rollercoasters. For the ultimate thrill seekers there's the 'XTreme' ride, or you can opt for some family favourites including Disco Fever, Sizzler and Frisbee. Then there's the Shock Wave Super Looper rollercoaster, Canoe River, a children's riverboat ride will have them shrieking with excitement, and Laser Quest provides thrills galore. For something a little gentler there's a 'Pony Adventure' – a children's themed pony ride.

Follow signs from junction 22 of the M5

3–4 hours

The new Super Looper rollercoaster

www.brean.com

Cheddar Caves and Gorge `265`

Cheddar

Cheddar Gorge, a place of wild and rugged beauty, is a karst limestone and calcareous grassland nature reserve and home to many rare plants and animals. Cheddar Caves, inhabited by our ancestors up to 40,000 years ago, were re-discovered in Victorian times, and are now famous for their spectacular stalactite and stalagmite decorations. Easy-to-use audio-guides tell the story of the caves' formation and discovery. There are a number of other attractions including an open-top bus tour, a Lookout Tower with magnificent views and a breathtaking cliff-top walk around Britain's biggest gorge.

Follow signs from junction 2 of the M5 or A38

3–4 hours

Gough's Cave

www.cheddarcaves.co.uk

Dunster Castle `266`

Dunster

The fortified home of the Luttrell family for more than 600 years stands dramatically on a wooded hill. It has an impressive medieval gatehouse and a ruined tower. The interior was remodelled in 1868 and now has a marvellous oak staircase and plasterwork ceiling. The castle is set in beautiful parkland and has a sunny, sheltered terraced garden of rare shrubs on which visitors can relax. Views over the surrounding countryside include Exmoor and the Bristol Channel.

Off the A39, 3 miles south-east of Minehead

2–3 hours

Leather wall hangings

www.nationaltrust.org.uk

Yarn Market
267

Dunster

This octagonal structure was built in 1609 by George Luttrell for local merchants to sell Dunster cloth and kerseymere, a fine woollen cloth with a twill weave. It also provided shelter during inclement weather. The floor is cobbled stone, and the structure is topped by a slate roof with a central wooden lantern. The building was damaged during the Civil War, when Dunster Castle was under siege for 160 days. The Yarn Market was restored in 1647, the date which appears on the weathervane that sits on top of it.

Dunster High Street

⚙ ⚙ ♣ ✳

⌛ 1 hour

★ A hole in the beams said to have been made by a Civil War cannonball

FREE

www.english-heritage.org.uk

Glastonbury Abbey
268

Glastonbury

Though now a ruin, there are several reasons to visit Glastonbury Abbey. First, it is still a living Christian sanctuary, may have been the site of the oldest church, and was certainly once the greatest abbey in the country. It is also the possible burial place of King Arthur. But another important attraction of this wonderful place is its peace and quiet. The relative seclusion of the 36 acres of parkland in which it stands provides the perfect atmosphere for people who want to forget their hectic lives and take it easy for a while.

Follow signs from Glastonbury town centre

⚙ ⚙ ♣

⌛ 1-2 hours

★ A stroll in the Abbey grounds

£

www.glastonburyabbey.com

Somerset Rural Life Museum
269

Glastonbury

The museum is housed in the attractive setting of a Victorian farmhouse, farm buildings and cider orchard. The social and domestic life of Victorian Somerset is described in reconstructed rooms and an exhibition, which tells the life story of a farm worker, John Hodges, from the cradle to the grave. The magnificent 14th-century Abbey Barn is the centrepiece. The barn and the farm buildings surrounding the courtyard contain displays showing the tools and techniques of farming in Victorian Somerset. Local activities like willow growing, mud horse fishing, peat digging and cider making are included.

Chilkwell Street, Glastonbury

⚙ ⚙ ♣ ✳

⌛ 1-2 hours

★ The Abbey Barn

FREE

www.somerset.gov.uk/museums

Glastonbury Tor 270

Glastonbury

The dramatic and evocative Tor dominates the surrounding countryside and offers spectacular views over Somerset, Dorset and Wiltshire. At the summit of this very steep hill an excavation has revealed the plans of two superimposed churches of St Michael, of which only a 15th-century tower remains. Rich in legend, the Tor is famous for its possible connections with King Arthur and New Age mysticism. Visitors can judge for themselves what a special and atmospheric place this is. The walk up takes about 20 minutes.

🔍 Follow signs from Glastonbury town centre
❄ ❄ ❄ ❄
⏳ 1–2 hours
⭐ Breathtaking views
FREE Donations welcome
www.nationaltrust.org.uk

Alstone Wildlife Park 271

Highbridge

This small, non-commercial, family-run park advertises itself with the slogan 'No rides, no slides, just animals'. And there are plenty of animals including 55 red deer, who will come to the gate and feed from your hand, Theodore the Bactrian camel, fascinating eagle owls and barn owls as well as a pair of chestnut mandibled toucans. The amusing emus and rheas have been here for at least 20 years. Visitors will also find Katie and Emily, the kune-kune pigs, very comical. All profits go into looking after the animals that live here.

🔍 Follow signs from the A38 at Highbridge
❄ ❄ ❄ ❄
⏳ 1–2 hours
⭐ Colin, the Green Squirrel Monkey
💲
www.visitsomerset.co.uk

Dunkery Vineyard

272

Minehead

Dunkery Vineyard is set in a beautiful part of the Exmoor National Park. The grapes grow in the most exquisite countryside where they are visited by an abundance of wildlife: including buzzards, red deer, roe deer, badgers, foxes, pheasants, red legged partridges, green woodpeckers, goldcrests, long tailed tits and large flocks of goldfinches. There are seven acres of vines, which are used to make delicious wines in the on-site winery especially dark red wines and Riesling. You can arrange guided tours of the winery and tastings (minimum 12 people) via the website.

🔍 Off the A396, near Wootton Courtenay, south-west of Minehead

⚙ ◎ ♣

⏳ 2–3 hours

⭐ Wine tastings

£

www.exmoor-excellence.com/dunkery

Haynes International Motor Museum

273

Sparkford

This is the UK's largest exhibition of the greatest cars from around the world. It covers a hundred years of motoring history over 400 amazing cars and bikes from nostalgic classics of the 1950s and 60s, glorious Bentleys and Rolls Royces to exciting super cars of today, like the Jaguar XJ220 and the Ferrari 360. Visitors can see the world famous Red Room, 11 huge display halls and one of the UK's largest speedway collections. Experience the outdoor military vehicle collection, the children's play area or relax in the cinema of motoring.

🔍 On the A359, just north of Sparkford

⚙ ◎ ♣ ❄

⏳ 2–3 hours

⭐ The incredible Red Room

£

www.haynesmotormuseum.com

Somerset Cricket Museum

274

Taunton

The long tradition of cricket in Somerset is celebrated in this good-sized museum at the County Ground, where weather can never affect your enjoyment. The museum explores the history of the club and the players that have taken to the pitch in Taunton, including greats such as Viv Richards, Ian Botham and Gary Sobers. From ceramics and cigarette cards to a Victorian hand press used to print scorecards and Joel Garner's boot, the permanent collection will appeal to fanatics and flirts alike, while this year's temporary exhibition looks at the county's Australian connections.

🔍 County Ground on Priory Avenue, Taunton

⚙ ◎ ♣

⏳ 1 hour

⭐ Botham's Ashes-winning bat from 1981

£

www.somersetcricketmuseum.co.uk

The Bishop's Palace and Gardens

275

Wells

This splendid medieval palace has been the home of the Bishops of Bath and Wells for 800 years. Visitors entering through the central porch step back almost 800 years into Bishop Jocelin's vaulted Entrance Hall. There are 14 acres of gardens including the springs from which the city takes its name. Visitors can also see the Bishop's private Chapel, ruined Great Hall and the Gatehouse with portcullis and drawbridge beside which the famous Mute Swans ring a bell for food.

🔍 Wells city centre, near the cathedral

⚙ ◎ ♣

⏳ 1–2 hours

⭐ The Mute Swans asking for lunch

£

www.bishopspalacewells.co.uk

Wells Cathedral `276`

Wells

Wells Cathedral is probably the finest example of Early English architecture (12th–14th century). Major interesting features include the magnificent West Front with over 300 carved figures of Saints and Kings. The inverted arches of the nave, which were added in 1338, to strengthen the base of the central tower, and the famous astronomical clock, one of the world's oldest working mechanical clocks (c. 1390), when it strikes the hour mounted knights ride into action.

🔍 Wells city centre

✿ ◯ ♣ ❄

⏳ 1–2 hours

★ The medieval stained glass Jesse Window

FREE Donations welcome

www.wellscathedral.org.uk

STAR ATTRACTION

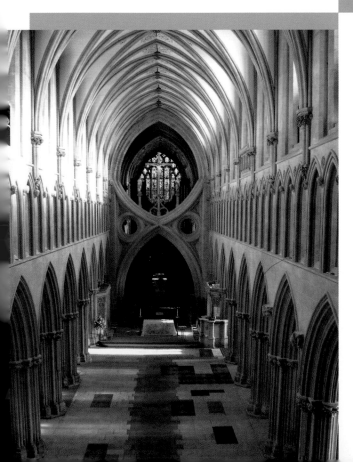

The Helicopter Museum `277`

Weston-super-Mare

The museum has over 70 full-size aircraft on display ranging from an impressive Russian gunship to a massive Super Frelon 36-seat helicopter, and from the Queen's own helicopters to the veterans of the Vietnam conflict. Also on display are the current world speed record holder and a selection of unusual gyrocopters. The museum also hosts regular Helicopter Experience Flights. During the 15-mile flight along the local coastline passengers can learn how rotorcraft work and fly via commentary from the experienced pilot.

🔍 Follow signs from junction 21 of the M5

✿ ◯ ♣ ❄

⏳ 2 hours

★ Helicopter Experience flights (charged separately)

£

www.helicoptermuseum.co.uk

Ebbor Gorge National Nature Reserve

`278`

Weston-super-Mare

Craggy limestone outcrops, scree slopes and wooded valleys are on offer in this glorious reserve. Some 200,000 years ago the huge cavern that formed Ebbor Gorge collapsed and left behind a number of small caves where reindeer, cave bear and wolf remains have been discovered. Artefacts and bones from Neolithic people who sheltered in these caves 5,000 years ago are on show at Wells museum. The humidity within Hope Wood valley makes it ideal for ferns, fungi, white letter hairstreak butterflies and greater and lesser horseshoe bats.

Off the A371 between Cheddar and Wells

1-2 hours

Waymarked trails

FREE

www.naturalengland.org.uk

Wookey Hole Caves

`279`

Wookey Hole

Situated in the heart of Somerset, evidence of early man inhabiting the site around Wookey Hole can be traced back over 50,000 years. As well as human artefacts, the many archaeological finds include the bones of tropical and Ice Age animals such as rhinoceros, bear, mammoth and lion. More recently, the Celts settled and farmed in the area before the Romans arrived approximately 2,000 years ago and took over the region for its rich mineral mines. There are other attractions at the site including the Ice Age Valley, Pirate Park golf, the Monster Mill and the Wookey Hole circus.

Follow signs from junction 22 of the M5

3-4 hours

The spectacular caves

www.wookey.co.uk

STAR ATTRACTION

Stonehenge   281
Amesbury

Mystery surrounds this 5,000-year-old monument. Visitors to this prehistoric site near Salisbury can decide for themselves whether Stonehenge was a place of sun worship, a healing sanctuary, a sacred burial site or something different altogether. Stonehenge is a powerful reminder of the once-great peoples of the late Stone and Bronze Ages. Erected between 3000 and 1600 BC, a number of the stones were carried hundreds of miles over land and sea, while antlers and bones were used to dig the pits that hold the stones whose ultimate purpose remains a fascinating and enduring mystery.

🔍 On the A303
☼ ☼ 🍁 ❄
⏳ 1 hour
⭐ Superb local walks
♿

www.english-heritage.org.uk

Fleet Air Arm Museum   280
Yeovil

This museum represents the flying arm of the Royal Navy. With four exhibition halls, over 90 aircraft, and 30,000 artefacts there's lots to see. The new Fly Navy hundred exhibition dramatically presents 100 years of naval aviation. Visitors can also see the first British built Concorde and the award winning Aircraft Carrier Experience. In the theatre, you'll 'fly' by helicopter to the flight deck of the aircraft carrier HMS *Ark Royal* where you'll see fighters and bombers. You can visit the 'Island' control rooms and bridge and even see a nuclear bomb.

🔍 Off the A303, near Yeovilton
☼ ☼ 🍁 ❄
⏳ 2-3 hours
⭐ The Aircraft Carrier Experience
♿ ♿

www.fleetairarm.com

Woodhenge
Amesbury

282

A similar size to nearby Stonehenge, Woodhenge was only discovered in 1925 when rings of dark spots were noticed in a crop of wheat. This Neolithic monument, dating from about 2300 BC, now consists of concrete markers replacing six concentric rings of timber posts, once possibly supporting a ring-shaped building. There is also evidence of a number of standing stones. There is speculation that this was the site of a child sacrifice as a skeleton was found at the centre of the rings. The skeleton of a teenager was also found nearby.

Just off the A345

1 hour

Sister site of the famous Stonehenge

FREE

www.english-heritage.org.uk

Avebury
Avebury

283

In the 1930s, the pretty village of Avebury was witness to the excavations of archaeologist Alexander Keiller. In re-erecting this great circle of stones, Keiller uncovered the true wonder of one of the most important megalithic monuments in Europe. The fascinating finds from his excavations are on display in the 17th-century threshing barn and stables galleries of the small on-site museum where interactive displays and activities for children bring the landscape to life. The 16th-century dovecote also displays a variety of alternating interpretations throughout the year.

Off the A4361 and B4003, 6 miles west of Marlborough

2 hours

Bronze Age burial mounds at nearby Windmill Hill

www.nationaltrust.org.uk

Figsbury Ring
Salisbury

284

Possibly a hill fort, possibly a henge, the secrets of Figsbury Ring have yet to be discovered. The site covers some 15 acres, with an outer bank and an inner ditch. The evidence suggests that Figsbury Ring was only occupied intermittently, either for gatherings or as a place of refuge. The most important find here was a Bronze Age leaf bladed sword, which is now held by the Ashmolean Museum in Oxford. Scatters of pottery and some animal bones have also been found but there are no signs of houses.

Off the A30, north-east of Salisbury

1–2 hours

Mysterious ancient site

FREE

www.wowheritage.org.uk

Larmer Tree Gardens
Salisbury

285

Created by General Pitt Rivers in 1880 as pleasure grounds for 'public enlightenment and entertainment', these gardens are an extraordinary example of Victorian extravagance and vision. The garden contains a wonderful collection of ornate buildings, majestic trees and intimate arbours. In spring there's a wonderful display of camellias and rhododendrons; in summer the hydrangeas are in vibrant colour, and towering over the ponds the eucryphias make a magnificent sight and in autumn the trees and shrubs of the garden and woodland beyond produce a rich tapestry of colour.

Follow signs from the A354, south-west of Salisbury

1–2 hours

King John's hunting grounds

www.larmertreegardens.co.uk

Old Sarum

Salisbury

286

This great earthwork, the original site of the city of
Salisbury, with 5,000 years of history and its huge
banks and ditches, was originally created by Iron Age
people around 500 BC, and later occupied by Romans,
Saxons and Normans. Today, visitors can see the
remains of the prehistoric fortress, the palace, castle and
cathedral. There are marvellous walks in the area or you
could enjoy a picnic while taking in the marvellous
views of the Wiltshire countryside.

🔍 Off the A345, 2 miles north of Salisbury
⚙ ⚙ ♣ ❋
⏳ 1–2 hours
★ Summer jousting tournaments
♿
www.english-heritage.org

Stourhead

Stourhead

287

Lying in secluded privacy in its own tranquil valley,
Stourhead features one of the world's finest 18th-
century landscape gardens. A magnificent lake is
central to the design, and there are classical temples,
enchanting grottos and rare and exotic trees. The Hoare
family history can be uncovered at Stourhead House, a
majestic Palladian mansion housing a unique Regency
library with fabulous collections of Chippendale
furniture and paintings, all set amid delightful lawns
and parkland. Stourhead is at the heart of a 2,650-acre
estate of chalk downs, ancient woods and farmland.

🔍 Off the A303, at Mere
⚙ ⚙ ♣
⏳ 2–3 hours
★ Views from the top of King Alfred's Tower
♿ ♿
www.nationaltrust.org.uk

Longleat

Warminster

Longleat has a lot to offer the visitor – from a marvellous safari park to an Elizabethan stately home, from miniature trains to mazes and boat rides, animal and castle adventures all set in 900 acres of 'Capability' Brown landscaped parkland with woodlands, lakes and farmland. There is almost too much to see in one day. Passport tickets, which allow visitors once-only entry into all Longleat attractions but on any day during that same visitor season, are available on the website and represent a 50 per cent saving.

🔍 Off the A36, between Bath and Salisbury

⚙ ☉ ♣

⏳ 5–6 hours

★ The drive-through safari

£ £ £

www.longleat.co.uk

STEAM – Museum of the Great Western Railway

Swindon

STEAM tells the remarkable story of the men and women who built, operated and travelled on 'God's Wonderful Railway'. Visitors are given the chance to experience the sights and sounds of the GWR works at Swindon – famous as the place where many of the best steam locomotives in the world were built – and to hear the stories of the men and women who worked there. The museum also brings to life the exploits of Isambard Kingdom Brunel – the flamboyant engineer, and acknowledged genius behind the creation of the GWR.

🔍 Follow signs from Swindon town centre

⚙ ☉ ♣ ❄

⏳ 2–3 hours

★ 175th birthday celebrations (see website for details)

£

www.swindon.gov.uk/steam

Westbury White Horse and Bratton Camp

Westbury

This famous landmark in west Wiltshire has marvellous views of the Wiltshire and Somerset countryside and in recent years has become a popular spot for kite flying and hang gliding. Cut into the steep chalk hillside in 1778, the white horse is thought to rest on the site of an older horse that commemorated the defeat of the Danes by King Alfred at Ethandun in AD 878. It is sited just below the Iron Age hill fort of Bratton Camp.

🔍 Off the B3098, 2 miles east of Westbury

⚙ ☉ ♣ ❄

⏳ 2 hours

★ The marvellous views

FREE

www.english-heritage.org.uk

Eastern

Bedfordshire
Cambridgeshire
Essex
Hertfordshire
Norfolk
Suffolk

Norfolk Broads

©MAPS IN MINUTES™/Collins Bartholomew 2010

Guide to the **East**

Wild Britain 291
Bedford

Wild Britain caters for families with small children. Starting in the tropical jungle, youngsters can earn their Safari Spotters badge. With conditions just like the tropics they'll come face-to-face with butterflies, terrapins and Speedo the tortoise, and will also be introduced to some not-so-common residents. Discover how soft a tarantula is, feel a cockroach scuttle across your palm and hold a large African Land Snail. You can also follow the Hedgehog Play Trail with fun puzzles and activities, cuddle fluffy rabbits in 'hands-on' corner and make your own arty creation to take home.

Follow signs from the A421

1–2 hours

The new Moley Mine

www.wild-britain.co.uk

English Falconry Birds of Prey Centre 292
Biggleswade

This family-run centre, located in woodland, has more than 300 birds including owls, eagles, hawks, falcons and vultures many of which are on static display and which also take part in the daily flying displays. Visitors are able to handle some of the birds under supervision. Photographic days and workshops are also held at the centre where the falconers present the birds in more natural looking settings. The centre runs an extensive events calendar during the warmer months, which are highly recommended (see website for details).

Off the B658, at Old Warden Aerodrome

2–3 hours

Handling and spectacular flying displays

www.birdsofpreycentre.co.uk

Shuttleworth Collection 293
Biggleswade

This world famous collection of aircraft, started by Richard Shuttleworth, depicts the history of the first hundred years of flight. Aeroplanes on show range from a 1909 Bleriot to a Second World War Spitfire and many others. During the season, the aircraft are flown in displays, alongside visiting aircraft from other operators. These displays recreate flying during the Edwardian period, the First World War, the peacetime years of the 1920s and 30s, the Second World War and up to the 1960s. There are eight hangars to visit, which house the planes, cars, motorcycles and carriages.

Off the B658, at Old Warden Aerodrome

2–3 hours

Regular flying displays

www.shuttleworth.org

Dunstable Downs, Chilterns Gateway Centre and Whipsnade Estate
Dunstable

`294`

There are acres of space to enjoy with fabulous views over the Vale of Aylesbury and along the Chiltern Ridge. Dunstable Downs is an Area of Outstanding Natural Beauty and a kite-flying hotspot. Chalk grassland, rich in wildlife, provides prime walking country. There's a visitor centre that has information on waymarked trails and guided walks across with a number of fascinating archaeological features. There is a regular programme of events including a monthly farmers' market.

On the B4541, west of Dunstable

2–3 hours

Annual kite festival (see website for details)

FREE Donations welcome

www.nationaltrust.org.uk

Stondon Transport Museum
Henlow

`296`

From vintage cars and vehicles to a horse-drawn Romany caravan, Stondon Transport Museum is a great place to while away a few hours. Featuring bygone vehicles from the beginning of the century to modern classics. The museum has a collection of over 400 exhibits, lovingly restored to their full glory.
The majority of the exhibits are under cover in five halls, and arranged to reduce a lot of walking for the very young or elderly. A brief synopsis of the vehicle's history is attached to each exhibit and volunteers are usually on hand to add detail.

Off the A600, at Lower Stondon

2 hours

Life-size replica ship of Captain Cook's *Endeavour*

www.transportmuseum.co.uk

ZSL Whipsnade
Dunstable

`295`

Set in 600 acres of Chiltern parkland, Whipsnade is home to over 2,500 wild animals: lions, tigers, rhinos and giraffes can be seen in almost natural conditions. The zoo has a worldwide reputation for its role in the breeding and conservation of rare animal species and breeds. A full-size steam railway, the Jumbo Express, takes visitors past wallabies and maras, which range freely throughout the park. Visitors may also drive their own vehicles through the parkland, seeing the animals close up, or take one of the regular shuttle buses through the park.

Follow signs from junctions 9 or 12 of the M1

3–5 hours

New Rhinos of Nepal exhibit

www.zsl.org

STAR ATTRACTION

Pitstone Green Museum 297
Leighton Buzzard

Housed in the buildings of an 1831 farm, this museum offers a fascinating day out for the family with many interesting displays and artefacts. Although mainly concerned with 200 years of local farming, country life, trades and professions, it has many other interesting exhibits including two model railways, a 37-HP Crossley gas engine, stationary engines, vintage wirelesses, photographic and electrical apparatus and a Second World War military aviation room, which includes a full-size reconstruction of the cockpit of an Avro Lancaster Bomber.

Off the B489

Only open on certain days, see website for details

2-3 hours

Wide range of rural events

website.lineone.net/~pitstonemus/

Woburn Abbey, Gardens and Deer Park 298
Woburn

Home to the Duke of Bedford, Woburn is open for visitors to experience the grandeur and extravagant decor of this palatial mansion. The dining room boasts a ceiling painted by Cipriani in 1770 and a fine collection of paintings including Venetian views by Canaletto. There are various staterooms to see including the dining room and bedrooms. Royal visitors who have stayed here include Elizabeth I, Charles I, Queen Victoria and Prince Albert. Outside, you can explore the 3,000-acre deer park where there are ten species of deer roaming freely.

Follow signs from junction 13 of the M1

3-4 hours

The Blue Drawing Room

www.woburn.co.uk/abbey

Woburn Safari Park 299
Woburn

Woburn Safari Park has 350 acres to explore and hundreds of animals to see in your car and on foot. The road safari includes a wide variety of animals with room to roam including elephants, rhinos, big cats, buffalo, camels and monkeys. You can also explore the Wild World Leisure Park, which includes Penguin World, Land of the Lemurs, a sea lion cove, swan boats and the Great Woburn Railway. During the main season there are daily events such as: sea lion display, birds of prey flying demonstrations and keeper talks at feeding time.

Follow signs from junction 13 of the M1

4-5 hours

Wolves, black bears and tigers

www.woburn.co.uk/safari

At Duxford, **keep an eye on the sky**, as you may well see some historic aircraft in flight

Fitzwilliam Museum 300

Cambridge

The Fitzwilliam Museum, founded in 1816, houses world-class collections of works of art and antiquities spanning centuries and civilisations. Highlights include masterpieces of painting from the 14th century to the present day by Titian, Canaletto, Rubens, Monet and Picasso among others, drawings and prints, sculpture, furniture, armour, pottery and glass, oriental art, illuminated manuscripts, coins and medals and antiquities from Egypt, the Ancient Near East, Greece, Rome and Cyprus.

🔍 In Cambridge city centre

✹ ✹ ✿ ✺ (closed Mondays)

⏳ 2-3 hours

★ Newly housed Egyptian collection

FREE

www.fitzmuseum.cam.ac.uk

Kettle's Yard 301

Cambridge

Entry to the home of former Tate curator Jim Ede's collection of early 20th-century art is gained by pulling on a doorbell. Once inside, you are invited to choose a book to read, take out your sketchpad, or simply sit and look at art. The collection of works here reads like a roll call of 20th-century art: Ben Nicholson, Joan Miro, Barbara Hepworth and Henry Moore are just a few. The building was originally constructed from four derelict cottages, but newer galleries used for temporary exhibitions of contemporary art, and regular recitals of chamber music, jazz and new music.

🔍 In Cambridge city centre

✹ ✹ ✿ ✺

⏳ 3-4 hours

★ The Cypriot jug, c. 700 BC

FREE

www. kettlesyard.co.uk

Imperial War Museum Duxford 302

Duxford

Imperial War Museum Duxford takes you on an unforgettable journey through the history of aviation, in times of war and peace. Visitors can wander among over 200 aircraft – including the Spitfire and Concorde – to discover the science, engineering and fascinating human stories behind the machines that changed our world forever. Duxford is huge and with over 10 acres undercover, it always delivers a good day out.

An operational air base since the closing stages of the First World War, Duxford was also the first RAF station to operate Spitfires, played its part in the Battle of Britain – co-ordinated from the historic operations room – and was used as a USAAF fighter base. Today, the museum includes exhibits on all these events in its history. With exhibitions covering aircraft development, the effects of submarines, torpedoes and aircraft on war at sea and a huge collection of land warfare tanks, military vehicles and artillery there is much to see.

During the summer months, Duxford runs a series of themed air shows at which visitors can see some of the world's most famous aeroplanes take to the skies again (see website for details and dates).

FIVE-STAR ATTRACTION

🔍 Near junction 10 of the M11

✹ ✹ ✿ ✺

⏳ 3-4 hours

★ World famous air shows

💷 💷

www. iwm.org.uk/duxford

Ely Cathedral

304

Ely

The remarkable architecture of Ely has meant that it is now regarded as one of the finest cathedrals in England. Work on the present building commenced in the early 1080s under Abbot Simeon, and the church became a cathedral in 1109. For more than 400 years it was part of a Benedictine monastery. After Henry VIII dissolved the monastery in 1539, it continued to exist as a cathedral. Highlights include the famous Octagon Tower built in 1322, the superb Norman carvings dating from 1135 and the uninterrupted views from the West Tower.

🔍 In Ely city centre
⚙ ◎ ❦ ❄
⏳ 2–3 hours
★ The Octagon Tower
£ £
www. cathedral.ely.anglican.org

Oliver Cromwell's House

303

Ely

Oliver Cromwell, Lord Protector of England, lived in Ely for ten years. Today the house, the only surviving former Cromwell residence other than Hampton Court, has been recreated to show how his family would have lived in the mid-17th century. The carefully restored house now contains a Civil War exhibition including weapons and armour. It also has illustrations on everyday life at the time and a history of the Fenlands and their transformation from marsh to farmland.

🔍 In Ely city centre (also Ely's Tourist Information Centre)
⚙ ◎ ❦ ❄
⏳ 1 hour
★ The haunted bedroom
£
www.olivercromwellshouse.co.uk

Linton Zoological Gardens   305

Linton

This is a great little zoo, which places great emphasis on conservation and is much cheaper than its big competitors. There's lots to see including tigers, snow leopards, lynx, tapir, zebras, wallabies, owls, toucans, storks, hornbills, lemur, parrots, spiders and many others set in 16 acres of spectacular gardens; many featuring aviaries landscaped with rockeries and waterfalls. There are lots of other children's activities too, such as a bouncy castle, (seasonally available), an exciting play area, picnic areas, keeper talks, animal feeds and animal encounters.

On the B1052, at Linton, 10 miles south-east of Cambridge

2–3 hours

The Big Cat Experience

www. lintonzoo.com

Anglesey Abbey, Gardens and Lode Mill   306

Lode

A passion for tradition and impressing guests inspired one man to transform a run-down country house and desolate landscape. At the age of 30, the future Lord Fairhaven created his home in a former Augustinian priory. He created a spectacular garden and a cosy house in which to entertain. Life revolved around horse racing and shooting, and guests enjoyed 1930s luxury. Inside, fine furnishings, books and paintings, silver and rare clocks give a feeling of opulence. Outside, 114 acres offer the simple pleasures of nature.

On the B1102, 6 miles north-east of Cambridge

3 hours

Astonishing clock collection

www. nationaltrust.org.uk

Wisbech and Fenland Museum   307

Wisbech

Opened in 1847, this was one of the very first purpose-built museums in the country. It is a grand building on a small scale, the steps leading up to the entrance columns helping to create the effect of a miniature Greek temple to learning. Inside, you'll find a fully preserved Victorian interior with original display cases still in use. Their contents reflect the founders' fascination with geology, archaeology, natural history and travel. In the museum library you can see the original manuscript of *Great Expectations* by Charles Dickens.

Wisbech town centre

1 hour

The history of Fenland folk

FREE Donations welcome

www. wisbechmuseum.org.uk

Barleylands Farm Park and Craft Village

308

Billericay

Mainly for families with small children, Barleylands is a rural paradise with education in mind, set in over 700 acres of unspoiled countryside. You can feed the animals while finding out where food comes from. There are tractor rides, big bouncy pillows and a fabulous new play area. Visitors can browse in the craft village, home to over 60 unique working craft studios including a blacksmith and a pottery barn. The facility also plays host to special events, like a farmers' market and the Essex Country show.

🔍 Follow signs from the A127

☼ ◎ ♣ ✳

⏳ 2 hours

★ The new Adventure Play Barn

£

www. barleylands.co.uk

The Original Great Maze

309

Braintree

The great maze offers more than 5 miles of pathways cut from 10 acres of maize, which grows to a height of almost 10 feet. A new maze is designed each year, so those ready to take the challenge can return time and time again to try their hand at finding their way home. Don't worry if you're new to the challenge as there's always the viewing platform and a Lost Souls map to help you find your way out. Don't forget your wellies if it's wet.

🔍 Follow the Blake House Craft Centre signs from the A120

◎ Open July to September – check website for dates

⏳ 1–2 hours

★ One of the greatest maze challenges in the world

£

www.greatmaze.info

Kelvedon Hatch Secret Nuclear Bunker `310`
Brentwood

This is the biggest and deepest Cold War bunker in south-east England. Excavated in 1952–53, the bunker is sited 125 feet underground with an entrance through an ordinary looking bungalow. The facility was designed to be used by more than 600 military and civilian personnel, possibly including the Prime Minister, in the event of a nuclear attack. Visitors can try on authentic military uniforms and gas masks and explore the labyrinth of rooms deep within the earth, hidden behind the massive 1.5 tonne blast doors.

On the A128 at Kelvedon Hatch

1–2 hours

Eerie atmosphere

www.secretnuclearbunker.co.uk

East Anglian Railway Museum `311`
Chappel and Wakes Colne

The East Anglian Railway Museum is an open-air site based at Chappel and Wakes Colne Railway station. The entire site forms the museum, which is made up of station buildings, signal boxes, goods shed and restoration shed. The museum, set on the operational line from Marks Tey to Sudbury, has the most comprehensive collection of railway architecture, locomotives, coaches, wagons, and ephemera in the region. There are events days throughout the summer season with steam, diesel and vintage trains to ride on.

Off the A12, 8 miles from Colchester

See website for special events days

2–3 hours

Steam days

www.earm.co.uk

Chelmsford Museum and Essex Regiment Museum `312`
Chelmsford

With two museums housed in the same building it's hard not to be tempted to visit Oaklands Park in Chelmsford. Set in a Victorian house, the regular museum has permanent displays on the Story of Chelmsford, natural history and geology, coins, art and social history.
There is also a temporary exhibition programme, which changes throughout the year, and a busy special events programme. The Essex Regiment Museum tells the story of the county regiment from its mid-18th century origins up to its incorporation into the Royal Anglian Regiment.

Oaklands Park, off Moulsham Street

1–2 hours

The famous Salamanca Eagle, a Napoleonic standard captured from the French in 1812

FREE

www. chelmsford.gov.uk

Hedingham Castle `313`
Halstead

Hedingham Castle's Norman keep, 110 feet high, was built c. 1140 by Aubrey de Vere and is still owned by one of his descendants. There are four floors to explore, including a magnificent Banqueting Hall spanned by a remarkable 28-foot arch, one of the largest Norman arches in England. A good view of this splendid room can be obtained from the Minstrels' Gallery, built within the thickness of the 12-foot walls. The castle is set in beautiful parkland and has a full calendar of special events during the warm summer months.

Off the A1017, at Halstead

1–2 hours

Summer jousting events

www.hedinghamcastle.co.uk

Wat Tyler Country Park | 314

Pitsea

This park consists of 125 acres of glorious countryside, with walking trails and a picturesque village green and pond bordered by pretty, historic cottages that's perfect for strolling in. Children will love the adventure playground and the Sculpture Trail, and you can try a spot of birdwatching in the secluded hides or just explore the landscape. An exhibition at the visitor centre explores the park's history as an explosives factory and its future as a public open space and natural habitat at the heart of developments in the Thames Gateway.

🔍 Off the A13, at Pitsea

⚙ ⚙ ♣ ❄

⏳ 3–4 hours

⭐ Incredible bird life

FREE

www.wattylercountrypark.org.uk

Mole Hall Wildlife Park | 316

Saffron Walden

Mole Hall Wildlife Park covers 25 acres in the grounds of Mole Hall, a fully moated manor house dating back to 1287 and featured in the *Domesday Book* (the house is not open to the public). Recently renovated, the park has a strong educational bias. Visitors can watch the animals, learn about the trees and study the plants and wetland inhabitants. There is a Butterfly Pavilion, which gives a unique opportunity to get up close and personal with some winged beauties. There is also a flock of black Welsh mountain sheep, a herd of Alpacas and many different birds.

🔍 Follow signs from the B1383, take junction 8 of the M11

⚙ ⚙ ♣

⏳ 2–3 hours

⭐ Waymarked footpath walks

💷

www.molehall.co.uk

Audley End House and Gardens | 315

Saffron Walden

Originally built for the first Earl of Suffolk, Audley End House is one of England's grandest country homes. It has marvellous neo-Classical State Apartments designed by Robert Adam and small, intimate dressing rooms used by royalty and the aristocracy. There is also an impressive collection of painting by Holbein, Lely and Canaletto. Visitors can also explore the magnificent grounds and pastoral parkland designed by 'Capability' Brown. Walk over to the lake or climb up to the Temple of Concord to admire the house in its wonderful setting.

🔍 On the B1383, 1 mile west of Saffron Walden

⚙ ⚙ ♣

⏳ 2–3 hours

⭐ The new Stables Experience

💷 💷

www.english-heritage.org.uk

Adventure Island | 317

Southend-on-Sea

A good value, small, family theme park, there are lots of rides here with something to suit all ages. The park has four rollercoasters including Rage with its 75ft-drop and 360-degree band roll, the only coaster of its kind in England, plus unique rides Ramba Zamba, The Archelon and Sky Drop among many other attractions. There are also special, gentle rides and a themed Jungle Jive Cafe for tiny tots. There is a lot to do here. The best advice is to buy wristbands on-line to get good prices and a guaranteed good time.

🔍 Follow signs from Southend waterfront

⚙ ⚙ ♣

⏳ 3–4 hours

⭐ Rage

💷 💷

www.adventureisland.co.uk

STAR ATTRACTION

Tilbury Fort
Tilbury

319

The artillery fort at Tilbury protected London's seaward approach from the 16th century through to the Second World War. Henry VIII built the first fort here, and Queen Elizabeth famously rallied her army nearby to face the threat of the Armada. The fort mounted powerful artillery to command the river, as well as landward defences. Perhaps because of its strength, Tilbury Fort has never been involved in the kind of action for which it was designed. The worst bloodshed within the fort occurred in 1776, when a fight following a Kent-Essex cricket match left two people dead.

🔍 Off the A126, 5 miles east of Tilbury
⚙ ⊙ ♣
⏳ 2-3 hours
⭐ Exhibition of the fort's role in the defence of London
£
www.english-heritage.org.uk

House on the Hill Toy Museum
Stansted

318

This incredible collection of over 80,000 toys, games and books from all over the world on show, will delight children and rekindle fond memories for their parents. The displays include toys from Victorian times to the present day including dolls and dolls' houses, Barbie and Sindy, TV and film related toys, puppets, tin toys, lead toys, trains, teddy bears, books, games, annuals, slot machines, rock 'n' roll memorabilia and everything else you can possibly think of. There is also a Golden Jubilee Exhibition, which features a collection of replica Crown Jewels.

🔍 Follow signs to Mountfitchet Castle from junction 8 of the M11
⚙ ⊙ ♣
⏳ 1-2 hours
⭐ A trip down memory lane
£
www.stanstedtoymuseum.com

Royal Gunpowder Mills
Waltham Abbey

320

Set in 170 acres of parkland, this site mixes history, exciting science and beautiful surroundings. The museum traces the evolution of gunpowder, made here for the defence of the realm for some 300 years, and explains the impact it has had on the history of Great Britain. Cut off from its surroundings because of the secrecy of its work, nature took over, creating a hidden world, a unique landscape and a thriving ecology of wildlife and woodlands. Visitors are able to explore a large section of the grounds from a network of boardwalks, bridges and footpaths.

🔍 Off the A121, from junctions 25 or 26 of the M25
⚙ ⊙ ♣
⏳ 2-3 hours
⭐ Rockets Exhibition
£
www.royalgunpowdermills.com

Ashridge Estate 321

Berkhamsted

The Ashridge Estate comprises a vast swathe of woodlands and chalk downland at the north end of the Chiltern Hills. Start at the visitor centre next to the Duke of Bridgewater Monument. From here you can enjoy superb panoramas and arm yourself with maps and information. There's a network of footpaths and bridleways to explore. Among the ancient woodlands, with carpets of spring bluebells or fine autumnal display, you can spot a wide variety of wildlife such as red kite and fallow deer. There are also a number of historical remains from the Iron Age to the Victorian era.

🔍 Off the B4506
☼ ⊙ ♣
⏳ 2-3 hours
⭐ Ivinghoe Beacon
FREE There's a charge to see the monument 💷
www.nationaltrust.org.uk

Berkhamsted Castle 322

Berkhamsted

This is a good example of a motte and bailey castle where the original wooden defences were later rebuilt in stone. It dates from the 11th to the 13th centuries, with surrounding walls, ditches and earthworks. A palace complex was added in the 13th century. The Norman structure was begun in 1066 by William the Conqueror. In the 12th century, the castle was home to Thomas Becket, Chancellor of England. In the 14th century, it became the residence of Edward, the Black Prince, and Geoffrey Chaucer was appointed Clerk to the Works.

🔍 Next to Berkhamsted railway station
☼ ⊙ ♣ ❄
⏳ 1-2 hours
⭐ Guided tours (see www.berkhamsted-castle.org.uk for details)
FREE Guided tours 💷
www.english-heritage.org.uk

Paradise Wildlife Park 323

Broxbourne

This is a fantastic place to meet lions, tigers, monkeys, zebras, tapirs, reptiles, birds and more at what is widely regarded as the most interactive zoo in the UK. There are many attractions including three themed adventure playgrounds, children's rides, Paradise Lagoon paddling pool, tractor trailer rides and for a small additional charge the Dinosaur Woodland Railway, On Safari Adventure Golf and Tiger Falls Gold Panning. More recent additions include penguins, white lion, white tiger, gibbons, the national Speedway Museum and the Tumble Jungle indoor play area.

🔍 Follow signs from the A10 at Broxbourne
☼ ⊙ ♣ ❄
⏳ 2-3 hours
⭐ Feed the big cats by hand
💷 💷
www.pwpark.com

Hatfield House 324

Hatfield

This fine Jacobean House and garden was built by Robert Cecil, Ist Earl of Salisbury and Chief Minister to King James I from 1607 to 1611. There is a marvellous collection of pictures, furnishings and historic armour on display. The Royal Palace of Hatfield (c. 1485) in the West Garden is where Elizabeth I spent most of her childhood. An oak tree marks the place where the young Princess Elizabeth first heard of her accession to the throne. The garden dates from the early 17th century and includes a scented garden, herb garden and knot garden.

🔍 Follow signs from junction 4 of the A1(M)
☼ ⊙ ♣
⏳ 2-3 hours
⭐ The Grand Staircase
💷 💷
www.hatfield-house.co.uk

Mill Green Museum and Mill 325
Hatfield

This museum, in the former miller's house, has three galleries. Two house local artefacts from Roman times to the present day, while the third features craft demonstrations and special events during summer weekends and staff are on hand to help with any enquiries. There is also a working, fully restored, 18th-century watermill adjacent to the museum. The mill was in regular use grinding corn grown by local farmers until 1911. A full restoration was carried out between 1979 and 1986 and it's now one of the few remaining water-powered corn mills still producing flour.

Follow signs from the A1000 or the A414

1-2 hours

Milling on Tuesday, Wednesdays and Sundays

FREE Donations welcome

www.welhat.gov.uk

Knebworth House 326
Knebworth

The Lytton family have lived here for 500 years. Queen Elizabeth I stayed here, Charles Dickens acted in theatricals in the house and Churchill's painting of the Banqueting Hall hangs in the room where he painted it. Originally a Tudor manor house, it was transformed in 1843 into the Gothic fantasy we see today. Interior rooms contrast the Gothic with the 20th-century designs of Sir Edwin Lutyens. The gardens date from Victorian and Edwardian times; with more recent additions including a self-guided trail of 72 life-size dinosaurs set among the rhododendrons and redwoods.

Follow signs from the A1(M) at Stevenage

(check website for details)

3-4 hours

The 'Stately Home of Rock Music'

www.knebworthhouse.com

Henry Moore Foundation

327

Much Hadham

Hoglands (Henry and Irina Moore's home for over 40 years), gardens, studios and galleries are open to the public between April and mid-October in Perry Green. Many of the buildings on this 72-acre estate remain as they were in his lifetime. Tours include the opportunity to see Moore's iconic sculptures in beautiful grounds, while displays in the original studios trace Moore's artistic process from the numerous found objects from which he took inspiration, to the enlarging and carving of his works. You have to book in advance before visiting.

🔍 Perry Green, near Much Hadham
✺ ⊙ ♣
⌛ 2 hours
★ A privileged insight into the working practices and immense output of the artist
£ £

www.henry-moore.org/pg

Batchworth Lock Canal Centre

328

Rickmansworth

Batchworth Lock on the Grand Union Canal is a great place for a day out. The Canal Centre is the hub of all the activity that takes place here when the sun is shining and is the starting point for boat trips, other canal-side events and for exploring the local area. A miniature working model canal next to Batchworth Lock shows how a lock and canal works. The centre also offers a great deal of information leaflets and maps on walking and cycling in the area.

🔍 Church Street, in Rickmansworth town centre
✺ ⊙ ♣ See website for opening times
⌛ 1–2 hours
★ Leisurely canal cruise
FREE Canal cruises charge £

www.rwt.org.uk

Verulamium Museum

329

St Albans

This is an award-winning museum of everyday life in Roman Britain. It is on the site of one of the major Roman settlements and set in attractive parkland near the Roman theatre, walls and hypocaust. There is a new Iron Age gallery, recreated Roman rooms, discovery areas and some of the best mosaics outside the Mediterranean. Every second weekend of the month the museum is invaded by Roman legionaries who recreate life as a foot soldier in the Roman Imperial Army.

🔍 Follow signs from St Albans town centre
✺ ⊙ ♣ ✷
⌛ 1–2 hours
★ Incredible Romano-British mosaics
£

www.stalbansmuseums.org.uk

Natural History Museum at Tring `330`
Tring

The remarkable collections in the galleries of the Natural History Museum at Tring were once the private passion of its founder, Lionel Walter, second Baron Rothschild. The Rothschild family gifted the entire museum and its collections to the nation in 1937. This fascinating 'Noah's Ark' is one of the finest collections of stuffed mammals, birds, reptiles and insects in the UK. It includes examples of several animals that are now extinct, and a model of a dodo. There is also a Discovery Room, where children can try more hands-on activities to explore their senses and the natural world.

🔍 In Tring town centre

⚙ ◐ ♣ ❄

⏳ 1–2 hours

⭐ The chance to see unusual, endangered and extinct creatures

FREE Some exhibitions may charge

www.nhm.ac.uk/tring

STAR ATTRACTION

Welwyn Roman Baths `331`
Welwyn

Tunnel through time to the world of the Romans with a visit to Welwyn Roman Baths. Learn about how the Romans liked to relax with an elegant culture of bathing, and admire their creativity and style. The bath house is ingeniously preserved in a steel vault under the A1(M) motorway. Once part of a fine villa, the layout of the cold, warm and hot rooms and the heating system are remarkably preserved. Also on display are archaeological finds and an exhibition devoted to the history of the site, which was uncovered during the 1960s and 70s.

🔍 Under the A1(M) at its junction with the A1000, just off the central roundabout of the Welwyn by-pass

⚙ ◐ ♣

⏳ 1 hour

⭐ Exhibition on how the vault was built

💷

www.hertsmuseums.org.uk

Blickling Hall, Gardens and Park `332`
Aylsham

At Blickling, you can follow four centuries of history. Imagine yourself a guest at one of Lord Lothian's house parties just before the outbreak of the Second World War, discussing the latest politics and religious matters. Learn what life was like as a servant and hear the stories of the real people who kept Blickling going. The estate is a treasure trove of romantic buildings, beautiful and extensive gardens and landscaped park. From herbaceous formal gardens to the stunning parterre and woodland wilderness, there is something to see at any time of the year.

🔍 Off the A140, north-west of Aylsham

⚙ ◐ ♣

⏳ 2–3 hours

⭐ Portraits of Blickling's famous residents and their guests

💷 💷

wwwnationaltrust.org.uk

Banham Zoo `333`
Banham

Set in 35 acres of countryside and landscaped gardens, Banham Zoo is home to over 1,000 animals from all over the world. Visitors can take part in any number of activities, including one of the most exciting birds of prey displays in the UK. There is also an Amazing Animals presentation and a Safari road train. A new attraction offers you and your family the chance to meet a group of meerkats or get up close and personal with one of the giraffes. These 15-minute experiences can be booked at reception on the day of your visit.

🔍 Follow signs from the A11 and A140

⚙ ◐ ♣ ❄

⏳ 3–5 hours

⭐ Meet the meerkats

💷 💷

www.banhamzoo.co.uk

North Norfolk Coastal Walk 334

Blakeney

You can do a bracing five-mile, circular walk along parts of the North Norfolk Coastal Path that takes you through the former trading ports of Blakeney, Cley-next-the-Sea and Wiveton. Head north from Blakeney harbour car park, following the coast past Blakeney Spit. At the ruins of what is known as Blakeney Chapel, the path turns inland along the river towards Cley. Keep on past Cley Windmill and carry on to Wiveton Bridge. From here you can pick up the road back to Blakeney.

Q Blakeney harbour

⚙ ⦿ ♣ ❄

⧗ 3 hours

★ Maritime history at Cley church

FREE

www.nationaltrail.co.uk/peddarsway/

Felbrigg Hall, Gardens and Park 336

Cromer

Truly a hidden gem, the Hall is full of surprises, a mixture of opulence and homeliness where each room has something to feed the imagination. The interior was remodelled in the 1750s to house superb art treasures, and the Staterooms contain exquisite 18th-century furniture and paintings. Outside, the walled garden is a gardener's delight, providing fruit and vegetables for the restaurant, flowers for the hall and inspiration to visitors. The park with a lake, 520 acres of woods and waymarked trails is a great place to explore the nature and wildlife on this bountiful estate.

Q Follow signs from the A140 and A148

⚙ ⦿ ♣

⧗ 2–3 hours

★ Dr Johnson's dictionary in the Gothic library

£

www.nationaltrust.org.uk

Grime's Graves 335

Brandon

This is the only Neolithic flint mine open to visitors in Britain. A grassy, lunar landscape of over 400 shafts, pits, quarries and spoil dumps, they were thought to be graves by the Anglo-Saxons. It was not until one of them was excavated in 1870 that they were found to be flint mines dug over 5,000 years ago. What the prehistoric miners sought here was the fine quality, jet-black flint floorstone, prized as a material for axes and other tools. Digging with red-deer antler picks, they sank shafts from which radiated gallery-tunnels, following the seams of flint.

Q On the A134, 7 miles north-west of Thetford

⚙ ⦿ ♣

⧗ 1 hour

★ A trip down into an excavated shaft

£

www.english-heritage.org.uk

Hillside Shire Horse Sanctuary   337
Cromer

The former Norfolk Shire Horse Centre is welcoming visitors again as part of the Hillside Animal Sanctuary. There are five breeds of the gentle but impressive heavy horses at their stables in West Runton. Visitors can meet them and listen to talks on the history of these breeds on certain days (see website for details). There are horse displays and other rescued animals to meet as well. The sanctuary also has a farming bygones exhibition, which includes an extensive collection of carts, wagons and other machinery, and runs Blacksmith Days during the season.

🔍 Follow signs from the A149
☼ ⊙ ❦
⌛ 1 hour
★ Gentle giants of the farming world
♿
www.hillside.org.uk/OpenDaysatWestRunton.htm

Gressenhall Museum and Workhouse
Dereham
338

Gressenhall brings together a museum of life on the land, a traditional farm, a historic workhouse and beautiful grounds. Explore atmospheric shops and homes, stunning displays and a treasure trove of fascinating objects. On the farm, meet chicks, piglets and more. Explore 50 beautiful acres of Norfolk countryside including gardens and a historic orchard. There are lots of things to do including cart rides, dressing up, kids activities and an adventure playground.

🔍 On the B1146, 3 miles north-west of Dereham
☼ ⊙ ❦
⌛ 3-4 hours
★ The awful workhouse punishment cell
♿
www.museums.norfolk.gov.uk

Bressingham Steam and Gardens   339
Diss

Take a trip on one of four railways; working steam locomotives will take you round the magnificent gardens and woodland, or ride on the steam carousel. A trip to the locomotive sheds brings the power of mighty steam engineering up close. The National *Dad's Army* collection lets you wander through Walmington-on-Sea looking at original props and vehicles from the famous TV series. The gardens are renowned for their horticultural excellence. With nearly 20 acres, they are truly tranquil, perfect for relaxing and enjoying the scenery.

🔍 On the A1066, 3 miles west of Diss
☼ ⊙ ❦
⌛ 4 hours
★ Days out with Thomas and Ivor
♿ ♿
www.bressingham.co.uk

Langham Glass   340
Fakenham

Langham Glass is based in a large, old, pantiled and flint-faced barn near Fakenham. Visitors can attend a glassmaking demonstration at the visitor centre where teams of glassmakers can be seen working with molten glass using blowing irons and hand tools in the traditional way that has changed little over the past 300 years. You will witness the production of batch (sand mixed with lead oxide, potash and soda), the furnace, the glasshouse, adding the colour and annealing, before moving on to the finishing house where the items are polished and finished.

🔍 Follow signs from the A148
☼ ⊙ ❦ ✳
⌛ 1-2 hours
★ Fascinating process of making the batch
♿
www.langhamglass.co.uk

Norfolk Nelson Museum 341
Great Yarmouth

The Nelson Museum is sited in a Georgian merchant's house by the waterside. Visitors can explore Nelson's career, from his Norfolk childhood through his famous battles to his heroic death. Find out about his mesmerising personality, his terrible wounds and his many illnesses – not to mention his love life. Avoid the rats and beware the cannonfire in Below Decks! Try out a hammock, play ship's games, examine cannons from Nelson's time or relax in the Maritime Courtyard. Learn about Nelson's genius as a leader, in a new exhibition entitled The Nelson Touch: Inspirational Leadership.

On South Quay, Great Yarmouth

1–2 hours

The story of one of the Greatest Britons

www.nelson-museum.co.uk

Pleasure Beach 342
Great Yarmouth

This theme park is on the seafront at the southern end of Great Yarmouth's Golden Mile. It has over 20 rides and includes all the standard favourites, including Disko, Sky Drop, dodgems and the Log Flume. There's the Big Apple Coaster for little ones and the bigger traditional wooden Rollercoaster for the big ones. The very bravest ride Evolution, which sends riders this way and that way at the same time. There are lots of other rides and attractions too set in lovely seaside gardens.

On Great Yarmouth Seafront

2–3 hours

The Rollercoaster

www.pleasure-beach.co.uk

Row 111 343
Great Yarmouth

Living space was at a premium in early 17th-century Great Yarmouth, then among the most prosperous fishing ports in England. Hence the inhabitants crowded into the town's distinctive 'Rows', a network of narrow alleyways. Many were damaged by Second World War bombing, but two properties remain. Both Row 111 and the nearby Old Merchant's House were originally built as larger residences, but later sub-divided into tenements. Row 111 house is shown as it was in 1942, displaying a wonderful collection of fixtures and fittings rescued from other now-demolished Row dwellings.

Follow signs for the Historic Quay

1–2 hours

Nostalgic period decoration

www.english-heritage.org.uk

Baconsthorpe Castle 344
Holt

These extensive ruins, of a moated and fortified 15th-century manor house, are a testament to a prominent Norfolk family, the Heydons. Over 200 years, successive generations built, then enlarged, and finally abandoned the castle. Sir John Heydon probably built the strong inner gatehouse during the Wars of the Roses, and his son Sir Henry completed the fortified house. In more peaceful times, their descendants converted part of the property into a textile factory, and then added the turreted Elizabethan outer gateway, inhabited until 1920. Information panels illustrate the story of the family.

In Baconsthorpe, 3 miles east of Holt

1 hour

Downloadable audio tour (see website for details)

FREE

www.english-heritage.org.uk

Sandringham   346
King's Lynn

Sandringham is the much-loved country retreat of Her Majesty The Queen, and has been the private home of four generations of British monarchs since 1862. The house, set in 60 acres of stunning gardens, is perhaps the most famous stately home in Norfolk and is at the heart of the 20,000-acre Sandringham Estate, 600 acres of which make up the woodland and heath of the Country Park. It is an informal place and visits include ground floor rooms of the house, a museum set in the stable block and beautiful grounds.

Follow signs from King's Lynn

4 hours

The handsome Edwardian-style ground floor rooms

www.sandringhamestate.co.uk

Sea Life Sanctuary   345
Hunstanton

At this impressive sanctuary you will see otters, penguins and more than 30 permanent displays and aquariums – including sharks, seahorses and rays – all showcasing the rich diversity of life under the waves. The oceans cover two thirds of the planet, yet mankind is only starting to explore the world beneath the waves. By recreating natural habitats, the Sea Life Sanctuary renders this amazing underwater kingdom available for everyone to see. The centre also provides a safe haven for a number of sick, injured or orphaned seal pups.

Hunstanton promenade

2 hours

The sharks

www.sealsanctuary.co.uk

Dinosaur Adventure 347

Lenwade

In this dinosaur-based theme park visitors will come face-to-face with life-size dinosaurs lurking on a trail through the woods. You can help the rangers discover how many T-Rex roam the woodland. There are lots of other fun things to see and do here. Around the park you will find stations where you can stamp the boxes on your passport and earn a medal. With brush in hand, enjoy unearthing a dinosaur fossil and discover which dinosaur you think it is. There's also the Lost World tribe to discover in the Lost World maze, play areas and a Secret Animal Garden.

Follow signs from the A47 and A1067, near Lenwade

3-4 hours

Raptor Racers

www.dinosauradventure.co.uk

Walsingham Abbey Gardens 348

Little Walsingham

Set in a picturesque medieval village, the Abbey grounds contain the ruins of an Augustinian Priory. A place of pilgrimage since the 11th century, visitors can enjoy the gardens and walks that lead into unspoilt woodland and parkland. In spring the grounds are home to perhaps an impressive display of snowdrops. Admission price includes entry to the Shirehall Museum. This 16th-century building was used as a magistrate's court until 1971. The Georgian courtroom has remained unaltered since it was last used. The museum also includes displays on the history of Walsingham.

Off the A149

1-2 hours

Snowdrop display in February

www.walsinghamabbey.com

Norwich Cathedral 349

Norwich

The splendour and tranquillity of Norwich Cathedral have attracted visitors for nearly 1,000 years. The Hostry Visitors and Education Centre has been constructed on the original footprint of the old monastic Hostry, which was the traditional point of welcome for worshippers, pilgrims and students the monastic community was founded in 1096. Norwich Cathedral is one of the finest complete Romanesque buildings in Europe. It has the second highest spire and largest monastic cloisters in England. The nave bosses are a unique and it also has world-renowned collection of medieval carvings.

🔍 Follow signs from Norwich city centre
✿ ◉ ♣ ✵
⏳ 1–2 hours
⭐ Guided tours
FREE Donations welcome
www.cathedral.org.uk

Sainsbury Centre for Visual Arts 351

Norwich

In an internationally renowned building on the UEA campus designed by Norman Foster, visitors can discover the delights of the Sainsbury art collection. There are over 1,200 items in the collection, which spans thousands of years and many cultures. Alongside African masks are works by Pablo Picasso, Henry Moore, Alberto Giacometti and Francis Bacon. Many of these artists drew their inspiration from world art, a fascination for which they shared with the Sainsburys. Alongside the permanent collection, the centre also runs a regular programme of special exhibitions, talks and workshops.

🔍 Follow signs to the UEA campus
✿ ◉ ♣ ✵
⏳ 2–3 hours
⭐ The Inca llama effigy
FREE Exhibitions may charge
www.scva.org.uk

Norwich Castle Museum and Art Gallery 350

Norwich

The Norman keep of Norwich Castle dominates the city below. Visitors can enjoy spectacular views from the battlements and reveal the castle's darker secrets from the depths of the dungeons. Once a royal palace, the castle is now a museum housing one of England's finest regional collections of natural history, art and archaeology. There are exhibits on the Anglo-Saxons, the Vikings and Boudica. The art gallery demonstrates the rich heritage of East Anglia with stunning English watercolours, paintings from the Norwich School and Dutch landscapes.

🔍 Norwich city centre
✿ ◉ ♣ ✵
⏳ 2–3 hours
⭐ Guided battlement and dungeon tours
♿
www.museums.norfolk.gov.uk

NWT Ranworth Broad Wildlife Centre 352

Ranworth

Ranworth is one of the most popular of the Norfolk Broads with plenty to see and do for both families and naturalists. An interpretive boardwalk explains the succession from open water to dry land and the many habitats you pass through. The floating Broads Wildlife Centre is located at the end of the boardwalk and has fabulous views over the water. Visitors can expect to see birds, including terns, warblers, grebes and cormorants among others, plus butterflies and a wide variety of plant life.

🔍 Follow signs from the B1140, near South Walsham
✿ ◉ ♣
⏳ 2–3 hours
⭐ Floating visitor centre
FREE
www.norfolkwildlifetrust.org.uk

Fairhaven Woodland and Water Garden

354

South Walsham

This gorgeous place comprises of over 130 acres of ancient woodland, water gardens and a private broad in the heart of the Norfolk Broads. There are woodland walks and boat trips run daily from April until the end of October. Visitors can take a relaxing 50-minute trip down the river to the historic ruins of St Benet's Abbey. There are also 20-minute trips around the broad throughout the day – it is a great way to see kingfishers, grebe and swans or maybe even an otter.

Follow signs from the A47, near South Walsham

2–3 hours

See the Broads from the water

Boat trips cost extra

www.fairhavengarden.co.uk

The Muckleburgh Collection

353

Sheringham

On the site of the former Weybourne Military Camp, there is now a collection of more than 120 military vehicles, tanks and guns, plus items from Operation Desert Storm, militaria from the 18th century and scale models. The collection boasts 16 working tanks and at least 3,000 other exhibits. There are model ships, anti-aircraft guns and an exhibit on the Norfolk and Suffolk Yeomanry, which dates back to 1700. On most Sundays throughout the season visitors can see a Panzer 68 tank put through its paces and take a ride on the six armoured personnel vehicles called Gama Goats.

Follow signs from the A149, 3 miles west of Sheringham

2 hours

Panzer and Chieftain tanks

www.muckleburgh.co.uk

Castle Acre Priory

355

Swaffham

One of best-preserved monastic sites in England, there's a lot to see in the ruins of Castle Acre Priory. First established in about 1090, the oldest remains are of a great 12th-century church. There's also a medieval porch, and an extremely well preserved prior's lodging. A mansion in itself, this includes a first-floor chapel, wall paintings and two fine Oriel windows. The herb garden next to the visitor centre grows herbs that the monks would have used for medicinal, culinary and decorative purposes. Visitors can find out more about this beautiful priory in an on-site exhibition.

At Castle Acre, 5 miles north of Swaffham

2 hours

Story of the Cluniac order of monks in England

www.english-heritage.org.uk

Ancient House Museum of Thetford Life

Thetford

This museum is housed in a beautiful Tudor building. Constructed in 1490 for a wealthy merchant, it is now rather crooked – a testament to the strength of the builders and the materials they used. Using 21st-century displays, the life and times of the town of Thetford and the Brecklands are explored through artefacts, audio commentary and educational films. Visitors can 'meet' local people from the city's past such as philosopher Thomas Paine and Sikh hero, Maharajah Duleep Singh, as well as rabbit warreners and railway workers.

Thetford town centre

1–2 hours

Relics from the Romano-British period

Free during winter months

www.museums.norfolk.gov.uk

Bank Boats and Canoe Hire

Wayford Bridge

The Norfolk Broads have been a favourite holiday destination for many years. The 125-mile network of rivers and broads surrounded by low-lying countryside forms Britain's largest protected wetland. Of course, the best way to explore the Norfolk Broads is by boat. Bank Boats, based at Wayford Bridge on the River Ant, supply boats and canoes by day or for longer periods. The location gives easy access to popular sites such as Hunset Mill, Stalham Staithe, Sutton Staithe and Neatishead. Longer Boat rentals have the chance to reach Ranworth Broad, Horning and Potter Heigham.

Off the A149, between Stalham and Wroxham

2–6 hours

Messing about on the river

www.bankboats.co.uk

Holkham Hall

Wells-Next-the-Sea

This grand, Palladian style mansion was built between 1734 and 1764 by Thomas Coke, 1st Earl of Leicester, to house a collection of treasures and antiquities that he had amassed during his Grand Tour. The house today is little altered and still features this marvellous collection of valuable and unique manuscripts and printed books, great works of art and statuary. The gardens and park, laid out by William Kent with later contributions by 'Capability' Brown and Humphrey Repton, also remain pretty much as they were with rare trees and shrubs including Holm oaks.

On the A149, 2 miles west of Wells-next-the-Sea

2–3 hours

A walk on nearby Holkham beach

www.holkham.co.uk

Barton House Railway

Wroxham

The Barton House Railway recreates a traditional railway atmosphere where the whole family can enjoy the nostalgia of the golden age of steam with a miniature steam passenger railway and a steam and battery-electric railway, a fully working signalling system and authentic tickets. During your visit you can also explore an extensive museum of railway artefacts with a Midland and Great Northern theme and also observe the signalman at work in our full-size original signal box, which acts as the nerve centre controlling the railways.

On the A1151, at Wroxham

Open third Sunday of the month, from April to October

1–2 hours

Candle and oil-lamp lit evening events (see website)

www.bartonhouserailway.org.uk

High Lodge Forest Centre 360
Brandon

Thetford Forest is Britain's largest lowland pine forest and a place of peace and tranquillity. There are walks and waymarked trails as well as cycle tracks of varying degrees of difficulty. The High Lodge Forest Centre can supply you with any information you need. It also has the wide range of recreational facilities. There's a large grassy area to play in with adventure trails and play furniture. For adults, it's easy to get away from the noise if you need to. Why not take a walk to the new Arboretum at Lynford, or simply stroll around the nearby lake.

🔍 On B1107, between Brandon and Thetford

⚙ ◎ ♣

⏳ 4-6 hours

⭐ Themed walks

FREE Car parking charges

www.forestry.gov.uk/highlodge

Norfolk and Suffolk Aviation Museum 361
Bungay

This unique museum has some 60 aircraft of every type, from the pioneer years through to the present, both civil and military. It also houses themed collections for the Royal Observer Corps No. 6 Group, the 446th (H) Bomb Group USAAF, RAF Bomber Command, RAF Air-Sea Rescue & Coastal Command and local aviation through the years. The museum's collection has recently expanded with an exhibition room featuring the interior of a 1940s cottage, plus a reconstruction of a Second World War bomb shelter.

🔍 On the B1062, 1 mile west of Bungay

⚙ ◎ ♣

⏳ 2 hours

⭐ LINK ANT18 RAF flight simulators

FREE

www.aviationmuseum.net

Ickworth House, Park and Gardens 362
Bury St Edmunds

Ickworth House is a truly remarkable building. Only by visiting it can you get a real idea of the elegance of this architectural oddity. The central rotunda and curving wings were built to house art treasures collected from all over Europe and Italy in particular. Today it does just that with paintings, portraits, furniture and other treasures displayed in sumptuous staterooms. Outside, it is just as impressive with an Italianate garden, a Spring and a Silver Garden and a Stumpery. There are also terraces, woodlands and a lake.

🔍 Off the A143, 3 miles south-west of Bury St Edmunds

⚙ ◎ ♣

⏳ 3-4 hours

⭐ The portrait collection

£

www.nationaltrust.org.uk

Manning's Amusement Park 363
Felixstowe

This traditional children's amusement park has been entertaining people for over 80 years. There are numerous rides and slides in the Junior Theme Park, with waltzers, roundabouts, swing boats, a ball pit, an indoor bouncy castle and a new mini karting track. There's also an amusement arcade, a Jackpot Casino, a bowling green, an indoor Adventure Golf-FX, a sports bar, a nightclub and a Sunday market.

Felixstowe promenade

✿ ◎ ♣ ❄

⏳ 2-3 hours

★ Traditional children's amusements

£

www.manningsamusements.co.uk

Framlingham Castle 365
Framlingham

Framlingham is a magnificent example of a late 12th-century castle. It has fulfilled a number of roles during its history. At the end of the 16th century it was a prison: later still a poorhouse was built here. Today the stone walls and crenellated towers with their ornate Tudor chimneys dominate, while the grassy earthworks are subdued reminders of its outer defences. Visitors can go on a self-guided journey around the site on themed trails with a lively audio tour, explore the Mere and the wall-walk with its spectacular views over the surrounding landscape.

Follow signs from Framlingham town centre

✿ ◎ ♣ ❄

⏳ 2-3 hours

★ A walk on the walls

£

www.english-heritage.org.uk

Bridge Cottage 364
Flatford

In the heart of the beautiful Dedham Vale, the charming hamlet of Flatford was the location for some of John Constable's most famous pastoral paintings. This thatched cottage, dating from the 16th century, now houses an exhibition on the artist's life and work. Constable's father owned the nearby Flatford Mill (which is still there but not open to the public), and Constable often painted the mill itself as well as Bridge Cottage, and Willie Lott's cottage nearby. You can then visit the sites of other Constable paintings around the vale.

Off the B1070

✿ ◎ ♣ ❄

⏳ 1-2 hours

★ Guided tours of Constable's painting locations

£ £

www.nationaltrust.org.uk

Christchurch Mansion 366
Ipswich

Discover Ipswich's historic past with a visit to the beautiful, Tudor, Christchurch Mansion, in Christchurch Park – one of the city's finest parks. Visitors can see period rooms from the sumptuous Georgian Saloon, to the more humble Victorian wing with its displays of children's toys and dolls' houses. The museum also houses the biggest collection of paintings by Gainsborough and Constable outside London, along with collections of other artists inspired by the beautiful landscapes of East Anglia such as John Moore, Thomas Churchyard and Alfred Munnings.

Follow signs from Ipswich town centre

✿ ◎ ♣ ❄

⏳ 1-2 hours

★ Gainsborough and Constable collection

FREE

www.ipswich.gov.uk/museums

Lavenham Guildhall   367

Lavenham

Lavenham is the most unspoiled medieval town in the country, and the magnificent timber-framed Guildhall building with its jettied upper floor and oriel windows dominates the market place. Built by Corpus Christi, one of three guilds founded in Lavenham to regulate the flourishing wool trade, the building later became Lavenham's town hall, and variously a prison, workhouse, wool store and World War Two housing for evacuees. It now contains a museum detailing Lavenham's history, agriculture and the story of the wool trade.

In Lavenham marketplace

2 hours

Strolling through the streets of Lavenham

www.nationaltrust.org.uk

Melford Hall   368

Long Melford

For almost five centuries the turrets of Melford Hall have dominated Long Melford's village green. Devastated by fire in 1942, the house was nurtured back to life by the Hyde Parker family and it remains their much-loved family home to this day. Their interior decoration and furnishings chart changing tastes over two centuries, but it is the stories of family life at Melford – from visits by their relation Beatrix Potter with her menagerie of animals, through to children sliding down the grand staircase on trays – that make this house more than just bricks and mortar.

Off the A134, 3 miles north of Sudbury

1-2 hours

Jemima Puddle-Duck

www.nationaltrust.org.uk

Pleasurewood Hills Theme Park   369

Lowestoft

This 50-acre theme park is set in beautiful coastal parkland. It caters for all tastes from adrenalin-fuelled white-knuckle thrill rides and coasters like Enigma, and Thunder Struck, to white-water family favourites including Timber Falls. There's also a great selection of rides for younger kids. Be sure to explore Main Street and it's unique, interactive maritime theme. A new ride – Wipeout – is the tallest and fastest rollercoaster in the east of England. There are also some shows to see such as the antics of the sea lions; the hilarious parrots and the Magic Circus tango spectacular.

Off the A12, north of Lowestoft

4-6 hours

Wipeout – ride if you dare!

www.pleasurewoodhills.com

STAR ATTRACTION

National Horseracing Museum   370

Newmarket

Visitors can see the history of horse racing over 300 years – from its royal origins to Lester Piggott, Frankie Dettori and others – in this museum housed in the old subscription rooms, early 19th-century betting rooms. There are fine paintings of famous horses, paintings on loan from Queen Elizabeth II, and copies of old parliamentary acts governing racing. An audio-visual presentation shows races and racehorses. The museum also offers equine tours of this historic town. Guides take you to watch morning gallops on the heath where you'll see bronzes of horses from the past.

Follow signs from Newmarket town centre

1-2 hours

Marvellous collection of British sporting art

Guided tours charge extra

www.nhrm.co.uk

Southwold Pier
372

Southwold

This splendid new pier, completed in 2002, has plenty of old-fashioned fun for everyone. There's an amusement arcade, gift shops, a fish and chip shop and the fabulous Under the Pier Show, which has a number of alternative slot machines. Why not stop off to Whack-a-Banker, test your ability on a Zimmer frame by walking the dog, have a quick brainwash, go on an instant holiday or enter the Booth of Truth.

On Southwold seafront

1–2 hours

Under the Pier Show

FREE

www.southwoldpier.co.uk

RSPB Minsmere
371

Saxmundum

Minsmere offers families and keen birdwatchers a great day out. Nature trails take you through a variety of habitats to excellent birdwatching hides. In spring, you can watch avocets and marsh harriers, or hear booming bitterns. On the beach, a special area is cordoned off to protect nesting little terns. In autumn and winter, many wading birds and swans, ducks and geese visit the reserve. There is a visitor centre where you can find out more about the wildlife. There are events all year and family explorer backpacks and trail booklets are available.

Follow signs from the A12 at Yoxford or Blythburgh

3–4 hours

Avocets, bitterns and nightingales

www.rspb.org.uk

Gainsborough's House
373

Sudbury

This is the birthplace of Thomas Gainsborough (1727-88), one of England's most celebrated artists. The attractive townhouse, in the centre of Sudbury, dates from around 1500 and retains many interesting features, including 18th-century furniture. Its collection of his work encompasses his entire career, from early portraits and Suffolk landscapes to later works from his London period. It is also home to a fascinating collection of memorabilia, including his studio cabinet, swordstick and pocket-watch. At the back of the house is a delightful walled garden with an ancient mulberry tree.

Follow signs from Sudbury town centre

1–2 hours

Huge collection of Gainsborough's work

www.gainsborough.org

Orford Castle
374
Woodbridge

The polygonal towerkeep of Orford Castle was built
between 1165 and 1173. Visitors can explore the
basement with its well, and the lower and upper halls.
Round these polygonal rooms is a maze of passages,
leading to the chapel, kitchen and the turrets. From the
roof there are magnificent views seaward to Orford Ness.
The upper hall now houses a display that includes local
finds of Roman brooches, medieval seals and coins.
Graphic panels display maps, documents, pictures and
photographs illustrating Orford's history down to the
20th century.

On B1084, in Orford

1–2 hours

Stunning views from the roof

www.english-heritage.org.uk

Orford Ness National Nature Reserve
375
Woodbridge

Orford Ness is a wild and remote shingle spit about
13 miles long. You can access it by ferry from Orford.
It's a short trip to a place of tranquillity but one with
an intriguing secret. Wetlands and grazing habitats are
home to a wealth of wildlife and there are colour-coded
trails to follow. You will also find a cluster of interesting,
historic buildings, which were used by the military in
the First and Second World Wars. There's an information
building where visitors can read about the site and view
archive photographs.

Ferry leaves from Orford Quay

2–3 hours

The atomic bomb 'Pagodas'

www.nationaltrust.org.uk

Sutton Hoo
376
Woodbridge

Excavations here in 1939 revealed a burial chamber
containing a 90-foot ship filled with treasures including
a warrior's helmet, weapons, armour, ornaments,
tableware and a purse with 37 gold coins in it – an
Anglo-Saxon king's most treasured possessions from
c. AD 620. Visitors can walk in the footsteps of royalty
around the atmospheric burial mounds and visit an
exhibition that includes a full-size reconstruction of the
burial chamber and some Anglo-Saxon treasure on loan
from the British Museum.

Follow signs from the A12, north of Woodbridge

2–3 hours

King Raedwald's burial chamber

www.nationaltrust.co.uk

STAR ATTRACTION

East Midlands

Derbyshire
Leicestershire
Lincolnshire
Northamptonshire
Nottinghamshire
Rutland

Stanage Edge, Peak District, Derbyshire

Guide to the **East Midlands**

Haddon Hall

377

Bakewell

Haddon Hall is a fortified medieval manor house dating from the 12th century, and is the home of Lord and Lady Edward Manners whose family have owned it since 1567. Described by Simon Jenkins in his book *1000 Best Houses* as 'the most perfect house to survive from the Middle Ages', this remarkable old house is surrounded by terraced Elizabethan gardens and is set among the rolling countryside of the Peak District National Park. Guided tours are available and adapted to suit all ages, abilities and interests.

🔍 On the A6, 2 miles south of Bakewell
⚙ 🔅 🍁
⧗ 2–3 hours
⭐ The Banqueting Hall
£
www.haddonhall.co.uk

Peak District National Park

378

Bakewell

The Peak District National Park, opened in 1951, was the first such park in Britain. It has an extensive network of short and long-distance trails (over 2,000 miles in total), as well as large open-access areas and bridleways, commonly used by mountain bikers as well as horse riders. The many gritstone outcrops, such as Stanage and the Roaches, are recognised as some of the finest rock climbing sites in the world. Some of the area's large reservoirs have become centres for water sports, including sailing, fishing and canoeing, in this most landlocked and beautiful part of the UK.

🔍 Bakewell Visitor Centre is in Bakewell town centre
⚙ 🔅 🍁 ❄
⧗ 6–8 hours
⭐ Snake Pass
FREE
www.peakdistrict.gov.uk

Bolsover Castle

379

Bolsover

Set on a hilltop overlooking the Vale of Scarsdale, Bolsover Castle enjoys panoramic views over the beautiful Derbyshire countryside. Children will love the fairytale Little Castle, designed as a fantasy entertainment house with magnificent wall paintings. You can visit the indoor Riding House where William, Duke of Newcastle indulged his passion for training horses in balletic movement and wander round the beautiful Venus Garden, with its secluded love seats, 23 statues and fountain which plays again for the first time in centuries. There are also audio-visual displays to enjoy in the Discovery Centre.

🔍 Follow signs from junction 29a of the M1
⚙ 🔅 🍁 ❄
⧗ 1–2 hours
⭐ Views of the beautiful castle from the grounds
£
www.english-heritage.org.uk

Buxton Museum and Art Gallery 380
Buxton

Explore the geology, archaeology and history of the
Peak District displayed in a seven-section time tunnel
– complete with sounds and smells! The museum is an
excellent place to find out more about the town's
fascinating history and to become more acquainted with
the Peak District landscape. On the first floor, the award
winning 'Wonders of the Peak' gallery illustrates how
the Peak District landscape developed, along with the
animals and people who once lived in the area. On the
same floor is an art gallery, which is used for regular
exhibitions by local artists.

In Buxton town centre
1–2 hours
Roman antiquities
FREE
www.derbyshire.gov.uk

Peak Cavern 382
Castleton

This is a spectacular cavern set within a 250-foot
vertical cliff. Within this entrance chamber you will
see the remains of a village where a whole community
lived and worked for more than 400 years. As you
venture deeper into the cavern you will hear the
remarkable acoustics of the Orchestra Gallery in the
Great Cave, see a perpetual cascade of water at Roger
Rain's House and enter the Devil's Cellar to hear the
source of the River Styx. Guided tours, including
rope-making demonstrations, are available at frequent
intervals, with information about the cavern's history.

On the A6187 in Castleton village
1–2 hours
Pluto's Dining Room
www.peakcavern.co.uk

Donington Grand Prix Exhibition 381
Castle Donington

The exhibition has over 130 exhibits illustrating the
story of motorsport from the turn of the 20th century
to the present day and includes cars driven by Mansell,
Prost, Moss, Senna, Fangio, Clark and Stewart. It also
houses the largest collection of McLaren racing cars in
the world. Notable exhibits include the 1936 twin-engine
500 bhp Alfa Romeo Bimotore which has a top speed
of 200 mph, Jim Clark's World Championship winning
Lotus 25, the 'howling' flat 12 Ferrari 312B, and Stirling
Moss's Lotus, in which he defeated the Ferrari works
team in the 1961 Monaco Grand Prix.

Donington Park Grand Prix Circuit, close to junctions 23a and 24 of the M1
2–3 hours
Senna's 1993 European Grand Prix-winning car
www.donington-park.co.uk

STAR ATTRACTION

Hardwick Hall
383
Chesterfield

One of the most splendid houses in England. Although it was built by Bess of Hardwick in the 1590s and unaltered since: its huge windows and high ceilings make it feel strikingly modern. Outside, stone gleams and glass glitters in the light. Its six towers make a dramatic skyline. Climbing up through the house, from one spectacular floor to the next, is a thrilling architectural experience. Rich tapestries, plaster friezes and alabaster fireplaces colour the rooms, culminating in the hauntingly atmospheric Long Gallery. Outside, walled courtyards contain a herb garden, orchards and lawns.

⌕ Follow signs from junction 29 of the M1
☼ ◷ ♣ Wednesdays to Sundays only
⧗ 2-3 hours
★ Embroidery and tapestry collection
♿ ♿
www.nationaltrust.org.uk

Denby Pottery Visitor Centre
384
Denby

Tours of the famous Denby Pottery are conducted in the working factory by experienced tour guides who explain how the pottery is made. There's a choice of tours – choose the Craftroom Tour if you have young children, while for a more in depth look at the making processes you should plump for the Factory Tour. On both tours visitors can watch a video, make their own clay souvenir to take home and have a go at painting in glaze onto a Denby plate. You can also see splendid examples of fine Denbyware.

⌕ On the B6179 at Denby, 8 miles north of Derby
☼ ◷ ♣ ❄
⧗ 1-2 hours
★ Free cookery demonstrations
Tours ♿ Extra charge if you take your piece home
www.denbyvisitorcentre.co.uk

Pickford's House Museum
385
Derby

This museum of Georgian life and costume is sited in an elegant townhouse designed, built in 1770 and lived in by the architect Joseph Pickford. Visitors can see a number of rooms decorated and furnished as they would have been around 1815. The kitchen, laundry, cellar, pantry and housekeeper's cupboard have also been reconstructed, giving an idea of life 'below stairs' too. The upper floors feature displays of toys and toy theatres, and several rooms showing some of the museum's excellent collection of historic costumes and textiles.

⌕ Derby city centre
☼ ◷ ♣ ❄
⧗ 1-2 hours
★ 19th-century period costume collection
FREE
www.derby.gov.uk/museums

The Silk Mill
386
Derby

The Silk Mill museum is on the site of the world's oldest factories, the Silk Mills, built by George Sorocold in 1702 and 1717. The foundations and parts of the tower from the 1717 mill are still visible. The displays tell the story of the industrial heritage and achievement of Derby and its people. There is a special emphasis on the development of Rolls Royce aero engines and the railway industry. Other displays cover local industries such as mining, pottery and foundry work. The Power Gallery covers the story of motive power in industry with hands-on exhibits.

⌕ In Derby city centre
☼ ◷ ♣ ❄
⧗ 1-2 hours
★ The Rolls-Royce story
FREE
www.derby.gov.uk/museums

Chatsworth `388`
Matlock

The 'Palace of the Peak' contains one of Europe's finest collections of treasures, displayed in more than 30 rooms, from the grandeur of the 1st Duke's hall and state apartments with their rich decoration and painted ceilings, to the 19th century library and dining room. A new display shows off some of the family's stunning jewellery collection. Outside too, in 1,000 acres of garden, there's just as much to see and do. A recent refurbishment has meant big changes but with new treasures on show the phrase 'a masterpiece in every room' has never been more apt.

🔍 Off the B6012, 8 miles north of Matlock

⚙ ⚙ 🍁

⏳ 2-3 hours

⭐ Astonishing collection of family portraits

💷 💷

www.chatsworth.org

Chestnut Centre Wildlife Park `387`
High Peak

This conservation and wildlife park is set in 50 acres of landscaped grounds and is home not only to a unique collection of birds and animals, but also to many wild birds and mammals. Visitors are invited to walk around the park and see some of Europe's largest gathering of otters, 16 species of owl and other indigenous wildlife including, buzzards, pine martens, polecats, foxes, Scottish wildcats and deer all in their natural surroundings. The park is also home to the UK's only giant otter. Native to South America and an endangered species, they are very rare in captivity.

🔍 Follow signs from the A625

⚙ ⚙ 🍁

⏳ 2-3 hours

⭐ Captivating otters

💷

www.chestnutcentre.co.uk

Crich Tramway Village `389`
Matlock

Crich Tramway Village is an open-air museum of trams and tramways. Visitors can see open, closed, single and double deckers, horse-drawn, steam and electric trams from all over the globe. This is also home to the National Tramway Museum. It is set up as an Edwardian village and has a street with shops and other buildings including the Red Lion pub from Stoke-on-Trent, Derby Assembly Rooms and Burnley tramway offices. There are tramlines that go out for about a mile from the village. There is also a collection of old street furniture from around the UK.

🔍 Follow signs from junction 28 of the M1

⚙ ⚙ 🍁

⏳ 2-3 hours

⭐ Working trams in an old style street setting

💷 💷

www.tramway.co.uk

Heights of Abraham
390

Matlock Bath

People have been climbing Masson Hill to the Heights of Abraham since a Regency style 'savage garden' was planted there in 1780. It wasn't until 200 years later that a cable car was introduced. As the observation cars rise from the valley floor, pulse-racing views unfold of the Derwent Valley and the Peak District. Mining began here in Roman times. In emptying the ground of the rich mineral deposits, they left behind a network of naturally formed caverns and passageways. Now, guided tours allow you to retrace the footsteps of the miners, and experience the spectacular caverns they left behind.

Off the A6, in Matlock Bath

2–3 hours

Hair-raising cable car journey

www.heightsofabraham.com

Melbourne Hall and Gardens
391

Melbourne

Melbourne Hall in beautiful, tranquil gardens in a lakeside setting. The hall became the home of Sir John Coke in 1628 and has been inherited by family members throughout the years. The house was home to William Lamb 2nd Viscount Melbourne, the Victorian Prime Minister, after whom the city of Melbourne in Australia was named. Today the hall is home to Lord and Lady Ralf Kerr and their family and so has limited opening times. The house contains a wealth of interesting history for visitors to discover.

Off the A514, 7 miles south of Derby

Gardens are open at other times

2–3 hours

Beautiful garden walks

www.melbournehall.com

Arbor Low Stone Circle and Gib Hill Barrow
392

Monyash

The region's most important prehistoric site, Arbor Low is a Neolithic henge monument atmospherically set amid high moorland. Within an earthen bank and ditch, a circle of some 50 white limestone slabs, all now fallen, surrounds a central stone 'cove' – a feature found only in major sacred sites. Nearby is enigmatic Gib Hill, a large burial mound, which takes its name from its use as a hanging site.

Off the A515, 2 miles south of Monyash

1 hour

Unspoiled, ancient countryside

www.english-heritage.org.uk

Calke Abbey
393

Ticknall

This baroque mansion, built in 1701 and set in stunning parkland, has become famous as an English country house in decline. Little restored, its interiors remain essentially unchanged since the 1880s. Its beauty is in the huge variety of contents, amassed over time and deposited here as the fortunes of its owners, the Harpur family, declined. In the walled gardens visitors can explore the orangery, the flower and kitchen gardens or walk around the stunning but fragile habitats of the surrounding Calke Park National Nature Reserve.

On the A514, 10 miles south of Derby

2–3 hours

Wonderful 18th-century silk bed

www.nationaltrust.org.uk

Ashby-de-la-Zouch Castle   394
Ashby-de-la-Zouch

This castle forms the backdrop to the famous jousting scenes in Sir Walter Scott's novel *Ivanhoe*. Now a ruin, the castle has a rich history. Between 1474 and his execution by Richard III in 1483, Edward IV's Chamberlain Lord Hastings added the chapel and the impressive keep-like Hastings Tower. Visitors can climb the 78-foot high tower, which offers fine views. Later it hosted many royal visitors, including Henry VII, Mary Queen of Scots, James I and Charles I. A Royalist stronghold during the Civil War, the castle finally fell to Parliament in 1646, and was then made unusable.

🔍 On the A511, in Ashby-de-la-Zouch town centre
✿ ◉ ❦ ❄
⏳ 1-2 hours
⭐ Secret, underground passages
💷
www.english-heritage.org.uk

Tropical Birdland   396
Desford

This is a beautiful tropical bird garden located in the heart of rural England. Visitors can see over two hundred exotic birds with over 50 species represented. These include macaws, parrots, parakeets, toucans and emus. You can wander through the walk-through aviaries, see where chicks are hatched and even sit and talk to some friendly, free-to-fly birds. There's also a 6-acre woodland to explore where you'll encounter all kinds of native wildlife, such as woodpeckers, kingfishers, squirrels and jays, as well as flourishing trees and shrubs.

🔍 Take junction 22 of the M1
✿ ◉ ❦ ❄
⏳ 2 hours
⭐ Snowy Owls
💷
www.tropicalbirdland.co.uk

Snibston Discovery Park   395
Coalville

This award-winning, interactive museum of science and discovery is set in a former colliery, created by the famous railway pioneer George Stephenson, and offers a mixture of art, technology and history through interactive exhibits for all ages (see right). From the earliest mining tools, proto-type jet engine to the largest fashion display outside London, there is plenty to explore. There are regular guided colliery tours, run by former miners, and rides on the colliery railway. If that's not enough then outside there are play areas, a Country Park and a nature reserve.

🔍 On the edge of Coalville town centre
✿ ◉ ❦ ❄
⏳ 2-3 hours
⭐ Guided Colliery Tours
💷
www.leics.gov.uk/museums

Learn all about the **Mars Rover Missions** with these programmable NXT Mars Rover Lego Robots

Belvoir Castle 397

Grantham

Belvoir Castle was built during the Regency period. Now open to the public, this stunning castle sits on a hilltop, with breathtaking views and beautiful gardens. It also houses many treasures, including one of the largest private art collections in the country in a series of lavish Staterooms. It also contains many fine pieces of French furniture, Italian sculpture and magnificent tapestries. In contrast, the Old Kitchen and Bakery give a taste of life below stairs in 1825. The School Room and Nursery look as they would have done when children of the Regency period arrived for the day.

Off the A52, 7 miles from Grantham

2-3 hours

Incredible art collection

www.belvoircastle.com

Jewry Wall Museum 398

Leicester

At Jewry Wall Museum you can discover the archaeology of Leicester's past and find out about its people from prehistoric times to the medieval period. The museum contains one of Leicester's most famous landmarks, the Jewry Wall, thought to be one of the tallest surviving pieces of Roman masonry in the country. The celebration of the city's history also includes detailed mosaics, intricate painted wall plaster and a beautiful Roman cavalry helmet cheek piece. There are also fascinating artefacts from other eras: from ancient stone tools to striking medieval decorated tiles from Leicester Abbey.

Leicester city centre

1-2 hours

Fascinating Roman artefacts

FREE

www.leicester.gov.uk

National Space Centre 399

Leicester

The centre is dedicated to astronomy and space science, and promotes an understanding of space, the history of its exploration and how it affects our future. Its distinctive, futuristic 42-metre high Rocket Tower has become part of the Leicester skyline since it opened in 2001. The Rocket Tower houses the attraction's biggest artefacts, including two huge rockets. Visitors then continue through a series of interactive exhibits, shows and simulators – including a 3D-simulator ride to the ice moon Europa, a NASA air-jet chair to manoeuvre and a moon rock to mine against the clock – that inform and entertain them and test the more intrepid to see if they are made of the right stuff to become deep space astronauts.

There is also a High-Tech gallery that reports the latest news from space and describing what wonders might be achieved in the next 50 years. But the best is saved till last as you take your seats in the Space Theatre. This is the UK's largest planetarium, and takes visitors on a breathtaking voyage of discovery in a 360° full-dome experience. The purpose of the National Space Centre is to inspire us all – particularly young people – to take a greater interest in science and engineering and it certainly delivers.

FIVE-STAR ATTRACTION

Off the A6, 2 miles north of Leicester city centre

3-4 hours

Planetarium show

www.spacecentre.co.uk

Newarke Houses Museum and Gardens

400

Leicester

Newarke Houses Museum is set in two historic houses, Wygston's Chantry House and Skeffington House, and tells the story of 20th-century Leicester. There are room settings from the 1950s and 1970s, a cinema, a collection of toys and a play area for children. Galleries tell the story of 'Moving Here' and settling in Leicester. Visitors can find out more about Leicester's famous son Daniel Lambert and visit a 1950s street scene that includes a pub, a grocer and a pawnbroker. There are also displays about the city at war.

Leicester city centre

1–2 hours

A stroll around this historic area of the city

FREE

www.leicester.gov.uk

Foxton Canal Museum

401

Market Harborough

The unique 'staircase' of ten locks at Foxton is at the centre of Britain's inland waterways network. The locks north of Foxton are 14 feet wide, as are the locks south of Watford Gap. The locks at Foxton and Watford were constructed at just 7 feet wide to save water and money. In 1900, the Foxton Inclined Plane Boat Lift was opened to widen the canal, speed up traffic and save water. This museum tells the story of the lift, the locks at Foxton and the social history of the people who worked and lived nearby.

Follow signs from the A6 or take junction 20 of the M1

2–3 hours

Guided tour and local walks

www.fipt.org.uk

Rockingham Castle

402

Market Harborough

Built by William the Conqueror more than 900 years ago, the castle stands in beautiful grounds with superb views over the Welland Valley. Visited by many Kings of England right through to the Medieval and Tudor periods, the castle underwent many changes until abandoned in 1485. It was subsequently bought by the Watson family and has remained in the family to the present day with various restorations throughout its history. The 18-acre gardens include its famous Elephant Yew Hedge, reputedly 450 years old, and the Wild Garden with its remarkable collection of fascinating plants and trees.

Off the A6003, 10 miles east of Market Harborough

2–3 hours

Collection of 20th-century paintings

www.rockinghamcastle.com

STAR ATTRACTION

Twinlakes Park `403`
Melton Mowbray

A family theme park that mixes traditional theme park rides and other attractions with a small zoo. There's lots of variety here set in 70 acres of countryside. Visitors can enjoy flying displays at the Falconry Centre and meet over 300 friendly animals at Red Rooster Farm. As for rides: the soaring flying sensation of the Icarus Sky Flyers and the speeding, rocking Mercury Minicoaster are favourites. There's also 125,000 square feet of indoor fun, with games, shows, adventure and soft play areas for the little ones. School holidays also see live entertainers, workshops and other special events.

🔍 Follow signs from the A607, 1 mile from Melton Mowbray

☼ ◎ ♣ ❄

⏳ 4–6 hours

⭐ Lilly, the lonely meerkat

💲 💲

www.twinlakespark.co.uk

STAR ATTRACTION

Bosworth Battlefield Heritage Centre and Country Park `404`
Sutton Cheney

This heritage centre is on the site of the Battle of Bosworth, 1485, the decisive battle of the War of the Roses where Richard III lost his life and his crown to the future Tudor king, Henry VII. The site offers diverse ways to re-live history from interactive displays to battle re-enactments. Visitors can handle weapons and armour in the detailed exhibition, watch a film explaining the events and walk around the battlefield with a blow-by-blow account of events.

🔍 Follow signs from the A5, A444 and B585, 3 miles south of Market Bosworth

☼ ◎ ♣

⏳ 2–3 hours

⭐ The lost site of this famous battle

💲

www.bosworthbattlefield.com

Claythorpe Watermill and Wildfowl Gardens `405`
Alford

Nestling at the tip of the Lincolnshire Wolds in a picture postcard setting, Claythorpe is home to over 300 birds that wander freely around the site. Visitors are able to experience their environment and habitat first hand. You can also visit the Old Bakery, which ceased milling in the 1970s, and now houses an Old Bygones exhibit that tell the story of the site's baking industry. The site also has a number of woodland walks on which visitors might see otters, red squirrels or even wallabies.

🔍 Follow signs from the A16

☼ ◎ ♣

⏳ 1–2 hours

⭐ Woodland picnics

💲

www.claythorpewatermill.fsbusiness.co.uk

Cleethorpes Coast Light Railway `406`
Cleethorpes

Operating along Cleethorpes foreshore and lakeside, this is Lincolnshire's premier narrow gauge (15-inch) railway and the last surviving steam light railway on the east coast of England. The trains, which can be caught at either Kingsway or Lakeside Stations, run for nearly one mile through attractive coastal scenery using an impressive array of steam and diesel locomotive engines. For keen railway enthusiasts there is the chance to learn to drive one of the trains – see website for details.

🔍 Follow signs for the Lakeside in Cleethorpes town centre

☼ ◎ ♣

⏳ 1 hour

⭐ The delights of Cleethorpes – in steam

💲

www.cleethorpescoastlightrailway.co.uk

The Jungle Zoo   `407`
Cleethorpes

This charming little zoo is ranged around a Tropical House with a spectacular jungle-like setting, which is home to red-eared and other terrapins and goldfish. Visitors can also see Caiman alligators, large lizards, marmosets, parrots and toucans among others. There's also a Reptile House, which houses snakes and spiders. Outdoor exhibits include capuchin monkeys, meerkats, ring-tailed lemurs, African pygmy goats, chipmunks, chickens and guinea pigs. There are also a number of bird exhibits housing species such as cockatoo, lorikeets and parakeets.

🔍 Follow signs for the Lakeside in Cleethorpes town centre

☀ ⚙ ♣ ❄

⏳ 1–2 hours

⭐ Giant snakes

£

www.thejunglezoo.co.uk

Gainsborough Old Hall   `408`
Gainsborough

This magnificent medieval manor is one of the finest 15th-century timber framed houses in Britain. The Great Hall with its splendid, arched, wooden roof forms the centrepiece of the building. The kitchens remain virtually unchanged and those who climb to the top of the brick built tower can enjoy magnificent views. Visitors can tread in the footsteps of some of its illustrious royal visitors, both Richard III and Henry VIII were guests of the Burgh family, who originally built and lived here. The Mayflower Pilgrims and John Wesley also worshipped within its walls.

🔍 Gainsborough town centre

☀ ⚙ ♣ ❄

⏳ 2–3 hours

⭐ The huge kitchen fireplace

£

www.lincolnshire.gov.uk

Gainsthorpe Medieval Village   `409`
Gainsthorpe

This is one of the best-preserved medieval village sites in England. The village is laid out on streets running parallel to the Roman Ermine Street, 500 metres to the east. The earthwork remains cover an area of about 5 hectares and include a fishpond, two dovecotes, barns, longhouses and croft buildings. According to local legend, the village was a haven for thieves, and this is what led to its destruction. The truth is unknown, though of course the devastating effects of the Black Death in the mid-14th century may have played a part.

🔍 West of the A15, 5 miles south-west of Brigg

☀ ⚙ ♣ ❄

⏳ 1 hour

⭐ Fascinating archaeological site

`FREE`

www.english-heritage.org.uk

Woolsthorpe Manor `410`
Grantham

Isaac Newton was born in this modest manor house in 1642 and he made many of his most important discoveries about light and gravity here. A complex figure, Newton notched up careers as diverse as Cambridge Professor and Master of the Royal Mint, spent years studying alchemy and the Bible as well as science, and was President of the Royal Society. You can still see the famous apple tree from Isaac's bedroom window and enjoy the brand new Discovery Centre.

🔍 Off B676, 8 miles south of Grantham
⚙ ◎ 🍁
⏳ 1–2 hours
⭐ The apple tree
💰
www.nationaltrust.org.uk

Fishing Heritage Centre `411`
Grimsby

This centre tells the story of the fishermen on North East Lincolnshire, their boats and the waters they fished in. The story underlines the dangers and hardships of life at sea and there is a reconstruction of a 1950s sea voyage, complete with authentic aromas and a moving deck. The centre also holds a wide-ranging collection of maritime artefacts including artworks, costumes, ship models, books, social history objects, fishing-related objects and much more. An important part of this is the Doughty Collection of maritime art, ship models and chinaware.

🔍 Next to Alexandra Dock, in Grimsby town centre
⚙ ◎ 🍁 ❄
⏳ 1–2 hours
⭐ Tour of the trawler *Ross Tiger* (costs extra)
💰
www.nelincs.gov.uk

Fantasy Island `412`
Ingoldmells

This is Britain's first themed indoor family resort and amusement park. It combines the best of seaside tradition with white-knuckle fun. Many of the attractions are set under a glass pyramid, but the really big rides are outdoors. The white-knucklers include the Jubilee Odyssey and the Millennium rollercoasters. Volcanic Impact, Amazing Confusion and the Beast will also shake you up! But there are also family rides, such as Fantasy Mouse, Rhombus Rocket and Dragon Mountain Descent, as well as children's attractions. A huge market also meanders around the park.

🔍 Follow signs from the A52, near Skegness
⚙ ◎ 🍁 ❄
⏳ 3–5 hours
⭐ Millennium Roller Coaster
💰 💰 💰
www.fantasyisland.co.uk

Lincoln Castle `413`
Lincoln

In Norman times, Lincoln was the third city of the realm. In 1068, two years after the Battle of Hastings, William the Conqueror began building Lincoln Castle on a site occupied since Roman times. For 900 years the castle was used as a court and prison. Many original features still remain and the wall walks provide visitors with magnificent views of the cathedral, the city and the surrounding countryside. Visitors can also see one of the four surviving originals of the Magna Carta, sealed by King John after his meeting with the Barons at Runnymede in 1215.

🔍 Lincoln city centre
⚙ ◎ 🍁 ❄
⏳ 1–2 hours
⭐ Free guided tours
💰
www.lincolnshire.gov.uk

Lincoln Medieval Bishop's Palace

414

Lincoln

Standing in the shadow of Lincoln cathedral, with sweeping views over the city, the medieval bishops' palace was once among the most important buildings in the country. Begun in the 12th century, the palace's most impressive feature is West Hall. The chapel range and entrance tower were added in the 1430s. The palace was sacked by Royalist troops during the Civil War. Built on hillside terraces, the palace has a vineyard and a Contemporary Heritage Garden inspired by the cathedral's medieval vaulting and the curves of the vines.

🔍 Next to the cathedral, in Lincoln town centre

⚙ ☀ 🍁

⏳ 1–2 hours

⭐ Medieval vaulting

♿

www.english-heritage.org.uk

Gibraltar Point NNR

416

Skegness

This reserve comprises three miles of unspoilt coastline from Skegness to the Wash. Habitats include sandy and muddy seashore, sand dunes, saltmarsh and freshwater marsh with ponds and lagoons. The reserve is recognised internationally for its important habitats and species. Visitors will be able to see a wealth of birds, rare plants and animals, including seals, water voles and pygmy shrews. There are five bird-watching hides, nature trials and lots of other activities, details of which can be found in the Visitor Centre.

🔍 Follow signs from Skegness town centre

⚙ ☀ 🍁 ❄

⏳ 2–3 hours

⭐ Oystercatchers and red-throated divers

FREE

www.lincstrust.org.uk

Bolingbroke Castle

415

Old Bolingbroke

The remains of a 13th-century hexagonal castle, birthplace in 1366 of the future King Henry IV, with adjacent earthworks. When the Civil War began the castle was uninhabitable but it's walls remained strong and a force of 200 Royalists were sent here to secure the countryside for the King. On 9 October 1643 a force of 6,000 Parliamentarians, led by Oliver Cromwell and Sir Thomas Fairfax, marched from Boston to take the castle. The castle held out until November, when the garrison surrendered and the castle was subsequently 'slighted'.

🔍 Off the A16, in Old Bolingbroke

⚙ ☀ 🍁 ❄

⏳ 1 hour

⭐ Mossy stones steeped in history

FREE

www.english-heritage.org.uk

Skegness Natureland Seal Sanctuary
Skegness

417

This sanctuary is well known for rescuing and rehabilitating orphaned and injured seal pups, but it also has crocodiles and other reptiles in the Tropical House, penguins, insects and birds to see. You shouldn't miss the regular seal and penguin feeding times, which are announced each day over the PA system. There's also an aquarium, Pet's Corner where visitors can meet goats, turkeys, rabbits and guinea pigs, as well as a Floral Palace where free-to-fly tropical birds, like flamingos, flit about among the bougainvillea flowers.

🔍 Follow signs from Skegness town centre
☀ ◎ ❦ ❆
⌛ 2 hours
⭐ Underwater viewing pool
£
www.skegnessnatureland.co.uk

Cogglesford Watermill
Sleaford

418

In a picturesque setting by the River Slea, this fully restored and working watermill, some parts of which date back to the 17th century, is thought to be the only Sheriff's Watermill still operating in England. Millers, like William Almond, have produced flour on this site for over a thousand years and the mill has been a major meeting place for local farmers and traders. Organic stone ground flour still produced in the mill is sold in the shop, together with locally sourced goods and produce.

🔍 Near the A163, close by Sleaford town centre
☀ ◎ ❦
⌛ 1 hour
⭐ Ingenious labour-saving sack hoists
FREE
www.n-kesteven.gov.uk/tic

Butterfly and Wildlife Park
Spalding

419

Set in the heart of the Fens, this park has some Tropical Gardens, with exotic species, lush plants, creepy crawlies and snakes, lizards, terrapins, iguanas and the new arrivals; a royal python and Moja, and an African white-throated monitor lizard. There is a tropical bird aviary and visitors also get the chance to meet friendly animals like raccoons, pygmy goats, pot bellied and curly-coated pigs. There are also displays by a number of impressive birds of prey. If that isn't enough, there's a fantastic outdoor play area with slides, nets and a climbing wall.

🔍 Follow signs from the A17, at Long Sutton
☀ ◎ ❦
⌛ 2-3 hours
⭐ The Birds of Prey
£
www.butterflyandwildlifepark.co.uk

Lincolnshire Aviation Heritage Centre

420

Spilsby

This marvellous Heritage Centre is set on a wartime bomber airfield. Visitors can experience the sights and sounds, smells and atmosphere of a bomber airfield during wartime. This is the only place in the country to see a Lancaster Bomber on an original wartime airfield (and even ride in it – see website for details). The centre also features the original Control Tower, welcoming NAAFI and an emotionally evocative Memorial Chapel containing the 848 names of personnel who gave their lives from this airfield.

On the A155, between Revesy and East Kirkby

1–2 hours

Lancaster Bomber on the move

www.lincsaviation.co.uk

Burghley House

421

Stamford

Built and mostly designed by William Cecil, Lord High Treasurer to Elizabeth I, between 1555 and 1587, the main part of the house has 35 major rooms. There are more than 80 lesser rooms and numerous halls, corridors, bathrooms and service areas. The lead roof extends to three quarters of an acre, restoration and rebuilding of which began in 1983 and took nearly ten years to complete. Visitors can also enjoy gardens and beautiful walks around the historic parkland laid out by 'Capability' Brown and still occupied by a herd of fallow deer.

Follow signs from Stamford town centre

2–3 hours

Grand Tour masterpieces

www.burghley.co.uk

Tattershall Castle

422

Tattershall

Explore the six floors of this rare red-brick medieval castle built by Ralph Cromwell, Lord Treasurer of England and one of the most powerful men in the country. Visitors can use an audio guide to create a picture of what life was like at Tattershall Castle in the 15th century. Climb the 150 steps from the basement to the battlements and enjoy the magnificent views of the Lincolnshire countryside, then explore the grounds, moats, bridges and neighbouring church, also built by Ralph Cromwell.

Off the A16, north of Boston

1–2 hours

Spectacular views from the battlements

www.nationaltrust.org.uk

Althorp

423

Althorp

Home of the Spencer family since 1508, Althorp is open to the public in July and August each year. Visitors can see the house with its beautiful interiors and one of Europe's finest private collections of furniture, paintings, photographs and ceramics. You can also see the award-winning exhibition 'Diana: A Celebration' that reflects on the life and work of Diana, Princess of Wales. There are also beautiful, tranquil gardens in which you can walk or have a picnic and in which you can visit the Round Oval where Diana is buried.

Off the A428, follow signs from junction 16 of the M1

3–4 hours

Wonderful collection of portraiture

www.althorp.com

Brixworth Country Park 424

Brixworth

This park has many facilities including a café, cycle hire, a superb children's play area, a sensory garden, a bird-watching hide and waymarked trails for walkers and cyclists. It is now the main gateway to Pitsford Water, for fishing and sailing, and a 10-kilometre safe walking/cycling route called the Pitsford Water Trail. The park is also linked to the Brampton Valley Way. There are also open spaces for ball games, kite flying and dog walking.

🔍 On the A508, close to Brixworth village

⚙ ⚙ ♣ ❄

⌛ 2-3 hours

★ Sculpture trail

FREE Car parking charges

www.northamptonshire.gov.uk

Boughton House 425

Kettering

A collection of modest medieval buildings were purchased by the Montagu family in 1528 and transformed into one of the great houses of Europe. Its special attraction lies in the superb collections of paintings, furniture, tapestries, needlework, carpets, porcelain, arms and silver, just as the artists, craftsmen and collectors of the Montagu family over the generations intended. Visitors can also walk in the walled garden and park and see the restored waterways and landscape features; and in August can enjoy the treasure house, which is at the heart of the estate.

🔍 Off the A43, 3 miles north of Kettering

⚙ Grounds open at other times, see website for details

⌛ 2-3 hours

★ Art treasures and armour collection

♿

www.boughtonhouse.org.uk

Rushton Triangular Lodge 426

Kettering

This delightful triangular building was designed by Sir Thomas Tresham and constructed between 1593 and 1597. It is a testament to Tresham's Roman Catholicism: the number three, symbolising the Holy Trinity, is apparent everywhere. There are three floors, trefoil windows and three triangular gables on each side. On the entrance front is the inscription *Tres Testimonium Dant* ('There are three that give witness'), a biblical quotation from St John's Gospel referring to the Trinity. It is also a pun on Tresham's name; his wife called him 'Good Tres' in her letters.

🔍 On unclassified road, 1 mile west of Rushton

⚙ ⚙ ♣

⌛ 1 hour

★ Extraordinary architectural oddity

♿

www.english-heritage.org.uk

Abington Park Museum 428
Northampton

Known as 'the Museum in the Park', this Grade I listed building, a 15th-century manor house with a beautiful Tudor hall, that was once home to Shakespeare's grand-daughter, is now home to a museum that combines social and military history. Displays illustrate Northamptonshire Life, the story of the Northamptonshire Regiment and Yeomanry – at home and abroad in two world wars, a room full of Victorian curiosities, a fine array of costumes and a unique collection of leathercraft.

Park Avenue South, 2 miles east of Northampton town centre

2-3 hours

Original 16th-century oak panelling

FREE

www.northampton.gov.uk/museums

Wicksteed Park 427
Kettering

Wicksteed Park is situated in 147 acres of landscaped English countryside and offers the elements of a family theme park and a country park rolled into one. The theme park has more than 30 rides including a rollercoaster, racing cars and a log flume. There's also a water park, a funfair and one of the largest free playgrounds in the UK. The Wicksteed Railway continues to be one of the Park's major attractions carrying in excess of 250,000 passengers a year making it the country's busiest commercial narrow gauge railways.

Follow signs from the A6 or the A14

3-5 hours

Traditional funfair rides

www.wicksteedpark.co.uk

Billing Aquadrome 429
Northampton

Billing Aquadrome is a leisure holiday park set in 235 acres of parkland, woods and lakes. Although many people stay there in static mobile homes or on the campsite, the facilities are open to the public for days out. The main attraction is the new indoor aqua park, but there is a host of other activities such as huge outdoor and indoor play areas, a funfair, golf, go-karting, an amusement arcade and the Billings train, which will take you round the park and enable you to see what's on offer.

Off the A45, 3 miles from Northampton

3 hours

Aqua park

But some activities will charge extra

www.billingaquadrome.com

Holdenby House and Gardens 430
Northampton

A stately home whose royal connections go back over 400 years. Built in 1583 by Sir Christopher Hatton to entertain Elizabeth I, it became the Palace of James I and the prison of his son, Charles I. Now a family home, the house is the splendid backdrop to a beautiful 20-acre garden, with lawns and hedges, an Elizabethan rose garden, King Charles's Walk and a Pond Garden. Visitors can also see the Falconry Centre, from where birds of prey soar over the scene of so much history.

🔍 Between the A428 and A5199, 6 miles north-west of Northampton
☀ Check website for details of dates the house is open
⏳ 2–3 hours
⭐ Elizabethan rose garden
£

www.holdenby.com

Nene Whitewater Centre 431
Northampton

This 300-metre artificial watercourse, on the banks of the River Nene, offers whitewater rafting, kayaking, canoeing and adrenalin-pumping whitewater tubing to people of all standards and skills. Flow rates can be controlled thereby altering the course's difficulty and the skill levels required to paddle it. Courses for beginners cover all aspects of safety before riding begins. There are changing and showering facilities on site. As space is limited, it is essential to book in advance to make sure that you can do what you want at a time that is most convenient for you.

🔍 On the A426, just on the edge of Northampton town
✳ ☀ ✚
⏳ 1–2 hours
⭐ Whitewater tubing
£ £ £

www.nenewhitewatercentre.co.uk

Derngate 432
Northampton

No.78 Derngate is a Georgian house originally built in the 1820s. It's noted for its interior, which was extensively remodelled by noted architect Charles Rennie Mackintosh, the only domestic commission Mackintosh undertook outside Scotland. Far ahead of its time, the house had central heating, indoor plumbing and lots of electrical gadgets in the kitchen. Mackintosh's design included a striking black room, a hall-lounge with yellow-stencilled wallpaper and a bedroom decorated with bold ultramarine, black and white stripes. There is a supporting museum next door at No.80.

Northampton town centre

1–2 hours

Revolutionary interior designs

www.78derngate.org.uk

National Waterways Museum 433
Stoke Bruerne

This museum is based in the canal-side village of Stoke Bruerne in the heart of rural Northamptonshire. It is housed in an atmospheric restored cornmill. Inside you'll find a treasure trove of stories, exhibits and collections that explain and bring to life the rich world of Britain's canals. And the towpath at Stoke Bruerne village is the perfect setting. It's alive with canal heritage and the Grand Union Canal on which it sits, built by William Jessop between 1783 and 1805, is a constantly moving picture of passing boats and wildlife.

On the towpath, in the centre of Stoke Bruerne village

1–2 hours

Working models of canal craft

www.nwm.org.uk/stoke/

Attenborough Nature Centre 434
Chilwell

Attenborough Nature Centre is an award-winning visitor and education facility surrounded by the tranquil waters of the beautiful Attenborough Nature Reserve. Situated within easy reach of Nottingham and Derby the centre provides a 'lifeline to the natural world'. The reserve is a complex of flooded gravel pits and islands, covers 360 acres and provides an ideal habitat for a wide range of plants and other wildlife. However, the reserve is best known for its birds and there are dozens of species to see during each season of the year.

Off the A6005, at Chilwell

3–4 hours

Egrets, sandpipers and kittiwakes

FREE Car parking charges

www.attenboroughnaturecentre.co.uk

D.H. Lawrence Birthplace Museum

435

Eastwood

This is the house where David Herbert Richards Lawrence was born in 1885. Visitors take a guided tour to learn about his family life and the type of working-class home and mining community that shaped his formative years. Knowledgeable guides will lead you through the rooms where the family lived, as well as the communal washhouse where the Victorian housewife would spend 'the hardest day of the week'. There is a DVD room and an exhibition room, displaying some of his original watercolours and personal items.

Off the A610, in Eastwood, north-west of Nottingham

1–2 hours

'Bert's' birthplace

www.broxtowe.gov.uk

Sherwood Forest National Nature Reserve

436

Edwinstowe

The legendary home of the outlaw Robin Hood is now part of a National Nature Reserve because of its national ecological importance. Within the 450-acre site there are 900 veteran oak trees, including the famous Major Oak. This ancient oak, one of Britain's most famous trees, is located just a ten-minute walk from the visitor centre. Waymarked trails allow visitors to see the forest's fascinating ecology and biodiversity. The natural decay of fallen timber means the woodland teems with insect life, fungi, birds and bats.

On the B6034, just north of Edwinstowe village

2–3 hours

The Major Oak

FREE Car park charge

www.nottinghamshire.gov.uk/countryparks

Newark Castle 437

Newark

Newark Castle sits next to the river Trent in the centre of the town. Its foundations date back to Saxon times but it was developed as a castle by the Bishop of Lincoln in 1123. The castle endured numerous sieges during the Baronial and English Civil War before it was partially destroyed in 1646. Today, visitors can take a guided tour into the castle's towers and dungeons or visit the heritage centre where there are historic exhibitions on display. The gardens have been painstakingly restored and have won a green flag award.

Newark town centre

1–2 hours

Castle where King John died

www.newark-sherwooddc.gov.uk

Wheelgate Adventure Park 438

Newark

Refurbished, renamed and with a whole range of new rides and other attractions, Wheelgate is catering for an increasing number of families each year. Centred around the huge, family-friendly play structure Pharaoh's Funderdrome, with slides, climbs, swings, bridges and giant ball pools, there's also an assault course, water fun, trampolines, mazes and other delights. Then there are the animals: some of whom live in a tropical house, others on Gruff Goat Farm and others still in the falconry centre which has impressive daily displays.

Off the A614, west of Newark

3–4 hours

World's best slides

www.wheelgatepark.com

Newark Air Museum 439

Newark

The museum is located on part of the former Second World War bomber-training base at Winthorpe. It has a diverse collection of aircraft and cockpit sections that cover the history of aviation. The impressive collection of over 60 aircraft includes transport, training and reconnaissance aircraft, helicopters, jet fighters and bombers. Highlights include De Havilland Sea Venom, a Canberra and a Hawker Hunter. In addition to the aircraft the museum displays a diverse display of aviation artefacts and a collection of more than 30 aero engines.

Near the A1, A46, A17, A1133, at Winthorpe, near Newark

2–3 hours

Bouncing bomb

www.newarkairmuseum.org

City of Caves 440

Nottingham

This attraction is part of a complex of up to 400 caves dating back to the Dark Ages, the last of which were in use until 1924. The caves were likely used for housing as early as the 11th century, and troglodytes were certainly recorded in the 17th century. Many were inhabited until 1845, when the St Mary's Enclosure Act banned the rental of cellars and caves as homes for the poor, though the practice doubtless continued in secret. Visitors can now tour the caves, which are arranged in various dedicated sections focusing on certain themes in their past.

Nottingham city centre

1–2 hours

Sam Hancock's Cave

www.cityofcaves.com

Galleries of Justice 441

Nottingham

England's history of crime and punishment is a shocking one. As are the sinister and grim stories of Nottingham's own outlaws, which are brought to life in the old courthouse and county gaol where they were judged, imprisoned and executed. To capture and explain this grim and gruesome history, the museum runs several tours using actors, audio guides, guide sheets and boards, lighting, sounds, set dressing and exhibitions. Visitors can also see a vast collection of spine chilling artefacts relating to crime and punishment over the last three centuries.

Nottingham city centre

2–3 hours

Crime and Punishment tour

www.galleriesofjustice.org.uk/

STAR ATTRACTION

Nottingham Castle 442

Nottingham

Nottingham Castle is a magnificent 17th-century ducal mansion built on the site of the original medieval castle, with spectacular views across the city. The castle has a turbulent past, linked to kings and conquerors and still has a maze of original caves hidden beneath its imposing walls. Today the castle is a vibrant museum and art gallery housing a vast collection of silver, glass, decorative items, visual arts, paintings and exhibits on Nottinghamshire archaeology and history. The gallery also brings the best regional, national and international artists' work to the city.

Nottingham city centre

2–3 hours

Interactive displays

www.nottinghamcity.gov.uk/museums

The Nottingham Experience 443

Nottingham

The Nottingham Experience was set up with the aim of helping visitors to the city get the best out of this beautiful city and surrounding countryside by providing a unique tailored service of tours to visitors whether on their own or in large groups or as corporate guests. Tours, which are designed specifically for the customer, include walking tours of the city for tourists or new students at the university. Examples of past tours include the Royal Tour of Nottingham, the Robin Hood Tour, the Sheriff's Tour, the Lace and Legend Tour, Sherwood Forest and the Major Oak Tour.

Beeston, Nottingham

4–8 hours

Your own tailored tour

See website for details

www.lifesense.org.uk

Wollaton Hall and Deer Park 444
Nottingham

Wollaton Hall is a spectacular Elizabethan mansion in the heart of Nottingham. It is a prominent Grade I listed building and following a major programme of restoration, it is open to visitors again. Built on a hill three miles west of Nottingham city centre, Wollaton Hall is set in 500 acres of spectacular gardens and parkland. In addition to the historic hall and its sumptuous grounds, visitors will find Nottingham's Natural History Museum, Nottingham's Industrial Museum and the Yard Gallery, all on the same site.

Off the A52, 3 miles west of Nottingham city centre

3–4 hours

Tudor kitchens and views from the Prospect Room

FREE Car parking charges

www.nottinghamcity.gov.uk/museums

Rufford Abbey 445
Ollerton

This ruined former Cistercian monastery was founded in the 12th century, but following its dissolution in 1536, its lands were given to George Talbot, 4th Earl of Shrewsbury. The Talbot family then went on to transform the buildings into a country house. The whole site is now set in Rufford Abbey Country Park, which also includes an exhibition on the life of Rufford's medieval monks, a camera obscura, a contemporary craft centre, gardens, woodland walks, a children's play village, sculpture trail and a lake.

Off the A614, 2 miles south of Ollerton

1–2 hours

Romantic ruins

FREE Car park may charge

www.nottinghamshire.gov.uk/ruffordcp

Bassetlaw Museum 446
Retford

Created in 1983 and set in an 18th-century townhouse, which retains many of its original features, the museum's collections include local history, archaeology, decorative and fine art, agriculture, costume and textiles. Of particular interest is the exhibition on the Pilgrim Fathers. The Separatist movement had its roots in the nearby villages of Scrooby and Babworth where Richard Clyfton was rector between 1586 and 1605. His followers included William Brewster, John Robinson and William Bradford, all of whom left aboard the *Mayflower* for the New World in 1620.

Retford town centre

1–2 hours

The story of the Pilgrim Fathers

FREE

www.bassetlawmuseum.org.uk

The Workhouse, Southwell   447

Southwell

Discover the most complete workhouse in existence. Meet the Reverend Becher, the founder of the workhouse, by watching the introductory film and immerse yourself in the unique atmosphere evoked by the audio guide. Based on real archive records, the guide helps bring the 19th-century inhabitants back to life. Discover how society dealt with poverty through the centuries. Explore the segregated work yards, dayrooms, dormitories, master's quarters and cellars, then see the recreated working 19th-century garden and find out what food the paupers would have eaten.

🔍 On the A612

✿ ◐ ♣

⌛ 1–2 hours

⭐ Hidden history of the poor

💲

www.nationaltrust.org.uk

Barnsdale Gardens   448

Exton

Made famous by BBC TV's Geoff Hamilton, Barnsdale Gardens continues to thrive as Britain's largest collection of individually designed gardens – 38 to be exact, in an 8-acre site. Described as a 'theme park for gardeners', the idea is that you will gain inspiration from this incredible range of garden styles and planting schemes. Visitors can stroll around the gardens, taking in the colours, plant types, the concepts and the designs, making a note of the ones you really like before buying them there and then at the nursery or later at the online shop.

🔍 Off the A606, near Exton

✿ ◐ ♣ ✽

⌛ 2–3 hours

⭐ Geoff Hamilton memorial garden

💲

www.barnsdalegardens.co.uk

Rutland County Museum and Visitor Centre

Oakham 449

This museum has an extensive rural life collection, which includes farm tools, tractors, a fine selection of wagons and a range of local tradesmen's tools – wheelwrights and carpenters, coopers, shoemakers and tinsmiths. The former local brewery, Ruddles, is also covered, and there is a simulation of a farm kitchen of the turn of the century. There is also an exhibition on Crime and Punishment, which includes the only surviving New Drop gallows in England. The museum garden is a beautiful place in which visitors can relax.

Oakham town centre

⚙ ⚙ ♣ ✳

⏳ 1 hour

⭐ The New Drop gallows

FREE

www.rutland.gov.uk

Rutland Water

Oakham 450

The western end of Rutland Water is now part of a nature reserve and one of the most important wildfowl sanctuaries in Great Britain. The reserve occupies a narrow strip of land running for 9 miles around the western end, covering a total of 600 acres. It has 27 bird hides and nature trails from two visitor centres with experts to help you with identification. Elsewhere on the reservoir you can take boat trips on the *Rutland Belle*, hire your own dinghy, go fishing or canoeing, or visit Normanton Church, which was saved when the reservoir was first flooded.

Off the A606

⚙ ⚙ ♣ ✳

⏳ 3–4 hours

⭐ Normanton Church

FREE Car parks and some activities charge

www.anglianwater.co.uk

Lyddington Bede House

Uppingham 451

Set beside the church of a picturesque ironstone village, Lyddington Bede House originated as the late medieval wing of a palace belonging to the Bishops of Lincoln. By 1600 it had passed to Sir Thomas Cecil, son of Queen Elizabeth's chief minister, who converted it into an almshouse for 12 poor 'bedesmen' over 30 years old and two women (over 45), all free of lunacy, leprosy or the French pox. Visitors can wander through the bedesmen's rooms, with their tiny windows and fireplaces, and view the former bishops' Great Chamber with its beautifully carved ceiling cornice.

Off A6003, near Uppingham

⚙ ⚙ ♣

⏳ 1 hour

⭐ Ceiling cornice in the Great Chamber

&

www.english-heritage.org.uk

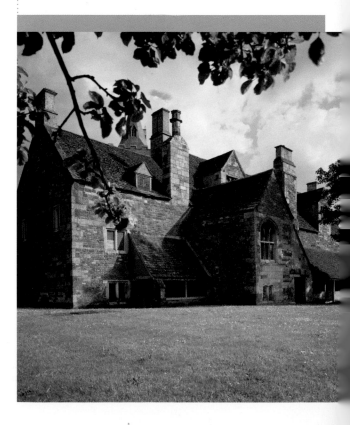

West Midlands

Herefordshire
Shropshire
Staffordshire
Warwickshire
West Midlands
Worcestershire

Bullring, Birmingham

Guide to the West Midlands

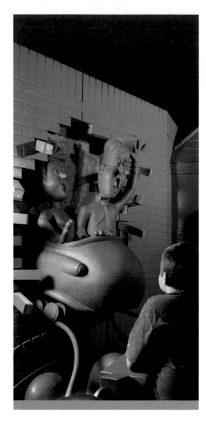

Brockhampton Estate   452
Bromyard

At the heart of this 1,700-acre estate lies Lower Brockhampton, a timber-framed manor house dating back to the late 1300s. The house is surrounded by a moat and entered via a timber-framed gatehouse. A rush-fringed pool on the edge of the parkland is a wonderful place to relax and savour the tranquil setting. In spring the surrounding damson trees produce a profusion of white blossom. Visitors can follow the Ash Walk to discover not only the elegant ash trees, but also the wonderful old oak trees, some of which were planted around the time of Henry VIII.

🔍 On the A44, 2 miles east of Bromyard
❁ ◉ ☘
⏳ 1 hour
⭐ Beautiful woodland walks
💷
www.nationaltrust.org.uk

Cider Museum   454
Hereford

Visit Hereford's famous Cider Museum and learn about the history of cider making – how the apples were milled and pressed and how the resulting juice was fermented to produce cider. Set in a former cider-making factory, visitors can explore original cider-champagne cellars and view cider-making equipment, a cooper's workshop and a vat house. Listen to oral history recordings and view 19th-century watercolours of cider apples and perry pears and appreciate the delicately engraved collection of English lead crystal cider glasses dating from the 18th century onwards.

🔍 In Hereford town centre
❁ ◉ ☘ ❄
⏳ 1–2 hours
⭐ Original cider-champagne cellars
💷
www.cidermuseum.co.uk

Time Machine Dr Who Museum   453
Bromyard

This small museum, based around a collection of science fiction TV and film memorabilia, has had such a success with its Dr Who exhibition that it has been refurbished and renamed in the Doctor's honour. It now includes new displays of BBC props, monsters and costumes from *Dr Who* from its beginnings in the 1960s right up to 2008. Visitors will come face to face with screen used Daleks, Cybermen, the Ood, Clockwork Droid, Silurian, K9, Zygon and others. There are also exhibits on *Star Wars*, *Red Dwarf*, Gerry Anderson and others.

🔍 On the A44, in Bromyard town centre
❁ ◉ ☘ ❄
⏳ 2–3 hours
⭐ The Daleks
💷
www.timemachineuk.com

Hereford Cathedral and the Mappa Mundi

455

Hereford

Standing on the peaceful banks of the beautiful River Wye, Hereford Cathedral occupies a site used for worship since Saxon times. The cathedral contains some of the finest examples of architecture from Norman times up to the present day, including the beautifully restored Shrine of St Thomas of Hereford. Housed within the Cathedral's 15th-century, south-west cloister is an exhibition that uses models and original artefacts to reveal the secrets of the Mappa Mundi, the largest and most elaborate complete pre-15th-century world map in existence.

Q Hereford town centre

✳ ◯ ♣ ❄

⏳ 2 hours

★ Mappa Mundi

£

www.herefordcathedral.org

The Old House

456

Hereford

The Old House is a remarkably well-preserved example of a 17th-century timber-framed building in the heart of Hereford. It is a startling sight, standing as the sole reminder of times-gone-by in the middle of a modern shopping precinct. Built in 1621, the house started life as a butcher's home and shop and finished as a bank in the late 1920s. Since 1929 it has been a museum of daily life in Jacobean times. It is furnished in period style with a marvellous collection of English oak furniture and there are interesting pieces in every room.

Q Hereford city centre

✳ ◯ ♣

⏳ 1 hour

★ Wall paintings

FREE Car parking charges

www.herefordshire.gov.uk/leisure

The Weir

457

Hereford

This unusual riverside garden of 10 acres, created in the 1920s, has sweeping views along the River Wye and the Black Mountains. It has been managed to create a varied habitat for a wide range of wildlife, and the garden is spectacular all year round – as drifts of spring bulbs give way to wild flowers, followed by autumn colour. A late 18th-century house (not open to the public) sits on top of steep slopes that fall away to the river. A walled garden has recently been opened to the public

Q Signposted from the A438, 5 miles west of Hereford

✳ ◯ ♣

⏳ 1-2 hours

★ Delightful walks through beech woodland high above the river

£

www.nationaltrust.org.uk

Eastnor Castle

458

Ledbury

This fairytale castle in the dramatic setting of the Malvern Hills is surrounded by a beautiful deer park, arboretum and lake. Visitors can tour the Great Hall, the Red Hall, the State Dining room and Gothic Drawing rooms and other impressive rooms decorated in Victorian and Edwardian styles with portraits, paintings, mirrors and a collection of medieval armour. Other attractions include the knight's maze, an assault course and pretty lakeside and woodland paths in the deer park in which there is a regular programme of special events during the summer months.

Q On the A438, 2 miles from Ledbury

✳ ◯ ♣

⏳ 2-3 hours

★ The Giant Redwood grove

£

www.eastnorcastle.com

Hampton Court Castle and Gardens 459

Leominster

Hampton Court is a castle on the meadows of the River Lugg, backed by a steep wooded escarpment and surrounded by woodland and grounds of 1,000 acres. Founded by King Henry in the early 15th century the castle has been completely restored. The panelled dining room is particularly impressive. The gardens are spectacular and, although a recent development, are now receiving national recognition. Water features highly here and there are canals, island pavilions, a waterfall, a sunken garden and two spectacular walled gardens.

On the A417, near the junction with the A49

2–3 hours

The 1,000-yew maze

www.hamptoncourt.org.uk

Goodrich Castle 460

Ross-on-Wye

Goodrich stands majestically on a wooded hill commanding the passage of the River Wye into the picturesque valley of Symonds Yat. The castle was begun in the late 11th century by the English thane Godric who gave it his name. Goodrich still boasts one of the most complete sets of medieval domestic buildings surviving in any English castle. During the Civil War, Goodrich was the scene of a series of sieges but eventually surrendered in 1646 under threats from 'Roaring Meg, a deadly Parliamentarian mortar. The visitor centre features an exhibition exploring life at the castle.

Off the A40, 5 miles south of Ross on Wye

2–3 hours

'Roaring Meg'

www.english-heritage.org.uk

Amazing Hedge Puzzle   `461`

Symonds Yat

Planted over 20 years ago by brothers Lindsay and
Edward Hayes, the fun of the Amazing Hedge Puzzle
has made it one of Herefordshire's most popular tourist
attractions. As well as finding your way through the
Jubilee Maze's 12 routes and 13 dead-ends; visitors can
also see the world's first permanent exhibition dedicated
to the history of mazes. There are also other maze-based
attractions, exhibits and puzzles. If you think you know
about mazes and how to solve them, a visit here will
make you change your mind.

🔍 Follow signs from the B4164

✷ ◎ ❖

⧗ 1–2 hours

★ Jubilee Maze

£

www.mazes.co.uk

Boscobel House and the   `462`
Royal Oak

Bishop's Wood

Boscobel was built in 1632, when John Giffard
converted a timber-framed farmhouse into a hunting
lodge. The Giffards were Roman Catholics at a time
when the religion suffered persecution. Following the
execution of Charles I in 1649, his eldest son was forced
to flee for his life. He sought refuge at Boscobel, hiding
in a tree, now known as the Royal Oak, and then
spending the night in a priest-hole in the attic before
escaping. Visitors can now see the dairy, farmyard,
smithy, gardens and a descendant of the Royal Oak.

🔍 On a minor road from the A41 to the A5

✷ ◎ ❖

⧗ 2–3 hours

★ The future King Charles II hiding places

£

www.english-heritage.org.uk

Severn Valley Railway   `463`

Bridgenorth

This full-size standard-gauge line runs regular steam-
hauled passenger trains between Bridgenorth and
Kidderminster, a distance of 16 miles. For most of the
way the route follows the meandering course of the
River Severn. The train stops at Hampton Lode, Highley
(where you can visit a superb collection of steam
locomotives and other railway artefacts and take in
some stunning view of the Severn Valley), Arley,
Bewdley and Kidderminster. The train crosses the famous
cast-iron arch bridge between Arley and Bewdley.

🔍 You can join the train at any of the stations

✷ ◎ ❖ ❄ See website for timetables

⧗ 3–4 hours

★ The station gardens

£ £

www.svr.co.uk

Secret Hills – Shropshire Hills Discovery Centre `465`
Craven Arms

This is the perfect place to start an exploration of the Shropshire Hills; the Secret Hills exhibition dips into the stories of the area and gives you endless ideas for places to visit. You can find out about the Ice Age and see a full-size replica of the Mammoth skeleton found at Condover, near Shrewsbury. You'll get a flavour of life in the Iron Age and discover the story of some of Shropshire's many medieval castles. You'll also see some of the people, places and products that continue to make the Shropshire Hills such a special place to visit.

Off the A49, 7 miles north of Ludlow

2-3 hours

Panoramic film shot from a hot air balloon

www.shropshire.gov.uk/shropshirehills.nsf

Acton Scott `464`
Church Stretton

Tucked away in the Shropshire Hills is the Acton Scott estate where visitors can experience life on a traditional 19th-century Victorian farm. Recently featured on BBC TV's *Victorian Farm* series, the estate offers a tremendous day out as well as short-stay holidays. Visitors see heavy horses working the land with vintage farm machines and milkmaids milking by hand and making butter in the dairy. The museum also holds a number of special events throughout the year, including sheep shearing, lambing, cider making and steam powered threshing.

Follow signs from the A49 at Marshbrook

3-4 hours

Tour of the Glebe farmstead

www.actonscott.com

Stokesay Castle `466`
Craven Arms

Stokesay Castle is a remarkable survivor, a fortified manor house that has hardly altered since the late 13th century. The house was built by Lawrence Ludlow, a leading wool merchant of his day, who created a comfortable residence with some defensive capabilities. In doing so, he took advantage of the newly established peace on the Welsh border following Edward I's defeat of the Welsh prince Llywelyn the Last. There is an audio tour to help visitors imagine Stokesay as the centre of local life in medieval times. Its grounds include cottage-style gardens and a moat walk.

On the A49, 1 mile from Craven Arms

1-2 hours

The Great Hall

www.english-heritage.org.uk

Ludlow Castle 467

Ludlow

Ludlow Castle is one of the finest medieval ruins in Britain, set in glorious Shropshire countryside at the heart of this bustling market town. Visitors can walk through the castle grounds, see the ancient houses of kings, queens, princes, judges and the nobility, and get a glimpse into the lifestyle of medieval society. Originally built to hold back the unconquered Welsh, the castle was abandoned in 1689. Since 1811 the castle has been owned by the Earls of Powis, who have arrested further decline, and allowed this magnificent historical monument to be open to the public.

In Ludlow town centre

1 hour

Spring festival

www.ludlowcastle.com

Wollerton Old Hall Garden 468

Market Drayton

Wollerton Old Hall Garden is a four-acre plantsman's garden developed around a 16th-century house (not open to the public) in rural Shropshire. It has developed into an important modern garden in the English garden tradition with echoes of Arts and Crafts. The strong formal design has created a number of separate gardens, each with its own character, and which use many rare and unusual plants to see. There is much in the garden for the plant enthusiast and the garden is bursting with design ideas. The range of plants is very wide resulting in significant collections of clematis, salvias, phlox and roses.

Follow signs from the A53 between the A41 junction at Tern Hill and Hodnet

Weekends only

2–3 hours

Lanhydrock Garden in summer

www.wollertonoldhallgarden.com

The RAF Museum Cosford 469

Shifnal

The RAF Museum Cosford tells the story of man's successes and failures in flying and missile development from the early days of aviation through two world wars to the present day. It houses one of the largest aviation collections in the UK, featuring over 80 historical aircraft, and one of the world's most comprehensive missile collections. You can examine more than 40 different aeroplane engines, from the rotary used in early biplanes, to the jet engine, which powers the modern Eurofighter. There is also a small collection of motor vehicles associated with both civil and military aircraft support.

Follow signs from the A41

3–4 hours

Cold War exhibition

FREE Car park charges

www.rafmuseum.org

Weston Park House and Gardens 470

Shifnal

Weston Park was built in 1671 and is set in glorious parkland with formal gardens and woodland walks. A favourite of Disraeli and P.G. Wodehouse, who used Weston as his inspiration for Blanding's Castle, today Weston can equally accommodate a summit of world leaders, yesteryear rallies, game fairs and even the annual V Festival. There's a miniature railway, adventure playground, auditorium, bars and restaurants but many prefer simply to take a gentle stroll around the park and admire the views.

On the A5, at Weston-under-Lizard

2–3 hours

Astonishing collection of fine art

www.weston-park.com

Attingham Park
471

Shrewsbury

Attingham Park was built for the 1st Lord Berwick in 1785 and was in continuous ownership by the family for more than 160 years. In the mansion – one of the great houses of the Midlands – highlights include the atmospheric Dining Room set for an evening banquet that reflects the Regency splendour, and the delicate decorative scheme in the Boudoir, which has recently been revealed. The mansion is at the heart of this great estate between Shrewsbury and the River Severn and is set in beautiful parkland.

On the B4380, 4 miles south-east of Shrewsbury

2–3 hours

Italian furniture

www.nationaltrust.org.uk

Hawkstone Historic Park and Follies
472

Shrewsbury

Created in the 18th century by the Hill family, Hawkstone is one of the greatest historic parklands in Europe. Centred around the Red Castle and the awe-inspiring Grotto Hill, it offers visitors hours of delight and stunning views of the Shropshire countryside and beyond. Hawkstone Follies is a historic parkland that covers 100 acres. Intricate pathways, ravines, arches and bridges, the towering cliffs and follies, the hermit in his hermitage and King Arthur addressing his troops in the awesome caves combine to create a magical visit.

Off the A49

3–4 hours

Tunnels and caves (bring a torch)

www.shropshiretourism.co.uk

Wroxeter Roman City
473

Shrewsbury

Wroxeter (or 'Viroconium') was the fourth largest city in Roman Britain. It began as a legionary fortress and later developed into a thriving civilian city. In February 1859 workmen began excavating and the site was soon thronged with fascinated visitors, including Charles Dickens. Wroxeter thus became one of the first archaeological visitor attractions in Britain. The most impressive features are the 2nd-century municipal baths, and the remains of the huge wall dividing them from the exercise hall. A museum reveals how Wroxeter worked in its heyday, and the health and beauty practices of its 5,000 citizens.

On the B4380, 5 miles east of Shrewsbury

1–2 hours

Ancient Roman city life

www.english-heritage.org.uk

Wroxeter Roman Vineyard
474

Shrewsbury

Wroxeter Roman Vineyard was planted in 1991. It nestles in the foothills of the Wrekin on a sandy plateau of the Roman city of Viroconium, enjoying a special microclimate. Visitors are welcome to stroll around the vineyards to soak up the atmosphere of this peaceful place, although conducted tours include an explanation of the history of the location and the vineyards and wine growing, as well as a visit to the winery, a look at the equipment used and tutored tastings. Tours must be booked in advance (see website).

On the B4380, 4 miles east of Shrewsbury

2–3 hours

Award-winning English wine

Tours cost extra

www.wroxetervineyard.co.uk

Alton Towers has pretty much cornered the market in terms of **thrilling, scary rides**.

Ironbridge Gorge Museums   475

Telford

There are ten award-winning museums spread along what is often called 'the valley that changed the world'. That valley, beside the River Severn, is still spanned by the world's first iron bridge. It was here that the Industrial Revolution started in the early 1700s. Though peaceful now, the valley was once filled with smoke, fire and blast furnaces, bearing the first iron rails, wheels, boats, the first steam locomotive, as well as the first iron bridge. Visitors today can see the products that set industry on its path and the machines that made them.

🔍 Follow signs from junction 4 of the M54

⌛ 3-4 hours

⭐ Blists Hill Victorian town

www.ironbridge.org.uk

Wonderland   476

Telford

A theme park especially for families with very small children, Wonderland features a series of walks that lead you through the world of fairytales where children can find their favourite characters and their houses around every corner. The characters come to life to tell stories and sing songs. The park is set in beautiful woodlands and also features a maze, a dinosaur valley where you can dig for dinosaur eggs, a diamond mine and crazy golf. There are also gentle rides and a giant indoor play area.

🔍 Follow signs from junctions 4 and 5 of the M54

⌛ 1-2 hours

⭐ The Wonderland Maze

www.wonderlandtelford.com

Alton Towers   477

Alton

FIVE-STAR ATTRACTION

The biggest, best and most famous theme park in the UK, Alton Towers has pretty much cornered the market in terms of thrilling, scary rides. All the latest rides are here – Thirteen, the Blade, Nemesis (see left), Air – where the lying-down riding position makes you feel like you're flying – Oblivion, the world's first vertical drop coaster and Rita Queen of Speed, which accelerates from 0 to100 kph in 2.5 seconds.

But there are also lots of attractions for families and those in search of slightly more sedate entertainment, including the Congo River Rapids, and Hex – The Legend of the Towers. Or you can climb aboard the Runaway Mine Train for a small child-friendly rollercoaster, or fight with ghosts and ghouls in Duel.

Little ones can have fun too with the huge selection of kiddie-friendly rides including the Squirrel Nutty Ride, which takes you on a trip through the treetops, and the Charlie and the Chocolate Factory. Kids can even learn to drive at the Peugeot Driving School, or get to know some farm animals on the Doodle Doo Derby.

The whole park is set in 200 acres of landscape gardens, with live entertainment and the historic Towers building.

🔍 Follow signs from junctions 23a or 28 of the M1

⌛ 6-8 hours

⭐ Thirteen

💷 💷 💷 Book online to save money

www.altontowers.com

Sudbury Hall
Ashbourne

478

The country home of the Lords Vernon is a delight of 17th-century craftsmanship, featuring exquisite plasterwork, woodcarvings and classical story-based murals. Be amazed by the grandeur of the Great Staircase and Long Gallery. The Hall is also home to the Museum of Childhood, which is a delight for all ages. Visitors can explore the childhoods of times gone by, make stories, play with toys and share your childhood with others. You can be a chimney sweep, a scullion or a Victorian pupil, and be captivated by some archive film, interactives and other displays.

🔍 Near junction of the A50 and the A515
✿ ☉ ❦
⌛ 2–3 hours
★ Guided tour of the house
♿
www.nationaltrust.org.uk

Biddulph Grange Garden
Biddulph

479

This unusual Victorian garden was created by James Bateman for his collection of plants from around the world. A visit takes you on a global journey from Italy to the pyramids of Egypt, a Victorian vision of China and a recreation of a Himalayan glen. The garden features rhododendrons, summer bedding displays, a stunning dahlia walk in late summer and the oldest surviving golden larch in Britain, brought from China in the 1850s. The Geological Gallery shows how Bateman reconciled geology and theology, allowing the visitor to travel through time as the gallery depicts the creation story.

🔍 Off the A527
✿ ☉ ❦
⌛ 1–2 hours
★ Egyptian obelisks made of yew
♿
www.nationaltrust.org.uk

Ceramica
Burslem

480

Ceramica was set up in the Old Town Hall in Burslem at the turn of the millennium to commemorate the glory of the Potteries. The museum will show you every step it takes to make a pot, from clay, to firing, to the finished product. Visitors can see the kiln that Josiah Wedgwood used to fire the first Wedgwood plates, learn about the life of a potter and have a go at throwing your own pot on a potter's wheel. An extensive set of other displays presents the past, present and future of the ceramics industry.

🔍 Burslem town centre
✿ ☉ ❦ ❄
⌛ 1–2 hours
★ Josiah Wedgwood's kiln
♿
www.ceramicauk.com

The National Brewery Centre
Burton upon Trent

481

The National Brewery Centre is a world-class museum and visitor centre that celebrates Burton upon Trent's brewing heritage. Visitors are taken through the story of brewing, from ancient times through to the latest methods – using actors, animatronics, holographics and multi-media technology. You'll be able to see a microbrewery at work, meet the famous Shire horses and browse through a museum that includes many brewing artefacts, a vintage vehicle collection and working steam engine. Over 18s can take part in a beer-tasting master class and a tour around the site.

🔍 In Burton-on-Trent town centre
✿ ☉ ❦ ❄
⌛ 2–3 hours
★ Pepper's Ghost
♿
www.nationalbrewerycentre.co.uk

Halfpenny Green Vineyards   482

Halfpenny Green

Visitors are welcome at one of the largest vineyards in the country. Individuals or small groups can follow the self-guided vineyard trail. This follows a relaxing route through the vineyard. Information boards describe many of the French, German and hybrid grape varieties planted. Guided tours are also available during which you can also inspect the state-of-the-art winery, enjoy a tutored wine tasting and film show, then eat a cream tea, a cold buffet lunch or evening meal. There is an on-site shop where visitors can taste and buy the wines at a discount price.

Off the B4176

1–2 hours

Award-winning British wines

Cold buffet costs extra

www.halfpenny-green-vineyards.co.uk

Erasmus Darwin's House   483

Lichfield

This elegant 18th-century house, near Lichfield Cathedral, was home to Erasmus Darwin, a renowned doctor, philosopher, inventor, scientist and poet, and grandfather of Charles Darwin. Period furnishings, an audio-visual presentation and interactive displays tell the story of this remarkable man. He lived, practised medicine and conducted scientific experiments in the house from 1758 until 1781. A founder member of the Lunar Society, it was here that he received many famous 18th-century characters including Josiah Wedgwood, Matthew Boulton, Benjamin Franklin and James Watt.

Lichfield town centre

1 hour

Erasmus' Study

www.erasmusdarwin.org

Letocetum Roman Baths and Museum

484

Lichfield

This was an important staging post or *mansio* on Watling Street, the Roman military road to North Wales. It provided overnight accommodation and a change of horse for travelling Roman officials and imperial messengers. The foundations of an inn and bathhouse can be seen, and many of the excavated finds are displayed in an on-site museum.

On the A5 in Wall, 3 miles south of Lichfield

1 hour

Fascinating Roman artefacts

FREE

www.english-heritage.org.uk

Gladstone Pottery Museum

485

Longton

Gladstone is the only complete Victorian pottery factory from the days when coal-burning ovens made the world's finest bone china. Explore the cobbled yard, with huge bottle kilns, sit in the waiting room of the Doctor's House and find out about diseases such as potters' rot that so afflicted workers in this industry, then visit the consulting rooms and Victorian kitchen. The museum also offers a range of group visit options including guided tours, Art Deco pottery painting and bone china flower-making workshops.

Longton town centre

2 hours

Famous bottle kilns

www.stoke.gov.uk

Shugborough Estate

486

Milford

The mysterious Shugborough Estate is the ancestral home of the Earls of Lichfield. With rumoured connections to the Holy Grail, the 900-acre landscape is peppered with unusual monuments. The fine Georgian house, with magnificent views over riverside garden terraces, includes a stunning collection of porcelain. Costumed characters work in the servants' quarters and farmstead: doing laundry, cheesemaking, milling, brewing and baking. The Estate includes reconstructed shops, Victorian schoolroom and puppet collection. The newly restored walled garden grows historic varieties of fruit and vegetables.

Follow signs from junction 13 of the M6

2–3 hours

Widest tree in Europe

www.shugborough.org.uk

British Wildlife Rescue Centre   488
Stafford

The British Wildlife Rescue Centre was set up as an extension of Stafford Wild Bird and Animal Rescue. It consists of a hospital with veterinary cover, a pool for the rehabilitation of water birds, spacious aviaries and enclosures and housing for reptiles. The centre cares for sick, injured and orphaned wildlife, which is often brought in by members of the public and the RSPCA. It is also home to a number of unwanted/mistreated pets such as rabbits, guinea pigs and sometimes gerbils and ferrets who stay there before being re-housed.

On the A518, at Stowe by Chartley near Stafford

1–2 hours

Fox enclosure

www.britishwildliferescue.co.uk

Ancient High House   487
Stafford

The Ancient High House is one of the finest Tudor buildings in the country. Once dominating the skyline of Stafford, it is the largest remaining timber framed town house in England. Royalty was welcomed to the house in 1642 when King Charles I and Prince Rupert stayed there en route to Shrewsbury, and the house retains an extensive collection of period furniture and architectural features in a series of spectacular rooms with period settings. It is also the home of the Staffordshire Yeomanry Museum.

Stafford town centre

1 hour

The Civil War Room

FREE   Some exhibitions may charge

www.staffordbc.gov.uk

Stafford Castle   489
Stafford

In the years shortly after the Norman invasion of 1066, William the Conqueror is believed to have ordered defences to be built here against a still hostile and rebellious native community. An existing timber fortress was rebuilt as a motte and bailey castle, a building that has dominated the Stafford skyline for 900 years. Ransacked by the Parliamentarians during the Civil War, the castle's fortunes have waxed and waned throughout history. Today a Visitor Centre relates its fascinating history with a display of arms, armour and costumes.

Off the A518, 1 mile south-west of Stafford

2–3 hours

Medieval herb garden

FREE   Some exhibitions may charge

www.staffordbc.gov.uk

Etruria Industrial Museum 490
Stoke-on-Trent

Etruria Industrial Museum is the last steam-powered potter's mill in Britain. The mill is 'in steam' seven times a year when the 1903 boiler is fired and historic machinery can be seen working. Situated on the Caldon, Trent and Mersey canals, the museum also includes a bone and flint Mill (used to make the raw materials for bone china), a 1903 coal-fired boiler engine called the 'Princess', a hands-on, interactive science gallery, a forge and a canal check office. It's also a great place to watch local wildfowl and nature.

🔍 Follow signs from the A500

✿ ◉ ♣

⧗ 1–2 hours

★ Mill 'in steam' (see website for details)

&

www.stoke.gov.uk

Wedgwood Visitor Centre and Museum 491
Stoke-on-Trent

Wedgwood is a name recognised instantly around the world. Josiah Wedgwood, the 'Father of English Potters', founded the company in 1759. This site offers a unique chance to immerse yourself in the heritage of Britain's greatest ceramics company. The award-winning facilities combine 250 years of history, craftsmanship and creativity into a rich experience for visitors, including a crafts skills demonstration area, stunning museum galleries, a fine art collection and excellent shopping facilities.

🔍 Follow signs from junction 15 of the M6

✿ ◉ ♣ ✳

⧗ 3–4 hours

★ Make or decorate your own pot

&

www.wedgwoodvisitorcentre.com

STAR ATTRACTION

Kinver Edge and the Rock Houses 492
Stourbridge

Kinver Edge is a hill ridge created from sand when this area was a desert over 200 million years ago. For centuries people dug here to create their homes, the last cave dwellers only moved out in the 1950s. One of the rock houses has been restored so you can imagine living here in Victorian times. It is now a popular spot for walking, with lots of open heath and woodland to explore. At the top of Kinver Edge is an Iron Age hill fort where you can enjoy fantastic panoramas over at least three counties.

🔍 Off the A458 or the A449, 4 miles west of Stourbridge

✿ ◉ ♣ ✳

⧗ 1–2 hours

★ Houses of Britain's last cave dwellers

&

www.nationaltrust.org.uk

Drayton Manor Theme Park | 494
Tamworth

Packed with a host of great rides and attractions and set in 280 acres of lakes and parkland, Drayton Manor features some of the biggest, wettest and scariest rides around. Apocalypse is the world's first stand up tower drop, Shockwave is Europe's only stand up rollercoaster, Stormforce 10 is 'the best water ride in the country', Maelstrom is the only gyro swing to make you face outwards and Pandemonium turns your world upside down. There's a host of other rides too, a 4D cinema, Excalibur the Drunken Barrels and a small zoo at this family fun park.

🔍 On the A4091, near Tamworth

⚙ ◉ ♣

⏳ 3-4 hours

★ 4D cinema

💷 💷 💷

www.draytonmanor.co.uk

The Snowdome | 493
Tamworth

Billed as 'the Ultimate Snow, Ice and Leisure Experience', that phrase pretty much sums up the Snowdome. As well as skiing and snowboarding, you can career down the slopes on inflatable tubes, do some ice-skating and even try your hand at driving a snow mobile. With real snow all year round, a 170-metre main slope and other training slopes, this is a great place for serious skiers and for those who want to build snowmen or have a snowball fight. Warm clothing and gloves are essential for all slope users.

🔍 Follow signs from junction 10 of the M42

⚙ ◉ ♣ ❄

⏳ 2-4 hours

★ Adrenalin tubing

💷 💷

www.snowdome.co.uk

Tutbury Castle | 495
Tutbury

Built in the 1070s for one of William the Conqueror's barons, Tutbury Castle has been involved in some of the most dramatic events in English history. Built on the banks of the River Dove, the ruins of this once impressive castle still dominate the historic village of Tutbury in which it stands. A bloody place of siege and battle, the castle played host to Henry VIII, Anne Boleyn and acted as a prison for Mary Queen of Scots. The castle is located on a picturesque knoll that provides expansive views into the Dove Valley.

🔍 Near the A50, take junction 24a from the M1 or junction 15 from the M6

⚙ ◉ ♣

⏳ 2-3 hours

★ The Great Hall

💷

www.tutburycastle.com

Blackbrook Zoological Park `496`
Winkhill

This charming little zoo is home to one of the largest wildfowl collections in Europe as well as a thriving colony of meerkats. The meerkat clan is always popular with visitors who can listen to daily talks about their feeding and way of life. However, they are just one example of the many species represented on the list of residents. At the gate you are likely to be met by one or more of the zoo's magnificent peacocks. Move further into the complex and you will come upon large flocks of geese, swans, pelicans, graceful storks, flamingos, penguins, reptiles, lemurs and others.

Off the A523, near Leek

3-4 hours

Meerkats

www.blackbrookzoo.co.uk

Moseley Old Hall `497`
Wolverhampton

This atmospheric Elizabethan farmhouse conceals a priest's hole and hiding places, in one of which Charles II hid after the Battle of Worcester in 1651. The bed on which the royal fugitive slept is also on view. Follow the story of the King's dramatic escape from Cromwell's troops and find out about 17th-century domestic life in this historic home. In 2010, enjoy the 350th anniversary celebrations of the restoration of the monarchy. The garden has varieties of plants in keeping with the period and has a striking knot garden following a 17th-century design.

Between the A449 and A460, 4 miles north of Wolverhampton

2-3 hours

Guided tours

www.nationaltrust.org.uk

Coughton Court `498`
Alcester

This beautiful Tudor house has been the home of the Throckmorton family since 1409. Coughton Court still has many original features including the 16th-century gate tower. It is one of the last remaining Roman Catholic houses in the country to retain its historic treasures and houses one of the very best collections of portraits and memorabilia of one family from the early Tudor times. Alongside family items on display, there are pieces such as the chemise reputedly worn by Mary Queen of Scots when she was executed and a bishop's cope believed to have been worked on by Catherine of Aragon.

On the A435, 2 miles north of Alcester

2-3 hours

The Gunpowder Plot story

www.coughtoncourt.co.uk

Upton House and Gardens 500
Banbury

Join the guests of Lord and Lady Bearsted at the weekend house party of a 1930s millionaire. Surrounded by the internationally important art and porcelain collections, hear and discover more about family life and join in the atmosphere. See the red and silver art deco bathroom and get close to artworks by El Greco, Stubbs and Bosch. The stunning gardens – being returned to their 1930s heyday – consist of a sweeping lawn, giving way to a series of terraces and herbaceous borders leading to a kitchen garden, tranquil water garden and the National Collection of Asters.

On the A422, 7 miles north-west of Banbury

1–2 hours

Fabulous collection of paintings

www.nationaltrust.org.uk

Twycross Zoo 499
Atherstone

Twycross is the leading primate zoo in the country but also houses hundreds of other animals from around the world, including elephants, big cats – including the Amur leopard – birds, reptiles and amphibians. Set in 50 acres of parkland, the zoo is home to 1,000 or so animals, most of which are endangered species. Its world famous primate collection ranges from tiny pygmy marmosets to the impressive silverback western lowland gorillas. Twycross is the only UK zoo to house mankind's 'closest relative' – the Bonobo.

On the A444, near Atherstone

3–4 hours

Himalaya

www.twycrosszoo.org

Brandon Marsh Nature Centre 501
Coventry

A visit to the Brandon Marsh Nature Centre should begin at the visitor centre, opened by Sir David Attenborough in 1998. This contains displays, hands-on activities and information useful for all visitors. Brandon Marsh is a 200-acre nature reserve and Site of Special Scientific Interest on the banks of the River Avon. Once an active sand and gravel quarry, the site is now a tranquil series of pools and wetlands, with nature trails and bird hides. Depending on when you visit you could see migrating waders, breeding warblers or year-round residents like kingfisher, coot or moorhen.

Off the A45, 3 miles south-east of Coventry

2–3 hours

Onyx Nature Trail

www.warwickshire-wildlife-trust.org.uk

Coventry Transport Museum   502

Coventry

Coventry is the birthplace of the British cycle and motor
industry. Discover the fascinating story behind the
development of road transport from the earliest cycles
to land speed record breakers. With thrills, nostalgia,
inspiration and a little bit of education, visitors can take
a surprising and emotional journey through 150 years
of innovation and find out about the people who made
it happen. With over 240 cars, commercial vehicles and
buses, 94 motorcycles, 200 cycles, 25,000 models and
around one million archive and ephemera items, visitors
have a lot to see and do.

🔍 Coventry city centre
⚙ ◎ 🍁 ❄
⏳ 2–3 hours
⭐ Thrust SSC (which reached c.763mph in 1997)
FREE

www.transport-museum.com

STAR ATTRACTION

Lunt Roman Fort   503

Coventry

The Lunt is a turf and timber Roman fort near Coventry.
It's AD 60; the Iceni of East Anglia, led by the legendary
Boudica, have rebelled against Roman rule, and have
just been defeated in a terrible battle fought somewhere
in the Midlands. As a result the Romans are building
a series of fortifications across the Midlands including
the Lunt. Come and explore this partially reconstructed
timber fort. Stand on the ramparts, explore the exhibition
in the granary and imagine yourself training horses in
the gyrus – a feature not found anywhere else in the
Roman Empire.

🔍 On the A45, the southern edge of Coventry
⚙ ◎ 🍁
⏳ 1 hour
⭐ Museum of Roman army life
♿

www.luntromanfort.org

Heritage Motor Centre 504
Gaydon

The centre features the world's largest collection of historic British cars, including names that have made Coventry famous – MG, Triumph, Land Rover and Jaguar. There are over 200 cars on display, charting the history of the British car industry from the turn of the century to the present day. It features interactive displays, as well as outside activities: go-karts, 4x4 off road driving skills and guided tours. There is also a nature trail and a picnic and play area.

🔍 Follow signs from junction 12 of the M40
✿ ◉ 🍁 ❄
⌛ 2–3 hours
★ Veteran cars
♿
www.heritage-motor-centre.co.uk

Henley-in-Arden Heritage Centre 505
Henley-in-Arden

The history of this charming town is recorded in its oldest house, parts of which have been dated back to 1345. What has now become the town's information centre also has exhibits including a model of the Norman castle that once stood on the mount, a history of the ancient market cross, the traditions of the local town criers, transport and trade, school and home. Visitors can also learn about the tradition of the town's ancient Court Leet, still an instrument of local government.

🔍 Henley-in-Arden town centre
✿ ◉ 🍁
⌛ 1 hour
★ The Crown Post
FREE Donations appreciated
www.heritagehenley.org.uk

The Saxon Sanctuary 506
Henley-in-Arden

Possibly the oldest building in Shakespeare Country, St Peter's, Wootton Wawen, has a Saxon tower and 'sanctuary' dating back to the 10th century or earlier. The minster's extraordinary mixture or architectural styles, complete with medieval glass and wall painting, provides an evocative venue for the 'Forest of Arden' exhibition in the Lady Chapel, which traces the history of the woodland village. A colourful handbook includes maps of spectacular local walks through history. The Ancient Britons first settled here, because they thought this was a sacred place. Today, Wootton Wawen still has its very own ambience.

🔍 On the A3400
✿ ◉ 🍁 ❄
⌛ 1 hour
★ Paintings by Philip Shepherd RWS
FREE
www.saxonsanctuary.org.uk

Kenilworth Castle and Elizabethan Garden 507
Kenilworth

Kenilworth Castle is one of most spectacular castle ruins in England. A day out for the whole family, Kenilworth Castle in Warwickshire is set in vast grounds perfect for exploring. It is best known as the home of Robert Dudley, the great love of Queen Elizabeth I. Dudley created an ornate palace here to impress his beloved Queen in 1575. The newly recreated Elizabethan Garden, lost for 400 years, is now open to visitors. A paradise for garden lovers, wander through this sumptuous landscape as Queen Elizabeth I would have done herself.

🔍 Kenilworth town centre
✿ ◉ 🍁 ❄
⌛ 2–3 hour
★ Walks to Old Kenilworth and its ruined abbey
♿
www.english-heritage.org.uk

Compton Verney Art Gallery 508
Kineton

Compton Verney offers a unique opportunity to view art in the setting of a Robert Adam house located in 120 acres of spectacular 'Capability' Brown parkland. There are six permanent collections: the 'Golden Age' of Neapolitan art 1600-1800; Germanic paintings and sculptures 1450-1650; British Portraits; Chinese bronzes; British folk art; and the Marx-Lambert collection of popular art. There is also a programme of international temporary exhibitions, supported by a diverse range of events, talks, tours and workshops.

🔍 Off the B4086, between Kineton and Stratford-upon-Avon
❀ ☼ ❧
⏳ 2-3 hours
⭐ Chinese bronzes
💷
www.comptonverney.org.uk

Baddesley Clinton 509
Knowle

This atmospheric moated manor house dates from the 15th century and was the home of the Ferrers family for 500 years. The house has a spectacular great hall, parlour and library and its interiors reflect its heyday in the Elizabethan era, when it was a haven for persecuted Catholics – there are three priest's holes hidden among the panelling. The house has extensive formal gardens and ponds, with many of the farm buildings dating back to the 18th century. St Michael's church, which shares much history with the house, is just a few hundred yards up a lane.

🔍 Off the A4141, 2 miles south of Knowle
❀ ☼ ❧
⏳ 1-2 hours
⭐ Priest's holes
💷
www.nationaltrust.org.uk

194

The Rollright Stones 510
Long Compton

The Rollright Stones is an ancient site located on top of a chalk ridge. The complex consists of three main elements: a stone circle known as the Kings Men, just across the road is a larger solitary stone, known as the King Stone, and a few hundred yards further on is a group of large stones known as the Whispering Knights. Visitors are presented with a series of theories as to what these stones were for and can enjoy an air of quiet mystery.

🔍 Just off the A44, near Long Compton
❀ ☼ ❧ ❀
⏳ 1-2 hours
⭐ Magical myths and legends
💷
www.rollrightstones.co.uk

Royal Pump Rooms   511
Royal Leamington Spa

The historic Royal Pump Rooms have been redeveloped into a cultural and tourism complex and now include a museum and an art gallery among other attractions. The museum tells the story of Leamington's development. Particular emphasis is placed on the discovery of spa water and how the local community used it to develop Leamington as a health resort in the 19th century. The art gallery features paintings and craft by major British artists. These include nationally important artists and makers from the region such as: Gillian Wearing, Terry Atkinson and Sir Terry Frost.

🔍 Leamington Spa town centre
⚙ ⊙ ♣ ❄
⌛ 1-2 hours
★ The Turkish Bath
FREE
www.warwickdc.gov.uk/royalpumprooms

Draycote Water   512
Rugby

The site's flat five-mile perimeter access road is ideal for a leisurely stroll, run or cycle. The hilltop car park at Hensborough Hill provides particularly good views, and provides access by footpath to waterside picnic areas, while the country park offers plenty of room for outdoor games, and also holds a squirrel scamper nature trail and orienteering courses. Everything is explained at the visitor centre, which is located next to the car park. Visitors can also go fly-fishing, bird watching and there's a whole range of water sports on offer.

🔍 Off the A426, near Rugby
⚙ ⊙ ♣ ❄
⌛ 3-4 hours
★ Bird watching
FREE Car park charge
www.moretoexperience.co.uk

Rugby Art Gallery and Museum   513
Rugby

Rugby Art Gallery and Museum is housed in a purpose built contemporary building. The art gallery hosts exhibitions of contemporary visual art and craft, and from the Rugby collection of contemporary British Art including Stanley Spencer, Bridget Riley, LS Lowry and Lucian Freud. The museum includes Roman artefacts and a gallery focusing on Rugby people and life. There is a separate museum, the Webb Ellis Rugby Football Museum, on the nearby site of the first rugby football workshop, which houses a fabulous collection of memorabilia.

🔍 Follow signs from Rugby town centre
⚙ ⊙ ♣ ❄
⌛ 2-3 hours
★ An 1851 rugby ball and Rugby's clock for the world
&
www.rugby.gov.uk

Tudor World at the Falstaff Experience   515

Stratford-upon-Avon

Situated along the cobbled courtyard of the magnificent Shrieves House is an award-winning attraction that brings the 16th century to life. As you make your way through the museum visitors will hear some remarkable tales relating to the history of Stratford and England. This genuinely haunted museum – which has borne witness to plague, religious persecution, treason, intrigue, war, fire, and of course, Shakespeare – has its own heady atmosphere, felt by many who pass through its labyrinth of theatrical settings.

Stratford town centre

1-2 hours

Evening ghost tours

www.falstaffsexperience.co.uk

Anne Hathaway's Cottage   514

Stratford-upon-Avon

This is the quintessential English country cottage – actually a 12-roomed farmhouse – where Anne Hathaway grew up and lived before she married Shakespeare in 1582. Visitors can enjoy the romantic setting where William wooed his beloved future bride. Nestling under a deep thatched roof, the cottage dates from the 16th and 17th century. The interior, little changed over the centuries, is lovely, with original panelling and an open hearth in the living room. The house is surrounded by stunning grounds overflowing with blooms, shrubs and traditional vegetables.

In Shottery, 1 mile from Stratford town centre

1 hour

Period furniture

www.shakespeare.org.uk

Hall's Croft   516

Stratford-upon-Avon

One of the finest half timbered, gabled houses in Stratford is named after Dr John Hall, husband of Shakespeare's daughter Susanna. Dr Hall was a pioneering medical practitioner and the elegant rooms with exquisite furnishings and paintings on display are in keeping with Dr Hall's wealth and status. Visitors can see Dr Hall's consulting room, with interesting medical artefacts and a first edition of his medical notes published in 1657. You can also enjoy the tranquil garden, filled with the beautiful roses and herbs mentioned by John Hall in his medical notes

Stratford town centre

1 hour

Paintings and furniture collection

www.shakespeare.org.uk

Nash's House and New Place   517
Stratford-upon-Avon

Shakespeare died at his house in New Place in 1616. Although the house was later destroyed, it stood in the gardens of what is now Nash's House, named after Thomas Nash, a rich property owner who married Shakespeare's granddaughter Elizabeth. Today visitors can wander through the picturesque gardens dedicated to the Bard's memory and see the ancient Mulberry tree, claimed to be from a cutting he planted. The garden is now the site of an archaeological dig to find out more about New Place and visitors are invited to take part.

🔍 Follow signs from Stratford town centre

⚙ ⊙ ♣ ✳

⧗ 1–2 hours

★ Elizabethan style knot-garden

💷

www.shakespeare.org.uk

Shakespeare's Birthplace   518
Stratford-upon-Avon

Shakespeare was born in this house in 1564 and it provides a marvellous and intimate picture of his childhood. The family rooms have been recreated to reflect Tudor times with furniture, utensils and wall hangings from the period. Entrance to the house is through a visitor centre, which has an exhibition about the life and background of Shakespeare. From the visitor centre, you are escorted to the house through a beautiful, traditional English garden. This has been planted with many of the trees, flowers and herbs, much loved by Shakespeare.

🔍 Follow signs from Stratford town centre

⚙ ⊙ ♣ ✳

⧗ 1–2 hours

★ First Folio of the Bard's works published in 1623

💷

www.shakespeare.org.uk

St John's House   519
Warwick

A charming Jacobean house dating from about 1620, St John's became a branch of the Warwickshire museum in 1961 and houses the towns's social history collection. The collection reflects the lives of Warwickshire people over the last 300 years. It includes costume and textiles, dolls and toys, and a variety of everyday objects from homes and places of work such as furniture, teapots, books and sewing machines. The museum also has recreations of a Victorian schoolroom and kitchen. The collection is part of an ongoing project in which visitors are encouraged to participate.

🔍 Follow signs from Warwick town centre

⚙ ⊙ ♣ ✳

⧗ 1–2 hours

★ Costume displays

FREE

www.warwickshire.gov.uk/museum

Warwick Castle   520
Warwick

Billed as Britain's 'greatest medieval castle', Warwick is indeed an impressive sight towering above the river. Rebuilt in the 14th century, most of what you see today was reconstructed in the 19th century. Visitors can explore the varied history of the castle's dungeons, fortifications and living quarters, as well as the Rose Garden and the formal gardens. The Private Apartments contain a display of waxwork figures, showing how the rooms would have looked in the late 19th century. The castle also hosts period events throughout the season including jousting and Birds of Prey displays.

🔍 Follow signs from junction 15 of the M40
⚙ ⊙ ♣ ❄
⏳ 3–4 hours
★ World's largest siege machine
💷 💷
www.warwick-castle.co.uk

Charlecote Park   521
Wellesbourne

The mellow brickwork and great chimneys sum up the essence of Tudor England. Home to the Lucy family since the 15th century, whose stories are told throughout the house by their portraits, the objects they collected from around the world and the design influence they had on the house and parkland. The house has associations with Elizabeth I and with Shakespeare, who knew the house well. The gardens include a formal parterre, sensory garden, woodland walk and the wider parkland (inspired by 'Capability' Brown), which offers miles of walks and views across the River Avon.

🔍 Off the B4086, 1 mile west of Wellesbourne
⚙ ⊙ ♣
⏳ 2–3 hours
★ Imposing Elizabethan gatehouse
💷
www.nationaltrust.org.uk

Wellesbourne Wartime Museum   522
Wellesbourne

This museum is located in a wartime command and control bunker, and comprises a collection of aviation artefacts. Displays cover the history of Wellesbourne Mountford airfield with aircraft and other memorabilia. There is a small aircraft park, including the nose of Vulcan XA903, used to test the Olympus engines of Concorde in the 1960s. A small, dedicated group of enthusiasts is trying to restore some of the additional test equipment used in this aircraft. Elsewhere on the airfield, a Vulcan XM655 undertakes taxi runs on occasions.

🔍 Off the B4086, near Wellesbourne
⚙ ⊙ ♣ Sundays and Bank Holidays only
⏳ 1–2 hours
★ Vulcan bomber
💷
www.wellesbourneairfield.com/history.htm

Aston Hall and Park 523

Aston

A fine, red brick, Jacobean mansion, built between 1618 and 1635 by Sir Thomas Holte, features elaborate plasterwork ceilings and friezes, a magnificent carved oak staircase and a spectacular 136-foot Long Gallery. Period rooms contain fine furniture, paintings, textiles and metalwork. Charles I stayed in the house on the eve of the battle of Edgehill in October 1642. There is a new award-winning exhibition space in the old stables, a spectacular new garden – Lady Holte's Garden – which sits on the edge of extensive parkland.

🔍 Take junction 6 of the M1, 3 miles north of Birmingham city centre

✸ ◎ ✚ Closed on Aston Villa weekend home match games

⏳ 1–2 hours

★ The Long Gallery

FREE

www.bmag.org.uk

Midland Air Museum 524

Baginton

Recognised as one of the biggest and longest-established independent museums, the Midland Air Museum houses a varied collection of exhibits. A large indoor area includes the Sir Frank Whittle Jet Heritage Centre and the Wings Over Coventry gallery. Visitors can see an Avro Vulcan bomber and more than 30 other historic aircraft, aero engines and other artefacts. The museum is particularly proud of the collection of material relating to Sir Frank Whittle, the Coventry-born engineer who designed the jet engine, which made modern high-speed aircraft and economical air travel possible.

🔍 Off the A45, near Baginton

✸ ◎ ✚ ✳

⏳ 2–3 hours

★ Avro Vulcan nuclear bomber

♿

www.midlandairmuseum.co.uk

EcoPark 525

Birmingham

The EcoPark is a demonstration of the principles of sustainability and provides a stimulating and educational environment in which to experience it. Although aimed at children, adults are also welcome to explore ponds, woodland, flowing meadows and heathland. The area is a haven for plants and animals and frogs, herons, dragonflies, sparrowhawks and foxes are seen regularly. Regular activities include growing trees and vegetables, pond dipping and minibeast hunts all helping people understand nature. There is also a regular programme of naturally themed arts and crafts.

🔍 Follow signs from A45

✸ ◎ ✚ See website for opening times and booking

⏳ 2 hours

★ Glorious trees

FREE

www.wild-net.org/wildbbc

Lapworth Museum of Geology 526

Birmingham

With over 250,000 specimens the Lapworth Museum of Geology has the finest and largest collection of fossils, minerals and rocks in the Midlands. In addition there are large collections of early geological maps, equipment, models, photographic material, and also zoological specimens and stone axes. The museum dates back to 1880, and is named after Charles Lapworth, the first Professor of Geology at Mason College, the forerunner of the University of Birmingham, and one of the most important and influential geologists in the late 19th and early 20th centuries.

🔍 On the A38, just south of Birmingham city centre

✸ ◎ ✚ ✳

⏳ 1–2 hours

★ 420-million-year-old fossils

FREE

www.lapworth.bham.ac.uk

Birmingham Museum and Art Gallery
527
Birmingham

It is 125 years since Birmingham Museum and Art Gallery first opened its doors beneath the clock tower on Chamberlain Square. Inside you will find everything from Renaissance masterpieces to 9,000-year-old Middle Eastern treasures. Famous for its Pre-Raphaelite paintings, it also has an extensive collection of Arts and Crafts items. Visitors can see art and objects spanning seven centuries of European and World history and culture including silver, sculpture and archaeology. You can find out more about Birmingham's history or see the Egyptian mummies.

Birmingham city centre
2-3 hours
Superb Pre-Raphaelite collection
FREE Some exhibitions may charge
www.bmag.org.uk

Birmingham Tours
528
Birmingham

Birmingham Tours specialises in providing friendly professional guides for walking and driving tours of Birmingham. The Big Brum Buz tours include a hop on, hop off tour of the city, a Tolkien Trail that begins at Sarehole, said to have been the model for the Shire home of the hobbits, a Rhythms of the City rock music tour that revisits the early years of some of this country's greatest bands from the 1960s and 1970s like Black Sabbath, Led Zeppelin and the Move and a Ghostbusters tour. See website for dates and bookings.

Various points in the city centre
See website for dates of individual tours
2-3 hours
Tolkien Trail
www.birmingham-tours.co.uk

National Sea Life Centre
529
Birmingham

This is a tropical paradise in the heart of a buzzing city. Visitors are invited to take a marine voyage beneath the waves and explore 60 spectacular displays: from the touch pool to a one million-litre ocean tunnel; and from starfish to seahorses, sharks and rays. The largest residents are two giant sea turtles – Molokai and Gulliver. Regular talks and feeding demonstrations provide an insight into the mysteries of the seas. The centre has just added a new attraction and is now the only aquarium in the UK where you can see the extraordinary hammerhead sharks.

Near the National Indoor Arena
2-3 hours
Giant turtles
www.sealifeeurope.com

Thinktank
530
Birmingham

Thinktank redefines the concept of a science museum. Think of it more as a way to discover the world around you and the life you lead. It covers the past, present and future of scientific investigation from the natural world to space travel. Visitors can explore everything from steam engines to taste buds and intestines; this exciting museum has over 200 hands-on displays, over four floors, on science and technology including a state-of-the-art Planetarium and IMAX cinema. The museum also runs a regularly changing programme of temporary exhibitions and events.

Follow signs from Birmingham city centre
3-4 hours
The robots
www.thinktank.ac

Selly Manor
Bourneville | 532 |

Selly Manor and Minworth Greaves are two timber-framed manor houses, originally built in the 13th and 14th centuries, and moved to Bourneville in the early 20th century by the chocolate manufacturer George Cadbury. They are good examples of medieval and Tudor architecture. Visitors can learn about medieval life through period furniture and other domestic fixtures and fittings. These impressive buildings are surrounded by beautiful gardens, accurately recreated from the Tudor period. They include a parterre and a small decorative garden with plants for cooking and medicinal purposes.

🔍 Bourneville village green
⚙ ◎ ♣ ❄
⧗ 1–2 hours
★ Guide tours (see website for details)
£
www.bvt.org.uk

Cadbury World: The Experience
Bourneville | 531 |

Cadbury World: The Experience is located within the Cadbury factory and the smell of melted chocolate is overwhelming. Tours are self-guided and visitors will learn about the history of chocolate, its manufacture and the Cadbury family. It then moves to the packaging plant where bars of chocolate fly overhead on conveyor belts. Next comes a ride through 'Cadabra', a fantasy world populated by cocoa beans, and the tour ends with a demonstration area and a section devoted to famous advertising campaigns (see above). Other exhibits tell the story of the village of Bourneville and the Dairy Milk bar.

🔍 Follow signs from the M42 and the M5
⚙ ◎ ♣
⧗ 2–3 hours
★ Melted chocolate tasting
£ £
www.cadburyworld.co.uk

Black Country Living Museum
Dudley | 533 |

This museum is set in an urban heritage park in the shadow of Dudley Castle at the heart of the Black Country. Historic buildings from all around the Black Country have been moved and authentically rebuilt here, in tribute to the traditional skills and enterprise of the people that once lived in the heart of industrial Britain. Visitors are transported back in time from the modern exhibition halls to the canal-side village, where costumed demonstrators and working craftsmen bring the buildings to life with their local knowledge, practical skills and unique Black Country humour.

🔍 On the A4037, 3 miles from junction 2 of the M5
⚙ ◎ ♣ ❄
⧗ 3–4 hours
★ Electric tramcars and trolleybuses
£ £
www.bclm.co.uk

Dudley Canal Trust   534

Dudley

Explore the network of underground canal routes that helped form the industrial Black Country and marvel at the limestone caverns carved by man in his search for raw materials with which to make iron. Learn about the formation of limestone and the fossilisation of small creatures and plant life through a fascinating audio-visual presentation. Visitors will be introduced to the art of 'legging' in a network of underground canals, often forgotten about today. Sit back and enjoy the skipper-guided tour as experienced boatmen take you on a magical journey that is informative, relaxed and exciting.

🔍 Off the A4123, north of Dudley
⚙ ⚙ ♣ ❄
⏳ 1–2 hours
⭐ Stunning limestone caverns
♿
www.dudleycanaltrust.org.uk

Dudley Zoological Gardens   535

Dudley

This modern zoo, set in 40 acres of woodland in the grounds of Dudley Castle, is home to some of the world's rarest and most exotic animals. Among the endangered species are Asian lions, Sumatran tigers, lemurs and Humboldt penguins. Dudley is the only zoo in Britain with spectacular prehistoric remains, and Iron Age fort, a medieval castle, a limestone escarpment, and mysterious underground caverns all on the same site. There are beautiful scenic walks for energetic adults and an Adventureland where children can burn off their surplus energy.

🔍 Take junction 2 of the M5
⚙ ⚙ ♣ ❄
⏳ 3–4 hours
⭐ The tigers
♿ ♿
www.dudleyzoo.org.uk

Birmingham Botanical Gardens   536
and Glasshouses

Edgbaston

Originally opened to the public in 1832, visitors are still enjoying the 15 acres of beautiful, tranquil gardens that have retained the feeling of a Victorian public park, complete with bandstand. There are a number of themed gardens with spectacular seasonal displays and waymarked walks to guide you through them. Visitors can also look inside the four glasshouses which feature tropical, subtropical, Mediterranean and arid conditions and include insectivorous plants, giant 'cacti', tree ferns and cycads, orchids, sugar cane, bananas and citrus fruits.

🔍 Follow signs from Edgbaston town centre
⚙ ⚙ ♣ ❄
⏳ 2–3 hours
⭐ Japanese Bonsai garden
♿
www.birminghambotanicalgardens.org.uk

Broadfield House Glass Museum   537

Kingswinford

Situated in the historic Stourbridge Glass Quarter, this museum has one of the best glass collections in the world, much of which was made locally. It includes everything from 18th-century tableware, to Victorian cameo vases and modern sculptural pieces and reveals the diversity of glass and the creativity of glassmakers through the ages. Permanent displays and temporary exhibitions celebrate the art of glassmaking. There is also a glassmaking studio on site where visitors can watch and wonder at the glassblowers' skills.

🔍 Follow signs from the A491
⚙ ⚙ ♣ ❄
⏳ 2–3 hours
⭐ New pieces by Max Jacquard
FREE
www.glassmuseum.org.uk

National Motorcycle Museum 538

Solihull

The National Motorcycle Museum is recognised as the finest and largest motorcycle museum in the world. It is a place where 'Legends Live On' and it is a tribute to and a living record of this once great British industry that dominated world markets for some 60 years. It is a place where an older generation can once again view with nostalgia the machines they rode in days gone by, and younger generations can study the development of the motorcycle from its earlier days to the golden years of the 1930s-60s, when British motorcycles 'ruled the world'.

🔍 Near junction 6 of the M42

⚙ ☀ ♣ ❄

⌛ 2–3 hours

★ 650 motorbikes on show

&

www.nationalmotorcyclemuseum.co.uk

Jerome K Jerome Birthplace 539

Walsall

Once a museum in his honour, Jerome's birthplace – Belsize House, a grade II listed building in Bradford Street, Walsall – is now a solicitors' office. However, Edmunds and Co., the solicitors in question, have done a magnificent job in restoring and upgrading the house and are welcoming visitors to come and see where the author of *Three Men in a Boat*, one of English literature's timeless classics, was born. The reception area features a copy of the De Lazlo portrait and a small display. The house was marked with a blue plaque in 2008.

🔍 Walsall town centre

⚙ ☀ ♣ ❄

⌛ 1 hour

★ Birthplace of this eccentric author

FREE

www.jeromekjerome.com/birthplace

New Art Gallery | 540
Walsall

This Arts Lottery-funded gallery opened in 2000 and is still one of the most exciting art galleries in the UK. It aims to collect, present and interpret historic, modern and contemporary art in innovative and challenging ways. On permanent display is the Garman Ryan Collection, which was donated by Lady Kathleen Garman, widow of sculptor Sir Jacob Epstein, in 1973. Visitors can also see works by well-known European artists, including Monet, Rembrandt, Constable, van Gogh and Picasso, which are displayed alongside beautiful artworks from many different cultures across the world.

Follow signs from Walsall town centre

2-3 hours

Disco interactive art space

FREE

www.thenewartgallerywalsall.org.uk

The Locksmith's House | 541
Willenhall

Part of the Black Country Living Museum (see entry 533) the Locksmith's House shows the lifestyle and working conditions of the Hodson lockmaking family at the turn of the century. The two-storey backyard workshop is where Edgar Hodson made padlocks in the traditional way. The gas-lit interiors of the house depict how the family lived, with parlour, kitchen, office and bedroom displays. The house and workshops are typical of the many small businesses which once flourished in a town that has been the heart of lockmaking since the Industrial Revolution.

Willenhall town centre

Wednesdays and Saturdays only

1 hour

Intimate Victorian period furnishings

FREE

www.localhistory.scit.wlv.ac.uk/Museum/locks/LocksmithsHouse.htm

West Midland Safari Park | 542
Bewdley

The park has four miles of safari trail. Its prize attraction is the only pride of white lions in the UK. You can also see elephants, rhinos, tigers, wild dogs, lion, wallabies, wolves and buffalo among others. You get the chance to feed some of the animals too – special food is available on arrival for a small charge. And, you can drive through as many times as you wish. Alternatively, you can book a guided minibus tour for an extra charge – please ask when you arrive – this is always very popular, so early booking is recommended.

Off the A456

3-4 hours

Rare white lions

www.wmsp.co.uk

Broadway Tower and Country Park   543
Broadway

The view from the top of Broadway Tower is regarded as the finest in England. This 18th century folly was built by architect James Wyatt and completed in 1798. It includes a wide range of architectural features in one small building, including battlementsand a roof viewing platform. The tower has hosted a number of well-known owners and occupants one of whom was William Morris, famous architect, designer, poet and revolutionary who used it as a holiday retreat together with his friends Edward Burne-Jones and Dante Gabriel Rossetti.

Off A44, 1 mile south-east of Broadway

1 hour

Finest view in England

www.broadwaytower.co.uk

Avoncroft Museum of Historic Buildings   544
Bromsgrove

Avoncroft is a fascinating museum of historic buildings rescued from imminent destruction and rebuilt on an open-air site. Among other buildings visitors can see a 16th-century merchant's house and inn; fine 19th-century buildings such as a 'tin chapel' from Herefordshire and a 1940s prefab showing how people lived after being re-housed following the Second World War. Working life is also represented through a windmill, a crushing mill for making Worcestershire cider and perry and a beautiful 16th-century cruck barn.

Off the A38, 2 miles south of Bromsgrove

2–3 hours

Guided tours

www.avoncroft.org.uk

Evesham Abbey and Park   545
Evesham

Of the once powerful Evesham Benedictine Abbey, founded in AD 714, relatively little remains, its grounds now a park that sweeps down to the banks of the Avon. The most impressive survivor is the bell tower built by Abbot Lichfield and completed in 1539. Happily it survived while all around was reduced to a heap of broken masonry during the Dissolution. A striking structure, the tower stands some 110 feet high in the centre of town, forming part of a spectacular group with the 12th-century All Saints Church and the 16th-century Church of St Lawrence.

Abbey Park, in Evesham town centre

1 hour

Simon de Montfort memorial

FREE

www.valeofevesham.net

Bodenham Arboretum   546

Kidderminster

A mile-long drive winding through undulating countryside gently climbs to the brow of the hills to reveal a secret garden nurtured since 1973. An oasis of plantations, pools and avenues beautifully landscaped including over 3,000 species of trees and shrubs from all over the world. Bodenham is an area of outstanding landscape beauty and interest. Its 156 acres contains mature woodland, specimen trees and shrubs and two acres of pools and lakes. There is also a working farm and an award-winning visitor centre set in the hillside and overlooking the Big Pool.

Off the B1489, 3 miles north of Kidderminster

2–3 hours

Award-winning visitor centre

www.bodenham-arboretum.co.uk

Harvington Hall   547

Kidderminster

Harvington Hall, a moated Elizabethan manor house, has rooms full of original Elizabethan paintings, stunning gardens, and the finest series of priest's holes anywhere in the country, built when it was an offence to be a Catholic priest in England. Catholic supporters often hid priests in their homes, at the risk of being accused of high treason. One of the priest's holes is under a stairway. During the 19th century it was stripped of furniture and panelling and the shell was left almost derelict. But in 1923 it was bought and restored and now it is open to the public.

Off the A450, 3 miles south-east of Kidderminster

2–3 hours

Priest holes

www.harvingtonhall.com

Worcestershire County Museum   548

Kidderminster

This museum is housed in the servants' quarters of Hartlebury Castle, home to the Bishop of Worcester since the 16th century. The main galleries include collections ranging from children's toys, archaeology, costumes and crafts. Two new galleries focus on the geological wonders of Worcestershire and the importance of water to the region including Victorian spa holidays, Malvern spring water and the canal at Stourport. The building also contains a number of room sets such as Victorian, Georgian and Civil War rooms and original rooms within the castle including the schoolroom, scullery and nursery.

Off the A449 at Hartlebury, 5 miles south of Kidderminster

2–3 hours

Viking jewellery

www.worcestershire.gov.uk

Great Malvern Priory 549

Malvern

Originally built as a Benedictine monastery in 1085, Great Malvern Priory is now one of the greatest parish churches in the country. On the Dissolution of the Monasteries in 1541, local people raised £20 to buy the building to replace their decaying parish church. Today it contains the finest collection of stained glass after York Minster, together with carved misericords from the 15th and 16th centuries and the largest collection of medieval floor and wall tiles.

🔍 Off A449, in Malvern town centre

✳ ⚙ ♣ ❄

⧗ 1 hour

★ Window showing the coronation of St Mary

FREE Donations welcome

www.greatmalvernpriory.org.uk

Croome Park 550

Pershore

Croome was 'Capability' Brown's first complete landscape, making his reputation and establishing a new style of garden design. The park has many different buildings, referred to as 'eye-catchers', many of them designed by Brown, Robert Adam and James Wyatt. Croome Court, sold by the Coventry family in 1948, has now been reunited with the parkland, allowing visitors to appreciate the owner's vision for the estate as a whole. The house is presented empty of contents, giving visitors an opportunity to follow the restoration progress over the coming years

🔍 Follow signs from the A38 and B4084

✳ ⚙ ♣

⧗ 2–3 hours

★ Influential landscape garden design

💷

www.nationaltrust.org.uk

Hagley Hall 551

Stourbridge

Hagley Hall and its park is a wonderful example of 18th-century English architecture. Boasting 350 acres of deer park with its own church, the hall houses Van Dyck paintings, fine Chippendale furniture and Rococo plasterwork. The property once belonged to George 1st Lord Lyttelton who was secretary to the Prince of Wales. The hall was completed in 1760. In 1925 a terrible fire destroyed much of the property and its contents. However, the damage was repaired and the hall restored to its former glory. Today it is a family home and therefore public access is limited.

🔍 Near the junction of the A546 and A491, south of Stourbridge

✳ ⚙ ❄ See website for details

⧗ 1–2 hours

★ Scene of the arrest of two of the Gunpowder Plotters

💷 💷

www.hagleyhall.com

Leigh Court Barn 552

Worcester

This outstanding piece of medieval English carpentry is a tithe barn – a building used in the Middle Ages for storing the tithes – a tenth of the farm's produce, which had to be given to the church. This mighty timber-framed building was erected in the 1300s to house the tithes for the monks of Pershore Abbey. It is considered to be England's largest and most significant cruck building, being 150 feet long by 34 feet wide.

🔍 On an unclassified road off the A4103, 5 miles west of Worcester

✳ ⚙ ♣

⧗ 1 hour

★ Unique historic carpentry

FREE

www.english-heritage.org.uk

The Commandery   553
Worcester

This museum focuses on six different periods of history that affected the building in which it sits: medieval times, when it was constructed as a hospital by the Catholic Church; the Tudor period, when the house was inhabited by a family of wool merchants; the Civil War, when it was used by Charles II's forces as headquarters during the Battle of Worcester; the Georgian period, when it was split into homes; the Victorian period, when it housed a school for the 'blind sons of gentlemen' and the 1950s, when it was used as a printing factory.

Just outside Worcester city centre at Sidbury Gate

1-2 hours

Story of the Battle of Worcester

www.worcestercitymuseums.org.uk

Elgar Birthplace Museum   554
Worcester

The composer of much of England's best classical music, Sir Edward Elgar, was born in this pretty country cottage in the heart of England on 2 June 1857. After his death in 1934, Elgar's daughter Carice set up a museum here, as her father had wished. Visitors can see his study which houses his gramophone, family photographs and countless other mementoes including his books and even his golf clubs. There is also an Elgar Centre on-site where manuscripts, music scores, letters, concert programmes, photographs and personal possessions illustrate Elgar's musical life.

On the A44, 3 miles from Worcester

1-2 hours

Personal effects of one of England's greatest composers

www.elgarmuseum.org

Spetchley Park Garden   555
Worcester

Virtually hidden from the road, and largely unaltered in the last century, this lovely 30-acre Victorian paradise, belonging to the Berkeley family, has been lovingly created by successive generations, and boasts an enviable collection of plant treasures from every corner of the globe. There is horticultural drama all through the year. Clumps of wild primrose push up randomly through sapphire carpets of crocus and swathes of sunny daffodils in spring, with billowing borders of blowsy perennials and tender exotics in summer, and a palette of burnt orange, ochre and fiery red in autumn.

On the A44, 2 miles east of Worcester

2-3 hours

A plantsman's paradise

www.spetchleygardens.co.uk

Upton Heritage Centre   556
Worcester

In recent years Upton, once an inland port on the Severn, has been gaining new fame as a centre for the popular arts. Displays in the Upton Heritage Centre illustrate the growth and development of this charming town. The centre is located in Upton's oldest surviving building, nicknamed 'the Pepperpot', a restored bell tower. Most impressive is the story of the Battle of Upton Bridge that took place here in 1651 during the Civil War, when the Church of St Peter and St Paul, of which this was the bell tower, was badly damaged by Parliamentarian soldiers.

Upton town centre

1 hour

Battle of Upton Bridge display

FREE

www.upton.uk.net

Wales

Mid Wales
North Wales
South Wales

Brecon Beacons National Park

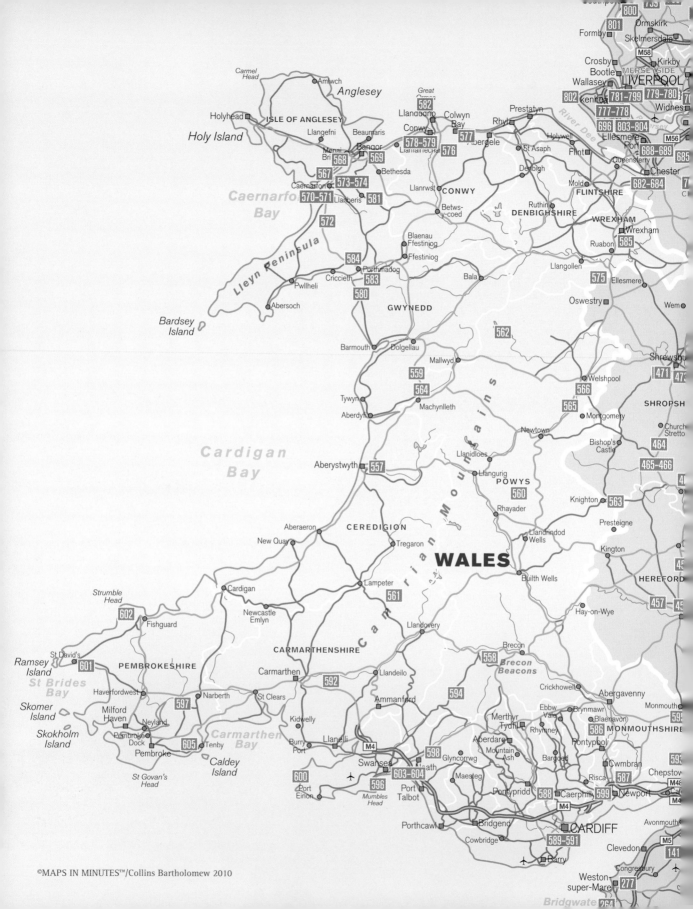

Carmel
Head

Amlwch

Anglesey

ISLE OF ANGLESEY

Holyhead

Holy Island

Great
Ormes
Llandudno **582**
Colwyn
Bay

Prestatyn

Formby

Ormskirk

Skelmersdale

Crosby

Kirkby

Bootle

Wallasey

MERSEYSIDE

LIVERPOOL

800

801

M58

802 kenhea

781-799 **779-780**

777-778 Widnes

M56

Conwy **578-579**

577

Rhyl

Holywell

696 **803-804**

Ellesmere

Port

685

Beaumaris

Llangefni

Llanfairfechan

576 Abergele

St Asaph

Menai
Bri **568** Bangor **569**

Bethesda

Derbigh

Mold

Queensferry

688-689

Caernarfon **567**

573-574

570-571 Llanberis **581**

Llanrwst

CONWY

Ruthin

DENBIGHSHIRE

FLINTSHIRE

682-684

Chester

Betws-
y-coed

Wrexham

WREXHAM

572

Blaenau
Ffestiniog

Ffestiniog

584

Porthmadog

Criccieth

583

Bala

Llangollen

Ruabon **585**

575 Ellesmere

Oswestry

Wem

Pwllheli

580

GWYNEDD

Lleyn Peninsula

Abersoch

Bardsey
Island

562

Welshpool

Shrewsbu

471 **47**

SHROPSH

Barmouth

Dolgellau

Mallwyd

559

564

566

565

Montgomery

Church
Stretto

Tywyn

Machynlleth

Newtown

464

Aberdyfi

**Cardigan
Bay**

Llanidloes

Bishop's
Castle

465-466

Aberystwyth **557**

Llangurig

Llanidloes

POWYS **560**

Rhayader

Knighton **563**

4

Presteigne

Aberaeron

CEREDIGION

Llandrindod
Wells

Kington

HEREFORD

New Quay

Tregaron

WALES

Builth Wells

Strumble
Head

Cardigan

Lampeter

561

Hay-on-Wye

457 **45**

602

Fishguard

Newcastle
Emlyn

Llandovery

Brecon

**Brecon
Beacons**

Crickhowell

Abergavenny

Monmouth

599

St David's

Ramsey
Island

601

PEMBROKESHIRE

CARMARTHENSHIRE

558

Merthyr
Tydfil

Ebbw
Vale

Brynmawr

Blaenavon

586 **MONMOUTHSHIRE**

**St Brides
Bay**

Haverfordwest

Narberth

St Clears

Carmarthen

592

Llandeilo

594

Rhymney

Bargoed

Pontypool

Skomer
Island

Milford
Haven

Neyland

597

Ammanford

Kidwelly

Aberdare

Mountain
Ash

Cwmbran

593

Skokholm
Island

Pembroke
Dock

Pembroke

605

Tenby

**Carmarthen
Bay**

Burry
Port

Llanelli

M4

598

Glyncorrwg

Pontypridd

Risca

Caerphilly **599**

Newport

587

M4

M4

Chepstow

Caldey
Island

600

Port
Einon

603-604

596

Mumbles
Head

Swansea

Neath

Port
Talbot

Maesteg

588

M4

Avonmouth

St Govan's
Head

Porthcawl

Bridgend

CARDIFF

Cowbridge

589-591

Clevedon

M5

Barry

Weston-
super-Mare

277

141

Congresbury

©MAPS IN MINUTES™/Collins Bartholomew 2010

Bridgwate

26

Guide to **Wales**

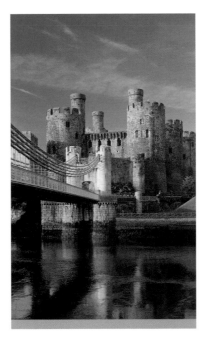

Vale of Rheidol Railway 557

Aberystwyth

The Vale of Rheidol Railway was the last steam railway owned by British Rail until it was privatised in 1989. The 11¾-mile journey between Aberystwyth and Devil's Bridge takes approximately one hour in each direction as the train overcomes a height difference of over 600 feet, affording superb views of the Rheidol Valley. At Devil's Bridge, where trains wait for an hour before returning to Aberystwyth, there is a cafe, toilets and a picnic area. The famous Mynach Falls, Jacob's Ladder and the Devil's Punchbowl are within walking distance of the station (but are operated as separate attractions).

Trains depart from Aberystwyth centre, beside main railway centre

3-4 hours

One of the Great Little Railways of Wales

www.rheidolrailway.co.uk

King Arthur's Labyrinth 559

Corris

Visitors to King Arthur's Labyrinth take an underground boat ride deep into the spectacular caverns under Braichgoch Mountain at Corris near Machynlleth. Once inside the Labyrinth, your hooded boatman guides you through tunnels and vast caverns, while you enjoy tales of King Arthur and other ancient Welsh legends. Stories of dragons, of giants, of battles and many more are told, complete with dramatic scenes, sound and light effects. Arthur is the hero of the earliest legends – a Dark Age warrior fighting the Saxon invader to bring peace to the Island of Britain.

On the A427, between Machynlleth and Dolgellau

2 hours

The Great Waterfall

www.kingarthurslabyrinth.com

Brecon Beacons National Park Visitor Centre 558

Brecon

The Brecon Beacons includes some of the finest walks in Britain and the peaks and valleys are crisscrossed by waymarked trails. It is also famous for its waterfalls, caves and gorges. The caves provided refuge for early settlers and remains of Stone Age settlements and burial chambers can be seen at Crickhowell, Talgarth, and Brecon. There are also stone circles scattered about the park. Other highlights are the Brecon and Monmouthshire Canal, the Cathedral Showcaves and Llanthony Priory. The Visitor Centre has details of all the attractions on offer.

Off the A470, 6 miles south-west of Brecon

1 hour

Circular nature trail

FREE Car park charges

www.breconbeacons.org

The Hall at Abbey-Cwm-Hir 560

Llandrindod Wells

Within a setting of breathtaking beauty, history and romance, the Hall and its 12 acres overlook St Mary's Church and the ruins of the 12th-century Cistercian Abbey of the Long Valley containing the monks' pond and the grave of Llewellyn the Last. The current owners have restored it into a building of Gothic splendour, boasting stunning interiors and fascinating collections. Tours of all 52 rooms of the house conducted by a family member, and access to the landscape gardens, are available daily through the year. Tours must be pre-booked. They start at 10.30 a.m. and 2.00 p.m.

Off the A44, A483 and A470, 10 miles north of Llandrindod Wells

2-3 hours

Fantastic interiors

www.abbeycwmhir.com

Dolaucothi Gold Mines   561
Llanwrda

These unique gold mines are set amid wooded hillsides overlooking the beautiful Cothi Valley. The Romans, who exploited the site almost 2,000 years ago, have left behind a glimpse of gold-mining methods. The harsh mining environment continued in the 19th and 20th centuries, ending in 1938. Guided tours take you back to experience the conditions of the Roman, Victorian and 1930s underground workings. See and hear the 1930s mine and mine machinery. Have a go at gold panning and take the opportunity to experience the frustrations of searching for real gold for yourself.

On the A428

2-3 hours

Guided underground tour

www.nationaltrust.org.uk

Lake Vyrnwy Nature Reserve   562
Llanwddyn

This man-made lake was completed in 1888 and has always been a haven for birds. The visitor centre is the best place to start. From here you can join a trail through the woodland and birds are soon all around you. You should be able to see and hear pied flycatchers and redstarts, while dippers nest by the lake and rocky streams, great crested grebes and goosanders bob on the water, and above you ravens, buzzards and perhaps a peregrine soar in the skies. There's plenty for children too, including nestbox trails and bat and owl walks.

On the B4393

2-3 hours

Spring birdsong

FREE

www.rspb.org.uk

Offa's Dyke Centre 563
Knighton

The Offas Dyke Footpath roughly traces the English-Welsh border, following the dyke for some 70 miles. Offa's Dyke is an 8th-century construction, built by the powerful King Offa of Mercia to mark the boundary of his kingdom. Stretching 150 miles in all, from the Severn to the North Wales coast. Knighton is officially the halfway point on the footpath, and it's here that you'll find the Offa's Dyke Centre, which provides a wealth of information on the history and geography of the dyke for walkers, cyclists and motorists.

🔍 Knighton town centre
☼ ⚙ 🍁 ⬛
⏳ 1 hour
⭐ Exhibition on Offa's Dyke
FREE
www.offasdyke.demon.co.uk

Centre for Alternative Technology 564
Machynlleth

Built in an old slate quarry in the foothills of Snowdonia, the CAT visitor centre has been set up to explain the importance of living more sustainably – saving money, creating green jobs, providing a healthier lifestyle and making real sense. It has recently launched a new vision for a low-carbon future called Zero Carbon Britain, and continually works on new messages, art pieces and displays for its 50,000 annual visitors. There are many solutions already available to tackle the issues our planet faces. Here you can find out what they are.

🔍 On the A487, towards Dolgellau from Machynlleth
☼ ⚙ 🍁 ❄
⏳ 2–3 hours
⭐ Positive solutions-based approach to looking after our planet
💷
www.cat.org.uk

Andrew Logan Museum of Sculpture 565
Welshpool

This museum houses a collection of works by renowned sculptor Andrew Logan. Visitors can see sculpture, mirrored portraits, watercolours, jewellery and photos from the mid 1960s to the present day. There are also personal items, created by Andrew for the late actor Divine, the late painter Luciana Martinez de la Rosa and Joan Simon Menkes, which have been left to the museum by their estates. In addition, you will find Andrew's series of Birds of a Feather, the Cosmic Egg, the Living Taj Mahal and Egypt Revisited inspired by his fantastic journeys.

🔍 On the A438, at Berriew
⚙ See website for opening times
⏳ 1 hour
⭐ Only museum in Europe dedicated to a living artist
💷
www.andrewlogan.com

Powis Castle and Garden 566
Welshpool

This world-famous garden is overhung with clipped yews, rare and tender plants. Laid out under the influence of Italian and French styles, it retains its original lead statues and an orangery on the terraces. High on a rock above the terraces, the castle, originally built c. 1200, began life as a medieval fortress. Remodelled and embellished over more than 400 years, it reflects the changing needs and ambitions of the Herbert family – each generation adding to the magnificent collection of paintings, sculpture, furniture and tapestries. A superb collection of treasures from India is displayed in the Clive Museum.

🔍 Follow signs from A438, 1 mile south of Welshpool
☼ ⚙ 🍁
⏳ 2–3 hours
⭐ Reynolds' portrait of the Countess of Powys (1758–1830)
💷 💷
www.nationaltrust.org.uk

Anglesey Sea Zoo   567

Anglesey

The biggest aquarium in Wales nestles on the shores of
the Menai Strait. Over 50 displays include a shipwreck
brimming with conger eels, shark pool grids to walk
over and a kelp forest full of huge fishes. Just opened
is the No Bone Zone, where you come face to face with
the cunning octopus and undersea peacocks. There are
also little seahorses and weird pipefish to baby sharks
and tiny lobsters. With daily feeds and interactive talks,
and the chance to see our local and international
conservation work, there's always something to see.

🔍 Follow signs from the A55
⚙ ◎ ✿ ❄
⌛ 2–3 hours
★ The Shark Pool
£

www.angleseyseazoo.co.uk

Plas Newydd   568

Anglesey

Set amid beautiful scenery on the Menai Strait, this
elegant house was designed by James Wyatt in the
18th century. The 1930s restyled interior is famous
for its Rex Whistler association, containing his largest
painting and exhibition. A military museum contains
relics of the 1st Marquess of Anglesey, who commanded
the cavalry at the Battle of Waterloo. There is a fine
spring garden and arboretum, with shrubs and wild
flowers, a summer terrace and massed hydrangeas,
which give autumn colour. A woodland walk gives
visitors access to a marine walk beside the Menai Strait.

🔍 Off the A55 at junctions 7 or 8
⚙ ◎ ✿
⌛ 2–3 hours
★ Home of the 'Ladies of Llangollen' who were visited by many famous writers
£

www.nationaltrust.org.uk

Penrhyn Castle 569
Bangor

This enormous 19th-century neo-Norman castle sits between Snowdonia and the Menai Strait. It is crammed with fascinating items, such as a one-ton slate bed made for Queen Victoria, elaborate carvings, plasterwork and mock-Norman furniture, in addition it has an outstanding collection of paintings. The restored kitchens are a delight and the stable block houses a fascinating industrial railway museum, a model railway museum and a superb dolls' museum. The 60 acres of grounds include parkland, an exotic tree and shrub collection as well as a Victorian walled garden.

🔍 On the A5122, 2 miles east of Bangor
✺ ◉ ❧
⏳ 2-3 hours
★ Finest art collection in Wales
♿
www.nationaltrust.org.uk

The Fun Centre 571
Caernarfon

With 14,000 square foot of family fun, including two 20-foot high drop slides, ball pools, tubes, bridges, maze, climbing walls, net and ropes, the Fun Centre, which takes up three floors of the building, will keep even the most energetic children (and adults) entertained for hours. There's also a driving school on the top floor where visitors can take the wheel of a variety of different vehicles ranging from a Ferrari to an American truck and then test their driving skills on the Fun Centre's oval track.

🔍 On the A487, just outside Caernarfon town centre
✺ ◉ ❧ ✺ See website for details
⏳ 1-2 hours
★ Adult nights
♿
www.thefuncentre.co.uk

Caernarfon Castle 570
Caernarfon

King Edward intended this castle to be a royal residence and seat of government for north Wales. Built between 1283 and 1323 and designed to replicate the walls of Constantinople, with polygonal towers, intimidating battlements and colour-banded masonry, the castle has always dominated the town. Its symbolic status was emphasised when Edward made sure that his son, the first English Prince of Wales, was born here in 1284. In 1969, the castle gained worldwide fame as the setting for the investiture of HRH Prince Charles as Prince of Wales.

🔍 Caernarfon town centre
✺ ◉ ❧
⏳ 2-3 hours
★ Queen's Tower
♿
www.cadw.wales.gov.uk

Inigo Jones Slate Works 572
Caernarfon

Founded in 1861, Inigo Slate Works first produced school writing slates. Today the company produces architectural memorial craft products and garden products from natural welsh slate and specialises in producing engraved slate nameplates and plaques. Visitors can tour the slate works, see Welsh craftsmanship at first hand and learn about the Welsh slate industry in a historical exhibition. The self-guided tour starts with a film showing how slate is mined. There is also geological, calligraphy, historical and lettercutting exhibitions. The works also runs engraving and calligraphy workshops.

On the A487, 6 miles from Caernarfon

1-2 hours

Last surviving example of a fully operational slate works in North Wales

www.inigojones.co.uk

Plas Menai National Watersports Centre 573
Caernarfon

Plas Menai enjoys a magnificent location on the Menai Strait. The waters here are ideal for sailing, windsurfing, canoeing and powerboating, with easy access to the sea and superb coastal scenery. It is also close to Snowdonia National Park, which provides canoeists and mountaineers with access to mountains, crags, rivers and lakes. There are residential and non-residential courses available all year round for every level of ability based in a purpose-built complex with comfortable and well-equipped accommodation.

On the A487, 2 miles north of Caernarfon

6-7 days

Some of Europe's best watersports training

www.plasmenai.co.uk

Welsh Highland Railway 574
Caernarfon

The Welsh Highland Railway is North Wales' newest railway. Trains run on a spectacular 19½-mile scenic journey from Caernarfon – climbing from sea level to over 650 feet as they cross the flanks of Mount Snowdon, before zigzagging dramatically down the steep hillside to reach the village of Beddgelert and the magnificent Aberglaslyn Pass (recently voted 'the most scenic view in the UK'). Riders can enjoy the spectacular scenery of lakes, mountains and forest en route to the heart of Snowdonia.

Main station is St Helens Road in Caernarfon, follow signs from the A487

4-5 hours

Pullman Observation carriage

www.festrail.co.uk

Chirk Castle
Chirk

575

Completed in 1310, Chirk was built by Roger Mortimer, 1st Earl of March, as part of King Edward I's chain of fortresses across North Wales. Features from its 700 years include the medieval tower and dungeon, 17th-century Long Gallery, grand 18th-century state apartments and servants' hall. The award-winning gardens contain clipped yews, herbaceous borders, shrub and rock gardens. A terrace with stunning views looks out over the Cheshire and Salop plains. The parkland provides a habitat for animals, wild flowers and mature trees and some splendid wrought-iron gates, made in 1719 by the Davies brothers.

Off the A5, south of Wrexham
2–3 hours
Collection of fine furniture
www.nationaltrust.org.uk

Welsh Mountain Zoo
Colwyn Bay

577

Set in North Wales, high above Colwyn Bay with panoramic views and breathtaking scenery, beautiful gardens are home to this caring conservation zoo. Visitors can roam the wooded pathways, relax on the grassy slopes and spend the day learning about rare and endangered species from around the world including snow leopards, chimpanzees, red pandas and Sumatran tigers. There's a Penguin Parade, Chimp Encounter, Bear Falls, New Condor Haven, Children's Farm and jungle playgrounds. Visit the new 'Sea Lions Rock' and watch Californian sea lions being trained.

Follow signs from the A55
3–4 hours
Arctic foxes
www.welshmountainzoo.org

Bodnant Garden
Colwyn Bay

576

Bodnant Garden is one of the most beautiful gardens in the UK. Spanning 80 acres, it is situated above the River Conwy on sloping ground looking across the valley towards Snowdonia. Bodnant's aim is to grow a wide range of interesting plants from all over the world, particularly China, North America, Europe and Japan that are suited to the Welsh climate and soil. As well as this, care has been taken to place the plants in such a way that they enhance each other and contribute to the general beauty of the garden throughout the seasons.

Off the A470, 7 miles south of Colwyn Bay
1–2 hours
Incredible seasonal colour
www.bodnantgarden.co.uk

Conwy Castle

578

Conwy

Built for King Edward I between 1283-87, Conwy remains one of the most outstanding achievements of medieval military architecture. Its distinctive appearance, with barbicans and towers, demands as much attention as the dramatic Snowdonia skyline behind it. The castle had started to fall into disrepair within a generation of its completion. Repairs and modifications were made by Edward, the Black Prince, in 1346. The castle saw some activity during the Civil War, but it was slighted at the end of the war and stripped of saleable materials leaving an empty shell.

🔍 Overlooking the Conwy Estuary

⚙ ◎ ❧ ❄

⏳ 1-2 hours

★ Night-time floodlit views

£

www.cadw.wales.gov.uk

The Royal Cambrian Society

579

Conwy

Constituted in 1881, the Royal Cambrian Academy is a centre for artistic excellence in Wales. It has over 100 artist members and aims to exhibit work by members of the Academy, to promote up and coming artists of quality, to mount historical exhibitions and offer a lively venue for education. Members come from all parts of the UK, including Wales. The work shown is a true reflection of contemporary Welsh art. No one knows what the true definition of Welsh Art is, but if it exists, it can be seen at the Royal Cambrian Academy.

🔍 Conwy town centre

⚙ ◎ ❧ ❄

⏳ 1-2 hours

★ Regular programme of temporary exhibitions

FREE

www.rcaconwy.org

Harlech Castle

580

Harlech

Like an all-seeing sentinel, Harlech Castle gazes out across land and sea, keeping a watchful eye over Snowdonia. The English monarch Edward I built the castle in the late 13th century to fulfil this very role. It was the most formidable of his 'iron ring' of fortresses designed to contain the Welsh in their mountain fastness. A long siege here during the Wars of the Roses inspired the song 'Men of Harlech'. A combination of magnificent medieval architecture and breathtaking location, Harlech is unmissable, a fact reinforced by its status as a World Heritage Site.

🔍 Harlech town centre

⚙ ◎ ❧ ❄

⏳ 1-2 hours

★ Marvellous views of the bay and Snowdonia

£

www.harlech.com

A **majestic** mountain top adventure

Snowdon Mountain Railway

Llanberis

581

FIVE-STAR ATTRACTION

Snowdon dominates the glorious, ancient landscape of North Wales. A place of legend, this 450 million-year-old mountain is said to be the burial place of the giant ogre Rhita, vanquished by King Arthur. You can have a truly great day out here on the Snowdon Mountain Railway. Visitors can ride Britain's only public rack-and-pinion railway to the summit of the tallest mountain (3,560 feet) in England and Wales. Built and opened in 1896, the railway passes through stunning scenery with awe-inspiring views of the Snowdonia National Park.

The journey starts at Llanberis station and immediately begins the steep incline up the first of the two amazing viaducts crossing Afon Hwch. You will then pass a beautiful waterfall and enter an ancient forest. Beyond the forest the train emerges into open countryside and you get a first glimpse of the sharp craggy peak of Snowdon. At the summit, you can rest and refuel at the visitor centre, which has spectacular panoramic windows with unimpaired views across the mighty Snowdonia range.

The return journey is equally spectacular. But for those wishing to walk down, single tickets to the summit are available.

Llanberis Station is on the A4086

2-3 hours

Journey of a lifetime

£ £ £

www.snowdonrailway.co.uk

Great Orme Mines

Llandudno

582

Uncovered in 1987 during a scheme to landscape an area of the Great Orme, these copper mines represent one of the most astounding archaeological discoveries of recent time. Dating back 4,000 years to the Bronze Age they change our views about the ancient people of Britain and their civilised and structured society 2,000 years before the Roman invasion. Over the past 21 years mining engineers, cavers and archaeologists have been slowly uncovering more tunnels and large areas of the surface landscape to reveal what is now thought to be the largest prehistoric mine in the world.

Follow signs from Llandudno

1-2 hours

Bronze Age cavern

£

www.greatormemines.info

Portmeirion

Minffordd

583

This unique village was created by Welsh architect Clough Williams-Ellis (1883–1978) to demonstrate how a naturally beautiful place could be developed without spoiling it. The fabulous architecture, sandy beaches and exotic gardens have inspired many illustrious artists, photographers and TV and film producers. Writers such as George Bernard Shaw, H.G. Wells, Aldous Huxley, Ernest Hemingway and Bertrand Russell were frequent visitors. Noel Coward wrote his best-known comedy, *Blithe Spirit*, here in 1941. Patrick McGoohan's enigmatic television series *The Prisoner* was filmed here in 1966–67.

Follow signs from the A487, near Minffordd

3-4 hours

Cottages to let by the Portmeirion Hotel

£

www.portmeirion-village.com

221

The Ffestiniog Railway　584
Porthmadog

The Ffestiniog Railway takes you on a 13½-mile journey from the harbour in Porthmadog to the slate-quarrying town of Blaenau Ffestiniog. These historic trains, already running for 140 years carrying slate from the quarries to the port, climb over 700 feet from sea level into the mountains through tranquil pastures, inaccessible by road undisturbed by the sights and sounds of modern life, through magnificent forests, past lakes and waterfalls, round horseshoe bends (even a complete spiral) clinging to the side of the mountain or even tunnelling through it.

🔍 Porthmadog harbour
✿ ◎ 🍁
⌛ 3–4 hours
★ Gardens at Plas Halt
♿ ♿
www.festrail.co.uk

Erddig　585
Wrexham

Widely acclaimed as one of Britain's finest historic houses, Erddig is a fascinating early 18th-century country house reflecting the upstairs–downstairs life of a gentry family over 250 years. The extensive downstairs area contains Erddig's unique collection of servants' portraits, while the upstairs rooms are a treasure trove of fine furniture, textiles and wallpapers. Outside, the outbuildings include stables, smithy, joiner's shop and sawmill. The setting is a superb 18th-century formal garden and romantic landscape park – which are the starting points for walks, bicycle and carriage rides through the estate.

🔍 Follow signs from the A525 and A483, 2 miles south of Wrexham
✿ ◎ 🍁
⌛ 2–3 hours
★ 18th and 19th-century furniture and furnishings
♿ ♿
www.nationaltrust.org.uk

Big Pit: National Coal Museum　586
Blaenafon

This is a real colliery. Kitted out in a helmet, with a cap-lamp and battery back visitors descend 300 feet to another world – a world of shafts, coal faces, different levels of underground roadways, airdoors and stables. You can also enjoy a multi-media tour of a modern coalmine with a virtual miner in the mining galleries, exhibitions in the pithead baths and historic colliery buildings, which are open to the public for the first time. The award-winning Big Pit is reminder of the coal industry in Wales and the people and society it created.

🔍 Follow signs from the M4 and A465
✿ ◎ 🍁
⌛ 2–3 hours
★ Underground tour
FREE
www.nmgw.ac.uk

Caerleon Amphitheatre, Barracks and Baths   587
Caerleon

This is the site of the 50-acre Roman legionary fortress of Isca, the permanent base of the Second Augustan Legion in Britain from about AD 75. There are impressive remains of the fortress baths (shown below), amphitheatre, barracks and fortress wall that give a good idea of how the fortress would have looked. The most famous monument here is the amphitheatre, which would have held about 6,000 people and been the scene of many gladitorial games. Many of the artefacts recovered here can be seen in the nearby Roman Legionary Museum.

🔍 Off the M4 and the A4042, at Caerleon
✺ ◉ ♣ ✲
⌛ 2–3 hours
⭐ Site exhibition
FREE
www.cadw.wales.gov.uk

Caerphilly Castle   588
Caerphilly

Caerphilly Castle, covering an area of 30 acres, is the largest castle in Wales and one of the biggest in all of Britain. In 1268, 'Red Gilbert' de Clare, Lord of Glamorgan, began building the castle to defend contested land during his conflict with Llywelyn the Last, Prince of Wales. The castle is a magnificent example of a medieval concentric design, with the curtain wall of the inner central ward surrounded by an outer curtain wall, which is surrounded by water defences and in some places by even more walls.

🔍 Caerphilly town centre
✺ ◉ ♣ ✲
⌛ 1–2 hours
⭐ Audio tours
♿
www.cadw.wales.gov.uk

Millennium Stadium Tours   589
Cardiff

Walk in the footsteps of Ryan Giggs... see where Madonna stood to sing. Lift the trophy like one of your heroes. Visitors can now explore the magnificent facets and features that make the Millennium Stadium one of the most impressive icons of modern Wales. Join one of the experienced tour guides to see the dressing rooms, feel the pre-match tension, hear the roar of the crowd, walk down the players' tunnel and raise the rafters like millions of others who have gone before you at Millennium Stadium Tours.

🔍 Cardiff city centre
✺ ◉ ♣ ✲
⌛ 1 hour
⭐ Sit in the royal box
♿
www.millenniumstadium.com/tours

St Fagan's: National History Museum 590
Cardiff

St Fagan's is one of Europe's leading open-air museums and Wales's most popular heritage attraction. It stands in the grounds of the magnificent St Fagan's Castle, a late 16th-century manor house donated to the people of Wales by the Earl of Plymouth. The museum shows how the people of Wales have lived, worked and spent their leisure time over the last 500 years. Over 40 buildings have been moved from various parts of Wales and reassembled in over a hundered acres of parkland. There are also galleries with exhibitions of costume, daily life and farming implements.

Just off the A4232, 4 miles west of Cardiff

2–3 hours

Regular traditional music and dance festivals

FREE

www.museumwales.ac.uk

Techniquest 591
Cardiff

This science discovery centre in Cardiff Bay has over 160 interactive exhibits that will bring science and technology to life. Among the amazing range of activities on offer, visitors can fire a rocket, launch a hot-air balloon, sink an oil rig, move half a ton of granite, study a colony of ants and play a giant keyboard. There's also a science theatre – which stages curriculum linked shows for schools during term time and shows for all the family at weekends and in the holidays. It also has a Planetarium.

Cardiff Bay

2–3 hours

Science theatre shows (see website for details)

£

www.techniquest.org

National Botanic Garden of Wales 592
Carmarthen

Created within a beautiful 568-acre Regency park, this landmark garden combines 200 year-old historical features with spectacular modern architecture and landscaping. The Great Glasshouse is the only place in the world you can visit the Mediterranean, South Africa, Australia, Chile and California on the same day. Outside, Europe's longest herbaceous border creates a colourful corridor with thousands of perennials and shrubs. And there are gardens within the garden, from the award-winning Japanese garden to bog and boulder gardens.

On the A48, 10 miles east of Carmarthen

2–3 hours

Seasonal displays

£

www.gardenofwales.org.uk

Tintern Abbey 593
Chepstow

This Cistercian abbey, founded in 1131 in the beautiful Wye valley, is one of the greatest monastic ruins in Wales. The remarkably complete abbey church was rebuilt in the later 13th and early 14th centuries and included cloisters and other associated monastic buildings. One of the most spectacular ruins in the country it has long been a favourite of writers and artists. It inspired the William Wordsworth poem 'Lines Composed a Few Miles above Tintern Abbey', Alfred Lord Tennyson's poem 'Tears, Idle Tears' and more than one painting by J.M.W. Turner.

Off the A466, 4 miles north of Chepstow

1–2 hours

The perfect ruined abbey

£

www.cadw.wales.gov.uk

National Showcaves Centre for Wales 594

Dan-yr-Ogof

Created 350 million years ago, these caves are situated in the Brecon Beacons National Park and were recently voted Britain's Finest Natural Wonder. With 10 different attractions on one ticket there is loads to do and see. At the heart of the site are three showcaves found by the Morgan brothers in 1912 with stalactites, waterfalls (shown below) and other cave formations extending for over 10 miles. But there's also a Dinosaur Park – where you'll come face to face with a Tyrannosaurus Rex – a museum, a farmyard, an Iron Age village and a Shire horse centre.

On the A4067, signposted from junction 45 of the M4

2-3 hours

Astonishing caves

www.showcaves.co.uk

STAR ATTRACTION

Nelson Museum 595

Monmouth

Though he had few connections with Monmouth, the Nelson Museum was founded here in 1924, following the bequest by Lady Llangattock of her collection of material relating to the famous admiral. This includes Nelson's sword (and those of the surrendered French and Spanish naval commanders at Trafalgar), letters and various artefacts commemorating his victories, his naval career and his visit, with the Hamiltons, to Monmouth town. Also on display are silverware, prints, paintings, glassware, pottery and models of the Battle of Trafalgar.

Monmouth town centre

1-2 hours

'Nelson's' glass eye

FREE

www.monmouthshire.gov.uk

Oystermouth Castle 596

Mumbles

There have been a number of castles on this site overlooking the town of Mumbles and Swansea Bay. Today visitors can see the ruins of the 13th century fortification built by the de Braose dynasty. Edward I visited the castle in December 1284, but the castle declined in importance during the 14th century. There is an on-site exhibit that explains a little of the castle history. The grounds afford marvellous views of Mumbles seafront and Swansea Bay and is an ideal point from which to start exploring the Gower Peninsula.

🔍 Mumbles town centre

⚙ ⊙ ✿

⏳ 1 hour

★ Glorious views of Swansea Bay

£

www.castlewales.com

Oakwood Theme Park 597

Narberth

One of Wales's largest tourist attractions, Oakwood has 400,000 visitors a year and boasts more than 30 rides and attractions. Rides include Megafobia, a wooden rollercoaster, voted 'Best in the World' for four years; Speed, a steel rollercoaster with a beyond vertical drop and the Bounce, a 160-foot shot 'n drop tower coaster which shoots riders into the air at speeds of 70 kph. There is also plenty of gentler attractions on offer, such as crazy golf, pedalos on the boating lake, Treetops – a small wooden rollercoaster in a woodland area, Brer Rabbit's Burrow and much more.

🔍 Follow signs from the A48 at Camarthen

⚙ ⊙ ✿

⏳ 4-5 hours

★ Megafobia

£ £

www.oakwoodthemepark.co.uk

STAR ATTRACTION

Aberdulais Falls 598

Neath

For over 400 years this famous waterfall, set in a deep gorge, provided the energy to drive the wheels of industry, from copper to tinplate. At its peak in the 1750s, the falls became popular with landscape painters, including J.M.W. Turner, whose work has been reproduced and can be seen in the Information Centre. Today the waters of the River Dulais are used to make Aberdulais Falls self-sufficient in environmentally friendly energy, with its waterwheel – the largest in Europe – generating electricity. Lifts enable visitors to access the upper levels for excellent views of the falls.

🔍 On the A465, 3 miles north-east of Neath

⚙ ⊙ ✿

⏳ 1 hour

★ A truly spectacular waterfall

£

www.nationaltrust.org.uk

Tredegar House 599

Newport

Set in a beautiful 90-acre park, Tredegar House is one of the best examples of a 17th-century Charles II mansion in Britain. It served as the ancestral home of the wealthy Morgan family until 1951 when it became a girls' school. The house is now open to the public who can see one of the region's hidden gems. Three centuries of changing fashions in interior design are represented. A guided tour is recommended to help you see all the highlights. The gardens and park are also worth seeing with an orangery, stables and a series of marvellous woodland walks.

🔍 Follow signs from the A48, 2 miles west of Newport

⚙ ⊙ ✿

⏳ 1-2 hours

★ Guided tours

£

www.newport.gov.uk/tredegarhouse

Rhossili Visitor Centre 600

Rhossili

Rhossili is one of the finest beaches in Britain and one of many on the Gower Peninsula. Skirting the National Nature Reserve of the South Gower Coast and overlooking Rhossili Bay, the National Trust visitor centre is situated adjacent to the Warren, the Down, Worm's Head, the beach and the coastal cliffs, and provides all the information you will need to explore one of the most beautiful areas of Wales and includes a regularly changing programme of exhibitions. The area is popular with walkers, hang-gliders, para-gliders and surfers.

🔍 On the cliffs at Rhossili
❋ ❋ ❋ ❋ Check website for opening hours
⧗ 3-4 hours
★ A walk on Rhossili beach
FREE
www.nationaltrust.org.uk

St David's Cathedral 601

St David's

St David is the patron saint of Wales. He was the founder of a strict monastic order and the most influential clergyman in Wales during the 'Age of Saints'. This cathedral became one of the most important shrines of medieval Christendom. Nowhere in Britain is there a more ancient cathedral settlement, for it reaches back 14 centuries and survived the plunder of the Norsemen in the Dark Ages. Visitors will find his shrine and many other fascinating things in the purple-stoned cathedral, which nestles in a grassy hollow beneath the rooftops of this tiny city.

🔍 St David's city centre
❋ ❋ ❋ ❋
⧗ 1-2 hours
★ Guided tours
FREE Suggested donation is £4
www.stdavidscathedral.org.uk

North Pembrokeshire Walk 602

Strumble Head

A challenging 5-mile, circular hike from Strumble Head will reward walkers with some stunning views and a chance to see some of Britain's rarer wildlife. Start from the cliff-top opposite the lighthouse and follow the coast southwards until you get to the Stone Age hill fort of Garn Fach from where you take the coast road back towards the lighthouse. This walk takes in high cliffs, steep ascents and long drops. It is essential that you stick to the well-trodden path. If you're lucky you'll see seals, snakes and a wide variety of bird life.

🔍 Follow signs from the A40, near Fishguard
❋ ❋ ❋
⧗ 3 hours
★ Basalt columns
FREE
www.pcnpa.org.uk

Dylan Thomas Centre   603

Swansea

The Dylan Thomas Centre is sited in Swansea's maritime quarter. Formerly the city's Guildhall, which was originally built in 1825, it was restored and refurbished to host the UK Year of Literature and Writing in 1995. The permanent 'Man and Myth' exhibition (shown above) is based on the largest collection of memorabilia of its kind in the world. It is designed to appeal to the Dylan Thomas expert and interested visitor alike. This interactive exhibition explores Dylan's life and work through a variety of media and includes letters, books, worksheets and photographs.

Q Swansea city centre
☼ ○ ♣ ❄
⧖ 1–2 hours
★ Annual Dylan Thomas Festival – 27 October to 9 November
FREE
www.dylanthomas.com

National Waterfront Museum   604

Swansea

The National Waterfront Museum at Swansea tells the story of industry and innovation in Wales, now and over the last 300 years. The nation's industrial and maritime heritage is presented via cutting-edge, interactive technology married with traditional displays. The museum is housed in an original waterfront warehouse linked to a new, ultra-modern slate and glass building. Here you can discover the transport, materials and networks that were so important and the 'big things' that contributed so much to the industrial history of Wales. Then look into the future in the Frontiers gallery.

Q Swansea marina
☼ ○ ♣ ❄
⧖ 2–3 hours
★ Innovative displays
FREE
www.museumwales.ac.uk

Tudor Merchant's House   605

Tenby

Step back 500 years and discover how the Tudor merchant and his family of ten would have lived and worked in this fascinating three-storey house, situated close to the harbour within the historic walled town of Tenby. Features of the house include a fine 'Flemish' round chimney, fireplace and the original scarfed roof trusses. The remains of early frescoes can be seen on three interior walls. There are costumes for children to try on, activity sheets and a small herb garden at the back of the house.

Q Tenby town centre
☼ ○ ♣
⧖ 1–2 hours
★ Recreated Tudor family home
&
www.nationaltrust.org.uk

Yorkshire

East Riding
North Yorkshire
South Yorkshire
West Yorkshire

Swaledale, Yorkshire Dales National Park

©MAPS IN MINUTES™/Collins Bartholomew 2010

Guide to **Yorkshire**

Beverley Minster 606
Beverley

John, Bishop of York, founded a monastery on the site where Beverley Minster now stands. John died in 721 and was buried in a chapel of the church. Throughout the Middle Ages miracles, which took place at his tomb, attracted pilgrims from far and wide. He was canonised in 1037. The present church was built around his tomb. Building work began in 1220 and was completed in 1425. Visitors can take guided tours of the ground floor or the roof. Roof tours, which include spectacular views, show how the building was constructed and maintained during the centuries.

🔍 Beverley town centre
✺ ☼ ♣ ❄
⌛ 1–2 hours
★ Guided tours
&
www.beverleyminster.org

Bempton Cliffs Nature Reserve 607
Bridlington

A family favourite, and easily the best place in England to see, hear and smell seabirds. Between April and August more than 200,000 birds make the cliffs seem alive – with adults bringing food to their nests, or young chicks making their first faltering flights. With huge numbers to watch, beginners can get superb close-up views of the birds and will easily learn the difference between gannets, guillemots, herring gulls, razorbills, kittiwakes and fulmars. The easily recognisable puffins (here between April and July) are always a delight.

🔍 On the B1229, follow signs from Bempton village
✺ ☼ ♣
⌛ 2–3 hours
★ Amazing cliff top views
& Car park charges
www.rspb.org.uk

Sewerby Hall and Gardens 608
Bridlington

Situated in a dramatic cliff-top position, forming the gateway to the Flamborough Heritage Coast, Sewerby Hall and Gardens, set in 50 acres of early 19th-century parkland, enjoy spectacular views over Bridlington Bay. The hall contains the magnificent orangery, period rooms, permanent displays on the history of East Yorkshire and local aviator Amy Johnson, art and craft galleries and a souvenir and gift shop. The award-winning gardens are among the best in the region and include pleasure gardens, walled gardens, pitch and putt golf course, putting green and a small children's zoo.

🔍 On the B1255, at Sewerby
✺ ☼ ♣ ❄
⌛ 2–3 hours
★ Glorious gardens
&
www.sewerby-hall.co.uk

Burton Agnes Hall 609
Driffield

Burton Agnes Hall is a magnificent example of Elizabethan architecture built in 1598 by Sir Henry Griffith and still lived in by his descendants. The house is fitted with treasures collected and commissioned by the family over the centuries – original Elizabethan carving and plasterwork and a marvellous collection of Impressionist paintings. Lawns and yew topiary bushes surround the house, while the old walled garden is filled with collections of roses, clematis, herbs and perennials contained in a potager, maze, jungle garden and coloured gardens with giant board games.

🔍 On the A614, between Driffield and Bridlington
✺ ☼ ♣
⌛ 2–3 hours
★ Impressionist paintings
&
www.burtonagnes.com

Flamborough Head Lighthouse 610
Flamborough

A lighthouse was first built on the Flamborough Headland in 1669 but was never lit. The current lighthouse was built in 1806 and acts as a waypoint for deep sea vessels and coastal traffic as well as marking the Flamborough Headland for vessels heading for the ports of Scarborough and Bridlington. It is 85 feet tall and stands on top of a chalk cliff 170 feet high. The top of the lighthouse offers some truly spectacular views of Bridlington and its bay and also towards Filey and shipping in the North Sea.

🔍 On the B1259, 1 mile from Flamborough village
✻ ⚙ ✤
⏳ 1 hour
★ Lighthouse keeper's views
♿
www.trinityhouse.co.uk

Hull Maritime Museum 612
Hull

If you would like to discover more about Hull's maritime heritage, explore the old Dock Offices in Queen Victoria Square, which is home to the city's Maritime Museum. The museum has galleries dedicated to the city's Arctic whaling and North Sea fishing industries, which includes whale skeletons, tools and weapons as well as models of various ocean-going vessels such as the *Arctic Corsair*. The city's tradition of ocean-going commerce is also covered. This dates from the Middle Ages and has historically targeted the nations of Scandinavia and the Baltic Sea.

🔍 Hull city centre
✻ ⚙ ✤ ✽
⏳ 1–2 hours
★ Scrimshaw (whaling) art collection
FREE
www.hullcc.gov.uk

The Deep 611
Hull

Hull's mammoth submarium/aquarium (see right) ranks with the best of the world aquariums elsewhere in Valencia Spain and Lisbon Portugal. The Deep marine life and sea-life history experience is one in a million. Housed in an innovatively designed building shaped like a ship, visitors can literally explore the depths via an underwater lift, which can take you 30 feet down. Exhibitions and living sea life are numerous, including the Corals, the Kingdom of Ice, exploring Arctic sea life, and the Evolving Sea that takes you back to before life began.

🔍 Hull city centre, on the banks of the Humber
✻ ⚙ ✤ ✽
⏳ 2–3 hours
★ Europe's deepest viewing tunnel
♿ ♿
www.thedeep.co.uk

STAR ATTRACTION

Streetlife Museum 613
Hull

This museum tells the story of 200 years of transport in Hull. Children will love boarding the old trams, getting their bones shaken on the simulated mail coach ride and be surprised at the sights, sounds and even smells of an old coaching yard. There are also extensive displays of early motorcars, bicycles and a pre-war replica street scene. Visitors are met by two original trams, and then make their way through an original bicycle workshop to the Motor Car Gallery. This features a corridor full of both petrol and steam cars from the earliest days of motoring.

Hull city centre

1-2 hours

1930s street scene

FREE

www.hullcc.gov.uk

Burnby Hall Gardens 615
Pocklington

These delightful gardens are home to a National Collection of hardy water lilies – the biggest such collection to be found in a natural setting in Europe. Two lakes are set in eight acres of beautiful gardens – including rock gardens, a natural shrubbery, formal beds, the secret garden and a Victorian garden. The gardens were the inspiration of Major Percy Stewart who, on his death in 1963, left his estate in trust for the enjoyment of anyone who cares to visit. The Stewart Museum in the gardens provides a fascinating glimpse into his life.

Off the A1079, in Pocklington town centre

2-3 hours

Sunday band concerts

www.burnbyhallgardens.com

Wilberforce House Museum 614
Hull

William Wilberforce is one of Hull's most famous sons, and his role in the anti-slavery campaign has left a long lasting worldwide legacy. This museum, opened in 1906 and recently refurbished, is sited in his birthplace. The museum explores the history of slavery, abolition and the legacy of slavery today. Visitors can see many objects relating to slavery and the campaign for its abolition; including paper documents, plantation and slavery records, Wedgwood medallions and anti-slavery ceramics. The museum also has exhibits relating to the remarkable character of the man who was born here.

Hull city centre

1-2 hours

The Brookes ship model and poster

FREE

www.hullcc.gov.uk

Ingleborough Cave 616
Clapham

Until 1837 the secrets of Ingleborough Cave were hidden behind large natural calcite dams behind which water had ponded, submerging much of the passage beyond. These were broken down following a flood, to reveal a wonderland of sculpted passages and beautiful cave formations which have been delighting visitors ever since. A well-laid concrete path allows you to traverse comfortably for half a mile into the mountain, and discrete lighting displays the calcite flows, the stalactites and stalagmites at their best. An expert guide will help you to interpret the features, enhancing your experience.

Off the A65 north-west of Skipton

2-3 hours

The nearby Yorkshire Dales National Park

www.ingleboroughcave.co.uk

RHS Garden Harlow Carr   617

Harrogate

Enjoy some of the best horticulture in Yorkshire, every day of the year, at this lovely garden just outside Harrogate. Harlow Carr is well planted but has more of the character of a public park than a well-designed garden. The 58-acre garden has many seasonal highlights including the UK's longest streamside garden, woodland, wildflower meadows, perennial borders and kitchen garden. Spend a spontaneous morning visit enjoying the best of the season and gathering planting tips. This is one of Yorkshire's most relaxing and surprising gardens and stands at the gateway to the Yorkshire Dales.

🔍 Off the B6162, about a mile and a half from Harrogate town centre

☼ ☀ ♣ ❄

⏳ 2-3 hours

★ The Alpine Zone

&

www.rhs.org.uk

Dales Country Museum   618

Hawes

This museum tells the story of the people and landscape of the Yorkshire Dales past and present, and stimulates visitors to think about its future. Displays interpret the development of the Dales from prehistoric times to the present day. Themes include: school days, home life, leisure time, religion, transport, communication and tourism, farming, local crafts and industries. The museum is housed in an imaginative conversion of Hawes railway station in Wensleydale in the north of the park. Outdoor displays includes a real steam train and carriages on the track bed of the former Wensleydale Railway.

🔍 Off the A684, in Wensleydale

☼ ☀ ♣ ❄

⏳ 1-2 hours

★ Time Tunnel

&

www.yorkshiredales.org.uk

Duncombe Park   619

Helmsley

This magnificent house is set in beautiful parkland overlooking the River Rye and Helmsley Castle. Built in 1713, it is the family home of Lord and Lady Feversham. Guided tours of the house with its elegant interior design, opulent rooms and treasures collected over many centuries are available. Visitors can enjoy stunning views from the landscaped 18th-century terraces, complete with temples, conservatory and secret 'scented garden'. The house is surrounded by 182 hectares of parkland, half of which is a National Nature Reserve and home to ancient trees and rare species of fungi and insects.

🔍 On the A170

☼ ☀ ♣

⏳ 2-3 hours

★ Stunning gardens and parkland

&

www.duncombepark.com

Ryedale Folk Museum 620
Hutton-le-Hole

Ryedale Folk Museum is a large open-air museum. Set up by a group of local men in the 1960s, it has continued to grow into the four acres that you see today. The wide range of historic buildings on show have been rescued from around the area and contain a large collection of historic artefacts bringing to life the lives of ordinary people from Ryedale's past. They include long houses, an Elizabethan manor house and furnished cottages. Visitors can see the oldest daylight photographic studio in the country and see archaeological displays from prehistory to the tenth century.

On the A170
1–2 hours
History brought to life
www.ryedalefolkmuseum.co.uk

White Scar Cave 621
Ingleton

Deep beneath Ingleborough Hill, in the Yorkshire Dales National Park, lies a hidden world which has been sculpted by nature over thousands of years. Imagine a subterranean landscape, beautifully lit, with gushing streams and waterfalls, exotic cave formations, and a huge ice-age cavern adorned with thousands of stalactites (shown right). This is White Scar Cave – the longest showcave in Britain. An 80-minute tour travels more than a mile deep into the ground and includes a visit to the 330-foot high Battlefield Cavern. Dress warmly; don't wear heels; a hard hat will be provided.

On the B6255, on the road from Ingleton to Hawes
1–2 hours
200,000-year-old caves
www.whitescarcave.co.uk

Flamingo Land Theme Park and Zoo 622
Kirby Misperton

Flamingo Land attracts visitors from all over the country by combining white-knuckle rides, a good zoo and attractions for the little ones too. The zoo is home to over 1,000 animals, including African lions, giraffes, rhinoceros, Siberian tigers, meerkats and, of course, the famous pink flamingos. But it is also home to some of the best rides in the UK including, Velocity, the UK's only motorbike coaster, and Cliff Hanger which will blast you 200 feet into the air. Attractions for youngsters include the Dragon Coaster and the Tea Cup ride.

Off the A169 Malton to Pickering road
4–5 hours
Kumali, a suspended coaster
www.flamingoland.co.uk

Mother Shipton's Cave 624
Knaresborough

Mother Shipton is England's most famous Prophetess. She lived some 500 years ago during the reigns of King Henry VIII and Queen Elizabeth I. Her prophetic visions became known and feared throughout England, with many of them still proving uncannily accurate today. The Cave, her legendary birthplace, is near to the famous, unique, geological phenomenon – the Petrifying Well. Visitors can still see its magical cascading waters turn items into stone. The Petrifying Well is England's oldest visitor attraction, first opening its gates in 1630.

🔍 Follow signs from the A59

⚙ ⊙ ♣

⧗ 1-2 hours

★ Walks in the riverside park

£

www.mothershipton.co.uk

Knaresborough Castle and Courthouse Museum 623
Knaresborough

A stronghold of medieval kings, Knaresborough Castle still stands towering over the River Nidd. A visit to the site includes a tour to discover what Royalty got up to in the King's Tower, get a glimpse of the dungeon and walk through the underground sallyport. You can also visit the Courthouse Museum, housed in one of the castle's oldest surviving buildings. Here visitors can find out about Knaresborough's fascinating history and the colourful characters who have contributed to it, such as Eugene Aram, the infamous 18th-century murderer.

🔍 Knaresborough town centre

⚙ ⊙ ♣

⧗ 2-3 hours

★ Life in a Castle exhibit

£

www.harrogate.gov.uk/museums

Eden Camp Modern History Theme Museum 625
Malton

This is one of Britain's most comprehensive museums covering British military and social history from 1914 onwards. Housed within the grounds of an original Second World War prisoner of war camp, it presents all aspects of the story of the Second World War, which is recreated using sights, sounds, smells and moving figures to create a unique atmosphere that makes it feel like you travelled back in time to wartime Britain. There are also exhibits on the First World War and the role played by British military forces around the world since 1945.

🔍 On the A169

⚙ ⊙ ♣ ❄

⧗ 3-4 hours

★ Assault course for youngsters

£

www.edencamp.co.uk

Ormesby Hall
Ormesby

626

Home of the Pennyman family for nearly 400 years, this classic Georgian mansion, with its Victorian kitchen and laundry, attractive gardens and estate walks, provide lively resources for schoolchildren learning their history, and a unique visitor attraction. Weekend visitors can experience the spirit of the intimate home of Colonel Jim Pennyman, the last of the Pennyman line, and his arts-loving wife Ruth, as well as the stylish legacy of the 18th-century character 'Wicked' Sir James Pennyman – so named due to his extravagant lifestyle and his gambling with the family fortune.

🔍 Follow signs from the A172
☀ ⚙ ♣ Weekends only
⌛ 2–3 hours
★ Working Victorian laundry and glorious gardens
£
www.nationaltrust.org.uk

North Yorkshire Moors Railway
Pickering

627

The North Yorkshire Moors Railway is one of the oldest historic train lines in the north of England; it was completed in 1836 on the orders of George Stephenson. The steam train takes visitors on an 18-mile journey from the small market town of Pickering to the village of Grosmont, near Whitby. A scenic ride through the North York Moors National Park features diverse scenery – everything from beautiful lakes to forest covered valleys and even some moorland. Along the way there are also numerous beautiful stations and villages in the countryside.

🔍 Pickering town centre
☀ ⚙ ♣
⌛ 3–4 hours
★ Special theme days and dining car specials
£ £
www.nymr.co.uk

Richmond Castle
Richmond

628

With its breathtaking views of the Yorkshire Dales, Richmond Castle fully deserves its place as one of the finest tourist attractions in North Yorkshire. The castle was originally built to subdue the unruly North of England and it is one of the greatest Norman fortresses in Britain. The rectangular keep is 100 feet high and is one of the finest in the country. Visitors can explore the impressive ruins and learn all about the castle's past in an interactive exhibition before taking a peaceful stroll round the secluded Cockpit Garden.

🔍 Richmond town centre
☀ ⚙ ♣ ❄
⌛ 1–2 hours
★ Views from the top of the keep
£
www.english-heritage.org.uk

Ripley Castle and Gardens
Ripley

629

Home to the Ingilby family for over 700 years, Ripley has a fascinating history. The castle featured heavily during the Civil War and is famous as the place where 'Trooper' Jane Ingilby held Oliver Cromwell at gunpoint. Visitors can see a marvellous display of Civil War artefacts. James 1 stayed here in 1603, but two years later was almost a victim of the Gunpowder Plot. In a fascinating irony, eleven of the conspirators were connected to the Ingilby family. The gardens and grounds are also splendid with massive herbaceous borders and fine views over lakes and a deer park.

🔍 On the A61, 3 miles north of Harrogate
☀ ⚙ ♣
⌛ 2–3 hours
★ Guided tours of the house
£
www.ripleycastle.co.uk

Fountains Abbey and Studley Royal Water Garden   630

Ripon

Set in 800 acres of beautiful countryside, this site offers the whole range of England's heritage. Visitors can see the magnificent 12th-century abbey ruins and the only surviving Cistercian corn mill. You can amble through the beautiful landscaped Georgian water garden of Studley Royal, complete with statues, follies and breathtaking views. Delight in the richly decorated Victorian St Mary's church and take time out to relax in the Reading Room in Elizabethan Fountains Hall. Complete a great day out by exploring the medieval deer park.

🔍 Off the B6265, 4 miles west of Ripon
☼ ◉ ♣ ❀
⏳ 2-3 hours
⭐ Cellarium's incredible vaulted ceiling
💲

www.nationaltrust.org.uk

Lightwater Valley Theme Park   631

Ripon

Lightwater Valley is one of the leading theme parks in the UK and jam packed with over 40 thrilling rides and attractions. The line-up comprises some amazing rides, including the Ultimate, Europe's longest rollercoaster, as well as the stomach churning, mighty Eagle's Claw and the Wild River Rapids. Plus, newly arrived, dare you step aboard the terrifying Whirlwind or risk a one-on-one encounter in Raptor Attack's abandoned mineshaft? Visitors will also find a host of other less terrifying rides, a Bird of Prey Centre and a shopping village all on the one site.

🔍 On the A6108, 2 miles north of Ripon
☼ ◉ ♣
⏳ 3-4 hours
⭐ The Ultimate
💲 💲

www.lightwatervalley.net

Newby Hall and Gardens   632

Ripon

One of England's renowned Adam houses, Newby Hall is an exceptional example of 18th-century interior decoration. Built in the 1690s in the style of Sir Christopher Wren, the house was later enlarged and adapted by John Carr and subsequently Robert Adam. The contents of the house, collected by Weddell, ancestor of the Compton family, on the Grand Tour include the magnificent Gobelins Tapestry Room, a renowned gallery of classical statuary and some of Chippendale's finest furniture. The 25 acres of glorious formal gardens are full of rare and beautiful plants.

🔍 Two miles from the A1 between Boroughbridge and Ripon
☼ ◉ ♣
⏳ 2-3 hours
⭐ Guided tours of the house and fantastic children's adventure garden with train rides
💲 💲

www.newbyhall.com

Scarborough Pleasure Steamers 633
Scarborough

This is the best way to see the town and its glorious coastline. The pleasure steamers sail daily from the lighthouse pier. Visitors get a full hour-long cruise along the Yorkshire Coast on the *Regal Lady* or the *Coronia*, with fully licensed bars, snacks and entertainment on most cruises. You can either sail north towards Ravenscar Cliffs, Smugglers Cove, Hayburn Wyke and Scalby Ness. Or sail south towards Filey Brigg, Gristhorpe Cliffs, Redcliffe and Cayton Bay. There are also evening cruises during the season that sail at 8.00 p.m. It's best to book in advance.

🔍 Scarborough harbour
☼ ◎ 🍁
⏳ 1–2 hours
★ Views of the glorious Yorkshire coastline
♿
www.scarborough;eveningnews.co.uk

Bolton Abbey 634
Skipton

The Bolton Abbey estate comprises 30,000 acres of the Yorkshire Dales. Visitors can examine medieval buildings, explore the 12th-century priory ruins and take in as much of the 80 miles of moorland, woodland and riverside walks as they like. The riverside walk encompasses the heart of the romantic landscape, which inspired some of Britain's great artists and poets. Wordsworth, Turner, Girtin and Landseer were some of those who captured the beauty of the place in words and paint. Little has changed over the centuries; the cattle still come to drink from the river opposite the priory.

🔍 On the B6160, between Skipton and Harrogate
☼ ◎ 🍁 ❄
⏳ 2–3 hours
★ Ruins of Barden Tower
♿
www.boltonabbey.com

Skipton Castle 635
Skipton

At the top of Skipton's main street stand the massive twin towers of Skipton Castle. Over 900 years old, Skipton Castle is one of the most complete and best-preserved medieval castles in England. Visitors can explore every corner of this impressive history-rich castle, which withstood a three-year siege during the Civil War and was the last Royalist bastion in the north. You can see the banqueting hall, the kitchen, the bedchamber and the privy. Climb from the depths of the dungeon to the top storey of the watchtower.

🔍 Skipton town centre
☼ ◎ 🍁 ❄
⏳ 1–2 hours
★ Guided tours
♿
www.skiptoncastle.co.uk

Dalby Forest Drive and Visitor Centre 636
Thornton-le-Dale

Dalby Forest is on the southern slopes of the North York Moors National Park. The forest is home to a wide variety of wildlife: birds such as the crossbill and the nightjar, roe deer abound and badgers are a very common sight. Burial mounds and earthworks can be found everywhere. A network of forest roads, including the 9-mile Dalby Forest Drive, provides access to this outstanding landscape. The visitor centre at Sneverdale, one mile from the Thornton-le-Dale entrance, is the place to start.

🔍 Follow signs from the A170 at Thornton-le-Dale
☼ ◎ 🍁 ❄
⏳ 2–3 hours
★ Dalby Forest Drive
FREE
www.forestry.gov.uk

'Silver Darlings' Walk

Whitby

637

Whitby has always had fishing in the blood. Herring, the 'silver darlings' as they were known, have always been the fish of choice. You can do an easy walk around this fascinating port starting at the Marina, once a bustling shipyard. Head over the bridge, where you will find the Captain Cook Museum. Check out the market square before crossing the bridge again. Turn right and head up Pier Road along the quayside. At the top you can see Whitby Abbey, the whalebone arch and the Royal Crescent before heading back through the town to your starting point.

🔍 Tourist Information Centre, in Langborne Road

⚙ ◯ ♣ ❄

⌛ 2 hours

★ Dracula's Gothic abbey

FREE

www.whitbyonline.co.uk

Castle Howard

York

638

One of Britain's finest stately homes, Castle Howard is located in the beautiful Howardian Hills and is distinguished by its famous dome, which can be seen for miles. The house has many superb rooms, filled with fine furniture, statues and beautiful china. Visitors can also see remarkable collection of paintings by Rubens, Tintoretto, Van Dyck, Canaletto and Reynolds. The gardens too are marvellous and proudly display seasonal collections of snowdrops, daffodils, rhododendrons, azaleas, roses and delphiniums among their 1,000 acres.

🔍 Off the A64, 15 miles north-east of York

⚙ ◯ ♣

⌛ 2–3 hours

★ Portrait of Henry VIII

♿ ♿

www.castlehoward.co.uk

York's NRM is the **biggest railway museum in the world**

Clifford's Tower
York   639

It's the stunning view you get of the historic city of York that makes Clifford's Tower one of the most popular attractions in Yorkshire. Set on a tall mound in the heart of Old York, this imposing tower is almost all that remains of York Castle, which was originally built by William the Conqueror. There's plenty to discover here. In its time, the tower has served as a prison and a royal mint, as well as the place where Henry VIII had the bodies of his enemies put on public display.

🔍 York city centre

❄️ ☀️ ♣️ ❅

⏳ 1 hour

⭐ Displays relating the tower's bloody history

♿

www.english-heritage.org.uk

Jorvik Viking Centre
York   640

Jorvik is an award-winning museum that recreates the sights, smells, sounds, and flavour of daily life in the tumultuous world of 10th-century York. On this site the York Archaeological Trust discovered perfectly preserved remains of Viking York (Jorvik) encased in wet mud. The centre recreates this world through a series of tableaux depicting markets, shops, streets scenes, and other aspects of daily life, including meal preparation and the ever-popular latrine scene. Audio-visual displays help you to investigate the information gathered from the 5-year-long dig here at Coppergate.

🔍 Follow signs from the city centre

❄️ ☀️ ♣️ ❅

⏳ 1–2 hours

⭐ An astonishing archaeological discovery

♿

www.jorvik-viking-centre.co.uk

National Railway Museum
York   641

This truly impressive collection, including over 100 locomotives and nearly 200 other items of rolling stock, tells the railway story from the early 19th century to the present day. Visitors can re-live a golden era and witness history brought to life. Among the many highlights are the Flying Scotsman – perhaps the most famous steam train in the world, a futuristic Japanese Bullet Train, a replica of Stephenson's Rocket and the carriage used by Queen Victoria.

There is a daily turntable demonstration to show how several tons of railway locomotive could be turned on a sixpence. You can explore the workings of steam locomotives and watch the complex mechanism work before your eyes. Train enthusiasts can get in the cab of a steam engine, build a loco, control a train and watch a live link to York's electronic signal box.

Visitors with more practical interests should make sure they visit The Works. Here you can witness the traditional skills of engineers as they conserve the magnificent railway vehicles in their care. Check out track train movements in and out of York Station at the Integrated Electronic Control Centre. You can finish off your visit with a ride on a real railway – miniature, steam or diesel.

FIVE-STAR ATTRACTION

🔍 Near York railway station

❄️ ☀️ ♣️ ❅

⏳ 3–4 hours

⭐ Railway art collection

FREE Car parks and some exhibitions may charge

www.nrm.org.uk

York Dungeons   `642`
York

Deep in the heart of historic York, buried beneath its paving stones, lies the north of England's most chilling attraction. It depicts local horrible history using actor led shows, special effects and displays of models and objects. The Great Plague show is set in 1551 with a recreation of medieval York streets. There is also a recreation of a York pub, the Golden Fleece Inn, where visitors are told ghost stories. Other shows include the Judgement of Sinners and the Torture Chamber where visitors are shown demonstrations of torture devices.

🔍 York city centre
⚙ ◉ ♣ ❄
⏳ 1–2 hours
⭐ The Ghosts of York
💷 💷
www.thedungeons.com

Yorkshire Air Museum   `644`
York

The Yorkshire Air Museum is a fascinating and dynamic museum, authentically based on a Second World War Bomber Command Station at Elvington. The unique displays include the original Control Tower, Air Gunners' Collection, Barnes Wallis' prototype 'bouncing bomb' and a superb Airborne Forces Display. The rapidly expanding collection of historical aircraft depicts aviation from its earliest days, through the Second World War with the awesome and unique Halifax rebuild to today's Middle East conflicts with the recently retired Nimrod MR2 jet.

🔍 On the B1228, just outside York
⚙ ◉ ♣ ❄
⏳ 3–4 hours
⭐ Pioneers of Aviation exhibit
💷
www.yorkshireairmuseum.co.uk

York Minster   `643`
York

Built between the 12th and 15th centuries, York Minster is the largest Gothic cathedral in England. There are free guided tours but visitors are also free to see the magnificent architecture for themselves. You can visit the Octagonal Chapter house, which contains some of the Minster's finest carvings. You can explore the Undercroft, Treasury and Crypt where you will find Roman, Norman and Viking remains and the jewels of the treasury. If you can scale the 275 steps of the tower you will be rewarded with fantastic views of the city.

🔍 York city centre
⚙ ◉ ♣ ❄
⏳ 2–3 hours
⭐ Free guided tours
💷
www.yorkminster.org

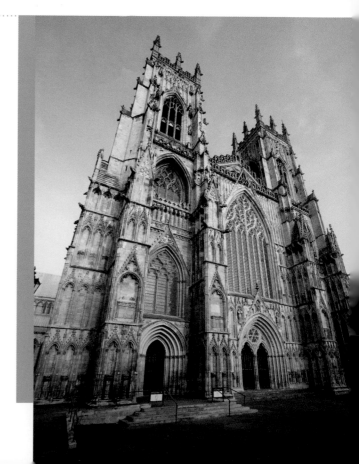

Yorkshire Museum and Gardens   645
York

Recently refurbished and upgraded, the Yorkshire Museum reopened to the public in August 2010 following a nine-month redevelopment called 'Letting in the Light'. The museum has re-displayed its internationally renowned collections in three major new exhibitions: Roman York – Meet the People of the Empire, Medieval York – the Power and the Glory, and Extinct: A Way of Life. In addition, the museum also offers a fascinating audio-visual guide to the history of York in its auditorium, making it an ideal port-of-call for first-time visitors to this historic city.

York city centre

2-3 hours

10-acre museum botanical gardens

www.yorkshiremuseum.org.uk

National Coal Mining Museum for England   646
Barnsley

The National Coal Mining Museum for England gives visitors the unique opportunity to travel 460 feet underground, down one of Britain's oldest working mines, where models and machinery depict methods and conditions of mining from the early 1800s to the present day. Experienced local miners guide parties around the underground workings. Above ground you can visit the pit ponies, find out more about the development of mining and its communities, take a train ride, see the steam winder and visit the pithead baths.

Off the A642, north-west of Barnsley

2-3 hours

Underground tour

FREE

www.ncm.org.uk

Conisbrough Castle `647`
Conisbrough

The lofty 12th-century keep of this very well preserved building, now complete with its restored roof and floors, is a spectacular sight. It had a major role to play in the Wars of the Roses and was once owned by Richard of York. Visitors can discover more about its history with the exciting audio tour and visual displays that bring the story of this great castle to life. Conisbrough Castle featured in Sir Walter Scott's *Ivanhoe*, and is redolent with reminders of the golden age of knights in armour.

On the A630, north-east of Conisbrough town centre

2 hours

Super views from the top

www.english-heritage.org.uk

AeroVenture `648`
Doncaster

This museum features many different examples of aircraft from all eras of aviation history, highlighting the region's influence during the early days of British aviation. The collection covers both civilian and military aircraft and has a few pieces that qualify as truly rare and are unlikely to be seen anywhere else in the world. Some of the models on display include Mach 2 jets, propeller based aircraft, machines from many decades ago on loan from the Royal Air Force, and even a huge collection of helicopters.

Follow signs from the M18, A6182 and A638

1–2 hours

Get inside a cockpit

www.aeroventure.org.uk

Brodsworth Hall and Gardens `649`
Doncaster

Time stands still at Brodsworth Hall, one of the most unusual visitor attractions in South Yorkshire. Inside this beautiful Victorian country house almost everything has been left exactly as it was when it was still a family home. Possessions that took more than 130 years to gather together, from the grandest piece of furniture to family mementoes and humble domestic items, are still in their original places. Meanwhile the grounds, a collection of grand gardens in miniature, have been restored to their full Victorian splendour, and feature a colourful array of seasonal displays.

Off the A635, 5 miles north-west of Doncaster

2–3 hours

Restored Victorian gardens

www.english-heritage.org.uk

Cusworth Hall, Museum and Park `650`
Doncaster

Cusworth Hall, Doncaster's premier beauty spot and one of only four Grade I listed properties in the district, was built in the 1740s in a parkland setting. Recently restored, stunning ceiling paintings in the Italianate Chapel have been revealed after being hidden under layers of paint for 50 years. The hall is now home to the Museum of South Yorkshire Life and its collections depict life in the locality over the last 200 years. The hall provides a beautiful backdrop to the lakeland landscape of the country park.

Off the A638, 2 miles north of Doncaster

1–2 hours

Parkland with marvellous views of Doncaster

FREE Car park charges

www.cusworth-hall.co.uk

Hatfield Water Park | 651
Doncaster

Hatfield Water Park is an all-round watersports centre offering challenging water and land based activities to all age groups and abilities. Activities include canoeing, dinghy sailing, wind surfing and sub-aqua; with courses run by highly qualified staff with a strong emphasis on water safety. You can visit for the day or on residential courses. The park also has a campsite and other residential accommodation. You can hire equipment or bring your own, but it is essential to book in advance (see website for details). Introductory two-hour Taster Courses in all watersports are available on request.

Off the A18, between Hatfield and Thorne

3–4 hours

Superb walking and cycling in the surrounding area

www.doncaster.gov.uk

Roche Abbey | 652
Maltby

Beautifully set in a valley landscaped by 'Capability' Brown in the 18th century, Roche Abbey has one of the most complete ground plans of any English Cistercian monastery, laid out as excavated foundations. The soaring early Gothic transepts of this Cistercian monastery, founded in 1147, still survive to their original height and are ranked in importance with the finest early Gothic architecture in Britain. These romantic ruins and the glorious countryside in which they sit offer the perfect place for a tranquil summer picnic.

Off the A634, 2 miles south of Maltby

2–3 hours

Super cliff-side views of these romantic ruins

www.english-heritage.org.uk

Magna Science Adventure Centre | 653
Rotherham

Set inside a huge former steelworks, Magna is an interactive science visitor attraction that explores the power of the elements – earth, air, fire and water. Aimed primarily at children, there is plenty here for the whole family and introduces educational science as fun. You can walk in a wind tunnel, fire a water cannon, explode a rock face, make waves and crawl through an underground tunnel. Set indoors and outdoors, the centre has four pavilions, a water park (bring towels and a change of clothes) and a fabulous adventure park.

On the A6178, take junctions 33 or 34 of the M1

3–4 hours

Hi-tech adventure park

www.visitmagna.co.uk

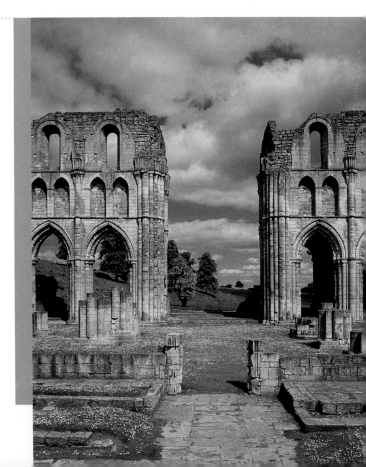

Rother Valley Country Park
Rotherham

654

This 750-acre country park offers the finest range of activities in the region. For the very active: windsurfing, dinghy sailing, cable water skiing and canoeing are available at the Watersports Centre. For the more sedate there are walks and cycling around the lakes. The very popular area for picnics and BBQs has beautiful views of the lake. An adventure playground will keep the kids amused for hours. Watersports courses run throughout the year and equipment hire is also available. The 18- and 9-hole golf courses provide an excellent venue for drier sport.

- 1 mile from junction 31 of the M1
- 3-4 hours
- Wide range of activities
- **FREE** Car parking and some activities will charge

www.rvcp.co.uk

Millennium Gallery
Sheffield

655

This is an outstanding venue for the visual arts, craft and design. With four individual galleries under one roof, there are all sorts of wonderful things to see. Be inspired by treasures from the past, admire master-pieces from Britain's national collections and discover new creations by artists and makers working today. The four galleries comprise a special exhibition space, craft and design, metalwork and a Ruskin gallery, which houses original artworks and copies of Renaissance masterpieces that the famous art critic and social historian John Ruskin felt everyone should see.

- Sheffield city centre
- 2-3 hours
- Metalwork gallery exploring the city's past glory
- **FREE**

www.museums-sheffield.org.uk

Renishaw Hall and Gardens
Sheffield

656

This house has been home to the Sitwell family, famous patrons of the arts, for nearly 400 years. Renishaw is still very much a family home, which adds to its unique atmosphere. The hall opened to the public for the first time in 2010. There are tours every Friday at 2.30 p.m., booking is recommended to avoid disappointment. A tour of the hall enables you to see some of the spectacular collections of art and furniture acquired by generations of Sitwells. Outside sits one of the most important classical Italianate gardens in Britain.

- On the A6135, 2 miles from junction 30 of the M1
- 2-3 hours
- Fabulous collections of art and furniture

www.sitwell.co.uk

Sheffield Ski Village   657
Sheffield

Europe's largest all-season ski resort caters for skiers and fun-seekers of all ages. The ski slopes are designed perfectly for beginners and advanced riders and a lesson programme will soon have you enjoying all that skiing and snowboarding have to offer. There is also a brilliant outdoor Adventure Mountain and an indoor Jungle Jim's play area, which provide the perfect alternatives for those members of the family who don't want to ski. The centre is also home to a new state-of-the-art, ten-pin bowling alley. It is advisable to book your activities in advance (see website).

Off the A61, 5 minutes from Sheffield city centre

3-4 hours

Fabulous all-year round snow fun

www.sheffieldskivillage.co.uk

Bagshaw Museum   658
Batley

A Victorian former mill owner's house set in 36 aces of parkland; the museum is host to a wide range of unusual collections from around the globe. Once the home of George Sheard, from 1875–1902, this Gothic house became a museum in 1911. Its purpose was to entertain visitors. It still does that with permanent displays on Egypt and decorative arts from the Far East. New displays include two local history galleries including exhibits on Fox's Biscuits and Batley Variety Club, the new Spirit of South Asia gallery and a new gallery showcasing saucy seaside postcards.

Off the A652, in Wilton Park, Batley

1-2 hours

Life and death in Ancient Egypt

FREE

www.kirklees.gov.uk

Oakwell Hall   659
Batley

This beautiful Elizabethan manor house delighted Charlotte Brontë who featured it as Fieldhead – the home of the heroine in *Shirley*. Built in 1583, the hall is now set out as it would have been in the 1690s. Visitors today can easily imagine themselves in post Civil War England when faced with the imposing great hall with its gallery, the elegant painted chamber and the beautifully panelled parlour. Set in beautiful countryside where you can stroll around the delightful period garden or check out the inhabitants of the wildlife access garden.

Follow signs from the A652

2–3 hours

Discover Oakwell gallery

www.kirklees.gov.uk

Bradford Industrial Museum   661
Bradford

Think of industry in Bradford and you think of wool, mills, machinery, steam engines and horses, all of which can be found at Bradford Industrial Museum. Housed in Moorside Mills, an original spinning mill, it's alive with magnificent machinery that once converted raw wool into the world's best worsted cloth. The yard rings to the sound of iron on stone as the Shire Horses give rides, pull a horse tram or haul a horse-bus. The mill-owner's house is furnished as at the turn of the century. You can also see the back-to-backs in which the mill workers lived.

Follow signs from the Bradford Ring Road or the A658

2–3 hours

Washday in Gaythorne Road

FREE

www.bradfordmuseums.org

Bolling Hall   660
Bradford

Situated in a quiet, leafy garden, Bolling Hall was for many years the seat of two important land-owning families, the Bollings and the Tempests. The hall is a rambling mixture of styles with every nook and cranny packed with history. During the Civil War the household supported the Royalist cause, and the house provided a stronghold during the siege of Bradford. Rooms are furnished and decorated to give an accurate taste of life at different periods of the house's history, and the fascinating furniture on display includes a superb bed made for Harewood House by Thomas Chippendale.

Follow signs from the A650, 1 mile from Bradford city centre

1–2 hours

Cromwell's death mask

FREE

www.bradfordmuseums.org

National Media Museum 662
Bradford

The National Media Museum is a fabulous free museum devoted to film, photography, TV, radio and the Internet. The museum has always set new standards in display and interactivity. Visitors can obtain a hands-on experience of the media, learning how television works and trying their hand at animation among other activities. Special events bring you face-to-face with leading photographers, stars and programme makers. Three film festivals bring you the very best in new and classic film. Above all, the museum invites you explore the media, the world it presents and to think again.

Bradford city centre

2–3 hours

IMAX cinema

FREE Except for cinemas

www.nationalmediamuseum.org.uk

Red House 663
Cleckheaton

This delightful 1830s cloth merchant's house has fascinating Brontë connections. Charlotte Brontë visited often and featured it in her novel *Shirley*. The red brick house, built in 1660, was home to the Taylor family. Mary Taylor was a close friend of Charlotte's. The house still looks very much as it would have in Charlotte's day. Each room brings you closer to the 1830s, from the elegant parlour to the stone-flagged kitchen. The stained glass windows are perfectly preserved in the dining room. And the 19th-century gardens help to capture the atmosphere of this fascinating bygone age.

On the A651 at Gomersal, near Cleckheaton

1–2 hours

The Secret's Out Brontë exhibit

FREE

www.kirklees.gov.uk

Bankfield Museum 664
Halifax

Set within an Italianate mansion, this former home of textile mill owner, MP and philanthropist Edward Ackroyd, houses an impressive, internationally renowned collection of textiles. Bankfield is steeped in history and has been a museum for over a hundred years. The house still retains many original features including an imposing entrance hall, painted ceilings, wall decoration, marble fireplaces and a private chapel. The collections date from prehistoric times to the 21st century and include an internationally important collection of costumes.

On the A647, 1 mile from Halifax town centre

1–2 hours

Textiles and costumes

FREE

www.calderdale.gov.uk

Shibden Hall
Halifax

666

Enter a house where you sense the family has just gone out and allow yourself to absorb 600 years of history. Built in 1420, this incredible building with its medieval timber frame, oak panelled interiors and atmospheric room settings has taken its place as Halifax's Historic Home. The on-site folk museum, which is a reconstruction of an early 19th-century village, and barn, also offer visitors a glimpse of a world without electricity, where craftsmen worked in wood and iron. The house is surrounded by stunning gardens, cascades and historic parkland.

🔍 Follow signs from Halifax town centre and the M62

⚙ ◉ 🍁

⏳ 1–2 hours

⭐ Painted glass windows

£

www.calderdale.gov.uk

Eureka! The National Children's Museum
Halifax

665

This award-winning museum features over 400 interactive exhibits that will inspire children aged 11 and under to learn about themselves and the world around them through imagination, play and discovery. In exploring the different galleries, children can see their own skeleton, catch a wave, save a polar bear, mix their own music, build a house and even get a job at the Post Office. Outdoors they can twist, turn, climb or play hide and seek at the new outdoor PlayScape and Sensory Trail then dig on the inland beach.

🔍 Halifax town centre

⚙ ◉ 🍁 ❄

⏳ 2–3 hours

⭐ Learning through play

£

www.eureka.org.uk

Bronte Boats
Hebden Bridge

667

The company specialises in hiring barges on the Rochdale Canal. It offers day trips, hiring by the day or the week. Your trip begins with a short but thorough training course before you set out on your voyage. A standard long boat is 58 feet long, equipped with central heating, spacious dining room and soft furnishings. You can travel on this picturesque and historic waterway at your own pace. The canal runs for 32 miles, has 91 locks and over 100 bridges. It navigates over the Pennines from Manchester to Sowerby Bridge in West Yorkshire.

🔍 Hebden Bridge town centre

⚙ ◉ 🍁 ❄

⏳ 8 hours (and longer)

⭐ Holiday at your own pace

£ £ £

www.bronteboats.co.uk

Last of the Summer Wine Exhibition

668

Holmfirth

This museum is dedicated to the long-running TV series. Visitors can walk through a rather familiar looking door into Compo's house. The house is filled with props, photographs and other artefacts from this much-loved programme. Display information captures many characters and situations from the show – including the world famous matchbox, which used to scare the more sensitive cast-members with one quick glimpse of its contents. There is a video featuring famous clips from the series introduced by Bill Owen.

🔍 Holmfirth town centre

⚙ ◎ ❤

⏳ 1-2 hours

⭐ Upperiscope!

♿

www.summerwineexhibition.co.uk

Brontë Parsonage Museum

669

Keighley

The Brontës are the world's most famous literary family and Haworth Parsonage was their home from 1820 to 1861. Charlotte, Emily and Anne Brontë were the authors of some of the best-loved books in the English language. The beautifully preserved museum has been opening its doors to visitors for over 75 years. Set between the unique village of Haworth, and the wild moorland beyond, this homely Georgian house still retains the atmosphere of the Brontës' time. The rooms they once used are filled with their furniture, clothes and personal possessions.

🔍 In Haworth, 3 miles south of Keithley

⚙ ◎ ❤ ❄

⏳ 1-2 hours

⭐ The moorland is thought to have inspired *Wuthering Heights*

♿

www.bronte.org.uk

Cliffe Castle Museum

670

Keighley

Cliffe Castle was originally the home of Victorian millionaire and textile manufacturer, Henry Isaac Butterfield. It stands in attractive hillside grounds with greenhouses, a garden centre, aviaries and a children's play area. The house is now a large museum with a wide variety of displays. These include an array of glittering minerals, local rocks and fossils (including a 2-metre long fossil amphibian), mounted birds and local mammals, original furnished rooms with chandeliers, William Morris stained-glass, old dolls, toys and domestic items and a programme of temporary exhibitions.

🔍 On the A629, north of Keighley town centre

⚙ ◎ ❤ ❄

⏳ 1-2 hours

⭐ Victorian Great Drawing Room

FREE

www.bradfordmuseums.org

Keighley and Worth Valley Railway

671

Keighley

This steam railway runs from Keighley to Oxenhope. The steep gradient up the Worth Valley has been a challenge for locomotives ever since it opened in 1867. The sound of a steam engine tackling it echoes from the steep sides of the valley, while great clouds of steam add drama to the scene. A few of the woollen mills that once stood here show why the line was built. The five-mile journey is a powerful reminder of our industrial heritage, as well as being a unique way of enjoying the beautiful countryside immortalised by the Brontë sisters.

🔍 Keighley railway station
⚙️ See website for details of other operating days
⏳ 2 hours
⭐ *The Railway Children* line
£

www.kwvr.co.uk

Harewood House

673

Leeds

Harewood House, one of the treasure houses of England, was built in the mid-18th century and has magnificent interiors by Robert Adam, furniture by Thomas Chippendale and paintings by J.M.W. Turner, Reynolds, Titian and El Greco, among others. An Italianate Terrace, designed by Sir Charles Barry, stretches along the South Front of the House and provides stunning views of Lancelot 'Capability' Brown's landscape and lake. The collection of paintings, furniture and porcelain is as fine as any in the land, and the setting is Yorkshire's most beautiful landscape.

🔍 On the A61, 7 miles from Leeds
⚙️ ⚙️ ♣
⏳ 2–3 hours
⭐ Turner's paintings of this spectacular house
£ £

www.harewood.org

Leeds Art Gallery

672

Leeds

Regarded as having the best collection of works of art outside London, the gallery is home to a world of treasures including sculptures by Rodin, Henry Moore, Jacob Kramer and Dame Barbara Hepworth. An internationally acclaimed collection of works on paper features Turner, Cotman, Cozens and Girtin. Popular Leeds artist Atkinson Grimshaw is represented by numerous evocative, moonlit scenes. The gallery has also always tried to support the work of living artists and continues to collect contemporary art including works by Paula Rego, Mark Wallinger, Alison Wilding and Bridget Riley.

🔍 Leeds city centre
⚙️ ⚙️ ♣ ✳️
⏳ 2–3 hours
⭐ Brilliant modern sculpture collection
FREE
www.leeds.gov.uk/artgallery

Temple Newsham   675
Leeds

Temple Newsam is one of the great historic estates in England. Set within over 1,500 acres of parkland and farmland landscaped by 'Capability' Brown in the 18th century, it is a magnificent Tudor-Jacobean mansion. Famous as the birthplace of Lord Darnley and home to the Ingram family for over 300 years, the mansion houses a rich art collection. The garden is renowned for its rhododendron and azalea walk and features the National Collections of delphinium, phlox and aster. Europe's largest working rare breeds farm is set within the original estate Home Farm.

🔍 On the A63, 4 miles from Leeds
⚙️
⏳ 2–3 hours
⭐ Collection of 18th-century English furniture
💷
www.leeds.gov.uk/templenewsam

Royal Armouries Museum   674
Leeds

The Royal Armouries is Britain's national collection of arms and armour. It has five galleries covering self-defence, war, armour of the Orient, hunting and tournaments. There is a wealth of objects on display, including over 7,500 swords, King Henry VIII's equestrian equipment, longbows excavated from the sunken British battleship the *Mary Rose*, 50 instruments of torture, and arms and armour from as far afield as central Asia, India, Africa and Japan. The museum has its own horses and a Tiltyard where visitors can see shows demonstrating jousting, fencing, archery and falconry.

🔍 South of Leeds city centre
⚙️ ⚙️ ♣️ ❄️
⏳ 3–4 hours
⭐ Jousting tournaments
FREE Car parking charge
www.armouries.org.uk

Thackray Museum   676
Leeds

This multi award-winning museum offers an unusual day out, transporting visitors into a living experience of health and medicine, past, present and future. You can take a walk down a back street of Victorian Leeds, and see, hear and smell what life would have been like. In Living Health you can explore the lives, ailments and treatments of eight Victorian characters. Learn how medicine has developed over the years. There is also an extensive collection of medical equipment including tools and replacement body parts.

🔍 Follow signs to St James's Hospital from Leeds city centre
⚙️ ⚙️ ♣️ ❄️
⏳ 2–3 hours
⭐ Step inside the human body in the Life Zone
💷
www.thackraymuseum.org

Pontefract Castle   677
Pontefract

In the Middle Ages, Pontefract Castle was one of the most important fortresses in the country. It became a royal castle in 1399 and Richard II died here the following year. During the Civil War it was in Royalist hands and, as a result, after 1649 it was largely demolished. The remains of the castle are open to visitors. The cellars of the 11th-century great hall were used as a magazine from medieval times through to the Civil War period. You can visit it cut out of the solid rock and see where Civil War prisoners carved their names into the cell walls.

Q Pontefract town centre
⚙
⌛ 1–2 hours
★ Guided tours
£
www.wakefieldmuseums.org

Saltaire Village   678
Shipley

Saltaire, near Shipley, is the finest example of Victorian philanthropy in Britain. The village was built in 1853 by Sir Titus Salt to house the 3,000 workers in his wool mill, which sat next to the Leeds–Liverpool canal. Salt built stone houses for his workers (much better than the slums of Bradford), wash-houses with running water, a hospital, an institute for recreation and education, with a library, a reading room, a concert hall, billiard room, science laboratory and gymnasium. The village also provided a school for the children of the workers, almshouses, allotments, a park and a boathouse.

Q On the A650, 4 miles north of Bradford
⚙ ⚙ ♣ ❄
⌛ 2–3 hours
★ David Hockney gallery in the original Salts Mill
FREE Car parks charge
www.saltairevillage.info

Nostell Priory   679
Wakefield

Built on the site of a medieval priory, Nostell has been the home of the Winn family for 300 years. Commissioned by Sir Rowland Winn in 1733, James Paine built the house. Later additions by Robert Adam created exceptional interiors. Visitors can explore 300 acres of parkland. Gardens include lakeside walks, a newly planted orchard and an adventure playground. Inside the house, see a collection of Chippendale furniture made especially for Nostell, paintings by Brueghel, Hogarth and Kauffmann, a John Harrison longcase clock and an 18th-century doll's house.

Q On the A638, 5 miles south-east of Wakefield
⚙ ⚙ ♣
⌛ 2–3 hours
★ Spectacular plasterwork interiors
£
www.nationaltrust.org.uk

Yorkshire Sculpture Park   680
Wakefield

Yorkshire Sculpture Park is an open-air centre showing modern and contemporary sculpture by leading British and international artists that sets out to challenge, inspire, inform and delight. Changing exhibitions and projects are sited in 500 acres of historic gardens and parkland, four indoor galleries and an award-winning visitor centre. This stunning setting brings together art and nature for everyone to discover and enjoy. Artists represented include: Henry Moore, Anthony Caro, Antony Gormley, Barbara Hepworth, James Turrell and Andy Goldsworthy.

Q On the A637, 1 mile from junction 38 of the M1
⚙ ⚙ ♣ ❄
⌛ 2–3 hours
★ Sculpture in a natural setting
FREE Car parks charges
www.ysp.co.uk

North West

Cheshire
Cumbria
Lancashire
Manchester
Merseyside

Wasdale Valley, The Lake District

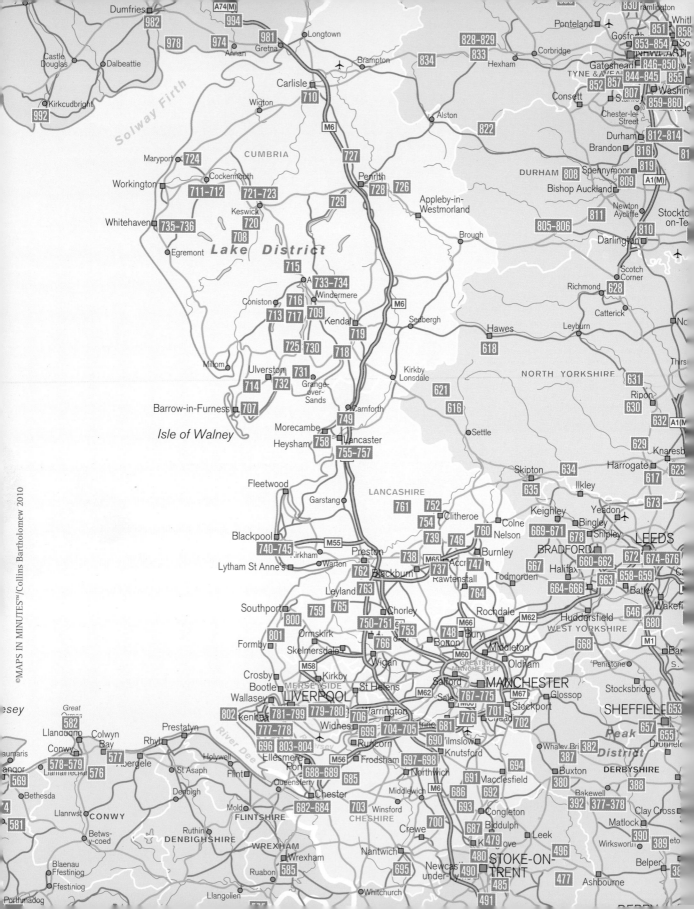

Guide to the **North West**

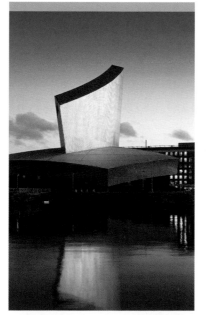

Dunham Massey 681
Altrincham

Set in a magnificent 300-acre deer park this Georgian house tells the story of the owners and the servants who lived here. Discover the salacious scandals of the 7th Earl of Stamford, who married Catherine Cocks, a former bareback circus rider, and the 2nd Earl of Warrington, who was so enamoured with his wife that he wrote a book anonymously on the desirability of divorce. Uncover these and other fascinating stories when you explore this treasure-packed house, then take a stroll in one of the north of England's great gardens, including Britain's largest winter garden.

Off the A56. 3 miles south-west of Altrincham

2-3 hours

Woodland walks

www.nationaltrust.org.uk

Chester City Walls 682
Chester

Chester is one of the best-preserved walled cities in UK. The walls, some parts of which date back to Roman times, are accessible in many places. Walking the walls is a great way to get an overview of the city. Along the 2-mile route, you'll see many of Chester's attractions including: Chester Cathedral, Chester Castle, the River Dee, the Eastgate Arch and clock and the Roman Garden. The main access is at each of the four main gateways – Northgate, Eastgate, Watergate and Bridgegate, but there are many other steps around the city, some including accessible ramps.

Around Chester city centre

1 hour

Roman amphitheatre

FREE

www.visitnorthwest.com

Grosvenor Museum 683
Chester

The Grosvenor Museum is home to a huge number of artefacts relating local and international history. Discover 2,000 years of life spread over three floors of a classic 19th-century building. Visitors can see the most impressive collection of Roman tombstones, along with fascinating displays that build a picture of Roman Chester (see below). Discover the world of Charles Kingsley, the famous naturalist of Victorian Chester, and explore hands-on the geology and natural history of the area. The museum also has a fine collection of paintings, sculpture and furniture in its art gallery.

Chester city centre

1-2 hours

Dazzling Deva

FREE

www.grosvenormuseum.co.uk

Chester Zoo has had **a profound influence** upon the style and development of zoological gardens all around the world

Chester Zoo
Chester

684   FIVE-STAR ATTRACTION

This is the UK's largest zoological garden. It has more than **7,000** animals housed in spacious enclosures. The zoo is set in 110 acres of beautifully landscaped gardens and has a number of themed play areas specially designed for children. Visitors get the 'wow' factor straight away, as the first animals you encounter are the elephants. Another innovation is that animals are grouped by geography, so that Realm of the Red Ape puts orang-utans and gibbons together with other species, like reptiles and squirrels that live in the same forest environment. Similarly, Spirit of the Jaguar lets you see the beautiful big cats alongside leaf-cutter ants and tree frogs, at one stroke putting the larger mammals into the context of their environment. But perhaps the main difference between Chester and most other urban zoos is the emphasis on space.

All your favourite animals are here including big cats, elephants, rhinos, giraffes, monkey, apes, birds, reptiles and amphibians. This is a big zoo with 11 miles of walkways, so come prepared for a long day. There are beautiful gardens for a picnic and all the facilities you would expect at a top class attraction.

🔍 Follow signs from Chester city centre

❄ ⊙ ♣ ✳

⏳ 3–4 hours

⭐ Innovative animal enclosures

💷 💷

www.chesterzoo.org

Mouldsworth Motor Museum   **685**
Chester

Hidden away in the glorious Cheshire countryside is an amazing 1930s Art Deco building that houses the Mouldsworth Motor Museum – four-wheel heaven for motor enthusiasts. This historical haven includes a century or more of motoring memorabilia, motors and memories. Visitors can see a rich motoring and transport heritage as told through a fascinating and ever-changing display of vehicles, motoring art, artefacts and set pieces. With more than 60 veteran and classic cars and motorcycles, there's also a 1920s garage, toys and pedal cars.

🔍 On the B5395, 6 miles east of Chester

❄ ⊙ ♣ Limited opening, see website for details

⏳ 1–2 hours

⭐ 1933 Alfa Romeo 8C

💷

www.mouldsworthmotormuseum.com

Dane Valley Walk   **686**
Congleton

Cheshire is fine walking country, and it doesn't get much better than the Dane Valley. There's a 4–5 mile route from Brereton Local Nature Reserve crossing the River Dane through to Swettenham. This is rich dairy country, with prime grazing for the county's famous cattle. Tucked away in the valley is Swettenham, a village that has changed little over the years. The woods behind are known as Daffodil Dell and are a favourite outing in the spring for local people. Swettenham Meadows above the brook are full of wildflowers all summer long.

🔍 On the A54, north of Congleton

❄ ⊙ ♣ ✳

⏳ 2–3 hours

⭐ Peaceful, rich pastures of England

FREE

www.welcometocongleton.com

Little Moreton Hall 687
Congleton

Gaze at the drunkenly reeling South Range, cross the moat and marvel at the cobbled courtyard before you enter a hall full of surprises. The skills of the 15th-century craftsmen are revealed as you climb the stairs to the Long Gallery and imagine life here in Tudor times. The various delights of this unique property include some remarkable wall paintings and a pretty knot garden. Colourful tales of both the Moreton family and this iconic building are revealed to you by knowledgeable tour guides.

On the A34, 4 miles south of Congleton

1–2 hours

Free guided tours

www.nationaltrust.org.uk

Blue Planet Aquarium 688
Ellesmere Port

At the largest aquarium anywhere in the UK, you're guaranteed to see more types of shark than anywhere else in Britain. And they are BIG! There are more than 10 different species from around the world including 3-metre-long sand tiger sharks. At the heart of this underwater adventure is Aquatunnel, one of the longest in the world at 70 metres with a moving walkway, and everywhere you look, you'll find a shark looming overhead. Other salt and freshwater tanks house a huge variety of sealife at this fascinating attraction.

Follow signs from junction 10 of the M53

2–3 hours

Big sharks

www.blueplanetaquarium.com

National Waterways Museum 689
Ellesmere Port

With its delightful waterside setting, flotillas of historic boats and fascinating displays housed in fine Victorian buildings, this museum is a great day out whatever the weather. Visitors can take a boat trip through an industrial landscape, soak up fascinating canal history, explore traditional narrow boats and homes through the ages, complete with cottage gardens. Its stunning location beside the Mersey and the Manchester Ship Canal makes the museum well placed to show how the waterways helped drive the UK's astonishing industrial revolution.

Follow signs from junction 9 of the M53

2–3 hours

Ellesmere Port Docks

www.nwm.org.uk

Tatton Park   690
Knutsford

This is one of the most complete historic estates open to visitors. The early 19th-century Wyatt house sits amid a landscaped deer park and is opulently decorated, providing a fine setting for the Egerton family's collections of pictures, books, china, glass, silver and specially commissioned Gillows furniture. The theme of Victorian grandeur extends into the garden, with its fernery, orangery, rose garden, tower garden, pinetum, walled garden with its glasshouses, Italian and Japanese gardens. Other features include a 1930s working rare breeds farm, a children's play area, and 1,000-acre deer park.

🔍 Follow signs from junction 7 of the M56 and junction 19 of the M6
☼ ⊙ ♣
⧗ 2–3 hours
★ Marvellous glasshouses
£
www.tattonpark.org.uk

Gawsworth Hall   692
Macclesfield

This ancient manor house was rebuilt in 1480 and again in 1701. A famous duel took place here in 1712 between Lord Mohun and the Duke of Hamilton who were both killed. Here lived Mary Fitton, who had a short but brilliant career at the Court of Elizabeth I, which ended in 1602 following an affair with the Earl of Pembroke. After Mary's disgrace the Fitton finances never recovered and a long legal battle began over the estate that culminated in the famous duel. Another famous resident of the house was Samuel Johnson, Britain's last professional jester, who lies buried in the grounds.

🔍 On the A536, between Macclesfield and Congleton
☼ ♣
⧗ 1–2 hours
★ The 'jewel in Cheshire's crown'
£
www.gawsworthhall.com

Capesthorne Hall   691
Macclesfield

This turreted, red brick 18th-century Jacobean style hall has been home to the Bromley Davenports since 1726. The original hall was built between 1719-32, and then rebuilt after a disastrous fire in 1861. This home has a fascinating collection of paintings, sculptures, furniture, tapestries and family treasures. Close to the house is a beautiful Georgian chapel dating from 1719 where services are still held. The gardens, lakes and park extend to over one hundred acres and contain many interesting features including herbaceous borders, an old icehouse, a fine gazebo (see right) and a variety of woodland walks.

🔍 On the A34
☼ ⊙ ♣ Sundays and Mondays only
⧗ 2–3 hours
★ Medieval family home
£
www.capesthorne.com

Jodrell Bank Visitor Centre and Arboretum
693

Macclesfield

The Jodrell Bank visitor centre is for the world famous Lovell Radio Telescope and the Jodrell Bank Observatory, the astronomy research centre of the University of Manchester. The new Observational Pathway, which stretches 180 degrees around the base of the telescope, is now open. The pathway allows visitors to get closer than ever before. There is also a 3D theatre, a small exhibition area, a 35-acre Arboretum with its National Collections of crab apple and mountain ash trees, and an award-winning Environmental Discovery Centre.

🔍 On the A535, 8 miles west of Macclesfield

✺ ◎ ♣

⧗ 2–3 hours

★ 3D trip to Mars

♿

www.jb.man.ac.uk/visitorcentre

Silk Museums
694

Macclesfield

The history of the Macclesfield silk industry is told on three sites around the town. The Silk Museum, built in 1877 to train designers for the silk industry, now houses exhibitions exploring the properties of silk, design, Macclesfield's diverse textile industries, workers' lives and historic machinery. Paradise Mill contains 26 restored jacquard handlooms, while exhibitions and room sets illustrate life in the mill in the 1930s. The Heritage Centre tells the story of the development of the silk industry through an award-winning, audio-visual programme. It also has a superb collection of silk costumes and textiles.

🔍 Macclesfield town centre

✺ ◎ ♣

⧗ 3–4 hours

★ Working silk mill

♿

www.macclesfield.silk.museum

Hack Green Secret Nuclear Bunker
695

Nantwich

For over 60 years this vast underground complex remained secret. The 35,000 square-foot underground bunker would have been the centre of regional government had nuclear war broken out. Entering through the massive blast doors, you are transported into the chilling world of the Cold War. Re-built at a cost of over £32 million, it contains decontamination facilities, a minister of State's office and life-support systems. Visitors can see government plans for nuclear war, step into the lives of those who worked here, and see fascinating displays of Cold War memorabilia.

🔍 Off the A530, a few miles outside Nantwich

✺ ◎ ♣

⧗ 1–2 hours

★ Simulated detonation of a nuclear bomb

♿

www.hackgreen.co.uk

Ness Botanic Garden 696
Neston

The superb garden at Ness was founded in 1898 by a Liverpool cotton merchant with a passion for plant collecting. The garden, which covers some 64 acres, houses a living collection of 15,000 plants many of which come from China, the Himalayas, Tibet and Burma. Ness's recent success has culminated in a new RHS Gold Medal award-winning garden 'Ness Botanische' created by Chris Beardshaw, which is a key feature at the site. Ness is an all-season garden with flowers, shrubs and trees, a beautiful rock garden, enchanting laburnum arch and spectacular herbaceous border.

🔍 Follow signs from the A540 and junction 4 of the M53

⚙ ◉ ❦ ❄

⏳ 1–2 hours

★ Spring flower display

💷

www.nessgardens.org.uk

Anderton Boat Lift 697
Northwich

Built in 1875, this was the world's first and currently England's only boat lift. One of the greatest monuments to the canal age, the lift is still operating. Visitors can see an exhibition, focusing upon the lift's history and the people who worked on it. The lift control centre is located within the exhibition, enabling visitors to see the lift in action on its busy daily schedule. You can then time travel through the unique structure on board the elegant *Edwin Clark* trip boat, journeying between the River Weaver and the Trent & Mersey Canal high above.

🔍 Off the A533, 3 miles from Northwich

⚙ ◉ ❦

⏳ 1–2 hours

★ River trip in a glass topped boat

💷 💷

www.andertonboatlift.co.uk

Weaver Hall Museum and Workhouse 698
Northwich

This museum is housed within the old Northwich Union Workhouse building and has displays about its history as a home for Victorian paupers. It was built in 1839 to a standard and in its heyday, the various wards could accommodate up to 300 inmates. The museum also has exhibits about the general history of the town with galleries on transport, domestic and community life and working life, including the salt industry and ship building. There are also special exhibitions, a vibrant programme of events and children's quizzes and activities.

🔍 Northwich town centre

⚙ ◉ ❦ ❄

⏳ 1–2 hours

★ Example of Victorian austerity

💷

www.saltmuseum.org.uk

Norton Priory Museum and Gardens

699

Runcorn

The beautiful gardens and grounds at Norton Priory
spread out over 38 acres. The ruins of a 12th-century
priory, a medieval sandstone statue of St Christopher,
a museum and beautiful undercroft are surrounded by
acres of mature woodland. These woodlands contain
picnic areas, sculpture trail, recreated medieval herb
garden, a tranquil stream and a sensory garden for
younger visitors. The glorious Georgian walled garden
boasts a rose walk, fruit trees, herbaceous borders and
a croquet lawn.

Follow signs from the A558

✿ ◉ ✤ ✱

⏳ 1 hour

★ Statue of St Christopher

♿

www.nortonpriory.org

Sandbach Crosses

700

Sandbach

The two massive Saxon stone crosses, elaborately
carved with animals and biblical scenes including the
Nativity of Christ and the Crucifixion, dominate the
cobbled market square of Sandbach. Probably dating
from the 9th century, and originally painted as well as
carved, they are among the finest surviving examples
of Anglo-Saxon high crosses. Brought to the town in
the Middle Ages, they were thrown down during the
Reformation or the Civil War and pieces were scattered
all over the area. They were put together and
reassembled here in 1816.

Sandbach town centre

✿ ◉ ✤ ✱

⏳ 1 hour

★ Incredible Saxon imagery

FREE

www.english-heritage.org.uk

Air Raid Shelters | 701
Stockport

These Air Raid Shelters consist of a network of tunnels nearly a mile long. They were hewn out of the red sandstone hills on which the town stands to provide air raid shelters for 6,500 people during the Second World War. They have now been imaginatively restored to give visitors the feel of the era and the struggle that Britain was facing. Come and explore this underground network and experience the way of life beneath Stockport's streets – fitted with electric light, wooden benches, bunk beds, wardens' post, a first-aid post and, unforgettably, the 16-seater toilets.

🔍 Stockport town centre
✿ ⚙ ♣ ❄
⏳ 1–2 hours
⭐ Guided tours (see website for details)
♿

www.airraidshelters.org.uk

Lyme Park | 702
Stockport

On the edge of the Peak District, nestling within sweeping moorland, Lyme Park is a magnificent estate. Its wild remoteness and powerful beauty contrast with one of the most famous country-house images in England – where Darcy met Elizabeth in the BBC's *Pride and Prejudice*. Discover a colourful family history – from rescuing the Black Prince, sailing into exile with the Duke of Windsor, to the writing of the hit TV series *Upstairs Downstairs*. Visitors can see impressive tapestries, clocks and beautifully furnished rooms, or escape to the park and feel miles from anywhere.

🔍 On the A6, 6 miles south of Stockport town centre
✿ ⚙ ♣
⏳ 2–3 hours
⭐ Rich Italianate interiors
♿

www.nationaltrust.org.uk

Beeston Castle and Woodland Park | 703
Tarporley

This 'Castle of the Rock' is famous for its spectacular views, which take in no less than eight counties on a clear day. From its lookout point at the top of a mighty crag, you can see from the Pennines all the way to the Welsh mountains. But that's not the only reason why Beeston Castle is one of the best-loved visitor attractions in Cheshire. There are beautiful woodlands to explore around the ruins, with wildlife trails for the children to follow, and even the chance to find the lost treasure of Richard II.

🔍 On a minor road off the A49, 11 miles south-east of Chester
✿ ⚙ ♣ ❄
⏳ Any time of year
⭐ Exhibition on the history of the castle
♿

www.english-heritage.org.uk

Gulliver's Family Theme Park | 704
Warrington

Gulliver's is a family theme park designed to cater for families with children between the ages of two and thirteen with all its rides and attractions tailored for the purpose. Set in a beautiful park, with towering trees and a lake as its centrepiece, visitors can see tumbling and juggling fun at Circus World, mosey on down to High Noon in Western World, walk with dinosaurs in the prehistoric Lost World, feel your knees tremble in the Count's Castle and shiver your timbers in Smugglers' Wharf. Be courageous and bold in Adventure World and splash around in the Splash Zone.

🔍 Follow signs from the M6 or the M62
✿ ⚙ ♣ ❄
⏳ 5–6 hours
⭐ The Splash Zone
♿ ♿

www.gulliversfun.co.uk

STAR ATTRACTION

Warrington Museum and Art Gallery
Warrington

705

Visitors to Warrington Museum and Art Gallery will be pleasantly surprised by the treasures on offer in galleries that retain many of their original features and distinctive Victorian atmosphere. Local history includes rare rocks, fossilised footprints and glittering gems, plus Warrington's very own 'dinosaur'. You can also see cases full of weird and wonderful objects from around the globe. See the freaky Feejee mermaids. See a shrunken head, grotesque mermaids and an Egyptian mummy. The art gallery houses works by renowned local and international artists.

🔍 Warrington town centre
❀ ◉ ♣ ✳
⏳ 1–2 hours
⭐ The Friary Manuscript
FREE
museum.warrington.gov.uk

Catalyst Science Discovery Centre
Widnes

706

Catalyst is an interactive science centre devoted to chemistry and how its products are used in everyday life. There are three galleries with over a hundred different exhibits to enjoy. Visitors can see panoramic views from the rooftop Observatory, and experience the fantastic Catalytic Discovery Lab, with activities such as Spies and Codes and the Catalyst Crime Scene Mystery. Take an unforgettable journey of discovery in the Alchemy Theatre; interactive shows with 3D and individual voting makes each showing unique.

🔍 Take junction 12 from the M56 or junction 7 from the M62
❀ ◉ ♣ ✳
⏳ 3–4 hours
⭐ Science education as fun
🎟
www.catalyst.org.uk

The Dock Museum
Barrow-in-Furness

707

This spectacular modern museum is built on the site of an original Victorian graving dock. Displays explore the history of Barrow-in-Furness and how it grew from a tiny hamlet in the 19th century to become the biggest iron and steel centre in the world and a major shipbuilding force in just 40 years. Its collection most relates to the shipbuilding, heavy engineering and armaments work of Barrow Shipyard. Other industries represented include iron and steel production and the Furness Railway. Also has a superb collection of ship models.

🔍 Follow signs from Barrow town centre
❀ ◉ ♣ ✳
⏳ 2–3 hours
⭐ Film show
FREE
www.dockmuseum.org.uk

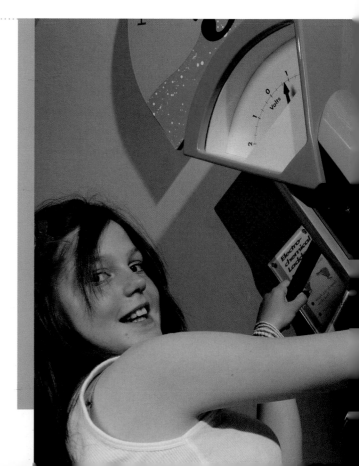

Honister Slate Mine
708
Borrowdale

Honister Slate Mine is at the top of the Honister Pass. Visitors can watch slate being riven (or split) using processes that have changed little over the past 300 years. Fully guided underground tours detail the history of the mine. The visitor centre has a series of information panels showing its characters, its triumphs and its disasters. Also on offer is the Via Ferrata – an adventure climbing system that uses a permanently fixed cable up the rock face of the old miners' route. Equipment and full safety instructions are provided and all climbs are guided (see website). Dress for wet weather.

On the B5289, at the top of the Honister Pass

1-2 hours

Hardhat mine tours

Visitor Centre **FREE** Tours 💷 Via Ferrata 💷 💷 💷

www.honister.com

STAR ATTRACTION

High Adventure Balloons
709
Bowness-on-Windermere

Hot air ballooning over the Lake District is the ultimate flying experience. Riders help inflate the balloon, which usually takes about 30 minutes. The first half-hour is spent at high altitude (5,000 feet) for panoramic views of the countryside. The second is at lower levels to see more detail. After the flight, in the balloonists' tradition, you will be presented with a glass of champagne, and a certificate. Flying is at the beginning and end of the day when the air is stable. Flight times are typically 6.00 a.m. and 6.30 p.m.

RM Travel, Rayrigg Road, Bowness-on-Windermere

3 hours

An unforgettable experience

💷 💷 💷

www.high-adventure.co.uk

Carlisle Castle
710
Carlisle

Standing strongly in the city it has dominated for nine centuries, Carlisle Castle is now a rich and varied visitor attraction reflecting its long and eventful history. Even before the medieval castle was begun, this site was an important Roman fortress. Visitors can explore fascinating and ancient chambers, stairways and dungeons and find the legendary 'licking stones'. Here, parched Jacobite prisoners found enough moisture to stay alive, only to be brutally executed on Gallows Hill. Uncover the fascinating history of William Rufus, Mary Queen of Scots and Bonnie Prince Charlie.

Carlisle city centre

1-2 hours

Border Regiment Museum

💷

www.english-heritage.org.uk

Jennings Brewery Tour `711`
Cockermouth

Jennings have been brewing beers in Cumbria for over 170 years. They still use the same methods that were used as long ago as 1828 in the small Cumbrian village of Lorton. The brewery moved to Cockermouth in 1874 and is still there today. Castle Brewery is in the shadow of Cockermouth Castle at the confluence of the River Cocker and River Derwent. You can take a tour of the brewery; find out how real ales are brewed, and then some of Jennings' superb Lakeland ales in the Old Cooperage.

🔍 Cockermouth town centre
✹ ⚙ ♣ ❄ Please book in advance via website
⏳ 1–2 hours
⭐ Traditional beer brewing
£
www.jenningsbrewery.co.uk

Wordsworth House and Garden `712`
Cockermouth

Step back to the 1770s and experience life as William and his sister Dorothy might have done at this beautiful, homely property. Enjoy a warm welcome from the Wordsworths' servants and find out more about the restoration of the house and garden. There are seven rooms furnished in Regency style, with some of the poet's personal effects. William's beloved garden inspired many of his later poems and contains flowers, fruit and vegetables popular in the 18th century – all of which are used in the house. The Discovery Room has fascinating research material and touchscreens.

🔍 Cockermouth town centre
✹ ⚙ ♣
⏳ 1–2 hours
⭐ The walled garden in May
£
www.nationaltrust.org.uk

Brantwood `713`
Coniston

The former home of John Ruskin, Brantwood is the most beautifully situated house in the Lake District. Brantwood is both a treasure house of historical importance and a lively centre of contemporary arts and the environment. Displays and activities in the house, gardens and estate reflect the wealth of cultural associations associated with Ruskin's legacy – from the Pre-Raphaelites and Arts and Crafts Movement to the founding of the National Trust and the Welfare State. With its many contemporary exhibitions, concerts, courses and special events, Brantwood continues in the Ruskin tradition today.

🔍 On the B5285, on the eastern shore of Lake Coniston
✹ ⚙ ♣
⏳ 2–3 hours
⭐ Ruskin's treasures and personal memorabilia
£
www.brantwood.org.uk

South Lakes Wild Animal Park `714`
Dalton-in-Furness

This is the Lake District's only zoo, which is recognised as one of Europe's leading conservation zoos. Its 17 acres are home to the rarest animals on earth, who are participants in co-ordinated breeding programmes to save them from extinction. This is the only zoo in Britain to hold both Amur and Sumatran tigers, the biggest and smallest tigers left in the world. Each day there are talks on the tiger conservation projects. In the Australian Bush area, many animals have complete freedom to wander at will, such as lemurs, exotic deer, emus, wallabies and kangaroos.

🔍 Follow signs from junction 36 of M6, 1 mile from Dalton-in-Furness
✹ ⚙ ♣ ❄
⏳ 3–4 hours
⭐ Hand feed lemurs, kangaroos and giraffes
£ £
www.wildanimalpark.co.uk

Dove Cottage and the Wordsworth Museum   `715`

Grasmere

Dove Cottage was the home of William Wordsworth from 1799 to 1808, the years of his supreme work as a poet. The cottage is located in the hamlet of Town End in the centre of the English Lake District where the poet lived, wrote and found inspiration. The cottage remains very much as it was in his time. The Wordsworths had many visitors to Dove Cottage – Walter Scott, Thomas De Quincey, Charles and Mary Lamb, Robert Southey and most of all Samuel Taylor Coleridge. The site also includes an award-winning museum.

🔍 On the A591, south of Grasmere
❀ ◉ ❀ ❄
⧗ 1–2 hours
★ Guided tours
♿
www.wordsworth.org.uk

Grizedale Forest Park   `716`

Hawkeshead

Grizedale Forest visitor centre is a good starting point for superb forest walks. The shop sells a guide showing the many miles of track suitable for walkers and cyclists. Here you will also find the largest 'Sculpture in the Forest' exhibition in the country. The park offers superb views of Coniston Water and Windermere. Take a walk up to the highest point at Carron Crag and enjoy a panorama of the central Lake District fells. Remember that the weather can change quickly especially on higher hills. Wear suitable clothing and footwear; take extra layers, food and drink.

🔍 Off the B5286, follow signs to Grizedale or Forest Park
❀ ◉ ❀ ❄
⧗ 3–4 hours
★ Variety of forest events
FREE Car parks charge
www.forestry.gov.uk

Levens Hall and Gardens

Kendal

718

Most famous for its stunning 17th-century topiary gardens, designed and laid out in the 1690s by Guillaume Beaumont who also laid out the gardens at Hampton Court, Levens is also a fine Elizabethan stately home. Now a family home, it contains fine furniture, paintings, one of the best examples in Europe of Spanish leather wall coverings, the earliest English patchwork, Wellingtoniana, clocks and miniatures. The Hall is said to be haunted, and people have claimed to have seen the ghost of a black dog who inhabits the stairs and an amicable lady in pink.

On the A6, 5 miles south of Kendal

2-3 hours

Incredible abstract topiary

www.levenshall.co.uk

Hill Top

Hawkeshead

717

Enjoy the tale of Beatrix Potter – Hill Top, a house bought in 1905 with earnings from her first book, *The Tale of Peter Rabbit*, is a time capsule of this amazing woman's life. Full of her favourite things, the house appears as if Beatrix had just stepped out for a walk. Every room contains a reference to a picture in a 'tale'. The lovely cottage garden is a haphazard mix of flowers, herbs, fruit and vegetables. Hill Top is a small house and can be busy so visitors may sometimes have to wait to enter the house.

2 miles south of Hawkshead

1-2 hours

Author's original pictures

www.nationaltrust.org.uk

Museum of Lakeland Life

Kendal

719

This award-winning museum takes you back through time to explore the story of the Lake District and its inhabitants. Isolated before the arrival of the railway and motorcar, this area developed its own unique customs and traditions. Recreated period rooms and workshops illustrate how people lived, worked and played and how different life was before the introduction of machinery. Lifelike displays narrate the stories of individuals who left their mark on the history of the Lake District, providing a rare insight into now lost trades and professions from this area of exceptional natural beauty.

Take junction 36 of the M6, follow signs to Abbot Hall

1-2 hours

Arthur Ransome exhibit

www.lakelandmuseum.org.uk

Borrowdale 720
Keswick

This rugged and dramatic valley is the heart of the central fells and the adventure capital of the north. There are many highlights here, particularly for walkers and cyclists. They include Watendlath, an isolated medieval hamlet high above the main valley; Derwent Water – a stunning lake surrounded by mountains, dotted with islands, fringed with rare Atlantic Oak woodlands and crowned with a Georgian mansion; Brandelhow, which provides tranquil walks around the water's edge, with spectacular views of Skiddaw and Blencathra; and Castlerigg Stone Circle.

On the B5289, but public transport is recommended

4–6 hours

Force Crag Mine

FREE

www.nationaltrust.org.uk

Cars of the Stars 721
Keswick

This fascinating museum brings together a huge collection of the most famous cars from film and TV. The vehicles are all presented in its individual film set, with atmospheric lighting and sound. Visitors can see the Batmobiles, Chitty Chitty Bang Bang, a number of James Bond's cars and gadgets (see right), Laurel and Hardy's Model T, Del Boy's Reliant Robin from *Only Fools and Horses*, the Flintstones's cars, Knightrider's KITT, Magnum's Ferrari, the A Team van, Herbie the Love Bug, Noddy's car and, of course, Lady Penelope's pink Rolls Royce FAB 1.

Keswick town centre

1–2 hours

James Bond's Aston Martin DB5 from *Goldfinger*

www.carsofthestars.com

Derwent Water Marina 722
Keswick

If you want to go sailing, windsurfing, canoeing, kayaking, ghyll scrambling, rock climbing or raft-building, this marina offers a whole host of RYA watersports courses. There are basic skills and refresher courses for all disciplines, and if you have your own equipment then the experts can show you how to get the best out of it. It is essential to book in advance if you are going on a course. Accommodation is available (see website). The centre also has canoes, kayaks, dinghys, windsurfers and rowing boats for hire by the day.

On the A66, at Portinscale

1–3 hours

Stunning watersports location

www.derwentwatermarina.co.uk

Friar's Crag 723
Keswick

Friar's Crag is a promontory jutting into Derwent Water. There is an easy path for walking with clear views over to Derwent Isle, and across the lake to Brandlehow Woods. It should be familiar to Arthur Ransome fans as one of the key settings in *Swallows and Amazons*; in the novel, the area was renamed Darien, and was the children's lookout spot. Visitors can walk around to a small bay boasting one of the finest views across the Lake District, with the Jaws of Borrowdale in the distance and the ridgeline of Cat Bells visible on the western shore.

🔍 On the A66, at Keswick
⚙
⏳ 1–2 hours
⭐ One of the finest views across the Lake District
FREE
www.visitcumbria.com

Lake District Coast Aquarium 724
Maryport

This small, independently owned aquarium is one of the best places to see some of the varied marine life of the Irish Sea. Visitors can see a huge variety of fish and invertebrates (starfish, lobsters and others) in 50 carefully themed and informative displays. These include fresh water and seawater creatures with rock pools, ray pools a Crashing Wave display, a Harbour Wall display and a deep-water feature. There are also radio-controlled boats to play with, an adventure playground and a mini-golf course.

🔍 Maryport quayside
✿ ⚙ ♣ ❄
⏳ 1–2 hours
⭐ Fish coming in on the tide
£
www.lakedistrict-coastaquarium.co.uk

Lakes Aquarium 725
Newby Bridge

Visitors can discover the fascinating wildlife of the Lake District on the tranquil shore of Lake Windermere. The aquarium has over 30 displays, which start with a dramatic mountain-top waterfall and leads down to a moorland stream. You can also see otters before moving on to see nocturnal life on the riverbank. You will see several varieties of trout, the pike, and Windermere's elusive char. Finally you will see the freshwater fish of the estuary, and the seawater inhabitants of the bay, including rays and sharks from around our coast.

🔍 On the A590, follow signs to Newby Bridge
✿ ⚙ ♣ ❄
⏳ 2–3 hours
⭐ Spectacular underwater tunnel
£
www.lakesaquarium.co.uk

Acorn Bank Garden and Watermill 726
Penrith

Acorn Bank is best known for its collection of 250 herbs and traditional fruit orchards. Ancient oak trees and high enclosing walls keep out the extremes of the Cumbrian climate, resulting in a spectacular display of shrubs, roses and herbaceous borders. The sheltered orchards contain a variety of fruit trees. Visitors can also wander along the Crowdundle Beck to the partially restored watermill, spot some wildlife then enjoy the views across the Eden Valley to the Lake District from the magnificent backdrop of the sandstone house.

🔍 On the A66, 6 miles east of Penrith
✿ ⚙ ♣ Wednesdays to Sundays
⏳ 1–2 hours
⭐ Astonishing variety of herbs
£
www.nationaltrust.org.uk

Hutton-in-the-Forest 727
Penrith

The historic home of Lord and Lady Inglewood, Hutton-in-the-Forest is a beautiful house of the north-eastern edge of the Lake District. It is surrounded by magnificent woodland of the medieval forest of Inglewood. Legend has it that it is the Green Knight's castle in the Arthurian tale of 'Sir Gawain and the Green Knight'. Originally a medieval stronghold with a pele tower, succeeding generations have altered and added to the house, and the outside and inside show a wide variety of architectural and decorative styles from the 17th century to the present day.

🔍 On the B5305, 6 miles north-west of Penrith
⚙ ◎ 🍁 Wednesdays, Thursdays and Sundays
⏳ 2–3 hours
⭐ Magnificent tree collection
💷
www.hutton-in-the-forest.co.uk

Brougham Castle 728
Penrith

In a picturesque setting beside the crossing of the River Eamont, Brougham Castle was founded in the early 13th century. The great keep largely survives, amid many later buildings – including the unusual double gatehouse and the impressive Tower of League. Both a formidable barrier against Scots invaders and a prestigious residence, the castle welcomed Edward I in 1300. Passages and spiral stairways makes Brougham a fascinating castle to explore, as well as an ideal picnic setting for a family day out. The keep top provides panoramic views over the Eden Valley.

🔍 Off the A66, 1 mile east of Penrith
⚙ ◎ 🍁
⏳ 1–2 hours
⭐ Marvellous views
💷
www.english-heritage.org.uk

Dalemain Historic House and Gardens 729
Penrith

Behind its Georgian facade, this lovely house contains a wealth of Tudor and medieval rooms and buildings. There has been a settlement at Dalemain since Saxon times. The Old Hall was added in the 14th century, along with another tower. In the 16th century, two projecting wings were added creating a typical Elizabethan manor house and in 1744, the impressive Georgian front was constructed to enclose an inner courtyard. Very few changes have been made to the buildings since those times giving the house an ancient and permanent atmosphere.

🔍 On the A592
⚙ ◎ 🍁
⏳ 2–3 hours
⭐ Stunning Tudor and Georgian interiors
💷
www.dalemain.com

Fell Foot Park 730
Ulverston

You can have a great time on a sunny, summer day at this restored 18-acre Victorian Park on the shores of Lake Windermere. Views of the lake are breathtaking. The lawns and garden sweep away to fine picnic areas and lakeshore. There is a cafe with a patio, where you can enjoy watching the boats and soaking up the tranquil atmosphere. There are rowing boats for hire should you fancy a trip on the water. Visitors can stroll around the grounds and let their children loose in the fabulous adventure playground.

🔍 On the A592, at the south end of Lake Windermere
⚙
⏳ 2-3 hours
⭐ A traditional summer picnic in beautiful surroundings
FREE Car park charges, donations welcome
www.nationaltrust.org.uk

Holker Hall and Gardens 731
Ulverston

Holker Hall is set in exceptionally beautiful countryside with gardens that merge into parkland framed by the Lakeland hills. This handsome rose coloured neo-Elizabethan mansion and its gardens provide a soft and gentle contrast to the ruggedness of the Lakeland countryside to the north. You can tour the house and see the distinguished library, elegant drawing room, and ornate dining room. You can visit the bedroom where Queen Mary stayed in 1937. The pleasure grounds cover 25 acres of formal and woodland gardens, with majestic water features including the limestone cascade.

🔍 On the A590, follow signs for Grange-over-Sands
⚙ ⚙ ♣
⏳ 2-3 hours
⭐ 72-foot high lime tree
£ £
www.holker-hall.co.uk

Laurel and Hardy Museum 732
Ulverston

You can visit the best museum in the world dedicated to Laurel and Hardy in Ulverston, the town where Stan was born on 16 June 1890. Everything you want to know about them is in the museum. The late Bill Cubin, the founder of the museum, devoted his life to these famous comedians and collected an amazing variety of memorabilia, believed to be the largest in the world, including letters, photographs, personal items and furniture. There is also a small cinema showing free films and documentaries all day.

🔍 On the A590
⚙ ⚙ ♣
⏳ 1 hour
⭐ The incredible story of two of England's best-loved comedy stars
£
www.laurel-and-hardy-museum.co.uk

Lake District National Park 733
Windermere

The best place to start your visit to the largest of the country's National Parks is at the Visitor Centre at Brockhole on Lake Windermere. From here you can get a better understanding of the area while enjoying dramatic mountain and lakeside scenery as well as an adventure playground and fabulous gardens. The centre will provide all the information you need for local walks and other attractions. England's largest National Park includes Scafell Pike – its highest mountain, Wastwater – its deepest lake and thriving communities like Keswick and Bowness-on-Windermere.

🔍 Follow signs from the A591, between Windermere and Ambleside
⚙
⏳ 2-3 hours
⭐ Newly installed climbing wall
FREE Car park charges
www.lake-district.gov.uk

The Beacon   735
Whitehaven

The Beacon, which was completely refurbished in 2007, presents the fascinating history of Whitehaven, west Cumbria's Georgian port, and the Copeland region that surrounds it. Situated on the harbourside, the museum tells the story of the town's maritime, social and industrial heritage through audio-visual, graphic and interactive presentations. You can absorb yourself in the amazing views through the powerful telescopes in the Viewing Gallery, present your very own weather forecast in the Weather Zone and explore the lighthouse style building to discover local history.

🔍 Whitehaven harbour
❀ ☼ 🍁 ❄
⏳ 1-2 hours
⭐ Join the crew of our very own ship
£
www.thebeacon-whitehaven.co.uk

Windermere Lake Cruises   734
Windermere

Steamers and launches sail daily throughout the year from Ambleside, Bowness and Lakeside with connections for the Lake District Visitor Centre at Brockdale, the World of Beatrix Potter, the Lakeside Aquarium and the Haverthwaite Steam Railway. These spectacular voyages give the traveller magnificent views of mountain scenery, secluded bays and the many wooded islands. There are a number of different cruises on offer or you can buy a 24-hour Freedom of the Lake ticket, which gives you access to any of them.

🔍 On the A591 at Windermere or Bowness, and the A590 at Lakeside
☼
⏳ 1-3 hours
⭐ Finest views in the Lake District
£
www.windermere-lakecruises.co.uk

Haig Colliery Mining Museum   736
Whitehaven

On the site of the former Haig Pit in Whitehaven, which closed in 1986, the winding engine house and headgear have been restored to their former glory and can now be seen at the Haig Colliery Mining Museum. The museum is open while development work is underway. Coal mining in this area dates back to the 13th century when the monks from St Bees Abbey supervised the opening of coalmines at Arrowthwaite. This long history ended in March 1986, when this pit, Cumbria's last deep coal mine, finally closed.

🔍 Follow signs from Whitehaven town centre
❀ ☼ 🍁 ❄
⏳ 2-3 hours
⭐ History of coal mining in Cumbria
FREE
www.haigpit.com

Haworth Art Gallery
Accrington

737

This Edwardian Tudor-style house stands in its own park with lovely views across the surrounding hills. The Haworth's unique collection of Tiffany Art Nouveau glass is on permanent display. Consisting of over 140 glass tiles, vases and mosaics, it is the largest public collection of Tiffany glass in Europe. It was given by Joseph Briggs who left Accrington in 1891 to seek his fortune in America. He worked with Tiffany in New York and sent his collection back in 1933. The collection includes some of the finest glass Tiffany ever produced.

🔍 On the A680, south of Accrington town centre

⚙ ⊙ ♣ ❄

⏳ 1-2 hours

★ Unique collection of glassware

FREE

www.hyndburnbc.gov.uk/hag

Blackburn Museum and Art Gallery
Blackburn

738

This museum is housed in a beautiful building near Blackburn Town Hall. It is best known as the home of the Hart bequest, the unique collection of local notable Robert Edward Hart (1876–1946). His gift of coins, manuscripts and books cannot be matched by any public collection outside London and gives the museum its international reputation. Opened in 1874, the museum also includes the history of Blackburn, the Egyptian Mummy, South Asian culture, Fine and Decorative Art and the Bowdler collection of world beetles, among other exhibits.

🔍 Blackburn town centre

⚙ ⊙ ♣ ❄

⏳ 1-2 hours

★ Marvellous coin collection

FREE

www.blackburn.gov.uk/museums

Whalley Abbey Gatehouse
Blackburn

739

Situated beside the River Calder, this 15th-century, two-storey stone building was the outer gatehouse of the nearby Cistercian abbey, the second wealthiest monastery in Lancashire. There was originally a chapel on the first floor. The adjacent parish church has further remains, including three pre-Norman Conquest cross shafts. The nearby abbey has a permanent exhibition. The abbey closed in 1537 as part of the Dissolution of the Monasteries. Also that year the Abbot Paslew was executed for high treason.

🔍 On a minor road off the A59, 6 miles north-east of Blackburn

⚙ ⊙ ♣ ❄

⏳ 1 hour

★ Extensive and fine ruins

FREE

www.english-heritage.org.uk

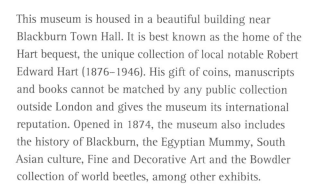

Blackpool Illuminations   740
Blackpool

At 6 miles long and using over one million bulbs, the Blackpool Illuminations are an awesome spectacle for 66 days each year from September to November. They consist of almost every kind of light display you can imagine: lasers, neon, light bulbs, fibre optics, searchlights and floodlighting. There are more than 500 scenic designs and features. Most are set pieces made out of wood studded with light bulbs: the characters and objects portrayed seem to 'move' by way of winking lights. Strings of lights along the structure of buildings pick out landmarks in luminous detail.

Central Promenade

2 hours

This unique lightshow

FREE

www.blackpool-illuminations.net

Blackpool Piers   741
Blackpool

Blackpool's three piers present the whole range of seaside entertainment between them. The North pier is the most relaxing and has the best views of the town's famous Promenade and the illuminations. The Central Pier is geared up for families with children's entertainers, shows and a fairground with a Ferris wheel. The South Pier is known as the 'Adrenalin Pier' and includes a full range of white-knuckle rides from traditional waltzers, the Crazy Mouse and then the real ultra rides of the reverse bungee Skyscreamer, and the Sky Coaster.

Blackpool Promenades

3-4 hours

The Big Wheel

North Pier   Rides charged individually

the-pier.co.uk/blackpool-piers

Blackpool Pleasure Beach   742
Blackpool

A theme park situated in Britain's most popular beach resort has to be good, and Blackpool Pleasure Beach is not a disappointment. With over 125 rides there is something for everyone. The newest ride is Infusion, ride it if you dare. Otherwise the park has more rollercoasters than any other park in the UK, including the Pepsi Max Big One. There are rides of all grades, from the monstrous Big Dipper, the Grand National and the Avalanche to the Log Flume and the River Caves. This park is 42 acres of fun.

Blackpool's South Shore

4-5 hours

Pepsi Max Big One

www.blackpoolpleasurebeach.com

Blackpool Sea Life Centre   743
Blackpool

One of the UK's best-known aquariums houses more than 50 spectacular displays and over 1,000 assorted sea creatures, taking visitors on a journey from the coastline and sandy shallows to the ocean depths. The highlight is an amazing walkthrough underwater tunnel. A new display – called Shark Frenzy! – brings together the world's largest variety of sharks and explodes the myths surrounding the most misunderstood creatures of the oceans. From native to tropical sharks including the impressive Bowmouth, watch these graceful, awe-inspiring beasts as they navigate the deep.

Blackpool Promenade, opposite the Central Pier

2-3 hours

Impressive jellyfish

www.sealifeeurope.com

Blackpool Tower and Circus
744
Blackpool

There is a lot to do here. There's a circus show – Mooky's Eastern Promise – starring the UK's favourite clown, Mooky, his long-suffering sidekick Mr Boo and a host of international circus acts. Visitors can also enjoy the sights and sounds of the stunning Tower Ballroom as seen on *Strictly Come Dancing*, play in Jungle Jim's Towering Adventureland, ride to the top of the tower, take the Walk of Faith (380 feet above the Promenade) as well as an aquarium, a 3D cinema, the Jurassic Walk and more.

Blackpool Promenade
3-4 hours
Tower top views

www.blackpooltower.co.uk

Sandcastle Waterpark
745
Blackpool

This is the UK's largest indoor waterpark with 18 slides and attractions. In an 84° tropical climate there are slides like Masterblaster – the longest indoor rollercoaster waterslide in the world – and Sidewinder – the world's first indoor vertical waterslide, or the more relaxing free-flowing Ushi Gushi Action River. For younger explorers there is the Caribbean Storm Treehouse, which is an interactive adventure play area with a giant tipping coconut that cascades over 600 galloons of water over unsuspecting victims, plus a range of water cannons, mini-slides and jets.

Blackpool's South Beach
2-3 hours
Masterblaster

www.sandcastle-waterpark.co.uk

Gawthorpe Hall
746
Burnley

Gawthorpe Hall is set in gardens and woodlands on the banks of the River Calder. The hall was built between 1600 and 1605 and was the home of the Kay-Shuttleworth family until 1970. Visitors can see how different generations of the family lived in the period rooms including: dining room with minstrel's gallery, an oak panelled salon and a long gallery. In the 1840s and 1850s Charlotte Bronte was a frequent visitor. Today the hall is home to the Kay-Shuttleworth collections of lace, embroidery and textiles – the largest collection outside the V&A in London.

North of the A671, on the outskirts of Padiham
2-3 hours
Marvellous interiors and furniture

www.nationaltrust.org.uk

Queen Street Mill Textile Museum
747
Burnley

On the outskirts of Burnley – a town once dominated by the textile industry – stands Queen Street Mill, the last surviving, operational steam powered weaving mill in the world. The mill is a time capsule of the late Victorian age, and produced cloth using Victorian steam driven power looms until its closure in 1982. Discover the story of cotton cloth production. Whether you're interested in local or social history, textiles and textile machinery, the sights, sounds and smells of Queen Street Mill bring the textile industry vividly back to life.

Off the A671, in Harle Syke
1 hour
300 Lancashire looms

www.lancashire.gov.uk

Brief Encounter Visitor Centre 749
Carnforth

This award-winning Visitor Centre is located within a busy working railway station. Housed in the beautifully restored historic buildings, it offers a number of attractions, facilities and a fascinating range of exhibitions. The 'Brief Encounter' exhibition is dedicated to the classic film, the actors and the film's famous connection with Carnforth Station. The Albert Halton Room commemorates Carnforth's contribution to the First and Second World Wars. There are also a number of other exhibitions, which explore the social history of Carnforth residents as well as the railway itself.

🔍 Carnforth railway station
☀ ☼ ♣ ❄
⏳ 1 hour
⭐ World-famous refreshment room and station clock
FREE Donations appreciated
www.carnforthstation.co.uk

East Lancashire Railway 748
Bury

This mainly steam-hauled service runs for 12 miles between Heywood and Rawtenstall. There are intermediate stations at Bury, Ramsbottom, Summerseat and Irwell Vale. From Heywood the line descends Broadfield bank, and after crossing the M66 and the River Roch the line climbs towards Bury town centre and the Irwell valley. On leaving Bury the line commences the long climb up the valley via Ramsbottom, crossing the River Irwell nine times before reaching the terminus at Rawtenstall.

🔍 Bury town centre
☀ ☼ ♣ See website for details
⏳ 3–4 hours
⭐ Bury Transport Museum (Entry fee 💷)
💷 💷
www.east-lancs-rly.co.uk

Astley Hall Museum and Art Gallery 750
Chorley

Astley Hall is one of the most significant buildings in the North West, with a fascinating history of families who lived there and some magnificent architecture. The history of the Hall is full of intrigue, with stories of plotting and religious turmoil. It dates back to Elizabethan times with changes and additions over the centuries. This Grade 1 listed building is the jewel in Chorley's crown, with stunning plasterwork and architectural features. As the town's museum and art gallery it is also home to items of local historical interest.

🔍 Off A581, west of Chorley town centre
☀ ☼ ♣
⏳ 1–2 hours
⭐ The Long Gallery
💷
www.chorley.gov.uk/astleyhall

Camelot Theme Park
Chorley

751

This theme park is filled with rides, shows and magical attractions on a medieval theme. There are some thrill rides for adrenalin junkies including Excalibur 2, the Whirlwind and the stomach-churning Galleon. There are also gentler family rides like Pendragon's Plunge and Falcon's Flight. Other Attractions at the park include Squire Bumpkin's Farm, an unmissable experience for the younger squires, and the Wizardry, where you will meet Merlin the talented magician. Visitors can also take their seats alongside King Arthur (see below) for daily jousting tournaments. Discounts available online.

🔍 Follow signs from junctions 27 and 28 of the M6 or junction 8 of the M61
☀ ◐ ♣
⏳ 3-4 hours
★ Jousting tournament
£ £ £
www.camelotthemepark.co.uk

Clitheroe Castle and Museum
Clitheroe

752

Standing on a rocky outcrop of limestone above the River Ribble, the keep of Clitheroe Castle has been a prominent landmark both in the town and the surrounding area for more than 800 years. It is one of the oldest buildings in Lancashire; it may be the smallest keep in England; and it is the only remaining castle in Lancashire that had a Royalist garrison during the Civil War. Views from the castle are breathtaking, as is the walk up the hill. You can break the journey by visiting the Castle museum.

🔍 Clitheroe town centre
☀ ◐ ♣ ❄
⏳ 1-2 hours
★ Ribble Valley views
Castle **FREE** Museum £
www.ribblevalley.gov.uk

Horwich Heritage Centre 753
Horwich

The Heritage Centre is home to a permanent exhibition on the rich history and industrial heritage of this area, and in particular the Horwich Locomotive Works. There are several exhibition areas, one of them centres on the locomotive factory and includes a scale model of a locomotive footplate. Other subjects include a Victorian kitchen, local industry, the Second World War and transport. Visitors can also see the entrance to Wilderswood Mine, the actual Fall Birch Tollgate post and The Way We Were display with more recent artefacts.

🔍 Horwich town centre
⚙ ⊙ ♣ ❄ Afternoons and Saturday mornings
⌛ 1 hour
⭐ Regular local history exhibitions
FREE
www.horwichheritage.co.uk

Tolkien Trail 754
Hurst Green

The village of Hurst Green, near Clitheroe, is the starting point for a 5–6 mile circular walk known as the Tolkien Trail. This is so-called because the writer was a regular visitor at a guesthouse in the grounds of nearby Stoneyhurst College while he was writing *The Lord of the Rings*. Tolkien wooded landscapes and the countryside around Stonyhurst is richly beautiful. A number of names used in the trilogy are similar to those found locally, including Shire Lane and the River Shirebourn. The ferry at Hacking Hall may have provided the inspiration for the Buckleberry Ferry.

🔍 Hurst Green village, on the B3264
⚙ ⊙ ♣ ❄
⌛ 2–3 hours
⭐ Glorious countryside of the lower Ribble Valley
FREE
www.ribblevalley.gov.uk

Judges' Lodgings 755
Lancaster

Sited in the centre of Lancaster, this elegant, Grade I listed building is Lancaster's oldest town house. The house was originally home to Thomas Covell, Keeper of Lancaster Castle and notorious witch hunter. Between 1776 and 1975 it became an impressive residence for judges visiting the Assize Court at nearby Lancaster Castle. The museum is now home to a renowned collection of Gillow furniture, which is displayed in fabulous Regency period room settings, fine art and also the enchanting Museum of Childhood, which explores toys and games from the 18th century to the present.

🔍 Lancaster town centre
⚙ ⊙ ♣ See website for details
⌛ 1 hour
⭐ Furniture, porcelain, silver and paintings
💷
www.lancashire.gov.uk

Lancaster Castle 756
Lancaster

One of the best-preserved castles in England, it is still used today as a court and a prison. Visitors can take guided tours of parts of the building. Known as John o' Gaunt's Castle, Lancaster Castle is one of the most historically interesting buildings in Lancashire. Its beginnings date back to Roman times and from its position on the hill overlooking the town and the River Lune, it stood as a bastion against the marauding forces of Picts and Scots. The tour includes the court where the Lancashire Witches were tried, the dungeons and the hanging corner.

🔍 Lancaster town centre
⚙ ⊙ ♣ ❄
⌛ 1 hour
⭐ The Old Cells
💷
www.lancastercastle.com

Lancaster Maritime Museum   757
Lancaster

This museum is housed in the Port of Lancaster Custom House and warehouses, which date from the 18th century. The buildings along the quayside developed as a result of the success of overseas trade. Alongside the museum are buildings that belonged to Quaker slave trader Dodshon Foster. This now peaceful stretch of the river would once have bustled with shipbuilding activity and the loading and unloading of goods. There is an ever-changing view across the river with the ebb and flow of the tide and the presence of the bird life that lives along its banks.

🔍 Lancaster quayside
✲ ◉ ♣ ❄
⏳ 2 hours
★ Lancaster's 'Golden Age' of trade
♿
www.lancaster.gov.uk

Eric Morecambe Statue   758
Morecambe

Unveiled by the Queen in 1999, the slightly larger than life-sized statue depicts Eric Morecambe in one of his characteristic poses with a pair of binoculars around his neck (he was a keen ornithologist). The statue is set against the stunning backdrop of Morecambe Bay and the Lake District hills, and people queue to have their photo taken alongside it. The statue and the arena below it are equally sensational at night, with superb lighting effects bathing the area.

🔍 Morecambe Central Promenade
✲ ◉ ♣ ❄
⏳ 1 hour
★ Great photo opportunity
FREE
www.visitlancashire.com

WWT Martin Mere   759
Ormskirk

Wilderness and family-friendliness combine at Martin Mere Wetland Centre. In the winter there are spectacular aerial displays of wild ducks, geese and swans, but year round the centre is home to resident water birds, otters (see below) and beavers. Visitors can hand feed the birds and look out for the baby goslings and ducklings in the waterfowl gardens, visit the beaver enclosure or go along to the otter and flamingo talks. You can also stroll along the nature trail taking in the sights, sounds and smells of wildflowers, insects and birds; or wander around the new reedbed walk.

🔍 On the A59, 6 miles from Ormskirk
✲ ◉ ♣ ❄
⏳ 2–3 hours
★ Spectacular aerial displays
♿
www.wwt.org.uk

Pendle Witches Trail
Pendle

In the early 17th century Lancashire was home to a significant number of Roman Catholics, a persecuted minority in James I's newly Protestant nation. In 1612 a number of women from around Pendle were convicted of witchcraft because of their beliefs. Visitors can follow the 45-mile route they took from their homes to their eventual trial and execution in Lancaster. The route passes through some of Lancashire's wildest and most spectacular scenery. The route starts at Pendle Heritage Centre where you can learn about the story and the route you need to take to Lancaster.

🔍 Follow signs Pendle Heritage centre from junction 13 of the M65

✳ ⚙ ♣ ❄

⏳ 3-4 hours

⭐ Malkin Tower on Pendle Hill

FREE

www.pendlelife.co.uk

Bowland Wild Boar Park
Preston

Bowland Wild Boar Park is set in the heart of the Forest of Bowland and offers a brilliant and fun day out for families. You can enjoy a picnic and go for a ramble around the footpaths of the park while viewing wild boars, llamas, wallabies, red squirrels, pet lambs and many more animals. Some of the animals can also be fed. There is also a Straw Barn play area and tractor and barrel rides are also available during the summer. There are also picturesque walks in the Trough of Bowland by the River Hodder.

🔍 Follow signs for Chipping, 10 miles north-east of Preston

✳ ⚙ ♣ ❄

⏳ 1-2 hours

⭐ Hand feeding llamas, red deer, goats and lambs

💷

www.wildboarpark.co.uk

British Commercial Vehicle Museum
Preston

This is one of Britain's most important heritage collections – a unique display of historic commercial vehicles and buses spanning a century of truck and bus building. Its exhibits contain not just examples of the vehicles themselves, but evidence of their interaction with daily life. Over one million people in the UK are employed in the road transport industry and its infrastructure. Trucks carry more than 98 per cent of the goods purchased and road transport carrying over five million people per day is literally the lifeline of the nation.

🔍 Follow signs from junction 28 of the M6

✳ ⚙ ♣

⏳ 2-3 hours

⭐ The last link to Leyland Trucks

💷

www.bcvm.co.uk

Harris Museum and Art Gallery
Preston

The Harris Museum and Art Gallery is an important regional museum that holds exciting collections including fine art, decorative art, costume and textiles, history and photography. Highlights include an important photography collection featuring images of Preston from 1850 and a collection of prints of the Crimea by Roger Fenton. Many of the artefacts in the collection were donated by the people of Preston and relate to local life, events and businesses making the museum ideally placed to tell the story of Preston and its heritage.

🔍 Preston city centre

✳ ⚙ ♣ ❄

⏳ 2-3 hours

⭐ Regular contemporary art shows

FREE

www.harrismuseum.org.uk

Ski Rossendale · 764
Rawtenstall

This is the north of England's premier outdoor skiing and snowboarding centre. Set amid trees and glorious parkland, it has superb views over the Rossendale Valley. The centre offers courses with top quality instructors for beginners, experts and those who have got a little rusty since their last winter holiday. You will need to book courses in advance. Equipment is available for hire. Recreational skiing and snowboarding is also available. You can also ride the Quarterpipe, a thrilling long run and steep upward finish, which give you one of the best tubing experiences available.

In Rawtenstall, easy access from the M66 and M65 and the A56

1-6 hours

The Quarterpipe

www.ski-rossendale.co.uk

Rufford Old Hall · 765
Rufford

This is one of Lancashire's finest 16th-century Tudor buildings, where a young Will Shakespeare is said to have performed. His stage, the Great Hall, is as spectacular today as when the Bard was performing for the owner, Sir Thomas Hesketh, and his raucous guests. Visitors can wander around the house and marvel over the fine collections of oak furniture, arms, armour and tapestries. Then step outside and enjoy the gardens, topiary and sculpture and a walk in the woodlands, alongside the canal.

On the A59

2-3 hours

Great Hall

www.nationaltrust.org.uk

Haigh Country Park · 766
Wigan

Haigh Country Park comprises 250 acres of park and woodland, with magnificent views across the Douglas Valley to the Welsh Hills. There is a wide variety of events and activities on offer to introduce people to these woodlands including a number of interesting themed walks. There are also three nature trails of varying lengths, woodland routes which are mapped to help you identify the trees and the wildlife you will see, a miniature ride-on railway and a programme of Conservation Task Days during which volunteers and community groups can learn about local green issues.

On the B5238 or B5239

3-4 hours

Guided walks (see website for details)

FREE

www.wlct.org/leisure/haigh/haighhome.htm

Chinese Arts Centre   767
Manchester

Manchester has the second largest Chinese population in the country. The city's youngest and most successful gallery offers a range of top-quality art Installations by contemporary Chinese artists and interesting design features that reference Chinese culture. The main gallery hosts a challenging and innovative exhibition programme showcasing the very best of contemporary Chinese art. The unique 'Breathe' residency project space provides resident artists with a living area, studio and exhibition space. There are also workshops, education programmes and information about Chinese art and culture.

🔍 Market Buildings, Thomas Street

⚙ ◎ ♣ ✳

⌛ 2–3 hours

⭐ Traditional Chinese tearooms

FREE

www.chinese-arts-centre.org

Manchester Jewish Museum   769
Manchester

This museum is a hidden treasure. Located in a former Spanish and Portuguese synagogue on Cheetham Hill Road, it is the oldest surviving synagogue building in Manchester, completed in 1874. It is a beautiful example of Victorian architecture, executed in Moorish style with fine stained glass windows. The building became redundant through the movement of the Jewish population away from the area. It has been returned to its former glory and is now a museum that chronicles the lives of Jewish people in Manchester and their contribution to making the city what it is today.

🔍 On the A655, 1 mile from Manchester city centre

⚙ ◎ ♣ ✳

⌛ 1–2 hours

⭐ Photographic archive

♿

www.manchesterjewishmuseum.com

Imperial War Museum North   768
Manchester

The multi-award winning Imperial War Museum North is one of the most celebrated museums in Britain today. The museum is about people, young and old, and their stories, about how lives have been and still are shaped by war and conflict during the 20th and 21st centuries. The stunning building, sited on the banks of the Manchester Ship Canal, by international architect Daniel Libeskind is a symbol of our world torn apart by conflict. There are free floor plans, trails, and regular tours to help navigate the fascinating building.

🔍 Trafford Wharf Road, Salford Quays

⚙ ◎ ♣ ✳

⌛ 1–2 hours

⭐ Big Picture Show

FREE

www.iwm.org.uk

STAR ATTRACTION

Manchester Museum
Manchester

770

This museum has four floors of displays and exhibitions in 15 galleries. It houses a huge collection of artefacts from diverse cultures and the natural world. Visitors can see the famous Egyptology galleries, including mummies, the Prehistoric gallery that features Stan, a full-size T Rex, a Science for Life gallery, and a zoology gallery, which contains mammals, birds and live animals. Made up of a series of impressive Gothic style buildings at the heart of the University of Manchester, the Museum was designed by Alfred Waterhouse in 1885.

🔍 Oxford Road, south of the city centre
✴ ✴ ❦ ✳
⌛ 2–3 hours
★ T Rex skeleton
FREE Some exhibitions may charge
www.museum.manchester.ac.uk

Museum of Science and Industry
Manchester

771

A city at the heart of the Industrial Revolution, a trip to MOSI allow visitors to discover Manchester's industrial past and learn about the fascinating stories of the people who contributed to the history and science of a city that helped shape the modern world. Located on the site of the world's oldest surviving passenger railway station, the museum's action-packed galleries, working exhibits and costumed characters tell the amazing story of revolutionary discoveries and remarkable inventions both past and present.

🔍 Follow signs from the city centre
✴ ✴ ❦ ✳
⌛ 3–4 hours
★ Crawling through a Victorian sewer
FREE Some exhibitions may charge
www.msim.org.uk

Manchester Music Tours   772
Manchester

Take an exclusive walking tour of landmarks synonymous with the Manchester music scene. Tours are hosted by Phill Gatenby and Craig Gill, two stalwarts of the scene. Phill has written books about Morrissey and the Smiths, while Craig is a founder member and drummer of Inspiral Carpets and resident DJ at the legendary Hacienda and Boardwalk nightclubs. Tours will give you first-hand accounts of what it's like to work with Noel Gallagher, Tony Wilson, Johnny Marr, Shaun Ryder, Mark E Smith and Peter Hook to name but a few. You can book your place online.

🔍 Starts at the Free Trade Hall
✴ ◎ ♣ ❄
⏳ 2 hours
⭐ Legendary rock landmarks
♿ ♿
www.manchestermusictours.com

Old Trafford Museum and Tour   773
Manchester

The story of Manchester United is unlike any other football club in the world. Beginning more than a century ago, it combines eras of total English and European domination with some of the greatest adversity faced by any club. Visitors to the Manchester United Museum and Tour can experience the story in all its glory, and immerse themselves in a legend still in the making. The tour allows you to see the stadium through the eyes of Manchester United greats themselves and the museum helps you to share 130 years of football history.

🔍 Old Trafford stadium
✴ ◎ ♣ ❄ Pre-booking recommended
⏳ 2–3 hours
⭐ Journey down the players' tunnel
♿ ♿
www.manutd.com

People's History Museum   774
Manchester

The People's History Museum tells the dramatic story of the British working class's struggle for democracy and social justice. The museum provides a journey through the lives, histories and issues of the working people of Britain in the last two centuries, and houses an unprecedented collection of almost 1,500 historic objects, including the world's oldest trade union and miners' banner, the Tinplate Workers (1821) and Ashover Miners (c.1825), and the table on which the 18th-century writer and revolutionary Thomas Paine wrote his ground-breaking publication *Rights of Man*.

🔍 Left Bank in Spinningfields in Manchester city centre
✴ ◎ ♣ ❄
⏳ 2–3 hours
⭐ The Peterloo Massacre exhibit
FREE
www.phm.org.uk

Trafford Ecology Park   775
Manchester

Set in the heart of what was an industrial wasteland, Trafford Ecology Park is now 11 acres of peace and natural tranquillity. It provides the opportunity for busy city dwellers to take a break from the hectic daily schedule and reconnect with wildlife. The site is well maintained, free of litter and provides many little corners for quiet contemplation. Benches and picnic tables are arranged at convenient points to highlight views or other natural features. There is a lake, ponds, a reed-bed marsh, woodlands and wildflower meadows.

🔍 Off the A576, near Salford Quays
✴ ◎ ♣ ❄
⏳ 1–2 hours
⭐ Visitor centre
FREE
www.actionfornature.co.uk

Wythenshawe Park
776

Manchester

This beautiful and spectacular regional park comprises 275 acres of open parkland, and hosts events and activities throughout the year, including an annual firework and bonfire extravaganza. There are three historic buildings to explore: North Lodge, the Statue of Oliver Cromwell and Wythenshawe Hall. This park comprises a variety of landscape features including historic and ornamental woodlands, herbaceous borders, formal bedding, amenity grassland and beautiful wildflower meadows. There's also a wide range of sports facilities, including football pitches, tennis courts, bowling greens and children's play areas.

Off the M56, 4 miles from Manchester airport

3-4 hours

Museum, gallery and glasshouses

FREE Charges for some activities

www.manchester.gov.uk

Birkenhead Priory and St Mary's Tower
777

Birkenhead

Founded in 1150, this Benedictine monastery is the oldest standing building on Merseyside but is surrounded by modern Birkenhead. The whole history of the town is wrapped up in one place. The monks of Birkenhead Priory looked after travellers for nearly 400 years and supervised the first ferry across the Mersey, up to the Dissolution in 1538. First restored over a century ago, the site is now a museum. St Mary's, the first parish church in town, survives now as only a tower. Visitors can climb this late-Georgian ruin for unrivalled views across the Mersey.

Follow signs from Birkenhead town centre

1-2 hours

The original Ferry Cross the Mersey

FREE

www.wirral.gov.uk

Williamson Art Gallery and Museum
778

Birkenhead

The Williamson has a strong reputation for the quality and variety of its exhibitions and houses the vast majority of Birkenhead's collection of art and history. The art collection is the largest, numbering some 6,000 oil paintings, watercolours, drawings and prints; many by artists with local connections. Always on show is a display of ship models, focusing on Cammell Laird shipbuilders and their contribution to marine history, and the Mersey. In addition there are important collections of local ceramics, including Della Robbia Pottery and 18th-century Liverpool Porcelain.

Slatey Road, Birkenhead

1-2 hours

Watercolour collection

FREE

www.wirral.gov.uk

National Wildflower Centre
779

Knowsley

The centre is set in the 35-acre Victorian Court Hey Park, approximately 5 miles from Liverpool city centre. Its purpose is the creation and management of new wildflower habitats for people to enjoy and where wildlife can flourish and develop. By promoting new places for wildflowers to develop and thrive, we are playing a part to preserve our valuable native species and providing places where birds, insects and other wildlife can flourish too. It is a tranquil, family-friendly venue to visit and an urban haven where you will be inspired by nature.

Follow signs from junction 5 of the M62

1-2 hours

A subtly tended wilderness

www.nwc.org.uk

Prescot Museum
780
Knowsley

Prescot Museum is located in a Georgian townhouse, which was once the site of the local cockerel-fighting pit. The town of Prescot has always been famous for its clock and watch making industry and became known as a 'town of little workshops', due to the different parts of the watches being made in workshops attached to houses throughout the town. Prescot Museum reflects this legacy through its permanent local history displays. It also explores other local industries, such as pottery manufacture, cable making and mining.

🔍 Follow signs from the A57 and A56
✿ ⊙ ♣ ❅
⧖ 1–2 hours
★ Clocks and watches
FREE
www.prescotmuseum.org.uk

Aintree Visitor Centre – The Grand National Experience
781
Liverpool

Gain an insight into the home of the most famous horse race in the world. The stories of Aintree winners, Red Rum, Ginger McCain, Jenny Pitman, are immortalised in history. The Grand National Experience explains how Liverpool hotelier, William Lynn, and Captain Becher conceived the race and how it was run for many years by a gaiety girl, Mrs Topham. The dominating feature of the Visitor Centre is the racecourse. This enormous green expanse fills the windows with a view full of expectation and gives visitors a memorable day out.

🔍 Follow signs from Liverpool city centre
⊙ ♣
⧖ 1–2 hours
★ Jockeys' weighing room
💷
www.aintree.co.uk

The Beatles Story
782
Liverpool

The Beatles Story follows the band's career from their early years to their break up and solo careers. There's a whole host of memorabilia, photographs and other artefacts on offer. Visitors can also see a recreated Cavern, a dark street in Hamburg, and a remarkable section where a powerful speaker system recreates Beatlemania. An interior of the Yellow Submarine leads through the final years, and an audio-visual consideration of each Beatle. A second site has recently opened at the Pier Head that picks up the story of the band members after the break up.

🔍 Albert Dock and the Pier Head
✿ ⊙ ♣ ❅
⧖ 2–3 hours
★ The new Fab4D Experience
💷 💷
www.beatlesstory.com

Beatles Tour   783
Liverpool

There are dozens of similar tours on offer but the Fab Four Taxi Tour will not let you down. After a city centre pick up, you will visit the homes of John, Paul, George and Ringo, birthplaces of John and Brian Epstein, the Penny Lane Experience, the Shelter in the middle of the Roundabout, Barbers showing photographs, Strawberry Fields, Eleanor Rigby's tombstone, the Cavern Club and lots more Beatles related places. The drivers are very knowledgeable and provide a good service. It is essential to book these tours and you can book online at the website address below.

🔍 Pick up in Liverpool city centre
✸ ◉ ♣ ❄
⧗ 3 hours
★ Penny Lane
💷 💷
www.fabfourtaxitours.com

Cains Brewery   784
Liverpool

Robert Cains' original Mersey brewery stands today as a fine example of Victorian brewhouse architecture. Renowned as a brewer of fine cask ales, visitors can tour the brewery and see an example of the tower brewing principle. You will get a fascinating insight into Merseyside's rich brewing heritage during a tour that includes two complimentary pints of Cains' award-winning ales. Tours take place Monday to Friday at 6.30 p.m. and on Saturdays and Sundays at 1.00 p.m. It is essential that you pre-book your tour (see website for details).

🔍 West Parliament Street, near Albert Dock
✸ ◉ ♣ ❄
⧗ 1-2 hours
★ Canning production line and brewhouse
💷
www.cains.co.uk

Croxteth Hall and Country Park   785
Liverpool

Imagine you are a guest at this Edwardian country house, enjoying the elegant surroundings and opulent lifestyle. Or imagine being a servant, rising early and toiling all day under the watchful eye of the housekeeper and butler. Generations of the Molyneux family, the Earls of Sefton, lived at Croxteth Hall from the 16th century until 1972. Today the rooms are open, showing a glimpse of life 'above' and 'below' stairs. Outside is a tranquil walled garden and beyond that magnificent woodland, grazing livestock and traditional cottages in a landscape that has changed little in over a century.

🔍 Take junction 4 of the M57, then A580 towards Liverpool
✸ ◉ ♣
⧗ 2-3 hours
★ Fabulous kids' adventure playground
💷
www.croxteth.co.uk

Echo Wheel
786
Liverpool

The new 60-metre high wheel is in place for at least a
year. It is positioned on the piazza outside the ECHO
Arena near Albert Dock and lights up the skyline after
dark. It includes 42 fully enclosed and air-conditioned
capsules which seat up to eight people and offers riders
spectacular views of the city including the River Mersey,
the Welsh mountains and World Heritage Site waterfront.
It also has a VIP luxury capsule with leather seating,
DVD player and a champagne fridge.

Albert Dock

1 hour

Fabulous views of the city's famous skyline

www.echoarena.com

Everton Football Club
787
Liverpool

Have you ever wondered just what goes on behind the
scenes at Goodison Park? Have you dreamed of walking
down the tunnel to the roar of 40,000 fans? Do you
want to know where your favourite players get changed
or relax after the game? If the answer's yes then you
can do just that on a Goodison Park stadium tour. Tours
take place on Mondays, Wednesdays and Fridays at
11 a.m. and 1 p.m. and Sundays at 11 a.m. Tours do not
operate on a match days. Booking is strongly advised.

3 miles north of Liverpool city centre

1–2 hours

Insight into the workings of a top-flight English club

www.evertonfc.com

International Slavery Museum
788
Liverpool

Visitors will learn about the millions of people, both in
the past and today, who have been taken into slavery.
In particular those who were part of the transatlantic
slave trade between about 1500 and 1865. Liverpool
was a major slaving port – its ships carried some
1.5 million enslaved Africans. The museum has sections
entitled Life in West Africa, Enslavement and the
Middle Passage, about the brutality and trauma suffered
on the voyage across the Atlantic, and Legacies of
Slavery about the modern day impact of transatlantic
slavery, such as racism and discrimination.

Albert Dock

2–3 hours

History of the slave trade

FREE

www.liverpoolmuseums.org.uk

Liverpool Football Club Museum and Tour
789

Liverpool

Go behind the scenes at one of the world's true sporting cathedrals – Anfield. Get fascinating insights into the club's history, taking in never seen before areas of the stadium. Enjoy an interactive experience in the Anfield Press Room and follow in the footsteps of legends like Shankly, Paisley and Dalglish. Sit in the same dressing room as the modern day icons. To the backdrop of spine tingling sound effects, walk down the tunnel, touch the world famous 'This is Anfield' sign and emerge to the roar of the Anfield faithful.

3 miles north of the city centre

⚙ ⚙ ♣ ❄

⏳ 1–2 hours

★ Liverpool FC trophy room

£ £

www.liverpoolfc.tv

Maritime Merseyside Walk
790

Liverpool

The best way to see the landmarks of one of England's major ports is on foot. Starting at the Merseyside Maritime Museum, head towards the river, taking in views of Birkenhead, turn right and you come to the Pier Head and the Three Graces. A little further is the place from where millions emigrated to the New World in the early 19th century. Turn inland, and walk up Water Street to the Town Hall, one of the oldest buildings in the city centre. Head back along James Street and turn right to find your way back.

Liverpool riverside

⚙ ⚙ ♣ ❄

⏳ 2 hours

★ The famous Mersey ferries

FREE

www.visitliverpool.com

Merseyside Maritime Museum
791

Liverpool

At Merseyside Maritime Museum you'll find out about the companies, people and ships connected to this great port. You can see boats, paintings, ship models, objects from wrecks, ships, uniforms and more. Exhibits include Seized, which tells the story of smuggling and Britain's taxes and duties and the Emigration gallery, where you'll find out about the nine million people who emigrated through the port. There's also the popular *Titanic*, *Lusitania* and *Empress of Ireland* gallery. You can learn about Liverpool's role in the Second World War, and what it's like to spend your Life At Sea.

Albert Dock

⚙ ⚙ ♣ ❄

⏳ 2–3 hours

★ Ships and shipping companies of Liverpool

FREE

www.liverpoolmuseums.org.uk

Mendips and 20 Forthlin Road
792

Liverpool

These unassuming houses are the childhood homes of John Lennon and Paul McCartney. Visiting the Beatles' houses in Liverpool is an absolute must for fans of the band of any ages. Visits provide a real insight in to the band's humble beginnings. John Lennon lived at Mendips with his Aunt Mimi and Uncle George. This is where his passion for music began and where some of his early songs were written. The McCartney family home is in Allerton, this is where the Beatles met, rehearsed and wrote many of their earliest songs. Displays include early Beatles memorabilia.

Tours depart from various points in the city

⚙ ⚙ ♣

⏳ 2–3 hours

★ The real Beatles story

£ £ Booking essential, see website

nationaltrust.org.uk

Mr Hardman's Photographic Studio
793
Liverpool

Step back in time to 1950 in this fascinating house at 59 Rodney Street – view the studio, darkroom and living quarters of the renowned portrait photographer E. Chambré Hardman and his wife Margaret. The memorabilia of post-war daily life is displayed alongside portraits of Liverpool people and landscape photographs of the surrounding countryside. Visitors can follow the photographic process from studio, to darkroom, to mounting room and even have their portrait taken in the studio.

Liverpool city centre
☀ ⊙ ♣ Timed ticket only
⌛ 1–2 hours
★ Photographic history of Liverpool
£
www.nationaltrust.org.uk

Sefton Park Palm House
794
Liverpool

This Grade II listed Victorian glasshouse is an octagonal, three-tiered structure showcasing the Liverpool botanical collection which was brought to the city from all over the world during its time as one of the world's greatest ports. Formal bedding within the grounds brings a spot of colour outside, while established plants from all over the world create lusciousness inside. Statues displayed inside and guarding the building perimeter hint at Liverpool's creative and trading history as a city and port. Seasonal planting displays showcase the variety of species held in the collection.

On the A5058
☀ ⊙ ♣ ✳
⌛ 1–2 hours
★ One of the largest municipal plant collections in the country
FREE
www.palmhouse.org.uk

Shiverpool Ghost Tours   795
Liverpool

Only visiting the most haunted sights and utilising Liverpool's darkest corners, and sourcing local, budding acting talent trained to the highest standard, Shiverpool Tours provide an unforgettable experience to brave audiences everywhere. These ghost tours are the best guided walks of the city designed to scare and reveal Liverpool's hidden mysteries, enabling audiences to look beyond the veneer on a magical journey through one of England's oldest towns – no wonder it's so full of ghosts. There are several tours on offer (see website for details and booking).

🔍 Tours start at various points in the city centre
✿ ◐ ♣ ❄
⧗ 1–2 hours
★ Ghostly appearances
♿ ♿
www.shiverpool.co.uk

Speke Hall, Garden and Estate   796
Liverpool

A rare Tudor manor house surrounded by fragrant gardens protected by a collar of woodland. Constructed by a devout Catholic family, keen to impress visitors with their home's grandeur, in particular the Great Hall, this beautiful building has witnessed more than 400 years of turbulent history. Priests fleeing persecution in the 16th century were offered sanctuary, hiding in the secret priest's hole. Fascinating insights into the lives and work of the Victorian servants are revealed in the kitchen and dairy, while Tudor servants slept in the roof space. It's a perfect oasis from modern life.

🔍 Follow signs from Liverpool airport
✿ ◐ ♣
⧗ 2–3 hours
★ Beautiful carved furniture
♿
www.nationaltrust.org.uk

Tate Liverpool   797
Liverpool

Tate Liverpool is the home of the National Collection of Modern Art in the north, and has been one of the most popular galleries in the city for over 20 years. It also hosts major exhibitions of international modern art, making it the ideal place to either see your favourite artworks or discover something new. The gallery has seen some fantastic exhibitions over recent years including work by Pablo Picasso, Gustav Klimt, Rodin, Duchamp, Peter Blake, Giacometti and the stunning work of 'Brit Art' movement including works by Damien Hurst, Antony Gormley, Tracey Emin and Rachel Whiteread.

🔍 Albert Dock
✿ ◐ ♣ ❄
⧗ 2–3 hours
★ World's finest contemporary art
FREE Some exhibitions will charge
www.tate.org.uk/liverpool

The Walker   798
Liverpool

The Walker holds one of the finest collections of fine and decorative art in Europe. As well as a stunning collection of paintings from the 13th century to the present, there is also a sculpture gallery, a craft and design gallery and a space specially designed for children. Amongst a huge collection of works by Old Masters and Pre-Raphaelite artists visitors can see work by Rembrandt, Hockney, Holbein, Waterhouse, Poussin, Turner, Lowry, Rossetti, Lord Leighton, Rubens, Sickert, Hogarth, Reynolds, Gainsborough, Stubbs, Millais, Nash and Freud to name but a few.

🔍 Liverpool city centre
✿ ◐ ♣ ❄
⧗ 2–3 hours
★ Decorative art of all kinds
FREE
www.liverpoolmuseums.org.uk

Yellow Duckmarine   799
Liverpool

The Duckmarine can move both on land and on water. Leaving from the Albert Dock, you will drive along the dockside, taking in all the major riverside sights before turning straight off the road, down the slipway and into Salthouse Dock. Imagine the looks on your children's faces. Once you've found your sea legs, the tour continues through the South Docks to Coburg Dock, before emerging from the water once more, right in front of the Albert Dock buildings. With a live commentary throughout, it's an unforgettable way of seeing this beautiful city.

🔍 Albert Dock
⚙ ◎ ♣ ✳
⏳ 1–2 hours
⭐ Unique views of Liverpool
£ £

www.theyellowduckmarine.co.uk

Botanic Gardens Museum   800
Southport

The Botanic Gardens Museum houses a number of fascinating objects within their permanent collections. Visitors can see photographs and paintings that tell the story of 19th-century Southport, a dugout canoe from AD. 535 that was found near Martin Mere in 1899, a Victorian parlour showing how a middle-class Victorian family would have lived, the history of the *Eagle* comic, which started in Southport in the 1950s, a collection of old toys that will appeal to both children and adults alike and a natural history room featuring a fascinating collection of birds and animals.

🔍 Botanic Road, Southport
⚙ ◎ ♣
⏳ 1–2 hours
⭐ Story of Dan Dare
FREE

www.seftonarts.co.uk

Formby Squirrel Reserve   801
Southport

A nature reserve that features beaches, sand dunes and pine woods along a stunning stretch of unspoiled coastline. Visitors can enjoy a stroll around the peaceful pine woodlands and look out for endangered red squirrels, which are here to feed on the ripe pinecones. Wide-open skies and an expanse of space make the beach at Formby a fantastic getaway from hectic urban life. Erosion of the sand has revealed footprints from animals and humans dating back to the late Neolithic/ early Bronze Age, about 3,500 to 7,000 years ago.

🔍 Off the A565, 6 miles south of Southport
⚙ ◎ ♣ ✳
⏳ 2 hours
⭐ Asparagus fields
FREE Car parking charge
www.nationaltrust.org.uk

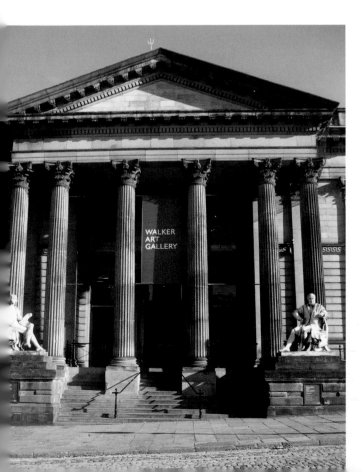

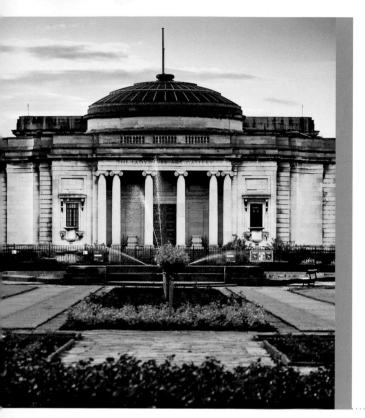

Lady Lever Art Gallery | 803
Wirral

This gallery is a real treasure. As well as a stunning collection of paintings visitors can also see beautiful furniture, Chinese collections, tapestries, sculpture, Wedgwood, classical antiquities and a beautiful building. There are several rooms in the gallery, centred around the main hall. The paintings on display includes pieces by Reynolds, Gainsborough, Stubbs, Turner, Millais, Burne-Jones, Lord Leighton, Rossetti and Waterhouse among others. Around the gallery you will also find beautiful furniture, Chinese ceramics, Wedgwood, tapestries and a room dedicated to Lord Leverhulme.

Follow signs from the A41, in Port Sunlight village

1-2 hours

J.M.W. Turner's 'The Falls of Clyde'

FREE

www.liverpoolmuseums.org.uk

Hilbre Island | 802
Wirral

There are three tidal islands lying at the mouth of the Dee Estuary: Little Eye, Middle Eye and Hilbre. They are designated as a local nature reserve. It's a marvellous place to watch migrating birds, wildfowl and waders as well as a whole range of other wildlife, including grey seals. There is also a lighthouse and a small museum. The islands are cut off from the mainland by the tide for up to four hours in twelve, so check the tide times before travelling.

Access is by foot, 2 miles west of Kirby

Check tide times at www.pol.ac.uk/ntslf/tidalp.html

2-3 hours

Nature in the raw

FREE

www.wirral.gov.uk

Port Sunlight Museum and Garden Village | 804
Wirral

Port Sunlight is a unique and beautiful 19th-century garden village created solely for the Sunlight Soap factory workers. The Port Sunlight Museum introduces the village's creator, 'Soap King' William Hesketh Lever, and explains his vision for the village and its residents. Find out about the architects who designed the buildings and landscapes. Experience what it was like to live and work here during the village's heyday. From the museum you can follow a trail around the village, enjoy the stunning architecture and beautiful parkland.

Follow signs from the A41, in Port Sunlight village

3-4 hours

Living history

www.portsunlightvillage.com

North East

Durham
Northumberland
Tyne and Wear

Dunstanburgh Castle, Northumberland

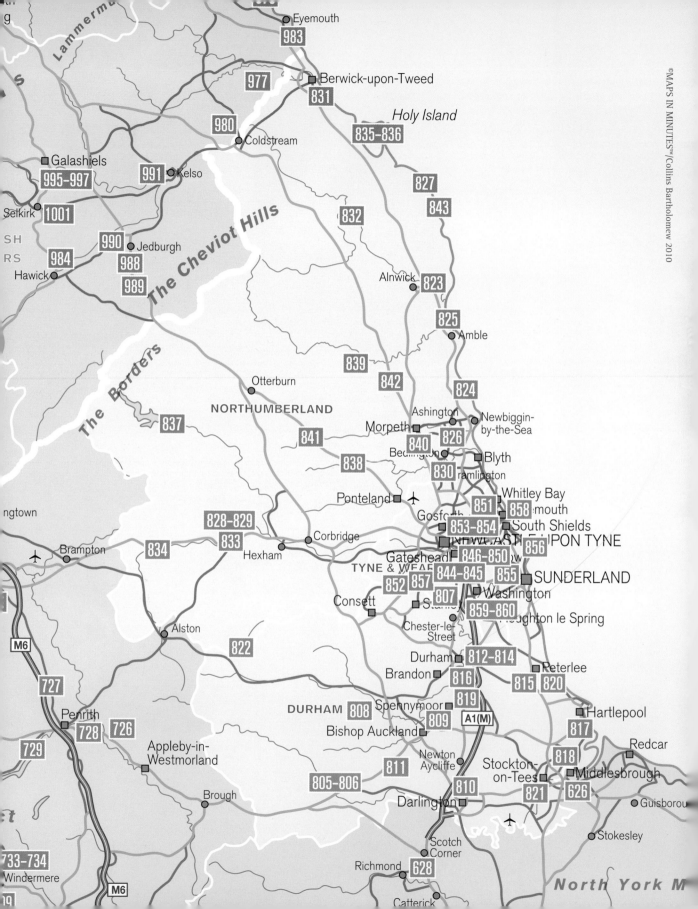

Guide to the **North East**

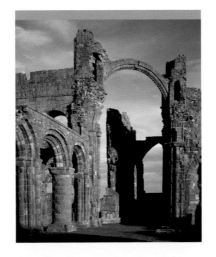

Rooted in history, brought to life by its people, this award-winning museum captures **the spirit of the North East**

Barnard Castle

805

Barnard Castle

Set on a high rock above the River Tees, Barnard Castle takes its name from its 12th-century founder, Bernard de Balliol. It was later developed by the Beauchamp family and then passed into the hands of Richard III. Try and spot Richard's boar emblem carved above a window in the inner ward or visit the 'sensory garden' of scented plants and tactile objects. With fantastic views over the Tees Gorge this fortress sits on the fringe of an attractive working market town also known as 'Barney' so there is plenty to do for families on a day out.

Barnard Castle town centre

1 hour

Castle associated with Richard III, Henry VII and Charles I

www.english-heritage.org.uk

Bowes Museum

806

Barnard Castle

Founded by local businessman, John Bowes, and his wife, this magnificent museum, opened in 1892, houses one of Britain's finest collection of paintings, ceramics, furniture and textiles. In every corner visitors can see important and precious works from all over Europe, and each piece has its own story to tell. The diverse collection spans three floors of the magnificent building and contains items too numerous to list including paintings by Canaletto and Goya, porcelain produced at Sèvres and marquetry attributed to André-Charles Boulle.

Barnard Castle town centre

2-3 hours

The Silver Swan

www.bowesmuseum.org.uk

Beamish – The North of England Open-Air Museum

807

Beamish

FIVE-STAR ATTRACTION

Follow signs from junction 63 of the A1M

3-4 hours

The Town 1913

www.beamish.org.uk

Beamish is a world famous open-air museum telling the story of the people of north-east England before and after the Industrial Revolution. Based around a number of buildings that were already here, such as Home Farm, Pockerley Old Hall and the Drift Mine, the other houses, shops and other buildings were all dismantled, brought to Beamish and rebuilt. All of the buildings are filled with furniture, machinery and objects – real artefacts from the museum's collections.

A good way to start your visit is to take a tram ride around the site to see what's on offer. You can then stroll around the shops and houses of the Edwardian town or go underground at the mine and then see where the miners lived. See the animals at Home Farm and relax in the cosy farmhouse kitchen. Explore Pockerley Old Hall, set in the beautiful Georgian landscape, and ride on a recreation of an early steam train.

This is not a traditional museum. What really sets Beamish apart from glass case museums is that the story is told not by labels but by costumed staff who are proud of their heritage and happy to share their knowledge with visitors.

Hamsterley Forest
808

Bishop Auckland

The forest comprises 5,000 acres of woodland lying between the Wear and Tees valleys on the edge of the North Pennines. Hamsterley is an oasis of broadleaved and coniferous woodland, sprawling along the sides of a sheltered valley. Visitors have no shortage of options when it comes to activities. With waymarked walks, bike hire, cycle routes and horse riding trails, all levels of fitness and ability are catered for. The visitor centre marks the start of a scenic four-mile drive that runs through the heart of the forest giving access to numerous picnic sites along the way.

🔍 Off the A68, follow signs to Hamsterley village
⚙ ◎ ♣
⏳ 2–4 hours
⭐ The largest forest in County Durham
FREE Car parks and some activities charge
www.forestry.gov.uk

Binchester Roman Fort
809

Bishop Auckland

Once the largest Roman fort in County Durham, Binchester was built in 1st century AD when the Roman army was asserting its power in the North East of England. Originally, the fort was wooden: when the Romans knew they were staying for a long time, it was rebuilt in stone. The soldiers came from all over the Roman Empire including Spain and Holland. Visitors can explore the remains of a Roman bathhouse with its 1,700-year-old under floor heating system and walk in the footsteps of the soldiers around the remains of the Commander's House.

🔍 On the A688, 2 miles north of Bishop Auckland
⚙ ◎ ♣
⏳ 2–3 hours
⭐ The Beast of Binchester
💷
www.durham.gov.uk

Head of Steam
810

Darlington

This newly refurbished museum offers a unique experience to visitors, telling the story of the history of Darlington and the impact of the railways. The museum is located on the 1825 route of the Stockton and Darlington Railway, the world's first steam-worked public railway. Exhibits include Stephenson's 'Locomotion No. 1', one of the oldest surviving steam engines in the world, and specially built for the opening of the railway, and 'Derwent', the earliest surviving Darlington built locomotive.

🔍 On the A167, follow signs from Darlington town centre
⚙ ◎ ♣ Weekends only in winter
⏳ 2 hours
⭐ Stephenson's 'Rocket'
💷
www.darlington.gov.uk

Raby Castle   811
Darlington

Built in the 14th century, Raby Castle is one of the largest and most impressive English medieval castles. Behind the powerful exterior of towers and fortifications every room, from the magnificent Barons' Hall, where 700 knights gathered to plot the 'Rising of the North', to the Mediaeval Kitchen, which was used until 1954, gives an insight to life throughout the ages. Raby also houses a fantastic art collection and splendid interiors. Treasures include an important collection of Meissen porcelain, tapestries, furnishings and paintings by leading artists such as Munnings, De Hooch, Teniers, Van Dyck and Reynolds.

On the A688, 1 mile north of Staindrop

2–3 hours

Barons' Hall

www.rabycastle.com

Crook Hall and Gardens   812
Durham

The Hall is a rare example of three eras of English domestic architecture. The Medieval Hall was built around 1208, the Jacobean Mansion was built in 1671 and in 1720 the Hopper family built the Georgian House. The main hall was restored in the 1980s. The circular turret was a late addition allowing the ancient wooden stairs to remain in place. The old stairs are now for the sole use of the White Lady, a niece of Cuthbert Billingham, who supposedly haunts the room. The hall is surrounded by glorious, tranquil themed gardens.

Durham city centre

1–2 hours

'History, romance and beauty'

www.crookhallgardens.co.uk

The DLI Museum and Durham Art Gallery   813
Durham

The Durham Light Infantry Museum has a collection of uniforms, equipment, weapons, silver, photographs and battlefield relics covering the history of the regiment from 1758–1968. The museum also has an outstanding medal room with eight original Victoria Crosses on show, plus over 3,000 other medals awarded to more than a thousand men who served. Your ticket also gets you in to Durham Art Gallery, the area's largest modern and contemporary art gallery.

Durham city centre, near the railway station

2–3 hours

Audio recordings of DLI Second World War soldiers

www.durham.gov.uk

Durham Castle   814
Durham

Durham Castle and Durham Cathedral sit side-by-side on a prominent hill top site, encircled by the wooded slopes of the meandering River Wear, and overlooking the medieval city of Durham with its fascinating narrow streets. Although the castle is now a residential building for the university, parts of it can be visited by guided tour. Built in 1072 by William the Conqueror, it has been in constant use for more than 900 years. Tours run every afternoon during term time and every morning during the vacations. It is essential to book in advance (see website for details).

Durham city centre

See website for details

1 hour

The Black Staircase

www.dur.ac.uk

Durham Heritage Coastal Path 815
Durham

You can take a spectacular 8-mile walk along part of Durham's Heritage Coastal Path starting at Limekiln Gill in Horden village. Head north along the cliff-top path, which is dotted with denes and gills, which are steep sided glacial valleys. Walk down Whitesides Gill, Warren House Gill and Foxholes Dene to see incredible geological features. Further on you will see the site of the Easington Colliery. Walk on to Shippersea Bay, Hawthorne Dean and stop at Beacon Hill for some fabulous views. You then have to retrace your steps to get back to the starting point.

Near Peterlee
4–5 hours
Setting for *Billy Elliot*
FREE
www.durhamheritagecoast.org

Museum of Archaeology 816
Durham

Once a key part of Durham's cloth-making industry, the 18th-century Old Fulling Mill is now home to Durham University's Museum of Archaeology. The collections on display provide a fascinating insight into the rich heritage of the North East of England, as well as showcasing items from across Europe. Highlights include outstanding Roman collections together with Anglo-Saxon, Medieval and Tudor finds from Durham city and the local area. The museum also has a regular programme of exhibitions devoted to local archaeology and history.

Durham city centre
Weekends only in winter
1 hour
Altars and stone inscriptions from Hadrian's Wall
www.dur.ac.uk/fulling.mill

Hartlepool's Maritime Experience 817
Hartlepool

This is a recreation of an 18th-century seaport. It brings to life the time of Nelson, Napoleon and the Battle of Trafalgar. Visitors can see how it was on board a real British naval frigate two centuries ago. You can explore the historic quayside, which features exhibitions, as well as realistic period shops and houses. There are plenty of guides, all in authentic period dress, to show you around. One of the highlights is HMS *Trincomalee*, Britain's oldest floating warship.

Follow signs for Hartlepool Historic Quay
2–4 hours
The Hartlepool monkey legend

www.hartlepoolsmaritimeexperience.com

Dorman Museum 818
Middlesbrough

Permanent displays include Town in Time, illustrating Middlesbrough's diverse history from prehistoric times, including hundreds of objects from the museum's collections. Other themed galleries include Earth in Space – space, geology and evolution on earth; Linthorpe Art Pottery; 20th-Century Woman – women's changing roles from a local viewpoint; H2O – a hands-on discovery centre for children and families and the T.H. Nelson Room – a 19th-century collection of birds and eggs presented in its original Edwardian museum setting.

Middlesbrough city centre
1–2 hours
Lion and zebra exhibit
FREE
www.dormanmuseum.co.uk

Whitworth Hall Country Park `819`
Spennymoor

You can experience 73 acres of historic parkland near Whitworth Hall, former home of the Shafto family (remember Bonny Bobby Shafto?) for over 300 years. You can hand-feed the resident red and fallow deer, stroll by or fish in the ornamental lake, go on a woodland walk and or visit the marvellous Victorian walled garden. There are also indoor and outdoor children's play areas. For a taste of old England why not come along to the newly built bandstand situated and listen to Spennymoor Town Band playing songs old and new.

🔍 Follow signs from Spennymoor town centre
☀ ☼ ♣ ❄
⏳ 2-3 hours
★ Victorian walled garden
FREE
www.thisisdurham.com

Castle Eden Dene NNR `820`
Peterlee

Castle Eden Dene is the largest area of semi-natural woodland in north-east England, renowned for yew trees. The tangled landscape is a survivor of the wildwood that once covered most of Britain. There are two marked walks around the reserve. The Dene, with its strange rocks and mysterious atmosphere, has fascinated people for thousands of years. The reserve covers 500 acres of woodland and lowland grassland, where post-glacial melt waters have carved out some spectacular limestone cliffs and gorges. There is a wide variety of wildlife to be seen in this tranquil place.

🔍 Follow signs from Peterlee town centre
☀ ☼ ♣ ❄
⏳ 2-3 hours
★ Magical waymarked walks
FREE
www.naturalengland.org.uk

Castlegate Quay Watersports Centre `821`
Stockton-on-Tees

Castlegate Quay Watersports Centre is sited on the Tees riverside. It offers a range of fun, water-based activities, such as kayaking, sailing and even power boating. Or you could opt for a multi-activity day, which lets you try a bit of everything. Fully qualified coaching staff offer tuition for all standards. Activities are suitable for people aged 8 and over. Equipment is provided, so all you need is a change of clothes. You should book courses in advance (see website).

🔍 Stockton town centre
☀ ☼ ♣ ❄
⏳ 4-6 hours
★ Multi-activity courses
♿ ♿ ♿
www.teesactive.co.uk

Killhope – the North of England Lead Mining Museum `822`
Upper Weardale

Killhope is a fully restored 19th-century lead mine, where visitors can experience the life and work of the lead mining families of the North Pennines. The enthusiastic and knowledgeable staff help visitors get the most from their visit. Putting on the museum's hard hats, cap-lamps and wellingtons and experiencing the mine tour is just one of the many exciting activities available here. You can also discover life in the mineshop where the miners lived, work as a washer boy on the washing floor or stroll through the woods and see the red squirrels. Dress warmly.

🔍 On the A689, between Stanhope and Alston
☀ ☼ ♣
⏳ 2-3 hours
★ 38-foot diameter waterwheel
♿
www.durham.gov.uk

Alnwick Castle   823

Alnwick

Built as a medieval fortress, this forbidding castle is known as the Windsor of the North. It has stunning State Rooms, fine furnishings and paintings by the likes of Canaletto, Van Dyck and Titian. The castle overlooks a 'Capability' Brown landscaped park in which there are peaceful walks and superb views. It was also the location for the filming of the *Harry Potter* movies. As well as the castle, there's magic and wizardry, archery, birds of prey and a host of other activities during the summer season.

🔍 Just off the A1, near Alnwick
✲ ⊙ 🍁
⏳ 2-3 hours
⭐ Guided tours of the castle
♿ ♿
www.alnwickcastle.com

Warkworth Castle and Hermitage   825

Amble

Warkworth Castle's magnificent cross-shaped keep crowns a hilltop above the River Coquet. It is one of the largest and most impressive fortresses in North East England. It was once home to Harry Hotspur, hero of many Border ballads and the bane of Scots raiders. Visitors can take an audio tour through the remains of a great hall, fine gatehouse and towering walls. You can also visit a medieval hermitage tucked away upstream and accessible only by boat.

🔍 On the A1068, 8 miles south of Alnwick
✲ ⊙ 🍁 ❄
⏳ 1-2 hours
⭐ Free audio tour
♿
www.english-heritage.org.uk

Druridge Bay Country Park   824

Amble

The park comprises three miles of beautiful beach and sand dunes, plus a large freshwater lake surrounded by woods and meadows. You can take a pleasant walk around Ladyburn Lake, or enjoy a sheltered picnic overlooking it. The lake is available for launching windsurfers and non-motorised boats (by permit), and sailing, windsurfing and canoeing courses are held each summer. You can enjoy watching birds on the lake and seashore, discover the many wild flowers on the dunes or fly a kite or take a dip in the sea.

🔍 Off the A1068, 3 miles south of Amble
✲ ⊙ 🍁
⏳ 2-4 hours
⭐ Glorious Cresswell Dunes
FREE Car parks charge
www.northumberland.gov.uk

Wansbeck Riverside Park   826

Ashington

Wansbeck Riverside Park covers over 250 acres of woodland, grassland and the river. The park is a popular area for informal activities such as walking, bird watching and picnicking as well as organised activities such as horse trails, nature trails, rowing and fishing. Flora and fauna is abundant and all kinds of animals, including red squirrels, bats and birds can be seen throughout the year. The woodlands too support a wealth of birds, mammals and insects. There is also a delightful camping and caravan site.

🔍 Between the A1068 and A189, south of Ashington
✲ ⊙ 🍁 ❄
⏳ 2-3 hours
⭐ Haven of English wildlife
FREE
www.wansbeck.gov.uk

Hadrian's Wall and Housesteads Fort 828
Bardon Mill

Running through an often wild landscape, Hadrian's Wall was one of the Roman Empire's most northerly outposts. Built around AD122, it has 16 permanent bases, of which Housesteads Fort is one of the best preserved. Set where the wall climbs to the top of a dramatic escarpment, there are some stunning views to enjoy. Imagine how life was for the 800 Roman soldiers based here as you wander the remains of the barrack blocks and the commandant's house. There's a fascinating museum too, complete with a model of how the fort looked in Roman times.

On the B6318, 4 miles from Bardon Mill

1-2 hours

2,000 years of history

www.nationaltrust.org.uk

Bamburgh Castle 827
Bamburgh

Standing high on a basalt outcrop, overlooking the North Sea, Bamburgh Castle is one of the most impressive looking castles in England. It is visible for many miles, and from its battlements offers views of Lindisfarne Castle on Holy Island, the Farne Islands and the Cheviot Hills. One of the oldest buildings remaining is a large Norman Keep, probably built by Henry II. The castle was restored and extended in the 18th and 19th centuries leaving little of the earlier fortifications. Tours include the magnificent King's Hall, Cross Hall, reception rooms and armoury.

By the B1342, 20 miles south of Berwick

2-3 hours

Guided tours

www.bamburghcastle.com

Roman Vindolanda 829
Bardon Mill

The Roman army occupied Vindolanda around AD 85. The remains of these early forts now lie below the turf, protected by later stone structures. Visitors can tour the ruins and visit the museum, which holds a vast range of artefacts. But the most highly prized of all are the slivers of wood, covered in spidery ink writing – the official and private correspondence of the men and women who lived here nearly 2,000 years ago. Their accounts, military documents, leave requests and even drawings form the earliest archive of written material in British history.

Follow signs from the A69

2-3 hours

Leather goods, textiles, wooden objects, bronze and iron objects

www.vindolanda.com

Bedlington Country Park   830
Bedlington

Bedlington Country Park covers 140 acres of woodland and grassland on the north banks of River Blyth. The earliest industrial use of the valley was the quarrying of sandstone. The quarries are now filled and are hidden and overgrown with mature trees. The area was made a Local Country Park in 1984 to protect its unique nature. The paths and bridle ways are now popular with locals and the area is teeming with wildlife such as otters, kingfishers, woodpeckers and red squirrels, as well as native trees, shrubs and rare flora.

🔍 Between the A189 and A1068, south of Bedlington
☼ ⚙ ♣ ❄
⏳ 2-3 hours
⭐ Historic industrial sites
FREE
www.northumberland.gov.uk

Berwick-upon-Tweed Barracks   831
and Main Guard
Berwick-upon-Tweed

Built in the early 18th century to the design of the distinguished architect Nicholas Hawksmoor, the barracks was among the first in England to be purpose built. The By Beat of Drum exhibition gives you an insight into the life of the British infantryman from the Civil War to the First World War. A stone's throw away from the Scottish borders and located in a Georgian market town it also boasts a range of other temporary and permanent exhibitions to explore including the Berwick Gymnasium Art Gallery and the Berwick Borough Museum.

🔍 Berwick town centre
☼ ⚙ ♣ ❄
⏳ 2 hours
⭐ Rampart walks with superb views
♿
www.english-heritage.org.uk

Chillingham Castle   832
Chillingham

This 12th-century stronghold, home of Sir Humphry Wakefield and his family, was the headquarters for the 1298 conquering attack on William Wallace by Hammer of the Scots, King Edward I. Wallace had raided the previous year, burning women and children to death in the local abbey. Battlements were added in 1344 by King Edward III (you can see the actual licence in the castle). The Elizabethans added Long Galleries and 'Capability' Brown designed the park in 1752. The glorious Italian garden was laid out in the 19th century by Sir Jeffrey Wyatville.

🔍 Follow signs from the A1 and A697
☼ ⚙ ♣
⏳ 2 hours
⭐ Ghost Tours (book online, in advance)
♿
www.chillingham-castle.com

Roman Army Museum   833
Greenhead

This museum houses a collection of replicas and real artefacts illustrating what life was like for the Roman soldiers stationed here on Rome's northern frontier. The collection of Roman armour and weapons includes shields, swords, body armour, shoes and javelins. Also on display are two Roman standards, a Roman chariot, a Celtic chariot and a Roman wagon. You can glimpse what life was like in the barrack room and listen to Gaius tell you about his Roman storeroom. There are numerous other displays including information about the Emperor Hadrian and his life.

🔍 Follow signs from the B6318
☼ ⚙ ♣
⏳ 2 hours
⭐ *Eagle's Eye* film of the Roman fort
♿
www.vindolanda.com

South Tyne Trail 834
Haltwhistle

The South Tyne Trail follows the route of the River South Tyne from Haltwhistle to the source. The whole route is almost 23 miles long, though you can join it at several points, and a great way to see the North Pennines. Much of the route follows the disused Haltwhistle railway line and includes the spectacular Lambley Viaduct. Walkers, cyclists and riders will share the journey with curlews and golden plovers, see miles of stone walls, or dykes, that are such a feature of the North Pennines landscape and visit Ashgill Force waterfall.

🔍 Best access from Haltwhistle or Alston
⚙️
⏳ 5–6 hours
⭐ Lambley Viaduct
FREE
www.northpennines.org.uk

Lindisfarne Castle 835
Holy Island/Lindisfarne

Dramatically perched on a rocky crag and accessible via a three-mile causeway at low tide only, the island castle presents an exciting and alluring aspect. Visitors must check tide times before crossing. Originally a Tudor fort, it was converted into a private house in 1903 by the young Edwin Lutyens. The small rooms are full of intimate decoration and design, with windows looking down upon the charming walled garden planned by Gertrude Jekyll. The property also has several extremely well preserved 19th-century limekilns.

🔍 6 miles east of the A1
⚙️ ⚙️ ♣
⏳ 1–2 hours
⭐ Some of the finest views in England
💷
www.nationaltrust.org.uk

Lindisfarne Priory 836
Holy Island/Lindisfarne

Sitting offshore on Holy Island and reached by causeway at low tide, the peaceful atmosphere and beautiful views make a visit here well worth the effort. Visitors must check tide times before crossing. Lindisfarne Priory, original home to the Lindisfarne Gospels, was an important centre of early Christianity, and the home of St Cuthbert. Visitors can see ornate carvings on the extensive ruins of the monastic buildings and enjoy the serenity that first drew the monks here. One of the most famous visitor attractions in North-East England, Lindisfarne Priory will stay in your memory forever.

🔍 6 miles east of the A1
⚙️ ⚙️ ♣
⏳ 1–2 hours
⭐ The 'Rainbow Arch'
💷
www.english-heritage.org.uk

Kielder Water and Forest Park 837
Kielder Water

Northern Europe's largest man-made lake and England's largest forest, Kielder Water and Forest Park is perfect for people that love nature, watersports, exploring, walking and cycling. There's mile upon mile of purpose-built trails. A haven for wildlife, visitors will see red squirrels, otters, red deer and ospreys. Waterskiing and sailing enthusiasts take to the water all year round and the lake offers a huge challenge to keen trout anglers. You can discover all you need to know about the park at various visitor centres including Kielder Castle, which also has an art gallery and exhibitions.

Access to the forest is from the C200

5–6 hours

Most tranquil spot in the England

FREE Car parks and activities charge

www.visitkielder.com

STAR ATTRACTION

Belsay Hall, Castle and Gardens 838
Morpeth

Belsay Hall, Castle and Gardens are the creation of the Middleton family. First came the castle, dominated by its massive 14th-century pele tower, and then in 1614 a Jacobean mansion wing was added. The Hall, a Classical Greek Revival villa, was designed by Sir Charles Monck (formerly Middleton), inspired by Ancient Greece and the buildings he had seen on his honeymoon in Athens. Despite its austere facade, it had a comfortable interior, arranged round a two-storey Pillar Hall. The vast gardens, which provide a magnificent setting for the castle and hall, are also largely Sir Charles's work.

On the A696, in Belsay

2 3 hours

Seasonal garden displays

www.english-heritage.org.uk

Cragside House and Gardens   839
Morpeth

The revolutionary home of Lord Armstrong, Victorian inventor and landscape genius, was a wonder of its age. Built on a rocky crag high above the Debdon Burn, Cragside is crammed with ingenious gadgets and was the first house in the world to be lit by hydroelectricity. Surrounding the house on all sides is one of the largest rock gardens in Europe. Across the iron bridge, in the formal garden, is the Orchard House, which still produces fresh fruit. The lakeside walks, adventure play area and labyrinth all make Cragside an attractive place for families.

🔍 On the B6341, 15 miles north-west of Morpeth

☀ ⚙ ♣

⏳ 2-3 hours

★ World of the Water Wizard

💷 💷

www.nationaltrust.org.uk

Scotch Gill Woods Local Nature Reserve   840
Morpeth

Scotch Gill Wood LNR is an ancient wild woodland nature reserve with a round walk of about a mile including footways along the steep slopes of the River Wansbeck valley. It is so named as the woodland was used by the Scots as a route to raid Newminster Abbey in medieval times. Today visitors can see abundant wildlife, including red squirrels, otters, kingfishers and crayfish, and special flora in the 20-acre park. There are footpaths throughout the woodland and you can park your car near Morpeth Rugby Club on the edge of town.

🔍 Mitford Road, Morpeth

☀ ⚙ ♣ ❄

⏳ 1-3 hours

★ Tranquil riverside walks

FREE

www.castlemorpeth.gov.uk

Wallington   841
Morpeth

Dating from 1688, Wallington is an impressive, yet friendly house with a magnificent interior and fine collections. The Pre-Raphaelite central hall is decorated to look like an Italian courtyard and features a series of paintings by William Bell Scott. The formality of the house is offset by the tranquil beauty of the surrounding landscape – with lawns, lakes, parkland and woodland. The beautiful walled garden, with its varied plant collection and conservatory, is an enchanting place to visit.

🔍 On the B6343, 12 miles west of Morpeth

☀ ⚙ ♣

⏳ 2-3 hours

★ Lady Wilson's Cabinet of Curiosities

💷 💷

www.nationaltrust.org.uk

Brinkburn Priory   842
Rothbury

Founded in 1135 as a house for the Augustinian canons, the beautiful church is the only surviving building of the Augustinian priory of Brinkburn. Picturesquely set by a bend in the River Coquet, it is reached by a scenic 10-minute walk from the car park. Outside there are remnants of the original medieval buildings, notably a stone arch, which is recognisable as the laver recess of the Refectory despite its dilapidated state. There is a manor house very close to the priory, which is Gothic in style and has recently been conserved for viewing by the public.

🔍 Off the B6344, 4 miles south-east of Rothbury

☀ ⚙ ♣

⏳ 1 hour

★ Glorious tranquil riverside setting

💷

www.english-heritage.org.uk

Farne Islands   843

Seahouses

Take the family on a boat trip to these rocky islands, now a sanctuary for seabirds and seals. They house a bird reserve hosting around 70,000 pairs of breeding birds from 21 different species. Puffins can be seen in season, and the islands are also home to a large colony of grey seals. You can visit a number of the islands including Inner Farne and Longstone Rock, from where Grace Darling and her father set out to rescue the survivors of a wrecked paddle-steamer, the *Forfarshire*, when it ran aground on a nearby islet in 1838.

🔍 Boats leave from Seahouses harbour
⚙
⏳ 3-4 hours
⭐ Nature in the wild
£ £
www.nationaltrust.org.uk

BALTIC   844

Gateshead

This major international centre for contemporary art is situated on the south bank of the River Tyne. Housed in a 1950s grain warehouse (part of the former Baltic Flour Mills), the gallery is used for the production, presentation and experience of contemporary art rather than to show off a collection. Artists whose works have been shown in the past include Damien Hurst, Martin Parr and Shahryar Nashat. Future exhibitions are planned by John Cage, Cornelia Parker and Tomas Saraceno. Many locals use the building as a meeting place, particularly the rooftop restaurant, which has stunning views.

🔍 Gateshead quayside
⚙ ⚙ ♣ ❄
⏳ 1-2 hours
⭐ Living contemporary art
FREE
www.balticmill.com

Shipley Art Gallery   845

Gateshead

The Shipley is the North East's leading gallery of design and contemporary craft. The stunning, new Designs for Life gallery, showcases over 300 objects. The Shipley's superb painting collection includes works from the 16th to the 20th centuries and features landscapes, seascapes, portraits and religious subjects including William Irving's 'The Blaydon Races'. Visitors can also see ceramics, glass, wood, metalwork, jewellery, textiles and furniture and exhibits on local history. There is also a regular programme of temporary exhibitions and events.

🔍 Prince Consort Road, Gateshead
⚙ ⚙ ♣ ❄
⏳ 2 hours
⭐ Designs for Life
FREE
www.twmuseums.org.uk

Bede's World and St Paul's Church

846

Jarrow

The extraordinary life of the Venerable Bede (AD 673-735) created a rich legacy that is celebrated today at Bede's World in Jarrow, where Bede lived and worked 1,300 years ago. Visitors can see the interactive Age of Bede exhibition in the stunning new museum building and can also visit the site of the medieval monastic ruins of the Anglo-Saxon monastery of St Paul. Outside there is a herb garden and an Anglo-Saxon demonstration farm based in recreated timber buildings and with rare breeds of animals.

🔍 Near the south entrance of the A19 Tyne Tunnel
❁ ◱ ❧ ❀
⌛ 2-3 hours
★ The life of early medieval Europe's greatest scholar
£

www.bedesworld.co.uk

Discovery Museum

847

Newcastle upon Tyne

Discover all about life in Newcastle and Tyneside, from the area's renowned maritime history and world-changing science and technology right through to fashion and military history. The museum is bursting with interactive displays, which makes it the perfect place to have fun while you're learning. One of the favourite exhibits – Turbinia – dominates the entrance to the museum. Invented on Tyneside, it is the first ship to be powered by a steam turbine. The 35-metre vessel was once the fastest ship in the world and her history is brought to life in a special display.

🔍 Newcastle city centre
❁ ◱ ❧ ❀
⌛ 2-3 hours
★ Family backpacks
FREE

www.twmuseums.org.uk/discovery

Life Science Centre

848

Newcastle upon Tyne

Newcastle's Centre for Life is aiming to inspire the next generation of scientists through an understanding of human life and its place in the scheme of living things. Exhibits explain complex issues, such as human evolution and physiology, in ways that children can understand and appreciate. At various times, floor space is occupied by moving models of perennial favourites, such as dinosaurs and mythical monsters. Other displays illustrate such issues as pollution, waste disposal and energy generation. There are also live creatures that children are encouraged to handle.

🔍 Newcastle city centre
❁ ◱ ❧ ❀
⌛ 2-3 hours
★ Dr Who exhibition
£

www.life.org.uk

Newcastle United FC

849

Newcastle upon Tyne

A tour of St James' Park will take you on an amazing journey through the history of Newcastle United. Your knowledgeable tour guide will show you many areas you will never have seen before – as well as some very famous ones. Visitors will be able to take a look inside the changing rooms, find out what it feels like to stand pitchside, see the dugouts, find out what happens in the Media Suite, see the view from the highest point in the stadium and then visit the club museum.

🔍 Newcastle city centre
❁ ◱ ❧ ❀ Book in advance online
⌛ 1-2 hours
★ Club museum
£ £

www.nufc.co.uk

Seven Stories
Newcastle upon Tyne

850

This innovative attraction allows visitors to explore the world of children's books as popular stories are brought to life through exhibitions, activities and special events. You can walk through the pages of your favourite books in a number of exhibitions. Get Up to Mischief with Horrid Henry celebrates one of literature's most fabulous naughty characters, and From Toad Hall to Pooh Corner is an enchanting new celebration of classic tales *The Wind in the Willows* and *Winnie-the Pooh*. With beautiful original illustrations and storybook settings this is the perfect place to enjoy stories and to inspire your own.

Newcastle city centre

2-3 hours

Innovative children's attractions

www.sevenstories.org.uk

Gibside
Rowlands Gill

852

The Column of Liberty, rising above the treetops, is the first sight visitors have of this impressive landscape garden created by the Bowes family in the 18th century. Spanning 450 acres, Gibside is a 'grand design' of spectacular vistas, winding paths and grassy open spaces much of which is designated as a Site of Special Scientific Interest. At key points there are decorative garden buildings, including the Palladian chapel, Georgian stables, greenhouse and ruins of a bathhouse and hall. There is a wonderfully tranquil atmosphere, attractive for people and for wildlife.

On the B6314, 6 miles south-west of Gateshead

1 2 hours

Search the skies for red kites

www.nationaltrust.org.uk

Stephenson Railway Museum
North Shields

851

Re-live the glorious days of the steam railway at Stephenson Railway Museum in North Shields. The museum is home to George Stephenson's Billy, a forerunner of the world-famous Rocket. Billy is joined by many other engines from the great age of steam including Jackie Milburn, named after the Newcastle United legend. Visitors can also take a ride on a steam train and discover how trains work with interactive exhibitions and learn about the impact of coal and electricity on ordinary people's lives.

Middle Engine Lane, off the A1058, east of North Shields

1-2 hours

Railways from the 1820s to the 1980s

FREE Train rides

www.twmuseums.org.uk

Arbeia Roman Fort and Museum
South Shields

853

Built around AD160, Arbeia Roman Fort once guarded the entrance to the River Tyne, playing an essential role in the mighty frontier system. Based four miles east of the end of Hadrian's Wall at South Shields, the fort was originally built to house a garrison and soon became the military supply base for the 17 forts along the wall. Today, the excavated remains, stunning reconstructions of original buildings and finds discovered at the Fort combine to give a unique insight into life in Roman Britain.

Baring Street, South Shields

1-2 hours

Time Quest 'excavation' site

FREE

www.twmuseums.org.uk

Souter Lighthouse and the Leas ⬛855
Sunderland

Boldly hooped in red and white, Souter is an iconic cliff-top beacon, offering a great family-friendly visit. When opened in 1871, it was a technological marvel, being the first lighthouse built to use electricity. Decommissioned in 1988, the machinery remains in working order and visitors can explore the compass room, the engine room and the fantastic views. To the north, the Leas has two and a half miles of beach, cliff and grassland with soaring seabirds and, to the south, Whitburn Coastal Park provides coastal walks and family trails.

🔍 On the A183, 3 miles south of South Shields

⚙ ◎ ♣

⏳ 1-2 hours

★ Victorian lighthouse-keeper's cottage

£

www.nationaltrust.org.uk

Ocean Beach Pleasure Park ⬛854
South Shields

If you are looking for theme park fun in the north-east then you have to head for Ocean Beach Pleasure Park on Sandhaven Beach, as it is the only surviving park in the Newcastle area. Not too big, not too expensive, Ocean Beach has over 50 rides, amusement arcades, Quasar, ten-pin bowling and a crazy golf course. Rides include Kickdown, Twist and the Wave Swinger. The park has free entry but there is a charge for individual rides and it is advisable to buy your ride wristbands online to save money.

🔍 On the seafront at South Shields

⚙ ◎ ♣

⏳ 2-3 hours

★ Ghost Hunt

FREE Individual rides charge

www.oceanbeach.co.uk

Sunderland Museum and Winter Gardens ⬛856
Sunderland

This family attraction combines a museum, art gallery, exhibition space and Winter Gardens. In the museum, visitors can learn about the history of Sunderland through exciting displays, hands-on exhibits, computer interactives and video presentations. The art gallery features paintings by L.S. Lowry together with Victorian masterpieces and artefacts from the four corners of the world. The stunning Winter Gardens have over 2,000 flowers and plants brought together in a spectacular showcase of the world's natural beauty.

🔍 Sunderland city centre

⚙ ◎ ♣ ✳

⏳ 1-2 hours

★ Local Lustreware pottery

FREE

www.twmuseums.org.uk

Tanfield Railway   857
Sunnyside

Few steam railways offer the variety and character of scenery, locomotives and rolling stock available on the Tanfield Railway. The carriages are a variety of small four- and six-wheeled vehicles dating back to the 1880s, with Victorian hardships like wooden seats. The opening windows let you soak up the sound and smell of the small steam engines working hard on the steep gradients. The opportunity to walk around the loco sheds and yards is unusual but extremely interesting.

On the A6076, Stanley to Gateshead road
Sundays, Bank holidays, Wednesdays and Thursdays during school holidays
2 hours
Oldest working railway in the world

www.tanfield-railway.co.uk

Tynemouth Priory and Castle   858
Tynemouth

Tynemouth Castle and Priory was once one of the largest fortified areas in England. Overlooking the North Sea and the River Tyne, it dominates the headland and has provided defence against the Vikings, the medieval Scots and Napoleon. The interactive Life in the Stronghold exhibition tells the story of the site from its original beginnings as an Anglo-Saxon settlement, an Anglican monastery, a royal castle, artillery fort and a coastal defence. Visitors can also explore the newly refurbished battery gun, which was designed to defend the Tyne in the First and Second World Wars.

Tynemouth, near North Pier
1–2 hours
Tranquil 13th-century chapel

www.english-heritage.org.uk

Washington Old Hall   859
Washington

At the heart of historic Washington village this picturesque stone manor house and its gardens provide a tranquil oasis, reflecting gentry life following the turbulence of the English Civil War. The building incorporates parts of the original medieval home of George Washington's direct ancestors, and it is from here that the family took their surname. The house remained in the family until 1613. Visitors can see mementoes of the American connection and the War of Independence as well as fine oak furniture and a splendid collection of blue and white Delftware.

On the A1231, 5 miles west of Sunderland
1–2 hours
Life and times of George Washington

www.nationaltrust.org.uk

Washington WWT   860
Washington

Ideally placed to provide a stopover and wintering habitat for migratory wildfowl after their passage over the North Sea, this 45-acre recreated wetland on the banks of the River Wear provides large flocks of curlew and redshank with a safe place to roost and herons with a place to breed. In warmer weather its varied landscape of wetlands, meadows and woodlands is also home to ducks, geese, waders, flamingos, cranes, frogs, bats and even goats. During the season family favourites include downy duckling days, a splashzone play area and daily bird feeds.

Off the A1(M), east of Washington
2–3 hours
All kinds of wildlife encounters

www.wwt.org.uk

Scotland

Central Scotland
Grampian
Highlands and Islands
Southern Scotland

Eilean Donan Castle, Highlands and Islands

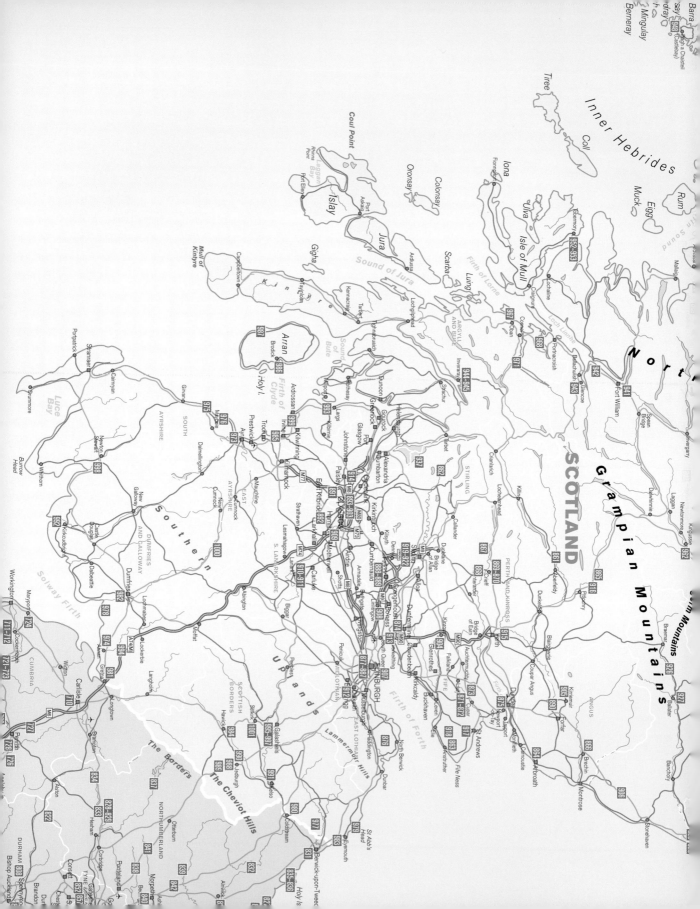

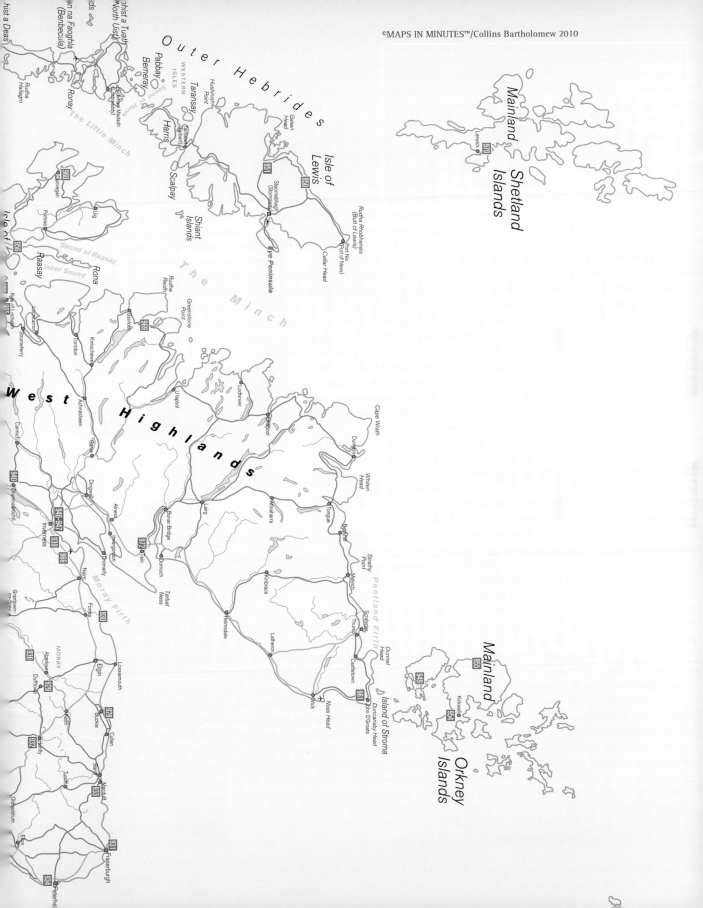

©MAPS IN MINUTES™/Collins Bartholomew 2010

Outer Hebrides

Isle of Lewis

Mainland
Shetland Islands

W e s t

H i g h l a n d s

Mainland
Orkney Islands

Guide to **Scotland**

Highland Adventure Safaris   861
Aberfeldy

This is an exciting way to experience the exhilaration and freedom in 250,000 acres of the beautiful southern Highlands Perthshire Estate. Visitors can immerse themselves in the great outdoors safaris, wildlife watching trips or on a thrilling off-road driving experience. You can head for the mountains or the ancient Caledonia pine forests on foot, on bikes, in a Land Rover or a self-drive 4x4. Experienced kilted guides will take you into Europe's last remaining wilderness on a wild adventure that you will never forget.

🔍 Follow signs from the B846

⚙ 🔆 ♣ ❄

⏳ 3-4 hours

★ Awe-inspiring nature

💷 💷 💷

www.highlandsafaris.net

Go Country   862
Aberfolye

This is the ultimate outdoor adventure park. Based on idyllic Loch Ard, within the Loch Lomond and Trossachs National Park, activities on offer include quad biking, a unique waterpark, canoeing, climbing/ abseiling, cliff jumping, archery, mountain biking, orienteering and many other activities. The centre has fully qualified instructors, equipment for hire and camping accommodation should you require it. It is essential that you book in advance via the website to ensure that your activity is available when you want it.

🔍 On the B829, at Kinlochard near Aberfoyle

⚙ 🔆 ♣ ❄

⏳ 3-6 hours

★ Hamster balling

💷 💷 / 💷 💷 💷   Depending on what you want to do

www.gocountry.co.uk

Scottish Fisheries Museum
Anstruther

863

This museum, housed in a range of historic buildings around a cobbled courtyard on Anstruther's harbour front, tells the story of fishing in Scotland and its people from earliest times to the present. The comprehensive collection includes ships, models, paintings, photographs, equipment and the written word. The buildings include an 18th-century merchant's dwelling, a mid-19th century storehouse on the foundations of the medieval chapel of St Ayles and the 16th-century Abbot's Lodging. There is a small chapel, which commemorates all those Scots who lost their lives at sea while fishing.

🔍 Anstruther harbour

✿ ◉ ❦ ❄

⏳ 1–2 hours

★ *Reaper*, the one hundred-year-old herring drifter

£

www.scotfishmuseum.org

Arbroath Abbey
Arbroath

864

Arbroath Abbey was founded in 1178 by King William I 'the Lion' as a memorial to his childhood friend Thomas Becket, Archbishop of Canterbury, who was murdered in 1170. William invited the Tironensian monks from Kelso Abbey, near the English border, to establish the monastery. When he died in 1214, his body was buried before the high altar. It was also the site of the signing of the Declaration of Arbroath in 1320, when Scotland's nobles affirmed their allegiance to Robert the Bruce as their king and is now one of Scotland's most important historical sites.

🔍 Arbroath town centre

✿ ◉ ❦ ❄

⏳ 1–2 hours

★ The Round-O

£

www.historic-scotland.gov.uk

Atholl Country Life Museum
Blair Atholl

865

Deep in the heart of Highland Perthshire, lying sheltered by the hills of Atholl, is the village of Blair Atholl, where the meeting of the rivers Tilt and Garry have witnessed so much of life over the centuries. At the Atholl Country Life Museum, once the village school, visitors can pay witness to that life and learn about the great characters of the area, their skills and achievements. Perhaps the most notable of these is Sgt Major Donald MacBeath of the Atholl Highlanders, gamekeeper, hero of the Crimean war and admired by Queen Victoria.

🔍 Off the A9 in Blair Atholl village

✿ ◉ ❦

⏳ 1 hour

★ Tales of Highland life

£

www.athollcountrylifemuseum.org

Auchingarrich Wildlife Centre 867
Crieff

Set in a hundred acres of Perthshire countryside, Auchingarrich Wildlife Centre features the magnificent Highland Cattle. You can see them, stroke them and feed them. Other animals on show include wallabies, raccoons, otters, chipmunks, porcupines and Scotland's largest collection of waterfowl, ornamental and game birds. Other attractions include falconry displays, indoor and outdoor play areas, animal and chick handling, a unique bird hatchery and the Highland Castle Centre.

On the B827, 2 miles south of Comrie

1–2 hours

Over 150 species of animals and birds

www.auchingarrich.co.uk

Pictavia 866
Brechin

Pictavia tells the fascinating story of the Picts, a Latin word for 'painted people', through a mixture of interactive exhibits, original artefacts and replicas. A visit begins with an audio-visual show narrated by Brian Cox, which tells the story of the Picts from the Roman invasion through to their battles with the Vikings. From there, you can listen to their music in the Tower of Sound, use touchscreen computers to investigate the mysteries of their carved stones, and experience the sights and sounds of Dunnichen in the Battle Tunnel.

Follow signs from the A90

1–2 hours

Story of the indigenous Scots

www.pictavia.org.uk

Drummond Castle Gardens 868
Crieff

Regarded as the most important formal gardens in Scotland, Drummond Castle Gardens are also among the finest in Europe. Visitors drive up a long beech avenue and then walk to the outer castle court. On passing into the inner courtyard and reaching the top of the terracing the full extent and majesty of the garden is suddenly revealed. The dominant feature of the parterre design is a St Andrew's Cross with a 17th-century sundial at its centre. First laid out by John Drummond, the gardens were renewed in the 1950.

Off the A822, 2 miles south of Crieff

1–2 hours

Statuary and topiary

www.drummondcastlegardens.co.uk

Famous Grouse Experience 869
Crieff

Glenturret is the oldest distillery in Scotland, established in 1775 and still uses traditional methods to produce and bottle single malt scotch. There are three tours available. Visitors can experience a brilliant, award-winning, interactive audio-visual display called *The Flight of the Grouse*, a video called *The Water of Life* and then walk through the museum portion of the distillery. After completing the distillery tour you can visit the unique sample room within Warehouse No 9 where to you will get to sample the Famous Grouse malt range.

🔍 Off the A85, 1 mile from Crieff
⚙ ◉ ✚ ❄
⧖ 2-3 hours
★ Incredible interactive show
£
www.famousgrouse.com

Drovers' Tryst 870
Crieff

The Crieff and Strathearn Drovers' Tryst annually celebrates the life, work and play of the people who made Crieff the cattle-droving crossroads of Scotland in the 1700s. The Tryst is built around a programme of guided walks and mountain bike events in the stunning scenery and autumn colours of Strathearn and its surrounding area. The walks vary in difficulty but all are enriched by wildlife, plants, trees, history and the company of like-minded people. Complementing the walks is a series of social events, with music, drama, film and dancing.

🔍 Crieff is on the A822 or the A85
✚
⧖ 2-6 hours
★ Fabulous walking festival
£
www.droverstryst.com

Fife Folk Museum 871
Cupar

Fife Folk Museum collects and displays artefacts illustrating the social, domestic and working lives of the Fife people from the 17th century till the present day. The collections are housed in the old Weigh House, adjoining cottages and a modern extension building in the High Street in Ceres. Collections include weights and measures, textiles, costume, ceramics, farming machinery and implements, craftsmen's tools, furniture and paintings.

🔍 Ceres town centre
⚙ ◉ ✚
⧖ 1 hour
★ Rural Scottish history
£
www.fife.gov.uk

Hill of Tarvit Mansionhouse and Garden 872
Cupar

This mansion house, built in 1906, reflects the period 1870-1920 when Scotland was the industrial workshop of the world. The house was designed as a showcase for a collection of Flemish tapestries, Chinese porcelain and bronzes, French and English furniture, paintings by Raeburn, Ramsay and eminent Dutch artists. Although built as a treasure house, the intimate scale gives Hill of Tarvit all the warmth of a family home. The gardens are perfect for a stroll, while the more energetic can tackle the walk up to Hill of Tarvit viewpoint.

🔍 Off the A916, 2 miles south of Cupar
⚙ ◉ ✚ Check website for dates
⧖ 2-3 hours
★ Extensive views from the Hill
£
www.nts.org.uk

Scottish Deer Centre
Cupar

873

You can have a day to remember at this beautiful countryside centre, where a large herd of deer roam free. Under the guidance of expert Rangers, visitors can meet different species of these majestic and gentle animals, even enjoying a nose-to-nose encounter or two. You can also see the resident wolf pack and learn about their importance to the Scottish countryside. There are also falconry displays where you can see these spectacular birds in action. Other attractions include trailer rides and a selection of adventure playgrounds for the children.

🔍 On the A91, just outside Cupar

✦ ◉ ♣ ❄

⌛ 3-4 hours

★ Treetop walkway

£

www.tsdc.co.uk

Dunfermline Abbey and Palace
Dunfermline

874

Dunfermline Abbey has a history stretching back to the 11th century – the time of King Malcolm III and Queen Margaret. In the 12th century, their son, David I, raised the little priory to the lofty status of abbey. The great nave still stands largely complete, the most visually stunning example of Romanesque architecture in Scotland. It is also famous as the mausoleum of Queen Margaret, David I and King Robert Bruce. As such, it occupies an especially important place in the national consciousness. The ill-fated Charles I was born here in 1600.

🔍 Dunfermline town centre

✦ ◉ ♣ ❄

⌛ 1 hour

★ Monks' refectory

£

www.historic-scotland.gov.uk

Discovery Point | 875
Dundee

Climb aboard Captain Scott's Royal Research Ship *Discovery* where you can follow in the footsteps of the great explorer and his crew, see how they lived, what they ate and witness their hardships and their triumphs. The ship, originally built in Dundee and the city's shipbuilders' greatest achievement, is now berthed on the River Tay. There is also a fascinating exhibition that commemorates Scott's fateful journey to the South Pole during his race against the Norwegian Roald Amundsen – one of the most famous stories in the history of exploration.

🔍 Dundee city centre
✳ ⚙ ♣ ✳
⏳ 1–2 hours
⭐ Race to the Pole
💲

www.rrsdiscoverpoint.com

National Museum of Flight | 876
East Fortune

East Fortune played an important role as an airfield during two World Wars. Now the National Museum of Flight, hangars are packed with aircraft, rockets, models and memorabilia that reveal how flight developed from the Wright brothers to Concorde. There are a number of special exhibits including Fantastic Flight, which gives visitors the chance to get to grips with the mechanics of flight, flight simulators where you have the chance to land an aeroplane and the Fortunes of War, which presents the human story of the historic military airfield on which the museum stands.

🔍 Follow signs from the A1
✳ ⚙ ♣ ✳
⏳ 1–2 hours
⭐ A trip on-board Concorde
💲

www.nms.ac.uk/flight

Cadies and Witchery Tours | 877
Edinburgh

These award-winning evening walking tours of Edinburgh explore the eerie alleyways and creepy courtyards of the Old Town with a mixture of laughter and stories witchcraft, plague and torture. There are various different walks available including the Ghost and Gore Tour and the Murder and Mystery Tour. The tours are authoritatively researched, and expertly presented by costumed guides (summoned from the spirit world, of course). Do not be surprised to encounter several mysterious apparitions along the way. You must book your place in advance (see website for details).

🔍 Edinburgh city centre
✳ ⚙ ♣ ✳
⏳ 1 hour
⭐ 'Jumper-ooters'
💲

www.witcherytours.com

Camera Obscura and World of Illusions | 878
Edinburgh

The Camera Obscura is Edinburgh's oldest purpose built visitor attraction. Opened in 1853 as Shorts Observatory, it has been enthralling visitors for over 150 years. The attraction now includes the World of Illusions and has three floors filled with interactive exhibits based on lights and visual trickery. The rooftop is home to a selection of powerful free telescopes, which gives unrivalled 360-degree views. Visitors are then able to see moving panoramas of the city via the extraordinary Victorian 'Eye in the Sky' Camera Obscura itself.

🔍 On the Royal Mile
✳ ⚙ ♣ ✳
⏳ 1–2 hours
⭐ Victorian visitor attraction
💲

www.camera-obscura.co.uk

Perched on an extinct volcano and offering stunning views, this instantly recognisable fortress is **a powerful national symbol**

Edinburgh Castle
Edinburgh

A majestic landmark that dominates the capital city's skyline, Edinburgh Castle is the best known and most visited of Scotland's historic buildings. Perched on an extinct volcano and offering stunning views, this instantly recognisable fortress has witnessed many of the defining events of Scottish history and is a powerful national symbol.

Visitors can see St Margaret's Chapel, which is the city's oldest building and dates from the 1100s, Crown Square which was developed in the 15th century, the Great Hall with its ornate wooden ceiling, was built by James IV in 1511 and has a collection of armour and weapons, and the Half Moon Battery was created in the late 16th century. A key attraction within the castle is the Scottish Crown Jewels. The crown, sword and sceptre are amongst the oldest regalia in Europe and are displayed with the Stone of Destiny, the coronation seat of Scottish Kings.

This is a poplar tourist destination and gets quite crowded in the summer months. It is advisable to buy your tickets on-line in advance which gets you fast-track entry. Early mornings and late afternoons are the best times for photography as the shadows cast by the sun are less harsh.

879

FIVE-STAR ATTRACTION

At the top of the Royal Mile

1-2 hours

Free guided tours

www.edinburghcastle.gov.uk

Edinburgh Zoo
Edinburgh

880

Scotland's most popular wildlife attraction is home to over 1,000 animals including meerkats, pygmy hippos, tigers, giraffes and blue poison arrow frogs. Set in beautiful city centre parkland, the zoo has the world's biggest penguin pool and Europe's largest colony of the likeable black and white birds. Visitors can follow the Bodongo chimpanzee Trail, get up close to the capuchin monkeys, take a Hilltop Safari, follow the penguin parade and meet the UK's only koala bears. There are also daily shows including the spectacular Animal Antics.

10 minutes from the city centre

3-4 hours

Penguin parade

www.edinburghzoo.org.uk

Murrayfield Stadium Tour
Edinburgh

881

Home to Scottish rugby union, Scotland's national rugby stadium at Murrayfield was officially opened in 1925 for a match against England. That was a memorable and victorious occasion for the Scottish team who won their first-ever Grand Slam title against their arch-rivals, securing a 14-11 victory. Over the course of its 70-year history, Murrayfield has hosted many such matches. Today, you can follow in the footsteps of legends as you visit the dressing rooms, players' tunnel, Royal Box, hospitality suites and, of course, the world famous pitch.

10 minutes from the city centre

1-2 hours

A walk to the pitch along the players tunnel

www.scottishrugby.org

Museum of Childhood
Edinburgh

882

The Museum of Childhood is a treasure house crammed full of objects telling of childhood past and present. The museum opened in 1955 and was the first in the world to specialise in the history of childhood. There are toys and games of all kinds from many parts of the world ranging from dolls and teddy bears to train sets and tricycles. Listen to the children chanting multiplication tables in the 1930s schoolroom. Watch the street games of Edinburgh children of the 1950s, and find out how children were brought up, dressed and educated in decades gone by.

🔍 On the Royal Mile
✳ ⚙ ❀ ❄
⌛ 1–2 hours
⭐ The 'noisiest museum in the world'
FREE
www.edinburgh.gov.uk

National Museum of Scotland
Edinburgh

883

This museum traces Scotland's story from fascinating fossils to popular culture. The collections cover life, the universe and everything in it. Visitors can see the Lewis Chessmen, made in Trondheim in the late 1100s, and found some time before 1831 in a sand dune at Uig on the Isle of Lewis. Elsewhere are the rather spooky Arthur's Seat Coffins, tiny coffins containing wooden figures unearthed in Edinburgh in 1837. Two other firm favourites are Dolly the Sheep, the world's first cloned sheep; and the Millennium Clock, whose incredibly elaborate chimes always attract a crowd.

🔍 Edinburgh city centre
✳ ⚙ ❀ ❄
⌛ 2–3 hours
⭐ Scotland from the very start
FREE
www.nms.ac.uk/scotland

Scottish National Galleries of Modern Art
Edinburgh

884

This complex consists of the Dean Gallery and the Scottish National Gallery of Modern Art. Both are set in extensive parkland, where visitors can discover works by Henry Moore, Rachel Whiteread and Barbara Hepworth. Highlights of the permanent collection include early 20th-century French paintings by Bonnard, Derain and Matisse; Cubist work by Braque, Léger and Picasso and early 20th century Russian art. The post-war collection includes work by Bacon, Hockney and Freud. Contemporary Scottish art is also well represented.

🔍 Bedford Road, west of Edinburgh's city centre
✳ ⚙ ❀ ❄
⌛ 2–3 hours
⭐ Dada and Surrealist art
FREE
www.nationalgalleries.org

Writers' Museum   885
Edinburgh

Located within the 17th-century Lady Stairs' House, the Writers' Museum is dedicated to the lives and work of Scotland's great literary figures. Particular attention is given to Robert Burns, Sir Walter Scott and Robert Louis Stevenson. The rich collection of manuscripts, first editions and portraits is complemented by personal exhibits including; the writing desk from Burns' house in Dumfries, a rocking horse Scott played with as a boy, and the riding boots that Stevenson wore while living in Samoa. Also on view is the printing press on which Scott's Waverley novels were originally published.

On the Royal Mile

1-2 hours

Scotland's rich literary past

FREE

www.edinburgh.gov.uk

Royal Botanic Garden   887
Edinburgh

The Royal Botanic Garden Edinburgh was founded in the 17th century as a physic garden. Known locally as the 'Botanics', the garden is a must-see element of any visit to Edinburgh, whatever the time of year. Its 75-acre site forms a remarkable haven of tranquillity within the city. The garden contains a unique collection of plants from around the world, housed in the world-famous Rock Garden, the Chinese Hillside and the Glasshouse Experience. Visitors can also see the Woodland Gardens and Arboretum and the Winter Garden, as well as enjoying spectacular views across the city of Edinburgh.

Off the A902, 1 mile north of Edinburgh city centre

2-3 hours

Themed guided tours

FREE Donations appreciated

www.rbge.org.uk

Palace of Holyroodhouse   886
Edinburgh

Founded as a monastery in 1128, the Palace of Holyroodhouse in Edinburgh is the Queen's official residence in Scotland. Situated at the end of the Royal Mile, it is closely associated with Scotland's turbulent past, including Mary Queen of Scots, who lived here between 1561 and 1567. Visitors can enjoy a tour of the Royal Apartments, which are renowned for their fine plasterwork ceilings and magnificent furnishings. One of the most famous rooms in the Palace is the Great Gallery, hung with Jacob de Wet's portraits of the real and legendary kings of Scotland.

Bottom end of the Royal Mile

1-2 hours

Brussels tapestries

www.royal.gov.uk

Callendar House Museum   888
Falkirk

Situated amid magnificent park and woodland, Callendar House tells stories spanning 600 years of Scottish history. Through wars, rebellions and the industrial revolution, the house has played host to many great figures over the centuries, including Mary, Queen of Scots, Cromwell and Bonnie Prince Charlie. Costumed interpreters bring history to life, creating the most exciting kind of interactive experience. A 1825 kitchen forms the centrepiece of this exhibition and you can sample authentic Georgian food, listen to stories about life below stairs, and watch kitchen staff go about their daily tasks.

East of Falkirk town centre

1-2 hours

Social history of Falkirk

FREE

www.falkirk.gov.uk

The Falkirk Wheel 889
Falkirk

These uplifting boat trips begin in the basin outside the Visitor Centre. On board one of the specially designed boats, visitors sail into the bottom gondola of the Wheel, which then makes a graceful sweep, lifting the boat up to join the Union Canal, 35 metres above. The ascent allows plenty of time to enjoy views of the spectacular surrounding scenery. Once lifted, the boat sails smoothly onto the Union Canal. This passes along the aqueduct, through the 180-metre Roughcastle Tunnel and under the historic Antonine Wall and back.

🔍 Follow signs from the M9
✳ ⊙ ♣ ✱
⌛ 1 hour
⭐ Canal walks and cycle paths
💷
www.thefalkirkwheel.co.uk

Glamis Castle 890
Glamis

Glamis Castle, famed as being the childhood home of the Queen Mother and the setting for Shakespeare's 'Macbeth', is situated in the beautiful and fertile valley of Strathmore. Visitors are given an escorted tour round many of the sumptuous apartments, including the dining room, the crypt, the magnificent drawing room, the private chapel with painted ceiling and the sitting room used by the Queen Mother. A surrounding park contains the Italian Garden – two acres enclosed within high yew hedges, and a nature trail among the magnificent Douglas Firs and hardwood trees.

🔍 On the A94, 5 miles south of Forfar
✳ ⊙ ♣
⌛ 1–2 hours
⭐ Guided tours
💷
www.glamis-castle.co.uk

The Burrell Collection 891
Glasgow

When shipping agent Sir William Burrell gifted his collection of over 9,000 works of art to Glasgow in 1944, the city acquired one its greatest collections. Visitors can see medieval art, tapestries, alabasters, stained glass and English oak furniture housed in a purpose built gallery. There are many European paintings, including works by Degas and Cézanne, an important collection of Islamic art, and modern sculpture including works by Epstein and Rodin. There is also a fine collection of works from ancient China, Egypt, Greece and Rome.

🔍 Pollok Country Park, 5 miles south of Glasgow city centre
✳ ⊙ ♣ ✱
⌛ 1–2 hours
⭐ Rodin's 'The Thinker'
FREE
www.glasgowmuseums.com

Calderglen Country Park 892
Glasgow

This beautiful country park, situated just outside Glasgow, has a conservatory, ornamental gardens, a children's zoo, extensive nature trails and walks. The Visitor Centre houses a wildlife experience called Hidden Worlds. Glorious at all times of the year, spring and early summer are the best times for woodland flowers and bird song. In summer visitors can explore the meadows looking for wild orchids and butterflies. In autumn the foliage on the trees takes on a wide variety of attractive colours and shades – and the toadstools and seasonal fruits are at their most abundant.

🔍 On the A726, in East Kilbride
✳ ⊙ ♣ ✱
⌛ 2–3 hours
⭐ Magical nature trails
💷
www.southlanarkshire.gov.uk

Clydebuilt
893
Glasgow

Part of the Scottish Maritime Museum, Clydebuilt traces the development of Glasgow and its river from the 18th-century tobacco lords to the present day. Exhibits allow visitors to experience the building of the MV *Rangitane* for the New Zealand Shipping Company through the eyes of the men who built her, from the riveters to the bowler-hatted gaffers of John Brown's Shipyard. Watch the history of Clyde shipbuilding in an award-winning audiovisual display, pilot the MV *Clan Alpine* on a virtual trip up the river or become a trader, buying, selling and transporting goods worldwide.

Take junctions 25 or 26 on the M8

2-3 hours

History of the QE2

www.scottishmaritimemuseum.org

Gallery of Modern Art
894
Glasgow

Located in the heart of the city, near George Square and Buchanan Street, and housed in an elegant, neo-classical building, the Gallery of Modern Art displays Glasgow's extraordinary range of post-war art and design. Four floors depict the natural elements – earth, water, fire and air. Exhibits include works by Niki de Saint Phalle, David Hockney, Sebastiao Salgado, Andy Warhol and Eduard Bersudsky as well as Scottish artists such as John Bellany and Ken Curry. It also offers a thought-provoking programme of temporary exhibitions.

Glasgow city centre

1-2 hours

Avril Paton's 'Windows in the West'

FREE

www.glasgowmuseums.com

Glasgow Science Centre
895
Glasgow

This is one of Glasgow's must-see attractions. Its heart is the Science Mall – a gleaming titanium crescent overlooking the Clyde, which has three floors packed with hundreds of hands-on exhibits, interactive workshops, live science shows and labs. But visitors can also visit the ScottishPower Planetarium to see the night sky as it should be, and see the latest IMAX® movies in a state-of-the-art cinema. In case that's not enough, you can also shoot to the top of the 105-metre Glasgow Tower for unbeatable views of the city.

Pacific Quay, next to the river

3-4 hours

Live science shows

If you do everything

www.glasgowsciencecentre.org

STAR ATTRACTION

Kelvingrove
896
Glasgow

Housed in a magnificent Victorian red sandstone building, one of Glasgow's most famous landmarks, Kelvingrove Art Gallery and Museum is a must-see for any visitors to the city. It houses a vast collection of paintings and sculptures, early firearms, Scottish arms and armour, medieval swords, crossbows, duelling weapons, silver, ceramics, clothing and furniture. There is also a major collection of the work of Charles Rennie MacKintosh and a fantastic art collection including masterpieces by Rembrandt, Van Gogh, Monet, Turner and Whistler.

Kelvingrove Park, on the west side of the city

2-3 hours

Dali's 'Christ of St. John on the Cross'

FREE

www.glasgowmuseums.com

The MacKintosh House
897
Glasgow

This is a reconstruction of the principal interiors from the Glasgow home of the Scottish architect and designer Charles Rennie Mackintosh (1868–1928) and the artist Margaret Macdonald Mackintosh (1864–1933). The original house, situated 100 yards away, was demolished in 1963. This new version has been furnished with the Mackintoshes' own furniture and decorated as closely as possible to the original. The selection of bric à brac, fitted carpets, curtains and other soft furnishings was based on descriptions of the house and photographs of Mackintosh interiors of the period.

🔍 Part of the Hunterian Art Gallery at Hillhead, 2 miles from the city centre

❄ ◎ ❈ ❋

⧗ 1–2 hours

★ Signature ladderback chairs

FREE

www.hunterian.gla.ac.uk

Necropolis
898
Glasgow

The Necropolis has been described as a 'unique representation of Victorian Glasgow, built when Glasgow was the second city of the empire. It reflects the feeling of confidence and wealth and security of that time.' It is a memorial to the merchant patriarchs of the city and contains the remains of almost every eminent Glaswegian of its day. Monuments designed by leading Glaswegian architects including Alexander 'Greek' Thompson, Bryce, Hamilton and Mackintosh adorn it. Their designs are executed by expert masons and sculptors who contributed ornate and sculptural detail of the finest quality.

🔍 Near Glasgow Cathedral

❄ ◎ ❈ ❋

⧗ 1–2 hours

★ John Knox monument

FREE

www.glasgow.gov.uk

People's Palace
899
Glasgow

The People's Palace tells the story of the people of Glasgow from 1750 to the present. You can see paintings, prints and photographs displayed alongside a wealth of historic artefacts, film and computer interactives, to find out how Glaswegians lived, worked and played in years gone by. Visit a traditional 'single end' and discover how a family lived in this typical one-room Glasgow tenement home of the 1930s, find out about home life during the Second World War and take a trip to the 'steamie' and do your washing.

🔍 On Glasgow Green

❄ ◎ ❈ ❋

⧗ 2–3 hours

★ Billy Connolly's Banana Boots

FREE

www.glasgowmuseums.com

Pollok Country Park
Glasgow

900

At 361 acres, this is Glasgow's largest park and its extensive woodlands and gardens provide a quiet sanctuary for both visitors and wildlife. Pollok offers a unique experience for a park visitor, providing an eclectic mix of countryside attractions set within the midst of a large cosmopolitan city. The park has a diverse range of environmental experiences from an award-winning herd of highland cattle through to formal and hidden gardens. Despite attracting in excess of a million visitors per annum, it is still possible to get lost in it.

🔍 Pollokshaws Road, 3 miles south-west of Glasgow city centre
✳ ⊙ ♣ ❄
⏳ 3-4 hours
⭐ White Cart Water
FREE
www.glasgow.gov.uk

Scottish Football Museum
Glasgow

901

With over 2,500 objects on display, the museum is home to the world's most impressive national collection of football related objects, history galleries, memorabilia and ephemera. The 14 galleries take you through the development of the modern game in Scotland, from the 19th-century to the present day. Visitors get the chance to see some of football's most exciting and unique objects, including the world's oldest national trophy, the Scottish Cup. The museum is housed at Hampden Park, the oldest continually used international ground in the world.

🔍 On the B768, take junction 1 of the M77
✳ ⊙ ♣ ❄
⏳ 2-3 hours
⭐ The Championship of the World trophy
£
www.scottishfootballmuseum.org.uk

Tall Ship at Glasgow Harbour
Glasgow

902

Visitors can explore the tall ship *Glenlee*, a three-masted barque, with length 245 feet, beam 37.5 feet and depth 22.5 feet. She is one of only five Clyde-built sailing ships that remain afloat. Built in 1896 in the Bay Yard in Port Glasgow, she operated as a long haul, bulk cargo vessel before being bought by the Spanish navy as a training ship. She has circumnavigated the world four times and steered through the wild waters of Cape Horn on 15 occasions.

🔍 Follow signs from junction 19 of the M8
✳ ⊙ ♣ ❄
⏳ 1-2 hours
⭐ The *Glenlee* Story
£
www.thetallship.com

Tenement House
Glasgow

903

In the 19th and early 20th centuries, most people in Glasgow lived in tenement flats then referred to as 'tenement houses'. The Tenement House is on the first floor of an ordinary red sandstone tenement in Buccleuch Street, in the city centre. It is preserved as an important part of the nation's heritage not only because it is typical of the flats so many Scots used to live in, but also because it has survived almost unchanged for over a century. Built in 1892, it has four rooms and most of its original features.

🔍 Glasgow city centre
✳ ⊙ ♣
⏳ 1 hour
⭐ Flat complete with domestic items of the time
£
www.nts.org.uk

Lochleven Castle
904
Kinross

The island stronghold of Lochleven has been visited by countless distinguished personalities during its history. Some took the boat across Loch Leven of their own accord, including King Robert Bruce (in 1313 and 1323). But the castle will be forever associated with Mary Queen of Scots. She first visited in 1561 as a guest of the owner, Sir William Douglas. But her last stay, in 1567–68, was as his prisoner. It was here that she was compelled to abdicate her throne in favour of her infant son, James VI.

🔍 By boat from Kinross, follow signs from the A922
✿ ◎ ☘
⌛ 2–3 hours
★ Stand in Mary's prison cell
♿
www.historic-scotland.gov.uk

J.M. Barrie's Birthplace
905
Kirriemuir

J.M. Barrie, the creator of Peter Pan, is one of Angus' most famous sons. The author was born here 150 years ago and you can visit the cottage where he grew up and enjoy a brand new exhibition celebrating his life and works, which shows how some of his earliest childhood memories inspired some of his greatest works. Stepping through the front door is like walking into Neverland. There are many fascinating items including costumes and manuscripts and some rooms look exactly like they would have done over a century ago when Barrie lived there.

🔍 Kirriemuir town centre
✿ ◎ ☘
⌛ 1 hour
★ Peter Pan Experience
♿
www.nts.org.uk

Fettercairn Distillery
906
Laurencekirk

Fettercairn distillery has been in operation since 1824, making it one of Scotland's oldest malt whisky distilleries. The distillery is snugly tucked away at the foot of the Cairngorm Mountains from which it takes spring water supplies. This area is one of Scotland's most fertile regions. These distinct characteristics combine to produce a balanced malt whisky with a fine character. Visitors can take tours of the distillery and warehouse, which include an audio-visual presentation and a whisky tasting of Fettercairn's 12-year-old single malt whisky.

🔍 On the B966
✿ ◎ ☘
⌛ 1–2 hours
★ Traditional distillery set in glorious farmland
♿
www.scotchwhisky.net

The Royal Yacht *Britannia*
907
Leith

As you step on board the Royal Yacht, you will be given an audio handset that is full of captivating stories and provides a rare glimpse into the life of the British Royal Family. From Sir Winston Churchill to Boris Yeltsin, Rajiv Gandhi to Nelson Mandela, some of the world's most influential people have been welcomed aboard *Britannia*. Starting at the Bridge, the self-guided tour covers five of *Britannia*'s magnificent decks, taking you through the fabulous State Apartments and crew's quarters, and ending in the gleaming Engine Room.

🔍 Leith Docks, follow signs from Edinburgh city centre
✿ ◎ ☘ ❄
⌛ 1–2 hours
★ State Dining Room
♿ ♿
www.royalyachtbritannia.co.uk

STAR ATTRACTION

Linlithgow Palace   908

Linlithgow

This majestic royal palace was begun by James I in 1424, following a fire that devastated its predecessor. It became a truly elegant 'pleasure palace', and a welcome stopping-place for the royal family along the busy road linking Edinburgh and Stirling. The Stewart queens especially liked its tranquillity and fresh air. The ancient palace served as the royal nursery for James V (born 1512) and Mary Queen of Scots (born 1542). But after 1603, when James VI moved the royal court to London following his coronation as James I of England, the palace fell quickly into decline.

🔍 Linlithgow town centre

❂ ❂ ♣ ❄

⧖ 1–2 hours

★ Magnificent ruins in a park by a loch

♿

www.historic-scotland.gov.uk

M&D's Theme Park   909

Motherwell

Scotland's biggest theme park has a host of rides and attractions for visitors of all ages. For white-knuckle riders there's the Tornado, Tsunami and the Express rollercoaster, while family rides include the Wave Swinger and the Big Apple. There's also a Big Wheel with fabulous views of the surrounding Strathclyde Country Park. For indoor fun, there's ten-pin bowling, pool, a gamezone, a carousel and a huge soft play area for the little ones.

🔍 At junction 5 of the M74

❂ ❂ ♣

⧖ 3–4 hours

★ Tornado

♿ ♿

www.scotlandthemepark.com

STAR ATTRACTION

Falls of Clyde Wildlife Reserve 910
New Lanark

This reserve stretches along both sides of the Clyde gorge,
from the historic village of New Lanark southwards to
Bonnington Weir. As well as the spectacular waterfalls
from which it takes its name, fringing the gorge on both
sides is a mosaic of woodland, both ancient natural and
modern mixed plantation. Pleasant riverside walks lead
through the reserve and provide fantastic views of the
waterfalls. The visitor centre at New Lanark has an
exhibition, information and full details of events and
walks in the reserve.

🔍 1 mile south of New Lanark
☼ ◉ ♣ ❄
⏳ 2-3 hours
★ Spectacular waterfalls
⚹
www.swt.org.uk

New Lanark World Heritage Site 911
New Lanark

Surrounded by native woodlands and close to the Falls
of Clyde, this cotton mill village was founded in 1785
and became famous as the site of mill-owner Robert
Owen's model community. Now beautifully restored
as both a living community and visitor attraction, the
history of the village is interpreted in an award-winning
Visitor Centre. Highlights include the 'Annie McLeod
Experience' dark ride, where the ghost of a mill-girl
takes you on a journey into the past. Visitors can also
relax in the 'sky high' mill roof garden that has lovely
views of the historic village below.

🔍 Follow signs from junction 13 of the M74
☼ ◉ ♣ ❄
⏳ 2-3 hours
★ Fascinating Victorian model community
⚹
www.newlanark.org

Scottish Mining Museum 912
Newtongrange

This museum is based at the Lady Victoria Colliery, one
of the finest surviving examples of a Victorian colliery
in Europe. The museum includes two exhibitions, which
describe the history of coal and the story of the mining
communities. You can also see the pithead, where
generations of miners descended 500 metres down into
the blackness, and a recreated underground roadway and
coalface where you will experience the atmosphere and
noise of a working pit. On your tour you will use unique
'magic helmets' (see above), which are fitted with remote-
controlled headphones to describe what you are looking at.

🔍 On the A7, 9 miles south of Edinburgh
☼ ◉ ♣ ❄
⏳ 2-3 hours
★ Personal anecdotes of the ex-miner guides
⚹
www.scottishminingmuseum.com

Deep Sea World   913
North Queensferry

Situated on the banks of the Firth of Forth, below the Forth railway bridge, Deep Sea World offers visitors a 'spectacular underwater safari'. Featuring the UK's longest underwater viewing tunnel and a fascinating array of marine life, you'll be amazed at what you find. This vast underwater world is home to one of the largest collections of sand tiger sharks in Europe, stingrays, conger eels, plus thousands of other weird and wonderful creatures. Themed tanks feature the Amazon, piranhas, Lake Malawi and the rocky shores. There is also a lovely seal sanctuary.

🔍 1 mile from the M90
✿ ◎ ♣ ❄
⏳ 2–3 hours
★ Godzilla, the 'killer' turtle
💷 ♿
www.deepseaworld.com

STAR ATTRACTION

Scone Palace   915
Perth

In a spectacular setting above the River Tay, Scone Palace has been the seat of parliaments and the crowning place of kings, including Robert the Bruce. It has housed the Stone of Destiny and is immortalised in Shakespeare's *Macbeth*. A breathtakingly beautiful place of power and mystery, Scone is regarded as a national treasure and is revered as the historic jewel in the crown of Scotland. Today, Scone offers visitors history, art and antiques, superb landscape and architecture and, of course, fun for the children.

🔍 On the A93, 2 miles north of Perth
✿ ◎ ♣
⏳ 2–3 hours
★ Magnificent formal rooms
💷
www.scone-palace.co.uk

Coats Observatory   914
Paisley

Coats Observatory is a unique attraction, housing astronomical equipment and displays, weather and earthquake recording equipment. Gifted to the people of Paisley by Thomas Coats and designed by Glasgow architect John Honeyman, the building opened in 1883 and has been welcoming visitors with an interest in astronomy ever since. On clear nights the telescope is trained on the moon, the planets and other interesting sights in the sky. The observatory also has a planetarium, which gives visitors a tour of the night sky without having to leave the comfort of their chair.

🔍 Access is via Paisley Museum on the High Street
✿ ◎ ♣ ❄
⏳ 1 hour
★ Wonders of the night sky
FREE
www.renfrewshire.gov.uk

Pass of Killiecrankie   `916`
Pitlochry

In 1689, the Pass of Killiecrankie echoed with the sounds of battle as a Jacobite army defeated government forces. The spectacular gorge is tranquil now and visitors can enjoy this magnificent wooded gorge with the River Garry flowing along its base. The Visitor Centre tells the story of the Pass's rich natural history and the battle and is the place to start your visit. There are lots of walks on offer here with stunning views of the Pass, to Soldier's Leap, Troopers Den and the Balfour Stone.

🔍 On the B8079, 3 miles north of Pitlochry
⚙ ⚙ ♣
⏳ 1–2 hours
⭐ Spectacular autumn display
FREE Car park charges
www.nts.org.uk

British Golf Museum   `917`
St Andrews

A visit to the British Golf Museum will transport you down a pathway of surprising facts and striking feats from 500 years of golf history. Using diverse displays and exciting exhibits, the museum traces the history of the game, both in Britain and abroad, from the Middle Ages to the present day. Visitors will encounter many famous professionals, amateurs of status, kings and queens and other curious golfing characters. Find out more about the evolution of equipment and marvel at the symbols of success on display.

🔍 Follow signs from St Andrews town centre
⚙ ⚙ ♣ ❋
⏳ 1–2 hours
⭐ Europe's largest collection of golfing memorabilia
♿
www.britishgolfmuseum.co.uk

Scotland's Secret Bunker   `918`
St Andrews

Discover the twilight world of the government's Cold War. Scotland's best-kept secret for over 40 years is hidden beneath an innocent Scottish farmhouse. A tunnel leads to Scotland's Secret Bunker – 24,000 square feet of secret accommodation. On two levels, 100 feet underground, the bunker includes staff accommodation on one level and operational areas on the other, with a control centre and Radar Room (see above). Had there been a nuclear war, this is from where post-apocalypse Scotland would have been governed. Take the opportunity to discover how they would have survived... and you wouldn't!

🔍 On the B940, south of St Andrews
⚙ ⚙ ♣
⏳ 1–2 hours
⭐ Nuclear Command Control Centre
♿
www.secretbunker.co.uk

Stirling Castle 919
Stirling

Without doubt one of Scotland's grandest castles due to its imposing position and impressive architecture, Stirling Castle commands the countryside for many miles around. Visitors can see the Great Hall – the largest medieval banqueting hall ever built in Scotland; the Chapel Royal – built especially for Prince Henry's baptism and elaborately redecorated for Charles I's coronation visit in 1633; and the Great Kitchens, which dramatically bring to life how lavish banquets were created in James IV's day. There are also stunning views from the battlements of two great battlefields: Stirling Bridge and Bannockburn.

🔍 Stirling Old Town
☀ ☼ ♣ ❄
⏳ 1–2 hours
⭐ Important symbol of Scottish independence
£
www.historic-scotland.gov.uk

Bannockburn 921
Stirling

This atmospheric spot is the site of Robert the Bruce's famous victory over the English. In June 1314, Bruce gathered his men to take on the professional army of King Edward II. Despite facing a greater number of troops, Bruce's men routed the English forces – a victory that meant freedom for Scotland from oppressive English rule. In 2004, archaeologists found an iron arrowhead here that could well have been fired at the Battle of Bannockburn. Visitors can find out what inspired this great Scottish victory at the on-site heritage centre.

🔍 On the A872, 2 miles south of Stirling
☀ ☼ ♣ ❄
⏳ 1 hour
⭐ One of Scotland's most famous battlefields
£
www.nts.org.uk

Argyll's Lodging 920
Stirling

Argyll's Lodging is the most complete 17th-century townhouse surviving in Scotland, and an important example of Renaissance architecture. It was purposefully situated on the approach to Stirling Castle, giving its aristocratic owner ready access to the royal court. It also provided a suitable environment within which he could receive, and impress, his sovereign. The principal rooms – including the Laigh Hall, drawing room and bedchamber, are magnificently restored and furnished as they would have appeared during the 9th Earl of Argyll's occupation around 1680.

🔍 Stirling Old Town
☀ ☼ ♣ ❄
⏳ 1–2 hours
⭐ Guided tours only (you must book in advance)
£
www.historic-scotland.gov.uk

Wallace Monument 922
Stirling

This monument stands tall and proud outside the city of Stirling, and overlooking the scene of Scotland's victory at the Battle of Stirling Bridge. This is a place where history is something you can touch and feel, as you follow the story of Sir William Wallace, patriot, martyr, and Guardian of Scotland. For over 140 years, this world-famous, 220-foot high landmark has fascinated visitors with its exhibits and displays, telling the story of Sir William Wallace. Visitors are also encouraged to explore the Abbey Craig, on which the monument stands, with its unspoilt land and beautiful woodland.

🔍 Follow signs from Stirling town centre
☀ ☼ ♣ ❄
⏳ 1–2 hours
⭐ Wallace's mighty broadsword
£
www.nationalwallacemonument.com

Aberdeen Maritime Museum 923
Aberdeen

Aberdeen Maritime Museum tells the story of the city's long relationship with the sea. This award-winning museum is located on the historic Shiprow and incorporates Provost Ross's house, which was built in 1593. It houses a unique collection covering shipbuilding, fast sailing ships, fishing and port history. Displays include ship and oilrig models, paintings, clipper ship and 'North Boats' material, fishing, whalers and commercial trawlers, North Sea oil industry, and the marine environment. It also offers visitors a spectacular viewpoint over the busy harbour.

Aberdeen harbour
1-2 hours
Marvellous art collection
FREE
www.aberdeencity.gov.uk

Archaeolink 924
Aberdeen

Archaeolink is a multi-award-winning living history park and visitor attraction, with a central focus on education, participation and fun. Travel 10,000 years in one day from the Mesolithic Age, the Bronze and Iron Ages to a Roman Marching Camp, with indoor and outdoor exhibitions featuring hands-on activities, workshops and guided tours every day. Situated in the beautiful countryside of Aberdeenshire in the shadow of the dramatic Bennachie mountain range, the park occupies a central location in the diverse archaeological landscape of north-east Scotland.

On the A96, north of Aberdeen
1-2 hours
Excellent family-friendly activities
£
www.archaeolink.co.uk

Codona's Aderdeen Beach 925
Aberdeen

A traditional amusement park, Codona's has been here for more than 25 years. It has all the standard outdoor rides including the Grampian Wheel, three rollercoasters (including one stomach-churner), the water flume and the Haunted House. Little ones can play their hearts out at Ramboland. In addition, Codona's has an indoor Sunset Boulevard complex with the latest simulator machines, video arcade games and slot machines. Upstairs there are 10 full-size American pool tables. There are also the dodgems and a 26-lane, ten-pin bowling alley.

Aberdeen beach
3-4 hours
The Aberdeen Eye
£
www.codonas.com

Balmoral Castle and Estate 926
Ballater

Set in the magnificent scenery of Royal Deeside in the shadows of Lochnagar, is the Balmoral Estate. Purchased by Queen Victoria in 1848, the Estate has been the Scottish home of the British Royal Family ever since. The Estate extends to just over 50,000 acres of heather-clad hills, ancient Caledonian woodland. Over the past 150 years careful stewardship by its owners has preserved the wildlife, scenery and architecture, which is now available for all generations to enjoy. Visitors can see parts of the house, the gardens and can enjoy a wide range of other activities on the Estate.

Off the A93, between Ballater and Braemar
2 hours
Tranquil Caledonian woodlands
£
www.balmoralcastle.com

The Old Royal Station | 927
Ballater

Ballater is beautiful village set in the heart of Deeside, with local fishing on the River Dee, walking and a number of other attractions. But the jewel in its crown is the recently restored Old Royal Station. Queen Victoria arrived here frequently on her way to Balmoral, and a museum inside the station contains exhibits on her visits and a reconstruction of the waiting room built here for her in 1886. The railway was vital to the development of the town but its royal use brought it to the attention of people all over the world.

On the A93, in the centre of Ballater

1 hour

The 'Royal' carriage

www.visitscotland.com

Dolphin Watching | 928
Buckie

Come and enjoy the famous wildlife and stunning coastal scenery on a Moray Firth dolphin trip and marine tour, sailing three times daily aboard the beautiful ex-Clyde class lifeboat *Gemini Explorer*. Leaving from Buckie, visitors will get the chance to see the Moray Firth dolphins, various species of whale and a wide variety of sea birds; the dolphins are regularly seen showing off around the boat. As the boat only holds 12 people, it is essential that you book your places in advance (see website for details).

Buckie quayside

Weather permitting

3 hours

Wildlife on the high seas

www.geminiexplorer.co.uk

Glenfiddich Distillery | 929
Dufftown

Visits to this famous distillery start with an evocative film about its history, after which you will be taken to the very heart of the operation. Feel the heat rising from the mash tun and discover the giant washbacks, hand-made from Douglas fir and five metres high. You will also see one of the traditional warehouses – whose earthen floors, stone walls and age-old atmosphere nurture this famous whisky to life. Connoisseur tours, which include a tutored nosing and tasting session of the finest whiskies, are also available (you must book in advance – see website).

On the A941, north of Dufftown

2-3 hours

Traditional Scottish industry

Distillery tours **FREE** Connoisseur Tours

www.glenfiddich.com

Findhorn Heritage Centre and Icehouse
Findhorn

930

Findhorn, a Moray village situated on the shore of Findhorn Bay opposite the Culbin Sands, was once a bustling port, full of trading ships and salmon fishing boats. The village icehouse has fascinating underground chambers built over 150 years ago to store ice for packing the salmon en route to London. In the heritage centre, you will learn the story of Findhorn from prehistoric times to the present day and discover the secrets of the Sands of Findhorn.

🔍 On the B9011, in Forres
✲ ◎ ♣
⌛ 1 hour
★ The unique Findhorn class yacht
FREE Donations appreciated
www.findhorn-heritage.co.uk

Museum of Scottish Lighthouses
Fraserburgh

931

The Museum of Scottish Lighthouses consists of the first lighthouse built on mainland Scotland and a purpose-built museum. The highlight of a visit is a guided tour of Kinnaird Head lighthouse. The museum also includes several galleries containing a fabulous collection of glass lenses, lighting technology and social history artefacts covering the lives of the men and families who guarded Scotland's coastline for over 200 years. There are audio-visual displays and interactive exhibits that will engage you both in science and history.

🔍 Follow signs from Fraserburgh town centre
✲ ◎ ♣ ❋
⌛ 1–2 hours
★ Fabulous views of the Moray Firth
£
www.lighthousemuseum.org.uk

Leith Hall
Huntly

932

A typical Scottish laird's residence brimming with family treasures, Leith Hall is set in 286 acres of scenic estate containing six acres of wonderful garden that overlooks some of Aberdeenshire's finest rolling countryside. The house contains many tapestries, several interesting clocks, some fine china and a wonderful collection of family portraits and paintings. It is also said to be haunted. The gardens are lovely and include a fascinating collection of Pictish stones including the Wolf Stone and the Percylieu stone. The estate contains several waymarked trails for visitors to explore.

🔍 On the B9002, 34 miles north-west of Aberdeen
✲ ◎ ♣ ❋ House only open on Sundays in July and August
⌛ 2–3 hours
★ Mysterious Pictish stones
£
www.nts.org.uk

MacDuff Marine Aquarium   933
Macduff

Situated on Aberdeenshire's scenic coast in the traditional fishing town of MacDuff, this award-winning aquarium features marine life from the Moray Firth, Scotland's largest bay, in a variety of exciting and innovative exhibits. Visitors come face to face with hundreds of native fish and invertebrates normally only seen by Scuba divers who brave the chilly waters of the North Sea. The aquarium's deep central exhibit, which displays a living kelp reef, is the only one of its kind in Britain and divers hand feed the fish on a regular basis.

East of MacDuff harbour

1-2 hours

Deep Reef and Sea Floor exhibit

www.macduff-aquarium.org.uk

Arbuthnot Museum   934
Peterhead

Discover the wealth of Peterhead's maritime history in one of Aberdeenshire's oldest museums, the Arbuthnot, named after Adam Arbuthnot, a member of a prominent local land-owning and merchant family. Visitors can see models showing the development of Peterhead's fishing boats and find out about the town's fishing, shipping and whaling past. As well as Inuit artefacts, the museum has displays on Arctic creatures, including a polar bear collected by Adam Arbuthnot, local history and one of Northern Scotland's largest coin collections.

Peterhead town centre

1 hour

History of Peterhead's ships

FREE

www.aberdeenshire.gov.uk

Strathspey Steam Railway   935
Aviemore

From its base at Aviemore through Boat of Garten and on to Broomhill, this steam railway takes you on a nostalgic 20-mile round trip along part of the original Highland Railway, which first opened in 1863. As the train passes over moorland, through woodlands and by great sweeps of the River Spey, the Cairngorm Mountains provide a spectacular backcloth to the scenery – it has all the ingredients for a great day out. Visitors can take a tour of the historic locomotive shed at Aviemore station on the first Saturday of each month.

Aviemore town centre; Boat of Garten and Broomhill are both off the A95

2-3 hours

Steam nostalgia and marvellous countryside

www.strathspeyrailway.co.uk

Ballindalloch Castle 936
Ballindalloch

Ballindalloch is one of the most beautiful castles in Scotland. Known as the Pearl of the North, it is located in the heart of Speyside, near to a number of famous whisky distilleries. Surrounded by majestic hills, and with the tumbling waters of the Rivers Spey and Avon flowing through the grounds, the setting is truly magnificent. Visitors can tour the house, which has a marvellous collection of 18th-century furniture and Spanish paintings. You can also tour the walled garden, a rock garden and the magnificent grounds.

On the A95, 14 miles north-east of Grantown-on-Spey

2-3 hours

Biggles author W.E. Johns' cottage in the grounds

£

www.ballindallochcastle.co.uk

Loch Lomond National Nature Reserve 937
Balmaha

This loch is famous for its beautiful wooded shores and islands. The reserve embraces five of the loch's islands, each supporting rich, mature oak woodland. Bluebells and wild garlic carpet the woodlands in spring when migrant warblers, flycatchers and redstarts start to return. It also includes the wetlands, around the mouth of the River Endrick, these flood most winters and host good numbers of wildfowl. Visitors can enjoy a wide range of activities on land and on the water in this marvellous landscape.

Off the B837

3-4 hours

Boat trip to the wooded island of Inchcailloch

FREE

www.lochlomond-trossachs.org

STAR ATTRACTION

Landmark Forest Adventure Park 938
Carrbridge

Landmark Forest Adventure Park is a theme park made up of outdoor activities. There are adventure rides, such as the Wild Watercoaster and a regular Runaway Timber Train coaster. But there are also a number of healthy, energetic pursuits too such as an Ultimate Challenge Assault Course (see above), a skydive 'parachute jump' simulator, a climbing wall, a Wild Forest Maze and Bamboozeleum – a hands-on, fun science and illusion exhibition. There's also an adventure play area, steam powered sawmill, working Clydesdale horse, a red squirrel nature trail, giant viewing tower, mini cars and diggers.

Just off the A9 at Carrbridge

3-4 hours

Views from the Fire Tower

£

www.landmarkpark.co.uk

Culloden Battlefield   939
Culloden Moor

Culloden was the last hand-to-hand battle fought on British soil. Part of a wider European religious and political conflict, the short but bloody fight, during which more than 1,5000 Jacobites were killed, changed the course of history. Today visitors can walk around the battlefield as it appeared to the opposing forces on 16 April 1746. You can then tour the visitor centre and exhibition that explains the whole Culloden story in an innovative and interactive way, which appeals to all the family. There's also a film, a battle table and rooftop view of the battlefield.

On the B9006, 5 miles east of Inverness

2-3 hours

Poignant and haunting moorland

www.nts.org.uk

STAR ATTRACTION

Jacobite Steam Train   941
Fort William

Described as one of the great railway journeys of the world, this 84-mile round trip takes you from Fort William to Mallaig. The train first passes Ben Nevis then crosses the Glenfinnan Viaduct used in the *Harry Potter* films, before continuing on to Arisaig. You may alight at Arisaig by request to the guard. From here, on a clear summer's day, you can see the 'Small Isles' of Rum, Eigg, Muck, Canna and the southern tip of Skye. From Arisaig it continues on, passing Morar and the silvery beaches used in the film *Local Hero*, until finally reaching the Atlantic Ocean at Mallaig.

Fort William town centre

6 hours

Harry Potter carriages

www.steamtrain.info

Loch Ness Monster Exhibition Centre   940
Drumnadrochit

Using photographs, descriptions and film footage, this exhibition presents the evidence about the existence of the legendary Loch Ness Monster. The exhibition includes up-to-the minute facts and documented evidence together with an account of the area's historical and cultural background. You can also visit a small cinema, which shows you real-life accounts and sightings of one of the world's most fascinating creatures. It also highlights the efforts made by various expeditions, such as Operation Deepscan, to find this intriguing monster.

On the A82, west of Inverness

1-2 hours

500 million years of history

www.lochness-centre.com

Vertical Descents

942

Fort William

Situated in the stunning scenery of the Highlands near Inchree Falls, this is a modern outdoor adventure activity centre offering a wide range of exhilarating activities including canyoning, white water rafting, fun yakking, bridge swing, paintball and mountain biking. Activities and courses of all standards are available from a team of highly trained instructors with safety as a top priority. Equipment and clothing is available for hire and information on local accommodation is also available should you require it.

🔍 Off the A82, 7 miles south of Fort William

☼ ◯ ✦

⏳ 3–5 hours

★ Adventure Activity Packages

💷 💷 💷

www.verticaldescents.com

Glencoe Visitor Centre

943

Glencoe

Glencoe features some of the finest climbing and walking country in the Highlands. It is the home of Scottish mountaineering, with 20 major climbing sites including eight Munros. There are also 49 miles of footpaths available. You can get all the information you need for any outdoor pursuits at the visitor centre, which also has exciting interactive displays including 'Living on the Edge', which explores the landscape, wildlife and history of Glencoe, and a film presentation about the infamous massacre that took place here in 1629.

🔍 On the A82, between Glasgow and Fort William

☼ ◯ ✦ ❄

⏳ 1–2 hours

★ Viewing platform

💷

www.nts.org.uk

Inveraray Castle 944

Inveraray

Originally the home of the Campbell clan, Inveraray is more of a mansion than a castle but it is impressive nonetheless. Although it is still the home of the Duke of Argyll, many of the rooms, with their French neo-classical decor, are open to the public. The main hall soars to the full height of the house and is decorated with a superb collection of weapons. There are collections of tapestries, paintings and items of special interest to members of Clan Campbell. Rob Roy McGregor's sporran and dirk handle are also on view.

On the A83, on the shores of Loch Fyne

2-3 hours

The 'Fairy Tale Castle'

www.inveraray-castle.com

Inveraray Jail 945

Inveraray

Inveraray Jail is more than just a museum – it's a historical experience brought to life. From the moment you walk through the door, you are free to explore at your leisure (not a privilege the prisoners had!) and interact with costumed staff who assume the roles of the jail's occupants. Visit the courthouse and witness early justice as you face the judge, try out a hammock after the warder locks your cell door, join the prisoners and sample the punishments for your criminal behaviour, then grab some swag as you make your escape.

Inveraray town centre

1 hour

A prison sentence in the 1820s

www.inverarayjail.co.uk

Inverness Dolphin Cruises 946

Inverness

These cruises depart from Inverness harbour and cruise the Moray Firth where you will have a chance of seeing the most northerly group of bottlenose dolphins in the world plus common seals, grey seals and porpoises. There is also abundant bird life such as terns, gannets, fulmars, razorbills, kittiwakes, red kites, ospreys, and a variety of wading birds at Munlochy Bay. The cruise features stunning views of the last Jacobite battlefield at Culloden Moor. You can also see the picturesque villages of Fortrose, Avoch and the lighthouse at Chanonry Point on the Black Isle.

Inverness harbour

1-2 hours

Fabulous wildlife

www.inverness-dolphin-cruises.co.uk

Inverness Terror Tour 947

Inverness

Led by Davy the Ghost, this walking tour of horror and laughter takes you through the back streets of Inverness. Hear gruesome tales along the way of witches, a number of local ghosts, hangings, murders, torture and other ghastly happenings, which will make you roar with nervous laughter, before ending the tour at the haunted tavern where you will be given a well-earned drink. Tours leave from the centre of town at 7.00 p.m. each night.

Tourist Information Centre, Bridge Street

1-2 hours

Chilling ghost stories

www.scotland.org.uk

Kisimul Castle 948
Isle of Barra

This is the traditional seat of the Chiefs of Clan MacNeil. The castle is spectacularly sited on a rock in the bay and is known locally as the 'Castle in the Sea'. Visitors can visit the castle by taking a short boat trip from the village of Castlebay. Hidden inside the massive curtain wall are a number of well-preserved buildings including a feasting hall, a chapel, a tanist's (heir's) house and a gokman's (watchman's) house. Stunning views of Castlebay are available from the walkway around the curtain wall.

🔍 Boats leave from Castlebay pier
☼ ☀ ✚ ❄
⏳ 1–2 hours
⭐ Spectacular and dramatic location
♿
www.historic-scotland.gov.uk

Scapa Flow Visitor Centre and Museum 949
Isle of Hoy

Scapa Flow, a small stretch of water sheltered by the surrounding Orkney Islands, is an atmospheric place. The visitor centre houses a large range of exhibits that give a real feel for Scapa Flow during the two World Wars. Visitors can see displays and models showing how its defences worked, plus models showing the scuttling of the German fleet in 1919. From large guns and torpedoes though to photographs and more personal memorabilia, visitors can get a sense of the people who spent a part of their lives here, and sometimes died here.

🔍 Lyness Pier
☼ ☀ ✚ ❄
⏳ 2–3 hours
⭐ 'Fortress Orkney' exhibit
FREE
www.orkney.gov.uk

The Black House Museum 950
Isle of Lewis

This site includes a traditional Lewis thatched crofter's cottage, or black house, with byre and stackyard, complete with a peat fire burning in the central hearth. The roof traditionally had no chimney, the smoke from the fire simply finding its own way out as it could. There is also a 'white house', a new style of housing brought in during the 1800s in an effort to modernise life here. Completing the complex is an excellent visitor centre in another nearby converted cottage. This provides background information and has a very helpful cutaway model of the black house.

🔍 Off the A858, in Arnol on the west side of the island
☼ ☀ ✚
⏳ 1–2 hours
⭐ Island life, 150 years ago
♿
www.historic-scotland.gov.uk

Calanais Standing Stones 951
Isle of Lewis

Calanais consists of a late Neolithic stone ring and associated lines of standing stones. Situated on a prominent ridge, it is visible from miles around. Excavations have revealed that the ring was set up between 2900 and 2600 BC, making it earlier than the main circle at Stonehenge. The layout of the site appears to have an association with astronomical events, the precise nature of which cannot be determined. The existence of Bronze Age monuments in the area implies that Calanais remained an active focus for prehistoric religious activity for at least 1,500 years.

🔍 Off the A859, 12 miles west of Stornaway
☼ ☀ ✚ ❄
⏳ 1–2 hours
⭐ Story of the Stones exhibition
♿
www.historic-scotland.gov.uk

Hebridean Whale and Dolphin Trust
Isle of Mull

952

The Isle of Mull has a greater variety and abundance of wildlife than any other Hebridean island. The HWDT is dedicated to enhancing knowledge and understanding of Scotland's whales, dolphins and porpoises (cetaceans) and the Hebridean marine environment. Its visitor centre in Tobermory has information on up-to-date wildlife sightings and can advise visitors on the whole range of wildlife 'safaris' available around this glorious island.

Tobermory harbour front

1 hour

Interpretative displays and information

FREE

www.hwdt.org

Whale Watching Trips
Isle of Mull

953

Explore the rugged coastline and rich waters around the Hebrides with award-winning Sea Life Surveys, searching for whales, sharks, dolphins, porpoises, seabirds and much more. Exploring the West Coast waters for 25 years, this family run business lets the wildlife and weather shape your journey, giving you a unique opportunity to see some of the ocean's largest and most mysterious inhabitants in their natural environment. There's a range of trips available but you must book in advance (see website).

East Brae, Tobermory

4 hours

Trip of a lifetime

www.sealifesurveys.com

The Orkney Museum 954
Isle of Orkney

For three centuries this house was the home of the Baikie family of Tankerness, whose estate gave the house its name. The Baikie library and drawing room are preserved here to give the visitor an idea of how the house looked when it was a family home. Today, the house is a museum that tells the history of Orkney from prehistory to the 20th century. The story is told through archaeological and social history exhibits, ranging from a Scar Viking ship burial through to a 300-year-old calculator.

🔍 Kirkwall town centre
❄ ❄ ♣ ❄
⧗ 1–2 hours
★ Orkney's War: Their Darkest Hour exhibition
FREE
www.orkneyheritage.com

Skara Brae Prehistoric Village 955
Isle of Orkney

This is the best-preserved prehistoric village in northern Europe, with eight dwellings linked by low alleyways. The site was uncovered by a storm in 1850, and presents a remarkable picture of life around 5,000 years ago. The beautifully constructed houses have stone beds, dressers, seats and boxes of provisions and a hearth where dried heather, bracken and seaweed were burned. A replica house has been created next to the site. Many original artefacts found at Skara Brae are on display in the on-site visitor centre.

🔍 On the B9056, 19 miles north-west of Kirkwall
❄ ❄ ♣ ❄
⧗ 1–2 hours
★ Real Neolithic village
£
www.historic-scotland.gov.uk

Raasay Outdoor Centre 956
Isle of Raasay

This outdoor activities centre is situated in the Borodale House Hotel, next to the historic mansion of Raasay House. All types of activities are available, including kayaking in Raasay's sheltered bay, sailing around the seas of Skye, climbing, coasteering and gorge walking, in some of the most beautiful locations in the British Isles. You can visit by the day or for longer as accommodation is available. All equipment is provided. Instructors are highly experienced, safety conscious and passionate about sharing their skills to people of all abilities.

🔍 You can be picked up from the ferry terminal at Sconser
❄ ❄ ♣
⧗ 4–6 hours
★ Real outdoor adventures
£ £ £
www.raasay-house.co.uk

Clan Donald Skye 957
Isle of Skye

Built by Lord MacDonald in 1815, the neo-gothic castle is today a sculptured ruin and focal point for the 40-acre garden. Here, sheltered by 200-year-old trees, many exotic plants shrubs and flowers flourish. The award-winning Museum of the Isles takes you through 1,500 years of the history and culture of the area known as the Kingdom of the Isles. The estate offers some stunning walks for all levels of fitness and with some stunning views. It is also home to iconic wildlife species including red deer, golden eagles and sea eagles.

🔍 On the A851 at Armadale, 16 miles south of Broadford
❄ ❄ ♣
⧗ 1–2 hours
★ History of Clan Donald
£
www.clandonald.com

STAR ATTRACTION

Bella Jane Boat Trips 958
Isle of Skye

No visit to the Isle of Skye is complete without a trip on the award-winning *Bella Jane*. This boat takes visitors to one of Scotland's most isolated and breathtaking lochs, Loch Coruisk, set in the heart of the stunningly beautiful Cuillin Mountains. Coruisk has fascinated visitors for generations and deservedly enjoys a magical and mysterious reputation, even in changeable weather. During the journey to the loch you get to visit the famous seal colony as well as glimpsing a variety of other animals, birds and sea life.

🔍 On the B8083, at Elgol
❀ ☼ ♣
⧗ 3 hours
★ Free tea on the trip home
£ £ £
www.bellajane.co.uk

Bright Water Visitor Centre 959
Isle of Skye

Situated between the Isle of Skye and Kyle of Lochalsh on mainland Scotland, Eilean Ban is a six-acre nature haven nestling below the Skye road bridge. Originally home to lighthouse keepers and their families, it later became the residence of the naturalist and author of *Ring of Bright Water*, Gavin Maxwell. Although famous for its association with otters, the island supports a wealth of wildlife of both local and national importance. Nature trails wind around the island leading to different points of interest, including the award-winning wildlife hide, a viewing platform and a sensory garden.

🔍 Take the Kyleakin exit at the roundabout at the end of Skye Bridge
❀ ☼ ♣ ❄
⧗ 1–2 hours
★ Stevenson lighthouse
FREE Donations requested
www.eileanban.org

Dunvegan Castle 960
Isle of Skye

Dunvegan Castle has been the stronghold of the Chiefs of MacLeod for nearly 800 years. Built on a rock, it has survived clan battles, the extremes of feast and famine and the profound social, political and economic changes through which the Western Highlands and Islands have passed. Originally designed to keep people out, romantic and historic Dunvegan Castle was first opened to the public in 1933. Over the years, it has played host to a number of distinguished visitors including Sir Walter Scott, Dr Johnson, Queen Elizabeth II and the Japanese Emperor Akihito.

🔍 1 mile north of Dunvegan
❀ ☼ ♣ ❄
⧗ 1–2 hours
★ The Fairy Flag
£
www.dunvegancastle.com

The Last House in Scotland 961
John o' Groats

John o' Goats is named after Dutchman Jan de Groot who ran the local ferry service from here to the Orkney Islands and charged a groat for the journey. Ferries still leave from here. This little museum offers a wealth of photographs of the area and boating history as well as a selection of wonderful historic artefacts that have been loaned to the museum by local residents. Visitors can have their postcards letters or parcels stamped with the official 'Last House' stamp and posted from inside the building.

🔍 17 miles north of Wick
❀ ☼ ♣ ❄
⧗ 1 hour
★ Stunning views of sea, cliffs and the lighthouse
FREE
www.visitjohnogroats.com

Highland Folk Museum `962`
Kingussie

The Highland Folk Museum brings to life the domestic and working conditions of the Highland peoples. Visitors to this open-air, living history museum can learn how our Scottish Highland ancestors lived, how they built their homes, how they tilled the soil and how they dressed. This award-winning visitor attraction not only encapsulates human endeavour and development in Highland life from the 1700s to the present day, but also offers an opportunity to explore a beautiful natural setting, home to red squirrels and tree creepers.

Kingussie village

2–3 hours

Highland textiles and tartans

FREE

www.highlandfolk.com

Highland Wildlife Park `963`
Kingussie

This unique safari-style park is home to native Scottish wildlife and endangered species from the world's mountain and tundra regions. Visitors can drive through the main reserve and see herds of European bison, red deer, yaks, Tibetan wild ass, reindeer and the Przewalski horse. You can then explore the rest of the park on foot to discover beaver, snow monkeys, red pandas, wolves, wildcats, lynx, Amur tigers and Mercedes the polar bear. Each day visitors can join feeding talks in the walkround area and find out more about our animals from the expert keepers.

On the B9152, north of Kingussie

2–3 hours

Beautiful wild cats

www.highlandwildlifepark.org

Eilean Donan Castle `964`
Kyle of Lochalsh

This castle, subject of one of the most famous views in Scotland, stands on a small island at the meeting point of three sea lochs near Dornie in Ross-shire. In a superbly romantic setting on the main tourist route to the Isle of Skye amid silent tree-clad hills, it has a rare and dream-like atmosphere. However, it is a formidable fortress made of solid stone that has played witness to hundreds of years of feudal history. Visitors can tour the ruins and then learn about this famous castle's history in the on-site visitor centre.

On the A87, 8 miles from Kyle of Lochalsh

1–2 hours

History of the MacRae clan

www.eileandonancastle.com

Seaprobe *Atlantis*
Kyle of Lochalsh

965

This is one of the top wildlife experiences in Scotland. Visitors embark on to the waters around Lochalsh and the Isle of Skye on board a semi-submersible, glass-bottomed boat. The underwater viewing gallery offers a truly astonishing panoramic underwater vision. Amongst the trips available, you can enjoy views of a kelp forest filled with fish, jellyfish, sea urchins and starfish, a Second World War shipwreck, seal and bird colonies. Also watch out for otters and occasionally dolphins, whales and even sharks.

🔍 Old Ferry slipway, Kyle of Lochalsh

☼ ◉ ♣

⧗ 1–2 hours

★ Superb underwater vistas

£ £

www.seaprobeatlantis.com

Cawdor Castle
Nairn

966

This superb fairytale castle (above), complete with fortress-like tower and drawbridge, is forever linked with Shakespeare's *Macbeth*. In vaults deep beneath it stands an ancient and mystical holly tree, around which the medieval tower was originally built by the Thane of Cawdor. Close by it is a secret dungeon. The castle is full of good furniture, fine portraits, pictures and outstanding tapestries. Outside, a series of paths wind through the Big Wood where visitors will see red deer and other native wildlife.

🔍 On the B9090, between Inverness and Nairn

☼ ◉ ♣

⧗ 2–3 hours

★ A tree growing since 1372

£

www.cawdorcastle.com

McCaig's Tower

`967`

Oban

Within Oban the most outstanding feature is McCaig's Tower. This is the Colosseum lookalike that stands above the town and features in many of the postcards you will find for sale in the shops in town. The tower was built by a local banker in 1897. The aim was to provide work for local stonemasons and provide a lasting monument to his family. First time visitors to the tower are in for a surprise. The interior consists of a grassy hilltop, with the wall of the tower encircling it like a crown on an uneven head.

🔍 Overlooking Oban town centre

✳ ⚙ ♣ ❄

⏳ 1 hour

★ Fantastic views of Oban Bay

FREE

www.oban.org.uk

Inverewe Gardens

`969`

Poolewe

This astonishing garden is built on a craggy hillside with a majestic setting on the water's edge of Loch Ewe. The warm currents of the North Atlantic Drift help nurture an oasis or colour and fertility enabling exotic plants from many countries to flourish on a latitude more northerly than Moscow. Inverewe has a famous walled garden with plants from around the world including Chinese rhododendrons, Tasmanian eucalypts and New Zealand daisy bushes as well as woodland containing a canopy of Scots pine trees. The Pinewood Trail and Kernsery Path are stunning all year round.

🔍 On the A832, 1 mile from Poolewe

✳ ⚙ ♣

⏳ 2-3 hours

★ Free guided walks during the summer

💰

www.nts.org.uk

Scottish Sealife Sanctuary

`968`

Oban

Nestling in a mature spruce forest on the shores of beautiful Loch Creran, the Scottish Sealife Sanctuary enjoys one of the most picturesque settings in Britain, and is home to some of the UK's most enchanting marine creatures. In crystal clear waters you can explore over 30 fascinating natural marine habitats containing everything from octopus to otters. Come nose to nose with the graceful rays as they swim to the surface to greet you or stand in the midst of hundreds of salmon as they swim around you in a unique shoaling ring.

🔍 On the A828, 10 miles north of Oban

✳ ⚙ ♣ ❄

⏳ 2-3 hours

★ Otter Creek

💰

www.sealsanctuary.co.uk

Up-Helly-Aa Exhibition 970
Shetland Islands

A traditional Viking fire festival has been celebrated in Lerwick every January since the 1880s. The dazzling Up-Helly-Aa ceremony sees a procession of a thousand flaming torches, which culminates in a huge blaze, as a replica longship is set alight. During the summer months there is an exhibition that relates the history of this incredible event and includes regalia, including the Jarl Squad suits of the previous 10 years, photographs and a short film on that year's event.

🔍 Follow signs from Lerwick town centre

⚙ ❀

⏳ 1 hour

★ Replica Viking longship

💲

www.uphellyaa.org

Inverawe Smokehouse 971
Taynuilt

Inverawe Smokehouse produces delicious, high-quality Scottish smoked salmon, made using the traditional smoking process. You can stop here and call in at the visitor centre to watch the whole production through viewing windows. There is also an exhibition covering the history of smoked food. The Smokehouse is set in glorious unspoiled countryside and visitors can enjoy the freedom of walking through the woods, parkland, down by the river and along Loch Etive side. There is wildlife everywhere. There is also a tearoom where you can try the delights on offer in the Smokehouse shop.

🔍 On the A85, between Glasgow and Oban

⚙ ⚙ ❀ ❄

⏳ 1 hour

★ A real Scottish tradition

FREE

www.smokedsalmon.co.uk

Glenmorangie Distillery Centre 972
Tain

Visitors can tour this fine distillery and see its unique swan-neck copper stills in the company of a guide who will explain the whisky-making progress from beginning to end. You will then be introduced to the Sixteen Men of Tain who make the whisky itself. Tours end in the tasking room where you can taste the results of their industry and skill. The visitor centre has a fine 130-year-old steam engine and exhibits including Glenmorangie's pioneering experiments on the effects of wood on whisky, which have led to the creation of their 'Wood Finish' malts.

🔍 On the A9, an hour north of Inverness

⚙ ⚙ ❀ ❄

⏳ 1–2 hours

★ Views of Dornoch Firth

💲

www.glenmorangie.com

Burns National Heritage Park 973
Alloway

On 25 January 1759, Scotland's best-loved poet, Robert Burns, was born amid a blast of icy wind in a humble cottage in Alloway. This cottage, now fully restored to its original state, forms the centrepiece of this attraction, offering a unique encounter with this exceptional man. Visitors can see the cottage, walk in the footsteps of Tam o' Shanter to the haunted Auld Kirk and Brig o' Doon, immortalised in Burns' much loved tale and brought to life in the audio-visual presentation within the Tam o' Shanter Experience. There is also a museum, a monument and beautiful commemorative gardens.

🔍 On the A719, south of Ayr

⚙ ⚙ ❀ ❄

⏳ 2–3 hours

★ An original manuscript of 'Auld Lang Syne'

💲

www.nts.com.uk

Devil's Porridge Exhibition 974
Annan

In 1915 the greatest munitions factory on earth was built on the Anglo-Scottish border near Gretna on the northern shore of the Solway Firth. The brainchild of David Lloyd George, the factory was 9 miles long and 2 miles wide, and 30,000 people moved here from all over the world to help Britain produce the quality ammunition it needed for the war. This exhibition tells the story of this remarkable venture, the people that came here to work and the secret towns that were created to accommodate them.

Follow signs on the A75 from Gretna

1–2 hours

One of the First World War's best-kept secrets

www.devilsporridge.co.uk

The Electric Brae 976
Ayr

The 'Electric Brae' runs a quarter of a mile from the bend overlooking Croy railway viaduct in the west to the wooded Craigencroy Glen in the east. If you stop your car here and take the handbrake off, it will appear to move *slowly* uphill. It would be better if there were weird forces at work here. But the truth is that while there is a slope of 1 in 86 upwards on this stretch of road, the configuration of the land on either side causes an optical illusion making it look as if the slope is going the other way.

On the A719, between Dunure and Croy Bay

1 hour

Weird science

FREE

www.mcintyre.demon.co.uk/local/electbrae.htm

Culzean Castle and Country Park 975
Ayr

The castle, built between 1772 and 1790 by Robert Adam, sits on a dramatic cliff-top site. It is notable for its oval staircase and circular saloon. The castle contains a good collection of pictures, 18th-century furniture, and an armoury. There is an Eisenhower Room recalling the president's links with Scotland. The country park surrounding the castle was Scotland's first and consists of 563 acres. There is a wealth of interest from the shoreline through to the deer park and gas house, with exhibitions, mature parklands and gardens.

Off the A719, 12 miles south of Ayr

2–3 hours

Glorious walled garden

www.nts.org.uk

STAR ATTRACTION

Paxton House and Country Park 977
Berwick-upon-Tweed

Built to the design of John Adam in 1758, Paxton House is one of the finest 18th-century Palladian country houses in Britain boasting interiors by Robert Adam and the pre-eminent collection of Chippendale furniture in Scotland. A magnificently restored picture gallery, the largest in a Scottish country house, exhibits over 70 paintings of British Art from 1760 to 1840. Here you will see masterpieces by Raeburn, Wilkie and Lawrence alongside many works of local interest. It also has over 80 acres of gardens, woodlands and parkland with a mile of riverside walks along the Tweed.

On the B6461, 4 miles from Berwick-upon-Tweed

1–2 hours

Superb period rooms

www.paxtonhouse.com

St Abb's Head National Nature Reserve | 979
Coldingham

St Abb's Head on the Berwickshire coast is a landmark site for birdwatchers and wildlife enthusiasts. This reserve is home to thousands of guillemots, kittiwakes, razorbills, shags, fulmars, puffins and herring gulls nesting on narrow ledges from April to August, and the cliffs here offer a spectacular vantage point for observing their behaviour. The Head boasts a wealth of other wildlife which you can learn about at the Nature Reserve Centre, or join a ranger-guided walk and enjoy the views along the coast as you go.

Off the A1107, 2 miles north of Coldingham

2-3 hours

Spectacular cliff-top walks

FREE Car park charge

www.nts.org.uk

Caerlaverock WWT | 978
Caerlaverock

Caerlaverock Wetland Centre is a spectacular 1,400-acre wild reserve situated on the north Solway coast. Its wintering birds include tens of thousands of Svalbard barnacle geese. Summer offers visitors the opportunity to explore rolling wildflower meadows, watch ospreys hunting over the Solway and even spot barn owls and badgers if you're lucky. From dawn to dusk, from January to December, in fair weather and in foul, its open, coastal landscape and wide skies are full of the sights and sounds of nature – and very little else.

Follow signs from the A75, 9 miles south-east of Dumfries

2-3 hours

Views from the observation towers

www.wwt.org.uk

Hirsel Country Park | 980
Coldstream

Set in the beautiful Scottish Borders, the 3,000-acre park attached to the Hirsel Estate can be found on the western outskirts of Coldstream, which marks the border between Scotland and England. There is something for everyone at the Hirsel: a variety of marvellous walks by lakeside, river and wood through the grounds of the Hirsel Estate, along the way catching sight of the well-known Douglas pedigree Highland Cattle and many other forms of local wildlife. There is also a visitor centre that has a small museum of country life, past and present.

On the A697

2-3 hours

Dundrock Wood

www.hirselcountrypark.co.uk

Gretna Green World Famous Old Blacksmith's Shop   981

Dumfries

Runaway marriages began in 1753 when it became illegal to marry under the age of 21 in England. However, in Scotland it was, and still is, possible to marry at the age of 16. Gretna Green is the first village across the border and many 'elopers' came here to the Blacksmith's Shop to get hitched. The Blacksmith's Anvil thus became the symbol of runaway weddings as not only were metals joined together on the heat of the fire but couples were also joined in marriage in the heat of the moment.

On the A74, just north of the border

1–2 hours

The famous marriage anvil

www.gretnagreen.com

Dumfries Museum and Camera Obscura   982

Dumfries

A treasure house of the history of south-west Scotland, Dumfries Museum is set in an 18th-century windmill. You will see fossil footprints left by prehistoric reptiles, the wildlife of the Solway marshes, tools and weapons of the earliest peoples of the region, stone carvings of Scotland's first Christians and a Victorian farm, workshop and home. On the top floor of the museum is the camera obscura; this historic astronomical instrument gives fascinating panoramic views over the town.

Dumfries town centre

1–2 hours

Skull cast of Robert the Bruce

www.dumfriesmuseum.demon.co.uk

Eyemouth Museum   983

Eyemouth

Housed in the Auld Kirk, now the town's Tourist Information Centre, this charming museum relates the history of Eyemouth and surrounding area and illustrates how its people have lived through the ages by land and sea. The centrepiece is a unique and moving tapestry worked to commemorate the centenary of the Great East Coast Fishing Disaster of 1881, when the community suffered the loss of 189 local fishermen at sea. Visitors can also see exhibitions on fishing, farming, milling, wheelwrighting and blacksmithing.

 Eyemouth town centre

1–2 hours

Incredible tapestry

www.eyemouthmuseum.org.uk

Drumlanrig's Tower   984

Hawick

This well-restored 15th-century building is an imposing landmark in the Scottish Borders town of Hawick. In the late 17th century it played a part in the religious struggles of the 'Killing Times' before it was transformed into the Duchess of Buccleuch's town house. It later became a coaching inn that remained open until 1981. Following restoration in the 1990s the building now houses period rooms, figures and audio-visuals in an exhibition of local history, with particular reference to Border Reivers.

Hawick town centre

1–2 hours

Turbulent local history

www.discovertheborders.co.uk

Scottish Maritime Museum 985
Irvine

The various parts of this interesting museum are scattered along the south side of the River Irvine. The main building is the vast Linthouse Engine Shop that includes an especially poignant resident in the Longhope Lifeboat, which was capsized by a huge wave with the loss of all eight crew in March 1969. Outside is a striking yellow and red Second World War lifesaving barge used to assist the crews of aircraft that had to ditch in the sea. Nearby is a recreation of a shipyard worker's tenement flat, used by workers and their families on the Clyde.

Irvine harbourside

1–2 hours

Collection of fascinating floating vessels

www.scottishmaritimemuseum.org

King's Cave 987
Isle of Arran

King's Cave on the Isle of Arran is the legendary place where Robert the Bruce fled, after murdering his rival John Comyn at the altar of Greyfriars Abbey. This less than heroic action divided Scots, and for a while Robert lost support amongst Scottish nobles and had to go into hiding. King's Cave was thought to have been his hiding place, or one of them. It is here that he was supposed to have been inspired to fight on by the tenacity of a spider spinning its web. Access to the cave is via the coastal footpath only.

Off the A481 near Blackwaterfoot

2 hours

Ancient Pictish wallcarvings

FREE

www.mysteriousbritain.co.uk

Brodick Castle, Garden and Country Park 986
Isle of Arran

Brodick Castle and Country Park is unique in being the only island country park in Britain. The castle offers 600 years of history, a fabulous collection of valuable artefacts including an impressive number of sporting pictures and trophies, paintings, furniture, silver and porcelain as well as stunning views over Brodick Bay to the Ayrshire Coast. The castle gardens provide an unrivalled experience from the formal walled garden to its superb network of woodland walks. The park includes Goatfell, the highest peak on Arran.

Cross by ferry from Ardrossan to the Isle of Arran

2–3 hours

Victorian Highland estate

www.nts.org.uk

Jedburgh Castle Jail and Museum 988
Jedburgh

This Victorian reform prison, now a museum of imprisonment and local history, is situated on the site of the Royal Castle of Jedburgh. Visitors can get a taste of life behind bars in this 1820s jail – a model prison in its day but now said to be one of the most haunted buildings in Scotland. The museum also covers the history of the Royal Burgh and houses a number of historical artefacts including finds made during excavations at nearby Dunion Hill Iron Age settlement. This impressive building has fine views of the town and surrounding countryside.

Jedburgh town centre

1 hour

Site of the town gallows

www.scotborders.gov.uk/museums

Jedforest Deer and Farm Park 989
Jedburgh

This 800-acre park is set in the beautiful rolling hills of the Scottish Borders. At its heart is a modern working farm where visitors can see magnificent herds of deer, a large conservation collection of rare breeds of sheep, pigs, cattle, chickens, ducks as well as spectacular birds of prey demonstrations. Within the farm there is also a conservation area pond, wildfowl and a barbecue and picnic area. The surrounding countryside offers grasslands, woodlands, and upland and lowland habitats in which there are colour-coded walks, nature trails and tree trails.

Off the A68, 5 miles south of the Jedburgh

2–3 hours

Wooded adventure playground

www.jedforestdeerpark.co.uk

Mary Queen of Scots Visitor Centre 990
Jedburgh

Mary Stuart visited Jedburgh in October 1566 and stayed in this house. Now a visitor centre in her honour, it offers a comprehensive look at Mary's turbulent life, with displays which include tapestries, paintings, furniture, personal items and arms and armour. Mary was on a brief tour of the Borders, undertaking local court duties. While staying here she rode to Hermitage Castle to visit the Earl of Bothwell. During the journey she caught a fever and nearly died. The house itself is a fine example of a 16th-century bastel house set within pretty public gardens.

Jedburgh town centre

1–2 hours

Mary's personal possessions

www.iknow-scotland.co.uk

Floors Castle 991
Kelso

Floors Castle has a towered central block and symmetrical Georgian ranges. In 1721 additions were made to an existing tower house to create a plain country house, which was then absorbed in the construction of a magnificent 19th-century baronial mansion. Treasures include Chinese and European porcelain and many other fine works of art. In the grounds is a holly tree, which marks the spot where James II was killed by an exploding cannon while besieging Roxburgh Castle. Extensive parkland and gardens overlooking the Tweed also provide a variety of wooded walks.

Off the A6089, north-west of Kelso

2 3 hours

The Needle Room

www.floorscastle.com

Galloway Wildlife Conservation Park 992
Kirkcudbright

This park, set in 27 acres of mixed woodland, is the wild animal conservation centre of southern Scotland. A collection of nearly 150 animals from all over the world can be seen in large and imaginative enclosures. The park's mission is to establish a conservation breeding centre for small animals, to conserve wildlife and sites of geological importance and to provide an opportunity for the public to enjoy them. Visitors can see red pandas, Scottish wildcats, otters, meerkats, foxes, owls and wallabies among others.

On the B727, 1 mile from Kirkcudbright

2–3 hours

Conservation in action

www.gallowaywildlife.co.uk

The Viking Experience 993
Largs

This multimedia attraction recounts the saga of the Vikings in Scotland, from their invasion to their defeat at the Battle of Largs in 1263. In the capable hands of costumed storytellers, you can experience the Viking adventure first hand as you are guided through 500 years of history, shown a Viking Longhouse and taken to meet the Viking gods and Valkyries in Valhalla, as Viking history is brought to life. Then take your seat for a 5-screen film presentation following one Viking family through generations of turmoil, battle and adventure.

⌕ Largs seafront
✿ ◉ ♣ ❄
⌛ 1–2 hours
★ Viking Hall of Knowledge
£
www.vikingar.co.uk

Thomas Carlyle's Birthplace 994
Lockerbie

Thomas Carlyle was born in 1795 in the Arched House built by his father and his uncle (both master masons) in Ecclefechan, near Lockerbie. At the Victorian-era house, visitors are able to explore the life of the famous writer, social historian and one of the most powerful influences on 19th-century British thought. The interior of the house is furnished to reflect domestic life in Carlyle's time and contains a fascinating collection of portraits and some of Carlyle's belongings.

⌕ On the A74, 6 miles south-east of Lockerbie
✿ ◉ ♣
⌛ 1 hour
★ Marvellous collection of portraits
£
www.nts.org.uk

Abbotsford 995
Melrose

This was the home of Sir Walter Scott, a 19th-century novelist and writer who did more for Scotland's reputation than anyone can imagine. The house, described by the writer as his 'Conundrum Castle', is on the banks of the River Tweed and was built to his designs in 1824. As well as his study and library, the house contains an impressive collection of historic relics, weapons and armour, which undoubtedly inspired him in writing timeless classics like *Waverley*, *Rob Roy* and *Ivanhoe*. The house is surrounded by glorious grounds and gardens.

⌕ On the A6091, 2 miles from Melrose
✿ ◉ ♣
⌛ 2–3 hours
★ Home of the world's first best-selling novelist
£
www.scottsabbotsford.co.uk

Melrose Abbey · 996
Melrose

Arguably the finest of Scotland's border abbeys, Melrose is a magnificent ruin on a grand scale with lavishly decorated masonry. Founded in 1136 by David I, it was the first monastery of the Cistercian order established in Scotland. The great abbey church loomed large in the lives of many people, on both sides of the border. Powerful people endowed it richly, and a hallowed few were privileged to be buried there. They included King Alexander II (d. 1249) and the heart of Robert Bruce (d. 1329), whose body was interred at Dunfermline Abbey.

🔍 Off the A7/A68 in Melrose
✿ ◯ ❀ ❄
⌛ 1–2 hours
★ Graceful 14th-century architecture
♿
www.historic-scotland.gov.uk

Three Hills Roman Centre and Fort · 997
Melrose

The Three Hills Roman Centre is full of information on the nearby Trimontium Roman fort. This includes illustrated panels and display cases, aerial photographs, drawings, models, maps, a blacksmith's workshop, a Roman kitchen and pottery and replica armour. The fort itself, which guarded the crossing of the River Tweed, is located in Newstead at the foot of the Eildon hills a mile from Melrose. The site can be visited any time, however, there are weekly guided walks that start from the museum on Thursday afternoons.

🔍 Melrose town centre
✿ ◯ ❀
⌛ 1–2 hours
★ A taste of Roman Frontier Life in Scotland
♿
www.discovertheborders.co.uk/places/66.html

Galloway Forest Park 998
Newton Stewart

The Galloway Forest Park offers 300 square miles of wild beauty. The glorious countryside comprises heather-clad hills, rugged rock faces, burns cascading down majestic slopes and the forest, moorland and lochs rising up to the grandeur of the mountains. The Merrick, Mulwharcher and the Rhinns of Kells stand proudly above much of the unspoilt, ancient woodland. The park is home to an outstanding variety of wildlife including red and roe deer, while mighty birds of prey patrol the skies. The park is easily accessed from the visitor centre at Kirroughtree.

Follow signs from the A75

3–5 hours

White-tailed sea eagles

FREE

www.gallowayforestpark.com

Sanquhar Tollbooth Museum 1000
Sanquhar

Sanquhar's 18th-century tollbooth is now home to this charming museum. Visitors can learn about Sanquhar knitting – a world famous tradition – the mines and miners of Sanquhar and Kirkconnel, the history and customs of the Royal Burgh of Sanquhar, three centuries of local literature, what life was like in Sanquhar jail, evidence of the earliest inhabitants of the area, native and Roman, and the everyday things of the people of Upper Nithsdale, at home and at work.

Sanquhar town centre

1–2 hours

Gloves knitted in the Sanquhar pattern

FREE

www.dumfriesmuseum.demon.co.uk

North Ayrshire Museum 999
Saltcoats

Housed in an old parish church dating from 1744. Changing displays illustrate the area's social history, maritime history, archaeology, transport and popular culture. On view is the famous Ardrossan Knights Templar stone coffin, a bronze-age burial cist from Stevenston, and Saltcoats' old hand operated fire engine. The surrounding churchyard is the final resting place of a number of interesting people including relations of Edgar Allan Poe, the Smiths of the City Shipping Line and Betsy Miller, the world's first female registered sea captain.

Saltcoats town centre

1 hour

Wedding Chair from Eglinton Castle

FREE

www.north-ayrshire.gov.uk/museums

Halliwell's House Museum 1001
Selkirk

This award-winning museum, housed in a row of 18th-century town cottages, recreates the building's former use as a home and ironmonger's shop. This museum explores and reveals the life of Selkirk through the ages. Visitors can learn about lives of the working people in majestic displays, follow the time-line, find out about 'The Souters' and see the Flodden Flag, brought home by the only local survivor from the battle. The attached Robson Gallery hosts regularly changing contemporary art, craft and local history exhibitions.

Selkirk town centre

1 hour

Flodden Flag

FREE

www.scotborders.gov.uk/museums

Index

Acknowledgements and picture credits

The Publishers would like to thank all the contributors who provided information, and particularly those who kindly supplied photographs for use with their entries. Unless otherwise stated the photography remains the copyright of the contributors.

Land's End Cliffs/istockphoto.com/©*William D Fergus McNeill*, pii; Liverpool Docks/istockphoto.com/©*ilbusca*, piii

Ightam Mote/istockphoto.com/©*RMAX*, p1; St Paul's Cathedral/©*Peter Smith*, p5, 34; Leeds Castle Kent/©*Leeds Castle Foundation*, p30; Chartwell House/©*Nick Heal*, p32; Holmes Study/©*The Sherlock Holmes Museum*, 221b Baker Street, London, England, www.sherlock-holmes.co.uk, p36; Natural History Museum/Moving T-REX ©*NHM* p40; National Gallery/©*Ian Crockart*, p42

Bedruthan Steps, Cornwall/istockphoto.com/©*Guy Sargent*, p55; At Bristol/©*courtenayphotography.co.uk*, p60; Paignton Zoo, Giraffe baby/©*Ray Wiltshire*, p58, 82; NMMC Flotilla/©*Hannah Rose* p64; Tintagel Castle/© & courtesy of *English Heritage*, p72; Berry Pomeroy Castle/© & courtesy of *English Heritage*, p85; Palmers Brewer Brewing Room/©*Carole Melbourne*, p87; Lulworth Castle/©*Nick Heal*, p89; Kingston Lacey/©*Nick Heal*, p93; Sea Life Park/©*Nick Heal*, p93; Ancient Roman Baths/ istockphoto.com/©*oversnap*, p100; Glastonbury Tor/©*Carole Melbourne*, p103; Stonehenge/© & courtesy of *English Heritage*, p107; Old Sarum/© & courtesy of *English Heritage*, p109

Norfolk Broads/istockphoto.com/©*Laurence Gough*, p111; Spitfire Cockpit/ istockphoto.com/©*Gary Blakeley*, 113, 118; Hatfield House/©Permission *Hatfield House*, p127; Sandringham/©By gracious permission of *H.M. The Queen*, p133

Stanage Edge, Peak District/istockphoto.com/©*Lesley Jacques*, p143; Gibralter Point NNR/©*Barrie Wilkinson*, p158; Sherwood Forest National Nature Reserve/istockphoto.com/©*Rey Rojo*, p165; Barnsdale Gardens/©*Hemant Jariwala*, p169

The Bullring, Birmingham/istockphoto.com/©*Chris Hepburn*, p171; Nemesis Ride, Alton Towers/©*Alton Towers Resort*, p182

Brecon Beacons National Park/istockphoto.com/©*fotoVoyager*, p209; Caerleon Amphitheatre, Barracks and Baths/©*Cadw (Crown Copyright)*, p223; Caernarfon Castle/©*Cadw, Welsh Assembly Government*, p216; Conwy Castle/©*Cadw, Welsh Assembly Government*, p211, 219; Welsh Highland Railway/©*Roger Dimmick*, p217; Big Pit: National Coal Museum/©*Amgueddfa Cymru National Museum Wales*, p222

Swaledale, Yorkshire Dales National Park/istockphoto.com/©*Paula Connelly*, p229; White Scar Cave/©*White Scar Cave/Robbie Shone*, p231, 236; Harlow Carr/©*RHS/Jon Enoch*, p235; Castle Howard/©*Mike Kipling*, p241; York Minster/©Reproduced by kind permission of the *Dean and Chapter*, p244; Statue of Mars/©*York Museums Trust/Joel Chester Fildes*, p245; National Media Museum/©*The National Media Museum*, p251

Wasdale Valley, The Lake District/istockphoto.com/©*Blackbeck*, p257; Imperial War Museum North/©*Imperial War Museum North/Tom Pollock*, p260, 289; Air Raid Shelters/©*Courtesy of Stockport Council*, p268; Lady Lever Art Gallery/©*fotografy.co.uk*, p300

Dunstanburgh Castle/istockphoto.com/©*Blackbeck*, p301; Hamsterley Forest/©*Hamsterley, The Forestry Commission*, p303, 306; Lindisfarne Priory/©*English Heritage Photo Library*, p303, 313; Kielder Water and Forest Park/©*Kielder Partnership*, p314

Eilean Donan Castle/istockphoto.com/©*Matthew Figgess*, p321; Museum of Flight/©*National Museums Scotland*, p324; Melrose Abbey/©Crown Copyright reproduced courtesy of *Historic Scotland*, p325, 368 Edinburgh Castle/istockphoto.com/©*Sascha Rosenau Njaa*, p332; Caerlaverock WWT/©*Brian Morrell WWT*, p363; Exterior Detail of MOS Tower/©*National Museums Scotland*, p334; The MacKintosh House/©*The Hunterian Museum and Art Gallery, University of Glasgow*, p339; Strathspey Steam Railway/©*Hendy Pollock*, p349; Calanais Standing Stones/©*Jan Schouten*, p354